# DISAPPEARANCES IN THE POST-TRANSITION ERA IN LATIN AMERICA

For over 100 years the *Proceedings of the British Academy* series has provided a unique record of British scholarship in the humanities and social sciences. Each themed volume drives scholarship forward and are landmarks in their field. For more information about the series and guidance on submitting a proposal for publication, please visit www.thebritishacademy.ac.uk/proceedings

PROCEEDINGS OF THE BRITISH ACADEMY • 237

# DISAPPEARANCES IN THE POST-TRANSITION ERA IN LATIN AMERICA

Edited by
KARINA ANSOLABEHERE, BARBARA A. FREY,
AND LEIGH A. PAYNE

*Published for* THE BRITISH ACADEMY
*by* OXFORD UNIVERSITY PRESS

*Oxford University Press, Great Clarendon Street, Oxford OX2 6DP*



*First edition published in 2021*



*British Library Cataloguing in Publication Data*
*Data available*

*Library of Congress Cataloging in Publication Data*
*Data available*

*Typeset by Newgen Publishing UK*
*Pod*

*ISBN 978-0-19-726722-6*
*ISSN 0068-1202*

# Contents

# List of Figures

# List of Tables

# Notes on Contributors

**Javier Amadeo** is associate professor in the Social Sciences Department at São Paulo Federal University (Unifesp). He has a Ph.D. in political science and undertook postdoctoral studies in history at São Paulo University (USP). He was Coordinator of the Anthropology and Archaeology Forensic Centre (Caaf–Unifesp), where he ran the project 'State Violence in Brazil: A Study of Crimes of May 2006 in the Perspective of Transitional Justice and Forensic Anthropology'. He organised the book *Violência de Estado na América Latina: direitos humanos, justiça de transição e antropologia forense* (*State Violence in Latin America: Human Rights, Transitional Justice and Forensic Anthropology*) (São Paulo, Editora da Unifesp, 2019) as part of the project.

**Karina Ansolabehere** is a researcher affiliated with the Instituto de Investigaciones Jurídicas of the UNAM (IIJ-UNAM) and the Latin American Faculty of Social Sciences (FLACSO-Mexico). Her areas of interest are: judicial politics, human rights, legal mobilisation, sociology of law, and political theory. She has a degree in sociology from the University of Buenos Aires, a master's in economic sociology from the Institute of Higher Social Studies of the National University of General San Martín, and a Ph.D. in social sciences research with a specialisation in political science from FLACSO-Mexico. She is a member of the National System of Researchers with Level III. She is currently principal investigator of the Observatory on Disappearances and Impunity in Mexico, an academic-advocacy collaborative that systematically investigates, analyses, and combats patterns of impunity currently surrounding enforced disappearances (the Observatory is administered in partnership with Oxford University and FLACSO-Mexico). She has produced multiple publications, the most recent being the *Routledge Handbook of Law and Society in Latin America*, co-edited with Rachel Sieder and Tatiana Alfonso (2019).

**Michelle Cañas Comas** is a researcher at the Centre of Legal and Social Studies (CELS) in Argentina. She has a bachelor's degree in international studies from Torcuato Di Tella University in Buenos Aires.

**Michael Chamberlin** is a human rights expert, an anthropologist with a master's degree in human rights and democracy (FLACSO-Mexico), and a member of the Board of the National Human Rights Institution in Mexico (CNDH). Currently, he works at the National Commission for Victims in Mexico, fostering reparations for communities and groups of victims. He formerly served as an external consultant for the Open Society Justice Initiative for transitional justice affirmative actions.

He is also the former deputy director of Fray Juan de Larios Human Rights Centre in Coahuila, where he developed a documentation strategy involving national and international human rights organisations in order to explore the linkages between criminal organisations, the private sector, and the government.

**Gastón Chillier** is the director of the International Team at the Centre of Legal and Social Studies (CELS) in Argentina. He served as executive director from 2006 to 2019. He has been co-chair of the International Network of Civil Liberties Organisations (INCLO) since 2011, and a board member of the European Centre for Constitutional and Human Rights since 2019. Gastón earned his law degree at the University of Buenos Aires (UBA) and obtained an LL.M. in international law and human rights at Notre Dame Law School in the United States.

**Paula Cuellar Cuellar** is a doctoral candidate in history and human rights at the University of Minnesota. Her dissertation is on violence against women and girls during the armed conflict in El Salvador. She holds a law degree from the Universidad Centroamericana 'José Simeón Cañas', an LL.M. in international human rights from the University of Notre Dame, an M.A. in human rights and peace studies from the University of El Salvador, and a postgraduate diploma in human rights and democratisation processes from the University of Chile. Currently, she is the Director of Consular Affairs at the Ministry of Foreign Relations in El Salvador. Previously, she held research and legal advisor positions in Mexico and in El Salvador on transitional justice, disappearances, violence against women, and journalists-at-risk projects.

**Natalia Federman** is a lawyer and a Ph.D. student in human rights at the University of Lanús, Argentina. She was the National Director of Human Rights at the Ministry of National Security between 2011 and 2014. She was also Programme Director of the National Directorate of Human Rights and International Humanitarian Law at the Ministry of Defence, and a lawyer of the Memory and Fight against Impunity Programme of the Centre of Legal and Social Studies (CELS) in Argentina.

**Barbara A. Frey,** J.D., is senior lecturer in the Institute for Global Studies and directs the Human Rights Program at the University of Minnesota. Frey is a principal investigator with the Observatory on Disappearances and Impunity in Mexico. She co-edited the 2018 volume *Mexico's Human Rights Crisis* with Alejandro Anaya-Muñoz. Frey is a leader of the University of Minnesota's Human Rights Lab. She was Principal Investigator for the Minnesota–Antioquia Human Rights Partnership in Medellin, Colombia (2012–15). She received two Fulbright-García Robles fellowships (2013 and 2019) for research in Mexico. Frey directed Minnesota Advocates for Human Rights from 1985 to 1997.

**Lulú Herrera** is the mother of Brandon Esteban Acosta Herrera and the wife of Esteban Acosta Rodríguez, who disappeared in Cuahuila, Mexico, in 2009. She is a founding member of the United Forces for Our Disappeared in Cuahuila (FUUNDEC).

**Rainer Huhle** holds a Ph.D. in political science. He teaches transitional justice for the master's in human rights at the University of Erlangen-Nürnberg, where he belongs to the Centre of Human Rights (CHREN). From 2003 through 2016 he was a member of the Board of the German Institute for Human Rights in Berlin, acting as vice-chairperson from 2007. From 2011 to 2019 he served as a member, and 2015 to 2019 as vice-president, of the UN Committee on Enforced Disappearances, where he was a Rapporteur charged with drafting the 'Guiding Principles for the Search for Disappeared Persons,' adopted in April 2019.

**Hunter Johnson** is a documentary filmmaker and photographer with a human rights focus. He holds a master's in human rights from the University of Minnesota, concentrating in arts advocacy. Working with the university's Human Rights Program, Hunter served as a lead researcher for the Observatory on Disappearances and Impunity in Mexico. Hunter is currently producing a film documenting Mexican independent journalists and state-level government officials who respond to the crisis of disappearance.

**The Maldonado family** are the brothers and parents of Santiago Maldonado, who was engaged in the struggles of the indigenous Mapuche communities in the Argentine province of Chubut. Santiago Maldonado disappeared on 1 August 2017 while participating in an act of resistance by the Lof de Cushamen community. The protest was repressed by Argentina's national gendarmerie. His whereabouts were unknown until 17 October 2017, when his lifeless body was found in the Chubut River. From the moment of his disappearance, his family led the search efforts and the demand for justice for Santiago. His brother Sergio Maldonado has led the demand for truth, justice, and remembrance in relation to his disappearance and death. He is joined by his brother Germán Maldonado, and their parents, Stella Peloso and Enrique Maldonado.

**Silvana Mandolessi** is assistant professor of cultural studies at KU Leuven, where she currently directs the ERC Starting Grant project 'We Are All Ayotzinapa: The Role of Digital Media in the Shaping of Transnational Memories on Disappearance'. Her latest book is *Digital Reason: A Guide to Meaning, Medium and Community in a Modern World* (with Jan Baetens and Ortwin De Graef, 2020). She is also the author of *Una literatura abyecta: Gombrowicz en la tradición argentina* (2012). She has co-edited *El pasado inasequible: desaparecidos, hijos y combatientes en el arte y la literatura del nuevo milenio* (2019), *Estudios de memoria* (2015), and special issues of the journals *European Review* and *Nuevo texto crítico*.

**Alvaro Martos** is a postdoctoral researcher within the CONACYT project PN-2017–6120, 'Observatorio sobre procuración e impartición de justicia en México en casos de desaparición forzada de personas: el deber de buscar e investigar' ('Observatory on Procuring and Imparting Justice in Mexico in Cases of Forced Disappearance of People: The Duty to Search and Investigate').

**María José Méndez** is a junior fellow at the Harvard Society of Fellows, and incoming assistant professor in the Political Science Department at the University of Toronto. Her current work examines the political, economic, and gender entanglements of transnational gang violence in Central America.

**Leigh A. Payne** is professor of sociology and Latin America at St Antony's College, Oxford. She is the author of numerous books, chapters, and articles on human rights, specifically focused on Latin America. Her research has been supported by grants from the British Academy, the Arts and Humanities Research Council, and the National Science Foundation, the Economic and Social Research Council, the Oak Foundation, the Open Society Foundation, the MacArthur Foundation, the Social Science Research Council, and the Oxford University Press John Fell Fund, among others. She was the co-principal investigator on the British Academy–Newton Fund project of Observatory on Disappearances and Impunity in Mexico.

**Marcela Perelman** has directed the Research Area of the Centre of Legal and Social Studies (CELS) in Argentina since October 2013, and she has been a member of CELS' staff since 2003. She works on all the main topics of the CELS agenda, and she focuses her work on the dynamics of violence and repression in democracy. Perelman holds a bachelor's degree in political science and a Ph.D. in social science from the University of Buenos Aires (UBA). Since 2002 she has taught urban sociology at UBA, and since 2007 she has been part of the Legal and Political Anthropology Team of UBA's School of Philosophy and Letters. She is a professor at the human rights Ph.D. programme of the University of Lanús.

**Volga de Pina Ravest** graduated *magna cum laude* from the undergraduate law programme at the Universidad de las Américas, Puebla, Mexico. She holds a master's in human rights and democracy from FLACSO-Mexico. Currently she is the assistant director of that master's programme. She is also a researcher at the Observatory on Disappearances and Impunity in Mexico at FLACSO-Mexico. She is a member of the Consejo Nacional Ciudadano del Sistema Nacional de Búsqueda de Personas (Citizens' Advisory Board for the National System for the Search for Missing Persons), a position she holds as an expert in the search for missing and disappeared persons. She participated in the advisory team for the Movimiento por Nuestros Desaparecidos en México (Movement for Our Disappeared in Mexico) in the discussion of the General Law for Disappeared Persons, approved in 2017.

**Sandra Serrano** is a research professor at FLACSO-Mexico. Her areas of investigation are serious violations of human rights, human rights institutions, gender, and the relationship between international and constitutional law and regional and national courts. Serrano has coordinated studies on access to justice, enforced disappearance, torture, and women's rights. She has also been a consultant for the Inter-American Court of Human Rights, the Inter-American Commission of Women, the Organization of American States, and the International Bar Association. She is currently a member of the Observatory on Disappearances and Impunity in Mexico.

**Raiane Patrícia Severino Assumpção** is professor at the Federal University of São Paulo (Unifesp – Baixada Santista campus) where she teaches the undergraduate course in social work and the graduate course in social work and social policy. She has a Ph.D. in sociology (2008). She is the coordinator of the Committee for the Promotion of Human Rights Education (Unifesp) and a researcher at the Anthropology and Archaeology Forensic Centre (Caaf-Unifesp), where she participated in the research project 'State Violence in Brazil: A Study of Crimes of May 2006 in the Perspective of Transitional Justice and Forensic Anthropology'.

**Débora Maria da Silva** is the founder and coordinator of the Independent Movement of May Mothers (Mães de Maio), formed in 2006 in Brazil by mothers, like herself, and other family members of victims. The Movement emerged to address the grave human rights violations in the state of São Paulo, in which security forces, especially the military police, have been implicated, and to demand investigation and legal remedy for these crimes. Débora Maria da Silva is also a researcher at the Anthropology and Archaeology Forensic Centre at the Federal University of São Paulo (Caaf-Unifesp).

**Marlon Weichert** has been a federal prosecutor in Brazil for 25 years. He acted as Deputy Federal Prosecutor for the Rights of the Citizen from 2016 to 2020. Weichert has extensive experience on transitional justice, public security, business and human rights, and mass atrocities prevention issues. He was the first scholar and prosecutor to argue that crimes against humanity were committed in Brazil during the military dictatorship. Weichert holds an M.A. degree in law and was a researcher at the New York University School of Law – Hauser Global Fellows Program. He has written more than 40 publications on human rights.

**'Wilson'** is a pseudonym, used to protect the identity of a Salvadoran man whose partner's son disappeared from their lives in 2014. He is a member of COFADEVI, the Comité de Familiares de Personas Desaparecidas por la Violencia en El Salvador (Committee of Relatives of People Disappeared by Violence in El Salvador).

# Acknowledgements

This study would not have been possible without the support of the families of the disappeared, their civil society advocates, our universities, and funding from external and internal sources. Our gratitude for this support is immense.

In each country we encountered families willing to share with us not only their experiences of pain and loss, but also their tireless struggles to search for their loved ones, and their commitments to discovering the truth, reparations, justice, and guarantees of non-recurrence. Their dedication did not stop at their nuclear or extended families, but broadened to include the community of those affected by disappearance. They were committed not only to a personal struggle, but to a society struggle. Their struggle was bolstered by the family and civil society organisations they formed and in which they actively participated.

In Mexico, these organisations included: Ciudadanos en Apoyo a los Derechos Humanos (Citizens in Support of Human Rights; CADHAC) of Nuevo León; the Centro Diocesano Fray Juan de Larios (Fray Juan de Larios Diocesan Centre; CDFJL) in Coahuila; I(dh)eas Litigio Estratégico en Derechos Humanos (I(dh)eas Human Rights Strategic Litigation), and the collectives of relatives AMORES, FUUNDEC/FUUNDEM, Grupo VIDA, Grupo Alas de Esperanza, and Grupo Familias Unidas.

External funding was also procured from a variety of sources for each of the projects. The research in Mexico benefited from funds provided by the Open Society Foundation; the British Academy's Newton Advance Fellowship; Consejo Nacional de Ciencia y Tecnología de México (CONACYT) Convocatoria Problemas Nacionales (National Council of Science and Technology of Mexico (CONACYT) National Problems Call); the University of Minnesota's Human Rights Initiative fund; and the Fulbright-US Scholar Program, which supported Barbara A. Frey's research in Mexico.

This book is the result of several years of research and reflection. It was a collaboration that grew out of friendship, shared commitment to human rights, and a desire to use our academic skills to address the continuing scourge of disappearances in the post-transitional era. Much of this work took place in seminars carried out at the University of Minnesota, FLACSO-Mexico, the Institute for Legal Research at the National Autonomous University of Mexico (UNAM), and the University of Oxford. Many academic colleagues, graduate students, and human rights activists participated in these workshops and we are grateful for their commentaries and critiques, which served to strengthen the central ideas in this book.

We want to thank all of the authors who graciously agreed to participate in this volume and to engage actively with us in this complex and painful subject matter. We benefited enormously from the depth of their regional and interdisciplinary expertise. We want to highlight the very personal contributions of Lulú Herrera, Débora Maria da Silva, the family of Santiago Maldonado, and 'Wilson', which formed the heart of this volume, demonstrating through their own stories the toll that the continuing practice of disappearance has on families and societies.

Portia Taylor of the British Academy deserves special mention for her steady support and assistance with this process, during which she unfailingly responded with patience and diligence to our various questions and consultations.

Finally, we want to thank those who helped in the editing process: Dorian Singh and Yaret Bautista, who revised the references and collected abstracts; Robert Whitelock for his copy-editing; Helen Flitton for production; and Nick Chown for the index. Their work was a key piece of this publication.

# Introduction

KARINA ANSOLABEHERE, BARBARA A. FREY,
AND LEIGH A. PAYNE*

LATIN AMERICA SITS at the centre of the third wave of democratisation that began in the early 1980s. It has advanced farther than any other region of the world in its accountability processes for past human rights violations perpetrated during authoritarian regimes and armed conflicts. Despite these human rights achievements, Latin America is known as the most violent global region. In the last two decades since the transitions, serious human rights violations, especially disappearances, have increased exponentially in several countries in the region. This volume seeks to understand these post-transition disappearances. It does so by examining four different countries in the region and the dynamics that play out within them. It considers a variety of voices and points of view: from the perspectives of victims and relatives; of activists, advocates, and public officials seeking truth and justice; and of scholars attempting to draw out the specificities in each case and the patterns across cases. The underlying objective behind the project is to gain knowledge and to draw on deep commitment to change within the region so as to overcome this tragedy.

After reading this volume, readers will not only have an overview of the practice of disappearances in the region, but will also be able to gauge how, despite the differences between countries, the social and political logics that support and even encourage disappearances in these places are similar. The disappearances of the past and those of the present are not the same, and it would be a mistake to consider them that way, but the social, political, and economic practices that make them possible are similar. These practices are what we call the logics of disappearance.

The focus on the phenomenon of disappearances in post-transitional Latin America fills a lacuna in academic research. Although there are many studies of disappearances during the region's past authoritarian rule and armed conflict, the widespread occurrence of these violations in the aftermath of transitions has not been addressed. Unfortunately, and as this book shows, the lack of studies does

*This chapter draws from Ansolabehere *et al.* (2017). Translation by Natalie Felsen.

not result from a lack of incidents. The time to understand the horrific practice of disappearance that is being carried out within the region's procedural democracies, and to confront it, is now.

The book approaches the phenomenon from an interdisciplinary perspective. The authors draw on their professional roles as historians, legal scholars, political scientists, and sociologists. They also include human rights practitioners and individuals who have personally experienced the disappearance of their family members. Thus, each country section includes powerful personal testimony to the impact of disappearance and efforts to address it alongside critical historical, social, political, and legal analysis.

Four country case studies are developed in the book: Argentina, Brazil, El Salvador, and Mexico. The case studies are not the only ones that this project could have undertaken. There is evidence of post-transition disappearances in other countries in Latin America: Guatemala, Peru (Dulitzky 2017: 53),[1] Chile, (Dulitzky 2017: 38),[2] and Colombia. There is also evidence of disappearances in democratic contexts outside Latin America, such as France, the Philippines, and Turkey (UN Human Rights Council 2020: para. 27). We have selected these four cases in Latin America because of the particular and paradigmatic dynamics of disappearance in the prior authoritarian and conflict situations and post-transition that these countries present for analysis.

Latin America is the region that has been referenced as starting and going farther than any other region in addressing human rights violations committed by state actors during its past authoritarian regimes and armed conflicts. Processes aimed at addressing past abuses, the accountability and deterrence mechanisms underlying 'transitional justice', were initiated in nearly every country. The originality of these processes – the first such processes of trials of state actors' abuses and truth commissions – were not only the first in the world, they also became models for countries in other regions. The concentration of these processes would suggest

[1] Ariel Dulitzky (2017: 53) notes 'the claim [to the UN Working Group] made by the relatives of Bruno Carlos Schell, an Argentine citizen who disappeared in Lima in June 2013 and whose whereabouts are unknown. Even though this is a recent case, according to the information received, the victim's relatives are facing the same problems as those faced by the relatives of persons who disappeared in the 1980s, such as the investigations being delayed or information being restricted by the authorities. It is worrying that, despite the years that have passed since the first cases of enforced disappearance in Peru, the Peruvian judicial system continues to suffer from legal and structural limitations that hinder the determination of the whereabouts or the discovery of the remains of disappeared persons.'

[2] The UN Working Group on Enforced or Involuntary Disappearances referred to the situation of 'a young Mapuche aged 16 years, José Huenante, who disappeared in 2005, investigation of which was assigned to the military justice system because those responsible were reportedly Carabineros. This contravenes article 16.2 of the Declaration and constitutes a major obstacle to efforts to end impunity in this case of enforced disappearance. Cases such as that of José Huenante should be investigated promptly and effectively by the ordinary justice system. Still today, the Chilean Carabineros are subject to military jurisdiction for any unlawful act committed by their members. The Working Group has been informed of a new bill to reform military jurisdiction and hopes that it will ultimately curtail its scope, in accordance with international standards.'

that stronger human rights institutions, more capable of dealing with abuses, would have acted to prevent the same sort of violations occurring in the post-transitional context, specifically disappearances. And yet, the figures from Brazil, El Salvador, and Mexico suggest that disappearances may have actually reached a higher level in the democratic period than during earlier authoritarian regimes and armed conflicts. The relatively smaller number of post-transition disappearances in Argentina seems to reflect that, where human rights organisations have remained poised as watchdogs of governments, they are able to mobilise and are more effective in addressing these violations when they occur. Another reason to focus on Latin America is the particular characteristics of the contemporary period. Democratisation in the region corresponds to at least four large social problems: extreme levels of inequality, violent crime, violent and illicit trade in resources, and corruption. Those factors are not mutually exclusive, they are interrelated – particularly in the phenomenon of disappearance. This book attempts to examine the logics behind disappearances and how they relate to the historical, political, social, and economic dynamics in the region.

The project is not, however, solely an academic enterprise. It aims to constitute itself the practice of human rights work. That is, it draws attention to an ongoing violation that until now has tended to receive recognition only in isolated and extreme situations, such as the case of the 43 students of the Ayotzinapa Rural Teachers' College in Iguala (Guerrero), Mexico, who disappeared in 2014. In general, disappearances under democratic governments have tended to be viewed as aberrations. This study aims to challenge that perspective and to make visible the widespread and, at times, systematic nature of disappearances in the post-transitional context. Visibility itself is an important impact. That disappearances begin to be viewed as widespread removes the stigma and invisibility surrounding these acts. Shedding light on the characteristics of this crime in Latin America may also heighten the vigilance of domestic and international human rights defenders, to ensure that this insidious practice is not allowed to spread to other procedurally democratic contexts.

In addition, this book has the objective of accompanying victims, their families, and their advocates, and of providing support and human rights tools to address and reduce these crimes.

The voices of relatives of the victims have thus been incorporated into the book. Each case study has a representative text from surviving family members who have sought redress from the state. They have formed their own organisations of victims and they have worked with existing human rights organisations in their attempts to promote their rights to life, truth, investigation, justice, and guarantees of non-recurrence.

These tasks are not without their challenges. A systematic study relies on information. And, yet, with the disappearance of a person, the facts surrounding the crime also disappear. Very little is known about who is disappeared, where, how, by whom. The studies in this book attempt to recover that information through testimony; through interviews with victims' relatives, state officials, and human rights advocates; through archives; through news reports; and through advocacy efforts.

The book has one section devoted to developing the tools to address victims' rights to truth, justice, and non-repetition. In this effort, advocates for the disappeared have to take advantage of potential pathways – from effective searches to engagement with international mechanisms – that can pierce the deniability and impunity that have shielded these post-transitional states from responsibility. These tools also draw upon the well-developed practices honed during past authoritarian and armed conflict situations in the region.

The patterns revealed from these analyses suggest two attributes that link past authoritarian and armed conflict disappearances with contemporary ones: disposability and deniability. Specifically, those who disappear are 'disposable peoples' (*desechables*). They can be disappeared without provoking massive protests because they are seen within governance institutions and among significant sectors in society as insignificant, or even as the cause of social or political disorder. Their disappearance is thus tolerated. Challenging the myths and beliefs that surround disappearances is part of the human rights work in which this book is engaged.

Those myths attempt to attribute the act of disappearance to the criminal or illegal activity in which the disappeared person was supposedly involved. During the authoritarian and armed conflict period, disappearance was attributed to the traitorous, seditious, subversive rebel elements in society who threatened the established political and economic order. In the contemporary era, disappearances are assumed to be the result of competition among criminal gangs. Even if they are not seen as gang-related, as in the case of Argentina today, the state disavows any role in these disappearances. That denial of responsibility is the second aspect of the human rights work in which this book is engaged.

The book examines two ways in which the state is involved in these contemporary disappearances, rendering them 'enforced disappearances' using the language of the International Convention for the Protection of All Persons from Enforced Disappearance. The International Convention recognises the involvement of the state in enforced disappearance where it directly carries out the disappearance, as well as where it 'acquiesces'. In this book, we consider the involvement of the state in the direct perpetration of disappearance, a crime of commission, in addition to its crime of omission. The crime of omission, acquiescence, occurs when the state fails to address the disappearance through the search for the missing, investigation into the disappearance, identification of those found in mass or unmarked graves, and judicial response related to the crime. The state does not have to have intended to cover up the crime to be complicit in it. In other words, it merely has to fail to carry out its human rights duties and obligations to victims and their families.

We do not expect democratic governments to be involved in either the act of commission or the act of omission. Obligations to protect citizens' security is paramount in democracies. For this reason, and because disappearance is commonly clandestine, it is often difficult to prove enforced disappearance in democracies.

The cases revealed in this book begin to show both types of state roles in enforced disappearances, commission and omission. Moreover, they connect the two types of involvements. Because the socio-demographic or political profiles of the disappeared render them disposable, the state feels little pressure – domestic or international – to address the occurrence. Moreover, the disposable nature of disappeared persons means that state agents may become engaged in the act of disappearance, alone or with other non-state actors, with impunity.

The who (disposable people) and the how (impunity) begin to reveal the logics of enforced disappearance to link the current phenomenon during democratic governments with those past forms of disappearance in authoritarian and armed conflict situations. Each of the empirical chapters in the 'Country Case Studies' section of this book further develops an explanation for these disappearances. In addition, the two chapters in the 'Theoretical Framework' section provide an overarching approach to disappearances from multidisciplinary and legal perspectives.

Finally, the book considers the tools available to families, civil society, legal actors, and international experts engaged in the efforts to stop disappearances, and to seek state responses to the disappearances. These include examples of past activities aimed at visibility, documentation, information, mobilisation, and pressure politics. They also include legal strategies that have been employed at the local, state, regional, and international level. The book thus hopes to put into the hands of those engaged in denouncing disappearance a set of tactics from which they might draw inspiration and method.

## Book Outline

The book is set up in three parts that present a theoretical and conceptual framework, case studies, and tools for human rights impact. In Part I the framework for understanding disappearances in post-transitional societies is presented in two chapters. Chapter 1 approaches the phenomenon of disappearances from a holistic perspective, drawing together the historical, political, sociological, economical, legal, and psychological dynamics of the phenomenon. Leigh A. Payne and Karina Ansolabehere specifically examine the degree to which current understandings of disappearances link up with past approaches. They do so by looking at the emblematic historical cases (Night and Fog; *los desaparecidos* in Argentina) and the legacy that such cases may suggest about how we understand disappearance and the ways to address it today.

The conceptual framework set out in this chapter relies on four overlapping logics. First, the logic of clandestine violent action contends that democracies may be just as likely to use disappearances as authoritarian and armed-conflict governments because of the perceived need of violent reprisals aimed at citizens. In such a context, state violence is hidden, or disappeared, from domestic public and international view. This logic is only likely to prevail, however, where the other three logics coexist. The second logic is the need for, and construction of, 'disposable people'. The state will only get away with its direct involvement in, or its failure to prevent or punish, disappearances if those who disappeared are not perceived to be rights-bearing citizens. An active process of creating official myths about the disappeared begins to justify the violence against them. They tend to be linked with enemies of the political, economic, or social order. The transition from authoritarian rule and armed conflict may place a different emphasis on the alleged characteristics of these disposable peoples – from political subversives to criminal elements – however, the underlying logic of disappearance persists.

Where the disappeared are widely maligned, the state faces little pressure to respond to the demands for investigation from the families. This puts victims and their families in the role of carrying out the investigations themselves, often accompanied by human rights advocates. In some cases, these groups are effective, as they were in the past, in bringing domestic and international pressure to bear on unresponsive states. To do so, these victims groups and their advocates have to overcome the third logic of disappearance examined in this chapter: social order through ambiguous loss. To make demands, families have to overcome social stigma, psychological paralysis resulting from ambiguous loss, and marginalisation and silencing resulting from their connection to disposable peoples. When this happens, there is some hope for social pressure on, and response from, the state. But such efforts are rare because of this set of deeply entrenched logics. Disappearances also have a political economy, or fourth, logic. Disappeared people are economically vulnerable. Many disappear in their workplaces – which raises questions about the role of employers in the political economy of disappearances – or else they cannot disassociate themselves from the crime economy, since many of the people who disappear are forcibly recruited or subjected to sexual slavery or forced labour.

Chapter 2 explains the international legal framework that sets out the obligations of states to address disappearances. Barbara A. Frey locates those obligations across several regimes of international law, including international humanitarian law, international human rights law, and international criminal law, in addition to the Inter-American System's legal framework pertinent to the four case studies in the volume. The Latin American experience with disappearances during the prior authoritarian and armed conflict period had a direct impact on the framing of the crime under international law. The post-transitional context calls for a re-examination of the definition of enforced disappearance to determine whether it is sufficiently flexible to account for variations of enforced disappearance, whether in countries utilising the national security doctrine, or in those experiencing terrorism, trafficking, or organised crime (Dulitzky 2019). Frey rejects the clear distinction between 'disappearances' by non-state actors, and 'enforced disappearances', where there is state involvement. The key question is what is the state linkage that is necessary to meet the international legal definition. The case studies presented in the volume demonstrate that many disappearances in democratic settings easily demonstrate state linkage because they are carried out (1) directly by state agents or (2) by other persons acting with the consent and support of the state. Frey observes, however, that a third category of disappearances has proven more difficult to account for under international law: crimes of acquiescence. A strategic legal response is required in order to reduce the space within which the state can employ systematic impunity to negate its own responsibility for enforced disappearances. Frey argues that in contexts of historical state involvement in disappearances, such as Argentina, or where there is systematic impunity so that the state consistently fails to search for victims or to investigate disappearances, the 'acquiescence' threshold for state responsibility is met under international law.

In democratic states experiencing high levels of normalised violence at the hands of state and non-state actors, crimes of disappearance are rarely solved. Frey argues that such states have few incentives to investigate disappearances because, by attributing the crimes to non-state actors, states are able to deny international legal responsibility for them. Instead of taking immediate steps to search for the victim and investigate the disappearance, therefore, state actors have incentives to point the finger elsewhere: by ignoring or hiding evidence, criminalising the victim, simulating investigations, or merely delaying long enough to endanger the life and personal integrity of the victim. Frey argues that only by tipping the burden of proof away from victims and back toward the states will governments have incentives to solve these crimes. Frey bases her approach on the due-diligence jurisprudence in the Inter-American System and the United Nations treaty bodies. She notes that, in practice, the key element of acquiescence is the one most frequently used by states to block their own human rights responsibility by insisting that the victims provide proof of actual knowledge of the crime. The due-diligence framework shifts that burden, supporting a more contextualised assessment of state action to determine whether state actors have actually taken timely and effective steps to prevent or minimise foreseeable human rights violations by private actors and to investigate, prosecute, punish, and provide reparations for victims of violations. Frey concludes her chapter by explaining how standards set forth in the Guiding Principles for the Search for Disappeared Persons (2019) and the Minnesota Protocol on the Investigation of Potentially Unlawful Death (2016) bring into focus the minimum steps states must take to demonstrate in good faith that they are not acquiescing in disappearances.

Part II of the volume sets out four sets of case studies selected for the book given the magnitude of disappearances (Mexico) as well as the emblematic types of disappearances, such as discriminatory practices related to race and class (Brazil), political protest (Argentina), and gang connections (El Salvador). To give voice to the victims, each case study begins with a testimony from relatives of the disappeared. These narratives emerge from family members, most of whom became unintentional activists and human rights defenders because of their life experiences and their encounters with disappearance. They were not born, or trained, or prepared, to take on the roles foisted on them. Their stories tell of the deepest personal pain imaginable: the inability to know what happened; to recover; to understand or accept the disappearance of a daughter, a son, a partner, a sibling, a parent. The stories also speak of an activism born of despair, a realisation that if one does not act, no one else will. This is a struggle against silence. It also attempts to combat shame imposed by others, to reclaim the dignity of the disappeared and their families. These stories do not speak of success, unless we see success in terms of perseverance. For years these activists have fought every day for a state response. Even without receiving it, they have continued to struggle.

These personal testimonies are followed by academic and practitioner studies that attempt to cast that personal event in a larger understanding of the phenomenon of disappearance in each country. They reveal the perverse logics of disappearance, the search for the missing persons, the struggle for missing justice. The studies approach the question through historical, political, social, and legal frameworks.

Mexico is the first case study. It is relevant because of the magnitude of cases. The government has acknowledged the enormous toll of disappearances since 2006, amounting to more than 60,000 disappeared persons and 3,631 clandestine graves (Sheridan 2020). These figures are higher than the symbolic numbers used by the families of the disappeared during the Argentine civil-military dictatorship. Despite these terrible numbers, experts have only been able to document the recovery of a small number of people, and only 93 legal actions are open. Thus, Mexico not only has an extreme level of disappearances, but is also characterised by systematic impunity for these disappearances.

The Mexican case study begins in Chapter 3 with the testimony of Lulú Herrera, one of the founding members of a collective of relatives of the disappeared in the state of Coahuila. She tells the story of learning of the disappearance of her husband, eight-year-old child, and two brothers-in-law. She also explains why, after six years without finding even one disappeared person in Coahuila, she and her collective of families continue to struggle in the search for their loved ones and the investigation of the crime. They have faced stigma for being families of disappeared, but they do not believe they have any other choice but to continue their fight. As she describes it, a mother does not give up until her child is found. Lulú Herrera and other mothers, through their perseverance and persistence, have not only raised attention to the disappeared, they have also won legal victories along the way. But their main objective – to find their loved ones – has not, yet, been achieved.

Chapter 4, by Karina Ansolabehere and Alvaro Martos, summarises the findings derived from the first phase of the Observatory on Disappearance and Impunity on the northern states of Coahuila, Tamaulipas, and Nuevo León. The Observatory attempts to answer the questions of who did what to whom, how, when, and where. Its findings contradict prevailing assumptions that disappearances in Mexico can be explained by organised crime alone. They show how the four logics of disappearances presented in the framework by Payne and Ansolabehere (Chapter 1) operate in northeastern Mexico, stressing the idea that, even when different contexts produce different types of disappearances, the logics of these disappearances are the same.

Chapter 5, also on Mexico, by Sandra Serrano and Volga de Pina Ravest, explores the legal strategies that have been developed and used in Mexico. In particular, a new General Law on Disappearances offers at the very least state recognition of the phenomenon and its responsibility to address victims' rights. The chapter explores the promises and limits of the new law based on an assessment of past efforts at searching for the disappeared and rendering justice for victims, as well as a review of the overlapping institutional configuration resulting from the legal changes.

The Mexico case study is followed by a focus on Brazil. In Brazil, disappearances are associated with summary executions by the security forces. In many of the cases, the individuals are eventually found dead in morgues or on the street. This pattern of disappearance is associated with a kind of policing that identifies certain socio-demographic features – young, male, poor, black – with security threats posed by criminal gangs. With only 400 documented cases of deaths and disappearances during the authoritarian period, the more than 200,000 disappearances registered in the democratic period seem to represent a very different and dangerous phenomenon.

Débora da Silva, the mother of a victim and an activist leader of the Brazilian May Mothers organisation, tells her story in Chapter 6. It is not only a personal reflection and expression of grief and anger, but is also a story of how someone turned loss into political mobilisation within Brazilian society. Her story is not an isolated case. She refers to the genocidal security policies that target those who look like her son (male, young, black) and who were born into the same poor neighbourhoods on the outskirts of the city. She found her son – murdered – but has not obtained justice for the wrongdoing. Her story reflects that of so many others.

The study presented by Javier Amadeo and Raiane Severino Assumpção in Chapter 7 provides the background to the events in May 2006 that gave rise to the May Mothers organisation. They cast the event within a broader understanding of the security policing in Brazil that has led to the executions–disappearances pattern. Disappearances have become a kind of security performance in which the state has targeted a specific class of people – poor, black males on the urban margins – for execution and disappearance as a way to demonstrate its commitment to fighting crime.

Chapter 8, by the São Paulo state prosecutor Marlon Weichert, considers how these deaths and disappearances at the hands of the official security apparatus and organised criminal groups can be approached theoretically as crimes against humanity, even though they are being carried out in a nominally democratic society. Given the magnitude of the crimes and their selective nature, Weichert argues that this pattern rises to the most serious level of international crimes. Weichert examines the legal apparatus in place that provides cover for security forces, rather than tools for victims and their families to obtain truth and justice regarding the violation. While, prior to 2019, it was possible to say that the killing of poor black youths constituted a policy of omission, Weichert argues, since then Brazilian security agents have crossed a threshold into actively committing a systematic crime against humanity.

The third country case study examined in the book is Argentina. Argentina is infamous for disappearances during the civil-military dictatorship of the 1970s and 1980s. Indeed, the word *desaparecido* is associated with those acts. So too is the emergence of mothers' groups (Mothers of the Plaza de Mayo) in searching for the disappeared. We include Argentina in this book not only because of its dramatic past, but also because of the profile of disappearances under the new democratic governments. Argentina represents civil society's demands for a heightened sense of state responsibility for prompt and thorough investigations into the disappearance of political protesters, or young persons of low social backgrounds. Failure to pursue truth, justice and reparations in these cases reveals the inability or unwillingness of democratic institutions to prevent a recurrence of the historical violence that continues to affect families of victims and the society as a whole.

The Argentine case study begins with Chapter 9, a series of letters by the family members of 28-year-old Santiago Maldonado, who disappeared in Chubut, Argentina. He had been part of a mobilisation by the Mapuche indigenous community regarding land claims against the Benetton company. Violence erupted around these demonstrations. When Maldonado disappeared, it was assumed by the protesters, the families, and their advocates that it was an enforced disappearance with direct involvement of the National Gendarmerie, which had suppressed the protests. Maldonado's body was recovered from the Chubut River without any signs of violence 80 days later, but the details of the disappearance remain unclear. Maldonado's brothers wrote open letters to pressure the state to find him. After he was found dead, the brothers and Maldonado's parents reflected on the vast support they received in the search efforts and in clarifying the facts of the disappearance. This social support distinguishes the Argentine case from others in the volume, where civil society actors face an uphill battle in their search for accountability for disappearances.

Chapter 10, by Natalia Federman, Marcela Perelman, Michelle Cañas Comas, and Gastón Chillier, presents the context in which the well-known Argentine human rights organisation Centro de Estudios Legales y Sociales (CELS) has begun to investigate disappearances under democratic governments. The organisation has a long history of experience investigating and prosecuting disappearances that occurred during the civil-military dictatorship. As the CELS staff present in this chapter, the approach that they used in the past cannot be taken out, dusted off, and applied to current cases of disappearance. Nonetheless, abstracting from the theory used for the crimes of the dictatorship provides insights. Federman *et al.* suggest that one difference may be motive. These disappearances may not be motivated by a systematic strategy to eliminate individuals. Nonetheless, the treatment of the disappeared individuals and their families when they were alive, once they had disappeared, and after their deaths were confirmed, reflects a systematic disregard for the human rights of certain marginalised communities. In addition, the institutional apparatus engaged in the recent disappearances is more extensive, including hospitals and morgues, judicial bodies, and security forces. Finally, the chapter explores a new security context in which political protesters are targeted, a situation that holds an eerie resemblance to the former dictatorship. These patterns are explored in the chapter through a general discussion and an application to two disappearances in which CELS is involved: Luciano Arruga and Santiago Maldonado.

The fourth case study is El Salvador, presented in Chapters 11 and 12. This is the least-studied case and also the one in which the least amount of activism and advocacy has occurred. We include it here because of the particular dynamic of disappearances in the context of gang-related violence. Such contexts seem to heighten a kind of tolerance for disappearance, by explaining away the acts as part of the unfettered violence used by gang members, accepting the use of disappearance by security forces as a form of control over the violence, or even using disappearance as a way to hide everyday forms of domestic and other kinds of violence.

From the perspective of the Salvadoran authorities, the arbitrary detention and disappearance of Yovani and Samuel by soldiers described in 'Wilson''s testimony in Chapter 11 is not a paradigmatic example of contemporary disappearances in El Salvador. In a way, their disappearance is more the exception than the rule in a country that has moved from the political violence of the 1980–92 civil war to the criminal violence of the post-conflict period. However, analysed from the perspective of everyday state presence in the peripheries of El Salvador, their disappearance is not an isolated case. Yovani and Samuel, who went missing in 2014, are two of many youths who have been swept up by state security forces in anti-gang operations. Their disappearance points to patterns of human rights violations that have been aggravated by the government's *mano dura* (iron fist) crackdown on violent crime. In his testimonial, Wilson registers some of these violations. He introduces his stepson's disappearance in relation to state abuse of authority – physical harassment, inhumane treatment, the falsification of evidence, arbitrary detention, extrajudicial killings, and disappearances – as well as in relation to patterns of state–criminal cooperation. His testimonial also gives us a sense of the innumerable obstacles that Salvadorans face in searching for their missing relatives.

The study on El Salvador, presented in Chapter 12 by María José Méndez, demonstrates that the story Wilson relates about his stepson is not unique. Based on interviews and archival research, the study highlights key dynamics of disappearances in El Salvador. On one hand, as Wilson's testimony suggests, the state itself has 'criminalised' the victims of disappearance as part of its security policies. On the other, the state has appeared to cede control to criminal gangs carrying out disappearances. Both dynamics render the state incapable of responding effectively to victims and their families in the demand for the search for the missing and justice for wrongdoing. Relatives find themselves standing in for the state in looking for their missing family members, often exposing themselves to danger in entering territory controlled by criminal elements. The chapter discusses efforts within El Salvador and internationally to try to address the gap that the victims experience: that is, that victims possess rights to investigation and justice in domestic and international law, but are blocked from accessing those rights because of the state's direct and indirect complicity in disappearance.

As the El Salvador case shows, more tools need to be put in the hands of victims, their families, and their advocates. This is the focus of Part III of the book. This section is organised around strategies used to achieve the objectives of visibility, search and investigation, accountability, and deterrence. In Chapter 13, Leigh A. Payne and Hunter Johnson consider the set of strategies used by families and non-governmental organisations to raise awareness of the everyday nature of disappearance. They attempt to erase the stigma of the disappearance on the victim and on families. By incorporating symbols of the home and of the family, these visibility strategies try to show that disappearance is part of the daily lives of families, but also disrupts them. These images reveal that disappearance happens to people like you, and it could happen to you. The campaigns thus draw attention to the crime and to the victims of crime, to overcome the stigma that allows these crimes to remain invisible and unaddressed. They reclaim the rights denied to families: to truth, to life, to redress, to justice. Many of the mechanisms described in this chapter can be employed with very few resources. And at times they have an impact.

In Chapter 14, Barbara A. Frey explains how international guidelines can be used in addressing disappearance cases through the Minnesota Protocol on the Investigation of Potentially Unlawful Death (2016). Frey sets forth the scope and content of the protocol's standards and explores what relevance they have for government authorities or for families searching for their loved ones. The processes of search and of investigation, while closely related, may involve different motivations, timelines, and standards of proof. The humanitarian search for the disappeared is conducted under the assumption that the missing person is still alive, and is therefore driven by the urgent need to locate the person before further harm may be done. The investigative process must meet the requirements of promptness, effectiveness, independence, and transparency, but is focused on gathering evidence for possible criminal charges and is therefore concerned with the thoroughness and reliability of the materials gathered. In most cases, the Minnesota Protocol is used to find a person presumed to be dead, and the investigative process is designed to locate the body, identify it, and return it to the family for a dignified disposal based on their personal beliefs. How these two processes – search and investigation – work together may be seen in the implementation of a law on disappearances in Mexico that prioritises search through a specialised set of state and federal mechanisms.

In Chapter 15, Rainer Huhle explains the process for sending urgent communications about disappearance cases to the United Nations (UN) system. Huhle introduces the work of two UN mechanisms that address the problem of disappearances: the UN Working Group on Enforced and Involuntary Disappearances (WGEID) and the UN Committee on Enforced Disappearances (CED). Both of these bodies have 'urgent action' procedures in disappearance cases, though advocates in these cases must tailor their requests to ensure the most impact. The chapter includes a summary version of the forms used to submit requests for urgent action to each of the two UN mechanisms, and what might be expected from each of the procedures. Huhle describes his experience working with this procedure as a member of the CED.

Michael Chamberlin explores in Chapter 16 how advocates are working to bring forward cases involving systematic patterns of enforced disappearance before the International Criminal Court. The Court, established in 2002 and based in The Hague, has jurisdiction over crimes against humanity, a category of crimes that includes the enforced disappearance of persons 'when committed as part of a widespread or systematic attack directed against any civilian population, with knowledge of the attack' (Rome Statute, article 7). Chamberlin describes the strategic reasons for bringing disappearance cases before the International Court, and briefly describes the grounds for admissibility and the procedure used by the prosecutor to review petitions. Every Latin American state, except for Cuba and Nicaragua, has ratified the Rome Statute and, thus, this process could provide an important strategic opportunity for bringing attention to widespread disappearances in the region.

The approach of strategic litigation in the Inter-American System is addressed by Sandra Serrano in Chapter 17. Serrano suggests various possibilities for engaging with the Inter-American Commission on Human Rights as well as the Court, which have both demonstrated a willingness to address the quintessentially Latin American violation of enforced disappearance. The chapter argues that the institutional history of the Inter-American System has been shaped by victims and their families, as well as by the region's human rights movement, itself forged in the struggle against the gravest human rights violations of authoritarian regimes, which were often committed against political opponents. The Inter-American System serves to respond to the new wave of disappearances in post-transitional contexts.

In Chapter 18, Volga de Pina Ravest discusses the experience of searching for the disappeared in Mexico. De Pina explains the principles and processes for searches that are set forth in Mexico's 2017 General Law on Enforced Disappearances. The product of a long and intense lobbying effort by networks of families of the disappeared, the law creates separate requirements and specialised tools, related to the search for victims and the criminal investigation of disappearances. This separation underscores the priority of the families, which is to find their disappeared loved ones. The law establishes a National Search Commission as well as requiring each of Mexico's 32 states to create a local search commission for the purpose of responding in a rapid and coordinated fashion to reports of disappearances. De Pina relates her observations on the successes and shortcomings of the search process, based on her participation in the Citizen's Council, which advises and oversees the work of the National Search Commission, and on her advocacy activities.

In the Conclusions to the book, Silvana Mandolessi draws out of the set of theoretical, case study, and tools chapters a set of 'best practices' or 'lessons learned'. She recognises the originality of the contribution of this volume in explaining that even when the context of disappearances changes there are logics that persist. In these more democratic contexts, families of victims of disappearance continue to face hurdles in attempting to access their rights to truth, investigation, justice, and guarantees of non-repetition. Mandolessi notes how this book contributes to an enhanced understanding of the multiple ways in which disappearances continue to occur in democratic countries. In the face of this continued suffering, the book does not leave the reader in despair, but instead offers a toolbox of best practices for civil society actors who continue to fight against disappearances, in Latin America and beyond. By reminding the reader of the power in the hands of civil society groups, Mandolessi recognises that the fight against disappearances must continue. The book is not an optimists' view based on wishful thinking, but sets forth the careful study of the efforts – and the outcomes of those efforts – to force democratic states to end this abhorrent practice.

## References

Ansolabehere, K., B. A. Frey, and L. A. Payne (2017), 'La "constitución" de la desaparición forzada: vínculos entre los significados legales y sociales de la desaparición', in *Desde y frente al estado: pensar, atender y resistir la desaparición de personas en México*, ed. J. Yankelovich (Mexico, Centro de Estudios Constitucionales de la Suprema Corte de Justicia de la Nación), pp. 1–26.

Dulitsky, A. (2017), 'Enforced Disappearances: General International Law Framework and Its Applicability to Transitional and Post-Transitional Periods', paper presented at *Limits of Transitional Justice: Post-Transition Disappearances and Impunity for Business Human Rights Violations*, St Antony's College, University of Oxford.

Dulitzky, A. (2019), 'The Latin American Flavor of Enforced Disappearances', *Chicago Journal of International Law*, 19 (Winter), 423–89.

Sheridan, M. (2020), 'More than 60,000 Mexicans Have Disappeared Amid Drug War, Officials Say', *Washington Post*, https://www.washingtonpost.com/world/the_americas/more-than-60000-mexicans-have-been-disappeared-amid-drug-war-officials-say/2020/01/06/07a4ea56-24f8-11ea-9cc9-e19cfbc87e51_story.html (accessed 13 March 2021).

United Nations Human Rights Council (2020), 'Report of the Working Group on Enforced or Involuntary Disappearances', A/HRC/45/13.

# Part I

# Theoretical Framework

# 1

# Conceptualising Post-Transition Disappearances

LEIGH A. PAYNE AND KARINA ANSOLABEHERE

THE QUESTION OF what explains disappearances in the post-authoritarian and post-conflict era motivates this chapter. Implicit in the question is the degree to which explanations for past disappearances, or disappearances in the context of dictatorships and armed conflicts, apply to the phenomenon of disappearances in democratic contexts. What are the similarities and the differences in disappearances in distinct political contexts?

To get at this question, we first probe historical repertoires: that is when, how, why, and where has widespread disappearance occurred? In exploring the legacies of disappearance, we find similarities with and differences from the current post-transition context. The temporal and contextual analysis leads us to develop four disappearance logics that bridge the two historical moments. In other words, these logics linger despite differences in the act of disappearance, in the characteristic of the disappeared person, and in the political context. These enduring logics include the clandestine nature of disappearance to hide acts of violence; the social construction of a 'disposable people' to avoid protest against such acts when discovered; the political economy, or utility, behind the acts; and the use of 'ambiguous loss' resulting from disappearance as a form of social control. We conclude with reflections on the holistic approach to post-transition disappearances that we develop in the chapter.

## Legacies of Disappearance

The first salient disappearances that we have found occurred with the Night and Fog ('Nacht und Nebel') decree issued by Adolf Hitler on 7 December 1941. Opponents of the Nazi regime, especially political activists and members of the resistance, were targeted for imprisonment and death. Primarily from Belgium, Denmark, France,

*Proceedings of the British Academy*, **237**, 17–36, © The British Academy 2021.

Luxembourg, the Netherlands, and Norway, these opponents were picked up in the middle of the night, taken far from their homes to detention centres, interrogated, and never heard from again. According to Edward Crankshaw (2011: 215), the decree originated with Hitler, was promulgated by Wilhelm Keitel, the head of the Nazi Armed Forces High Command, and ordered by Heinrich Himmler as the head of the Schutzstaffel (SS) in the following way: the targeted individuals were 'to be transported to Germany secretly, and further treatment of the offenders will take place here; these measures will have a deterrent effect because: (*a*) the prisoners will vanish without leaving a trace; (*b*) no information may be given as to their whereabouts or their fate'. The Nazis referred to the victims as 'vanished' or 'transformed into mist'.

A logic of disappearance emerged – hiding crimes through the clandestine nature of disappearance – that continues today, as the cases and testimonies of this book show. The acts physically removed regime opponents and dominated the rest of the population by instilling fear, thereby permitting the consolidation of political power. Disappearance could also be viewed as a way Nazi Germany could deny accusations of inhumane treatment during the war, by removing evidence of wrongdoing. The evidence disappeared with the individuals. Uncertainty prevails to this day; there is no confirmed or verifiable count of those who disappeared in the Night and Fog. The crime of disappearance carried out by the Nazi regime is recognised, however. Disappearances were deemed war crimes and crimes against humanity in the Allied Forces' Nuremberg Trials, and were subsequently included in international human rights covenants and treaties, as shown by Barbara A. Frey (Chapter 2).

Despite the legal architecture that developed following the Second World War, disappearances did not end. The very term 'the disappeared' (*los desaparecidos*) is associated with the period of state terror in Argentina (1976–83). Military groups, sometimes with their civilian informants or accomplices, broke into the houses of political opponents at night, dragged their victims out of the house in front of their families, and forced them into cars, in which they were taken to clandestine detention centres, tortured, and sometimes killed, often never to be seen again. The pattern meant that the figure of the disappeared sometimes came with additional designations based on some knowledge of the events: 'detained – disappeared' or 'disappeared – assassinated'. The fact of disappearance was not always disputed. Even one of Argentina's infamous Junta leaders spoke of the disappeared. Shortly after the visit by the Inter-American Commission of Human Rights to Argentina in 1979, Junta leader General Jorge Videla mentioned the disappeared in a press conference:

> Regarding the disappeared as such, he is an unknown. If the man appeared, he would get Treatment X. And if the appearance confirms his death, Treatment Z would apply. But as long as he is disappeared, there is no special treatment. He is a disappeared, he has no entity. He is neither dead nor alive, he is disappeared. Regarding that situation, we cannot do anything'. (Aprea 2015, 275)[1]

[1] In Spanish: 'frente al desaparecido en tanto esté como tal, es una incognita el desaparecido. Si el hombre apareciera tendría un tratamiento X. Y si la aparición se convirtiera en certeza de su

Videla's statement was the first official Argentine acknowledgement of 'the disappeared'. Yet its widespread practice in the dictatorship meant that it was already well known within and outside the country. Not all sectors of Argentine society shunned the practice of disappearance. Some explained it away, suggesting that there must be a reason (*por algo será*), implying that the disappeared individuals themselves were culpable of wrongdoing to have ended up in such a situation. But others had already mobilised before Videla made his statement to denounce the disappearances. Groups of mothers and grandmothers, whose sons, daughters (sometimes pregnant), and grandchildren were disappeared by the repressive apparatus, had found each other searching for their family members in hospitals, morgues, police stations, and prisons. In Buenos Aires, they organised walking together every Thursday afternoon in the Plaza de Mayo, facing the government palace (Casa Rosada). They defied the dictatorship by demanding a response: 'our children were taken alive, we want them returned alive'. As shown by Leigh A. Payne and Hunter Johnson (Chapter 13), human rights groups mobilised together with the families of the disappeared in visibility and information campaigns, within the country and outside, to pressure the authoritarian state to end the violence, to return the disappeared, and to seek remedy for wrongdoing. Still today the Mothers of the Plaza de Mayo meet on Thursday afternoons to demand that attention be given to past disappearances and to raise new human rights concerns. They have protested post-dictatorship disappearances in Argentina – Julio López and Santiago Maldonado (see Federman *et al.*, Chapter 10).[2] They have become the iconic form of mobilisation around disappearances, spawning countless academic, journalistic, fictional, and artistic works, and inspiring anti-disappearance mobilisation in other parts of the world.

Recently attention has increased to new groups of mothers of disappeared inspired by the Argentine Mothers of the Plaza de Mayo. The Kurdish 'Saturday Mothers' (Cumartesi Anneleri), for example, have met since the mid-1990s at noon on Saturday in the Galatasary district of Istanbul in a silent vigil calling for the return alive of their sons, daughters, husbands, and other loved ones (Bozkurt and Kaya 2014). Signalling their impact, they have had to shut down their protest from time to time on account of repression. Such repression seems to have backfired, however, by expanding, rather than reducing, the numbers who turn out for these events. From the original 30 mothers, some thousands have joined in solidarity.

Despite the paradigmatic figure of the Argentine disappeared, Guatemala is recognised as the first case of systematic disappearances during Latin America's

fallecimiento, tiene un tratamiento Z. Pero mientras sea desaparecido no puede tener un tratamiento especial. Es un desaparecido, no tiene entidad. No está ni muerto ni vivo, está desaparecido. … Frente a eso no podemos hacer nada.'

[2] Former bricklayer Jorge Julio López became one of the disappeared during the period of state terror when he was kidnapped and placed in several clandestine torture centres. López survived and aimed to testify at the trial of the head of the Buenos Aires Provincial Police, Miguel Etchecolatz. On the eve of his court appearance in 2006, López disappeared again. There is still no evidence of his whereabouts in 2020.

period of authoritarian rule. Following the violent overthrow of the democratically elected government of Jacobo Árbenz in 1954, framed by Cold War ideology and the National Security Doctrine, four decades of systematic disappearance ensued in the country's civil war and authoritarian rule. The practice of enforced disappearance was widespread, aimed at eliminating sectors of society presumed to be linked to left-wing groups. This tactic overlapped with ethnic cleansing; Guatemalans of Mayan origin constituted 83 per cent of the estimated 200,000 dead and disappeared. In this sense, disappearance grew out of a logic of eliminating internal threats to privileged social and economic classes and the regime protecting them. The social construction of 'disposable peoples' who could be disappeared without protest – because of political ideology; social, class, and ethnic origin; and perceived deviance – emerged as a logic that continues today.

In El Salvador too the involvement of the 'death squads' – a co-conspiracy of military, paramilitary, self-defence, and civil forces – used disappearance as part of the strategy to eliminate those who challenged authoritarian, capitalist, western, Christian, rule. The disappeared included so-called political subversives, guerrilla rebels, Communists, or others associated with left-leaning or opposition politics. The 1981 massacre of an estimated 800 Salvadorans in El Mozote revealed the efforts made to 'disappear' the evidence of killing, and the responsibility of US-supported and trained Salvadoran troops, by attempting to eliminate all witnesses and burning the village and the evidence to the ground. The disappearance logic aimed to hide evidence of wrongdoing through clandestine activity. Had it not been for the testimony of a single survivor, and journalists' reports in the international press, the cover-up might have succeeded. Instead, while preparing this volume, a trial for the massacre is ongoing. Unfortunately, so too are the disappearances, as documented in Chapters 11 and 12 through 'Wilson''s testimony and María José Méndez's analysis.

Gender has also been identified as an important element of disappearances in the armed-conflict and authoritarian regimes in the region. The Grandmothers of the Disappeared in Argentina originated because of the disappearance of pregnant daughters and daughters-in-law who gave birth while in clandestine detention centres to babies who were abducted into homes of families close to the military regime (Arditti 1999). The use of sexual violence as part of the genocidal practices aimed at the indigenous communities in Guatemala during the armed conflict is an issue that continues to demand accountability (Sanford 2008; Burt 2017). Testimony of political prisoners and evidence of rape and other forms of sexual torture on the bodies of women found in clandestine graves attest to the systematic use of gender-based violence during the authoritarian and armed-conflict periods. Women constitute 'disposable people' in particular historical and contemporary contexts.

The logics of hiding wrongdoing, rendering internal enemies 'disposable', and generating social control through ambiguous loss are evident in the Brazilian dictatorship. It is also an example of the political economy of disappearance. Systematic disappearance of mineworkers, rural workers, and trade unionists in urban factories was a key feature of the country's search for truth in its 1985 Torture Never Again unofficial report, the 1995 Special Commission of Deaths and Disappearances, the 2015 Rubens Paiva (São Paulo) State Truth Commission, and the 2014 National Truth Commission final report. In 2018, the body of disappeared trade unionist Aluísio Palhano Pedreira Ferreira was found, 47 years after he had disappeared in 1971. He had been an activist in the bank workers' union, and ardently fought for the rights of democratic workers and the disenfranchised. As a visible political activist on the left, he was targeted by the authoritarian regime. Subsequent documents showed he had been under surveillance since the beginning of the authoritarian regime, which took power in the 1964 coup; through his self-exile; and after his secret return to the country in 1970, when he joined the armed left-wing Popular Revolutionary Vanguard (Vanguarda Popular Revolucionária (VPR)). Witnesses heard, and saw the effects of, his torture sessions in various of the regime's detention centres. His body was found in a mass clandestine grave in the São Paulo cemetery of Perus. This case illustrates the particular targeting by the authoritarian regimes not only of political enemies, but also of enemies of the capitalist development projects instigated by an authoritarian regime closely connected to domestic and international big business. This was not unique to Brazil; it represents a broader logic around the political economy of disappearance during the authoritarian and armed-conflict periods in the region. The conjunction of these logics prevails beyond the dictatorship, as Chapter 4 by Karina Ansolabehere and Álvaro Matos, about Mexico's post-transitional disappearances illustrates.

It is difficult to find a country that, during the authoritarian and armed-conflict period of the 1960s to the 1980s, did not systematically disappear perceived enemies. Although an extensive literature exists on these historic examples of disappearances in the region, we have not found a single study of disappearances in democratic contexts, either in Latin America or elsewhere. This is not because disappearances do not occur in democracies. Contemporary disappearances explored in this book in democratic systems in Argentina, Brazil, El Salvador, and Mexico are evidence that they do. These four country examples suggest that the practice of disappearances in an earlier authoritarian or armed-conflict period may have an enduring legacy when a violent context prevails. Yet disappearance is not a historical repertoire in all countries of the region; we have not found examples of such disappearances in Uruguay, for example. In addition, there is great variation in post-transition disappearances across the region, suggesting that legacy alone is not enough to explain the phenomenon.

Disappearances, in other words, are not an inevitable legacy of authoritarian rule or armed conflict in the region. Nonetheless, they constitute a repertoire of political action, a way of doing politics, that can re-emerge as a strategy even after the transition from authoritarian rule or armed conflict. Thus, even when political regimes change, logics of disappearance can endure and shape the practices of governments and armed groups.

## Logics of Disappearance

These historic examples suggest a set of logics of disappearance from the past that still resonate today, even after transitions from authoritarian rule and armed conflict. These four overlapping logics include: (1) hiding wrongdoing from view through clandestine acts of disappearance; (2) disappearing populations deemed 'disposable' because of their social class, race and ethnicity, gender, geographic location, or political views; (3) disappearing those who potentially challenge the unfolding political economy of development; and (4) establishing social control through ambiguous loss. Underlying these logics is the recognition that social intolerance for open violence exists in democratic systems. This drives the violence underground. In addition, a process of social construction transforms citizens into marginalised, and therefore disposable, subjects who do not provoke outcry or a demand for accountability. Indeed, family members and communities find their efforts at making demands stifled by their own weak status in society. Simultaneously, victims and survivors face the ambiguity of loss from disappearance, complicating their capacity to mobilise. We delve into each of these logics before constructing our holistic approach to disappearances.

### Clandestine Acts of Disappearance

By hiding the act of violence, disappearance lessens the potential reputational and legal costs to states of human rights abuses. The abusive acts disappear along with the person. Authoritarian regimes and armed conflicts would seem to be immune to these types of costs. Yet international attention to disappearances has historically raised the costs of committing such acts to authoritarian states and armed actors. Following this logic, state actors, security forces, and/or powerful private groups in specific areas in democratic systems are even more likely to want to avoid the costs associated with committing or tolerating violence against populations. Moreover, pressure on democratic states to comply with human rights standards is likely to be higher given mobilised citizens and groups, institutional checks and balances, powerful democratic states, and international human rights and governance organisations. Violence carried out or tolerated by democratic states is thus more likely to be clandestine than overt. If the other logics behind disappearance prevail, therefore (i.e. the need to eliminate disposable peoples, the economic benefit from disappearing populations, and the social control rendered through ambiguous loss), and a repertoire of past disappearances exists, democracies will probably engage in or tolerate clandestine acts of disappearance.

The repertoire of disappearance may relate to the notion developed by Paloma Aguilar and Iosif Kovras (2019) of 'collaboration years'. Those years allow for authoritarian regimes to establish sophisticated systems of control over information and to adapt strategies to changing domestic and international responses to disappearances. Aguilar and Kovras suggest that as the pressure for accountability for human rights violations increases, disappearances are also likely to increase to hide abuses from public scrutiny. It would thus follow that when democracies face such scrutiny, disappearances may increase to hide violence. Where a legacy of past disappearance practices in authoritarian or armed-conflict situations prevails, these practices need not be constructed anew, but rather can be reactivated and adapted within a democratic system.

Disappearances occurring in democracies, moreover, may involve the kinds of 'clandestine linkages' identified by Javier Auyero (2010). Adapting Auyero, an agreement is forged among key actors to avoid reputational and legal costs by carrying out violence clandestinely. The underground nature of this violence allows democratic states to respond to the call for investigation into disappearance from international organisations and domestic groups, by denying the acts. Because the evidence of wrongdoing tends to disappear with the person, investigations and redress only rarely move forward in holding states responsible for complicity in these acts. Perpetrators do not cease committing human rights abuses; they hide them better. The logic behind disappearances depends in part on an implicit agreement, a pact of silence, that recognises the necessity to hide acts of violence because of the costs associated with visibility.

Yet these disappearances rarely remain fully invisible. Missing peoples begin to have a presence in domestic or international campaigns carried out by their colleagues, friends, and relatives. State denial usually fails to suppress these mobilisations. Accompanying such denial, therefore, is an active process of socially constructing the disappeared person in a way that removes their dignity, their humanity, and thus diminishes the likelihood of outcry against the wrongdoing. This is the process of constructing disposable peoples.

## Constructing Disposable Peoples

Forms of security and development narratives behind disappearances in authoritarian regimes and armed conflicts resurface in democracies. In authoritarian and armed-conflict situations, the disappeared subjects were 'subversives', enemies of social, political, and economic order and security. In democratic systems, too, there are those who are perceived as 'deviants', who threaten physical security and the social, political, and economic order. The same perceived need to remove these threats persists in both types of regimes. Because democracies are more constrained by laws, institutions, and social mobilisation, they may prove more actively engaged in the process of demonising the disappeared subjects as a way to defuse public outcry.

The disappeared in post-transition contexts, therefore, tend to be from socially, economically, and culturally marginalised populations. These populations, after all, are perceived as having the potential to disrupt the economic, social, and political status quo. As such, they constitute an implicit, if not explicit, threat to order, security, and stability. In addition, the disappearance of marginalised populations is less likely to provoke outcry than if more elite segments of society – citizens with rights – were disappeared. Because of their marginality, the disappeared lack the power of visibility and voice. If the middle and upper classes were systematically victimised, tolerance for disappearances would certainly diminish. Outcry and mobilisation would increase, heightening the reputational and legal cost to governments. Pressure on states from within and outside the country would probably lead to an ending of the practice and the increased likelihood that the state would respond to relatives' demand for the search for the missing and justice for wrongdoing. Without visibility, voice, and equality as citizens, marginalised groups are disappeared with impunity.

This attitude toward the disappeared results from histories of prejudice and discrimination. But it also involves active social construction of the disappeared person. The disappeared are transformed from citizens with equal rights into 'disposable people'. In so doing, they appear in public narratives as enemies of national values, order, stability, security, and economic progress. These public narratives are a form of myth-making that begins to justify disappearance. The language used during the Argentine period of state terror of 'there must be a reason' (*por algo será*) takes on a similar tone in post-transition Mexico: 'they are involved in something' (*está metido en algo*), as described in the testimony of Lulú Herrera (Chapter 3). An explanation is provided for why certain people have disappeared and not others. Those who are disappeared begin to be seen as somehow deserving of that treatment. This process of demonising disappeared victims translates into a lack of pressure on the government to search for the missing, investigate wrongdoing, and initiate accountability efforts. They disappear with impunity.

An arbitrary or random act might be more likely to prompt an investigation than the systematic disappearance of those who are perceived to have been involved in something, particularly in contexts of prolonged and generalised violence. The history of disappearance suggests that victims of widespread disappearance are often viewed as culpable in their own disappearance, because of their transgressive acts. They are seen as enemies of the state and civilisation, such as political subversives, traitors, Communists, criminal elements. Or they are perceived to be contaminants of 'good' society: Jews, Roma people, homosexuals, atheists, the indigenous, the brown- or black-skinned, the poor. The classification of people as deserving mistreatment renders them disposable: what Graham Denyer Willis (2015) calls 'killable subjects' and Judith Butler (2015) refers to as 'ungrievable lives'.

Becoming killable, ungrievable, or disposable is also gendered, as studies of gender-based violence and feminicide show. While the figure of the disappeared is disproportionately male, killing and disappearing girls and women are a form of social cleansing with impunity. Females become disposable because of misogyny, patriarchy, perceived threatening behaviour when they transgress traditional gendered roles (e.g. through working outside the home, their appearance, their sexual choices and identity, their family life, their social life), their race, or ethnicity. Victoria Sanford (2008: 112–13) notes that gender-based violence with impunity 'reveals the very social character of the killing of women as a product of power between men and women … and implicates the state as a responsible party, whether by commission, toleration, or omission'. Their disappearance 'means the destruction of the material bases of the community as well as its reproductive capacity' (Sanford 2008: 107). Sanford refers to ways in which the disappeared are framed as 'disposable' by highlighting certain facts, such as branding a woman found with a 'belly ring … as a gang member and/or prostitute' (111).

Demonising victims does not require the existence of an authoritarian state or armed conflict. Democratic states and societies can render 'disposable' certain classifications of people. These are the people who do not deserve to be searched for, who do not enjoy the right to life, investigation, justice, dignity. They lack democratic citizenship and democratic rights even under a democratic state and in a democratic society. They can be rendered as such through compelling narratives. In situations of high levels of violent crime, those who are assumed to perpetuate the violence are transformed into the enemy of the democratic state and society. Security and stability involve removing those violent groups by whatever means necessary. The ends justify the means. The perceived criminal becomes disposable in the interest of protecting rightful citizens and legal order.

Paradoxically, the act of disappearing suspected criminals violates the very rule of law such acts aim to protect. Where order becomes increasingly undermined by political, social, and criminal violence, the notion of the enemy is broadened, and tolerance for the disappearance of the presumed culprits of this violence grows. Certain peoples become disposable. But because such acts of violence against peoples should not be tolerated in rule-of-law systems, they must be hidden. Hence, a logic behind the disappearance of certain peoples, of hiding the violence against certain peoples with impunity, emerges.

In the cases explored in this book, disposable peoples are those without social and economic resources, who live in marginalised communities, who are brown or black. These individuals in El Salvador and Brazil are socially constructed as criminal elements because of their class, skin colour, geographic location. As criminals, or potential criminals, they are perceived as not deserving rights, as disposable. The disappeared examined in this book also include those who protest the political, social, and economic status quo. In Mexico, the disappeared include journalists who dig for the truth, human rights advocates, and survivors. These are groups that push the state to protect the security of all citizens, and not only elites.

In sum, the logic of disappearance is to remove peoples who can be construed in some way as a threat. To do so without a backlash requires two steps. First, the acts must be clandestine to avoid reprisals – because when disappearances occur on a large scale they become knowable by the public. The second step is to transform the disappeared into 'disposable peoples', those without value, without voice, without rights, without protection. By doing so, a complicit silence, tolerance, and impunity surround disappearance, creating a permissible environment for disappearances to continue.

## The Political Economy of Disappearance

Related to 'who' is disappeared is a corresponding logic of 'why'. Specifically, the economic utility of disappearance transcends authoritarian and armed-conflict situations into democratic ones. In the dictatorships and armed conflicts of the past in the region, economic actors allied with authoritarian state actors and paramilitary forces to eliminate challenges to business. Economic actors supported, directly and indirectly, the national security states' detention, torture, death, and disappearance of union leaders and workers as a means of eliminating barriers to the particular capitalist-deepening projects underway (O'Donnell 1973). Those targeted by the alliance of economic actors with military and paramilitary forces in armed conflicts and authoritarian regimes were those who protested cuts in wages, social benefits, and labour rights (Payne *et al.* 2020). Iconic cases from the Brazilian civil military regime and the Salvadoran civil war reflect this economic logic. The use of the term 'a coup and a regime against workers' (Fontes and Corrêa 2018) for Brazil's civil-military dictatorship refers to the torture, killing, and disappearance of rural and urban workers and trade unionists. One example of a disappeared worker during the Brazilian dictatorship is Olavo Hanssen. Secretly detained while distributing pamphlets on International Workers' Day (1 May) in 1970, Hanssen was subsequently tortured to death by state security agents of the Departamento de Ordem Política e Social (DOPS). After injecting a pesticide into his veins, state authorities buried his body in a clandestine grave. They then reported to Hanssen's family that they found his body, and evidence that he had committed suicide by poison. In El Salvador, a report from a United States Senate hearing (United States Senate 1981), based largely on evidence gathered by Amnesty International, reported on violations that had 'intensified sharply', including 'arbitrary detentions, "disappearances" and killings primarily of *campesinos* [rural workers, or peasants] by military and security forces, as well as by the paramilitary body ORDEN, which has continued to operate in spite of a government decree … declaring it dissolved' (244). The rural violence described resembled 'scorched earth' techniques on behalf of private rural landholders and businesses. As the hearing report states:

> Initial eye-witness reports … affirm that troop movement by Army and National Guard units that were announced as measures for the implementation of the land reform have in fact involved the disappearance and killing of hundreds of campesinos in villages supporting opposition labour organisations in Morazán, Cuscatlán, Chalatenango and San Salvador departments. Reports say that Army, National Guard, and ORDEN forces virtually wiped out several hamlets in Cuscatlán on 13 March, killing four persons outright, and detaining and causing to 'disappear' 30 others. (246)

The political-economy logic behind types of disappearances in authoritarian and armed-conflict situations also have a 'democratic' variant. In Argentina, the disappearance of Santiago Maldonado (see Chapters 9 and 10) occurred after his involvement in protest activities with indigenous communities against the Benetton company's practices of environmental and human exploitation for profit. While openly engaging in state violence against protesters on behalf of the company might have costly reputational effects, the disappearance of a single protester could send a clear warning about the consequences of challenging businesses. The political-economy logic of disappearance is thus to reduce labour and community constraints on business activity.

Another aspect of the political-economy logic behind disappearance relates to workers who become disposable after they have served their utility function. While Kevin Bales (1999) does not focus on disappearance, he identifies the phenomenon of 'disposable people' resulting from 'new slavery in the global economy'. He defines modern slavery as 'total control of one person by another for the purpose of economic exploitation ... [people] controlled by violence and denied all of their personal freedom to make money for someone else' (6). 'Slaves', he argues, 'keep your costs low and returns on your investment high ... People get rich by using slaves ... And when they've finished with their slaves, they just throw these people away ... People become completely disposable tools for making money' (4). Extending Bales' notion, disappearing those disposable individuals who have exhausted their economic utility provides the means to hide violent and illegal modern slavery systems. Bales identifies this disposable labour force as the result of economic vulnerability owing to extreme levels of unemployed, underemployed, impoverished, and often racial and ethnic social marginalisation. As Bales argues, 'predators are keenly aware of weakness' in which '[t]he common denominator is poverty, not color' (11). He explains that '[w]ithout work and with increasing fear as resources diminish, people become desperate and life becomes cheap' (12). Bales recognises, however, that luring workers into modern slavery is not the only means of acquiring them; some are captured or kidnapped (19).

The political-economy logic of disappearance begins with the systems of marginality that Bales describes. The lure of employment for the unemployed or underemployed, or their capture, is the first part of the process. The second step is coercion behind the work: locking in, chaining, or threatening with or using violence to force workers to work and making it nearly impossible for them to leave. The third step is money. Despite atrocious working and living conditions, a form of debt peonage involves deducting the costs workers incur (e.g. equipment, clothes, food, housing) from their pay, leaving them with little or no wages. A fourth step is what to do with workers once they have exhausted their utility. The overseer has very little investment in these workers. As Bales contends, modern slavery has 'all of the benefits of ownership without the legalities ... [t]hey get total control without any responsibility for what they own' (5). Thus, when workers become unable to work because they are weak or sick, or when they have completed the work and no longer have utility, they are discarded. Disappearing them hides modern slavery systems.

Disappearance with impunity adds an additional step. As Bales states, 'The extreme profitability of slavery means that slaveholders can buy political power and acceptance' (29). They can influence government officials, police, politicians, and others with bribery. They can incorporate those officials into the business. They can also use violence, or the threat of violence, against state officials to avoid repercussions. The political-economy logic behind disappearance thus gains from guarantees of impunity owing to the power and influence of those who engage in such activity, and the economic and social benefits that result from turning a blind eye to the enslavement of disposable people.

State officials in this sense may become complicit with economic enterprises in guaranteeing impunity for disappearances related to exploitative work in remote mines or agriculture, urban sweat shops, or sex work. This complicity may also extend to other types of economic activity, such as toxic dumping or other violating behaviours by legal businesses that affect indigenous or other marginalised communities. Disappearances in these cases may target those who protest such business activity, as evident in the Maldonado case.

The Mexico chapters in this book (Chapters 3, 4, and 5) address a different type of disappearance related to a political-economy logic. Organised crime groups require labour to design and build tunnels for the trafficking of illegal commodities across the USA–Mexico border, and also to produce and transport those commodities. To carry out this economic activity, organised crime groups prey on people in marginalised communities, kidnapping or enticing them into forced labour. They hide these systems of illegal trafficking in commodities and labour by disposing of – disappearing – those workers. These illicit activities are carried out within networks of macro-criminality, in which states, licit businesses, and even communities share in the economic benefits that come from forced labour and the subsequent disappearance of the enslaved. Profits generated by eliminating the cost of labour are recirculated in ways that reward complicit state actors, provide investments in the legal economy, and offer social prestige for those who participate. Luis Daniel Vázquez Valencia (2019: 61–3) defined macro-criminality as a situation of heightened corruption in which private actors, criminals, and state officials work through the state to realise the objectives of the criminal network, without regard for the public good. Vázquez explains that in the northeastern states of Mexico, this form of corruption includes conspiring with the criminal network to murder, traffic, and disappear people, all for the primary purpose of maintaining the power of the criminal network (63). The political economy of disappearance can take another form when criminal groups remove their adversaries, or competition, by killing and disappearing them. This allows certain criminal groups to consolidate territorial and business control in certain regions.

Those who do escape, as well as other witnesses, fear their own disappearance if they reveal what they know. In systems of widespread violence, clandestine linkages raise doubts that state authorities would be likely to respond effectively. Indeed, reporting to state authorities may heighten risks to personal security given linkages with organised crime. Bales claims that even in some democratic states, 'the police *are* organized crime' (Bales 1999: 29).

The political-economy logic of disappearances is differentiated by gender. Among the slave labour practices related to the disappearance of women are human-trafficking networks, in many cases related to sexual exploitation. Certain accepted practices of gendered violence include the disappearance of women who work as adult dancers. The prevailing view of their profession renders them 'disposable', and thus leaves their families without the possibility of official recourse to investigation and justice.

Disappearance is thus not anomalous to democracies. In democratic states where illegal activities permeate the economic, political, and social order, economic motivations for disappearances prevail, characterised by networks of sex- and labour-trafficking that operate with impunity through complicity and corruption. Organised crime is not the only form of political-economy logic that operates in democratic systems. It also prevails where labour is cheap, abundant, where workers are un- or underemployed and marginalised, and where the capacity exists to bribe underpaid and undertrained state authorities. In these systems, too, workers disappear with impunity after they have exhausted their economic utility. Those who witness these acts face implicit or explicit threats to keep quiet. And those who have engaged in them have sufficient power to infiltrate or control the state to guarantee continued violent economic exploitation with impunity.

## Social Control through Ambiguous Loss

One logic behind the tolerance of disappearance is the elimination of the enemies and undesirables of the state. Disappearance thus becomes a strategy of social control, identified explicitly in the Night and Fog decree. Ambiguous loss that results from the uncertainty related to disappearance has the effect of paralysing survivors and reinforcing order through fear. Triple victimhood results: in the first place with the disappearance of a family member; then through the association of the disappeared person with crime or other anti-state/society activity; and third by the loss of citizenship rights experienced by survivors and their advocates when their demands for truth, investigation, justice, and guarantees of non-repetition are ignored by state actors in the context of widespread impunity.

In past authoritarian state and armed-conflict violence, victims could count on international pressure on states to advance these rights. The international community may prove less willing to intervene on behalf of victims in democratic states, either because of the legitimacy of those states or the belief that rule-of-law systems exist to protect victims. In democratic contexts, therefore, naming-and-shaming strategies become much less effective in attracting international pressure. Moreover, the myth-making around these victims, rendering them criminal deviants, makes them less appealing for international campaigns in defence of 'innocent' victims. Although there are some cases in which international outcry has resulted from disappearance – consider, for example, the 43 students from Azyotzinapa or the Maldonado case in Argentina (see Chapters 9 and 10 in this book) – such examples prove to be the exceptions that confirm the rule. In those cases, families and human rights groups fought against the image of these disappeared peoples as criminal protesters, and instead focused on their role as aspiring teachers and advocates of social justice. Thus, humanising the victims is fundamental to effective international advocacy.

Although legal frameworks do not distinguish between types of citizens disappeared (see Chapter 2 by Barbara A. Frey), disappearances are very difficult to investigate and advance through judicial systems. It is often difficult to find sufficient evidence to link disappearances to perpetrators. After all, when the person is disappeared, the information about that person and the violation also disappears: i.e. the identity of the disappeared, the identity of the perpetrator, the details of the act, sometimes even the witnesses. Government actors use the difficulty of investigating the cases as a justification for systematic impunity, which is a context that breeds further disappearances.

As this book shows, in Argentina, Brazil, El Salvador, and Mexico, evidence of enforced disappearance is often linked to the direct actions of state officials. That evidence points to a pattern of direct state involvement in systematic human rights violations through the disappearance of the person. In other cases, non-state criminal violence, including disappearance, is carried out with the acquiescence of state authorities, whether through institutional complicity; corruption; or fear that results in the failure to protect, to prevent, or to punish the crime. In this way, contemporary disappearances in democratic systems are distinct from historical periods, such as in Latin America's period of civil-military dictatorships, and in Nazi Germany, where disappearances took place in clandestine torture and extermination centres run by the state.

There is little doubt that historic disappearances functioned as a form of overt political and social control. The Night and Fog decree already mentioned was about not only eliminating presumed enemies of the regime, but also controlling populations; thwarting the emergence of more opposition and resistance; and creating terrorised citizens unable to challenge the state for fear of their own, or their relatives', disappearance. If the disappeared lack social, legal, political, or economic capital, they do not have the resources to denounce the crime. Disappearances in contemporary democracies provide the means to carry out social and political cleansing without accountability. They also provide a means of social control by guaranteeing that populations will avoid challenges to authority to protect their security. Who can denounce state action (either commission of the crime or failure to investigation and prosecute) if the crime is not verifiable? In this context, which allows the state to hide its involvement, advances in domestic and international law and advocacy regarding enforced disappearances have had a limited effect.

Ambiguous loss, defined as the uncertainty and lack of information about a missing person, is itself a form of social control (Boss 1999). The missing person is both present and absent. There is a lack of closure or an ability to move forward through the grieving process if there is no certainty that the person is gone. Without having the very facts of the violation, basic information – what happened, to whom, by whom – disappears with the person.

In past authoritarian and armed-conflict situations, relatives of the disappeared attempted to pursue a crime that did not exist given the state of law or the state of emergency. This left victims' relatives helpless and without hope. The disappearances analysed in this book, however, occur in the context of existing domestic and international legal frameworks that recognise the crime of disappearance. In such a context, ambiguous loss assumes a different dimension. First, the act of disappearance is rhetorically denied. Disappearances can be rhetorically denied by using other designations of the act or the victim: kidnapping, missing persons, confrontations between armed or criminal groups. These terms can be used to absolve the state of responsibility for failing to investigate the crime of disappearance, and its own direct or indirect (acquiescent) role in that crime. Thus, in democratic contexts the disappearance itself creates ambiguous loss, but the official denial of the disappearance through rhetorical and legal mechanisms can deepen the harm. The particular form that ambiguous loss takes in democratic contexts – naming the crime as something else – deepens the sense of helplessness by removing an important tool of legal redress for disappearance. Without that legal designation of the disappeared, without state action to investigate, without certainty, and in the context of social myths regarding the disappeared, the logic of ambiguous loss as a form of social control prevails in democratic contexts.

And yet, despite ambiguous loss, families and communities do mobilise around disappearance. They find their voice. Indeed, organising and acting politically have allowed victims and their families to overcome ambiguous loss, as evident in the testimonies presented in this book. They look for the amplification of their demand for rights within and outside the country. But they are only sometimes heard.

Understanding how and when the rights of victims and their families are recognised is one of the objectives of this book. It operates on the assumption, drawn from historical examples, that if there is no mobilisation, no anti-impunity demand, then disappearances will continue. One explanation for the persistence of disappearance, therefore, is the lack of mobilisation, or the lack of resonance with survivors' demands.

The key efforts identified in the book aim to show that the disappeared are not disposable, but are citizens with rights, who form part of our everyday lives. These are people who live in our homes, go to our schools and churches, walk our streets. They are not different from us in that sense. They disappear from everyday life, but relatives aim to make them reappear, to be present, with photographs and other images (see Chapter 13 by Leigh A. Payne and Hunter Johnson). Human rights defenders, as presented in the empirical case studies in this book, work to reveal the state's role in carrying out, hiding, and otherwise failing to address these violent acts. They attempt in this context to construct viable pathways toward truth, justice, memory, and reparations.

## Toward a Holistic Framework

The four logics presented here prevail in authoritarian and armed conflicts and find new meaning in post-transitional contexts. Each separately contributes to the understanding of why disappearances occur, how they impact individuals and societies, and the challenges they present for human rights work. Constituting a multidisciplinary approach, these logics are the basis for constructing a theoretical framework to explain disappearances in the post-transition. We call this a holistic approach. In philosophy, holism recognises the interconnected nature of the parts. Only by recognising these parts – these four logics – as interconnected is the phenomenon of disappearance explicable. This holistic approach further links the logics and dynamics of disappearance to past historical repertoires in authoritarian and armed-conflict contexts with contemporary democratic contexts. We attempt to explain the logics behind how, why, and when disappearance occurs.

The starting point is the political context in which a perceived need for social order emerges. Historically, threats to the economic, social, and political order posed by left-wing radical redistribution movements, or the perceived social contamination of ethnic or religious groups, motivated disappearances. Eliminating so-called 'subversives' and ethnic cleansing required clandestine operations – disappearances – to avoid a backlash from within and outside the country. A paradoxical process of both admitting and denying disappearances occurs. Just enough information had to be released for social control to be effective – the logic of ambiguous loss – without too much evidence of wrongdoing being revealed that could halt the process. Historic examples shed light on past disappearances, but the dynamics and logics behind those acts did not end with authoritarian regimes or armed conflict.

The argument we make in this chapter is that political contexts of disappearances transcend particular types of political regimes and conflicts. There is nothing about the post-transition that makes systems immune to the four logics of disappearance set out here. Though the motivations behind disappearances, the state responses to them, the direct perpetrators, and the targeted victims alter from the authoritarian and armed-conflict periods to the democratic ones, the logics of hiding wrongdoing to avoid accountability and constructing disposable peoples, the economic gain from disappearance, and creation of social order through ambiguous loss persist. The differences in the two periods may involve particular emphases – from a discourse of ideological threat to a discourse of criminal threat – rather than a shift in underlying logics of disappearance.

The study of disappearances in post-transitional societies suggests certain sociological dynamics at work. To avoid a backlash against the disappearance of social groups, an active process of associating or constructing those figures as deviant, stigmatising them and those who search for them, becomes necessary (Goffman 1963). Targeted individuals and groups are framed as undeserving of state or social care and concern. Certain attitudes and actions are associated with them as a form of justification of their disappearance. The framing process predisposes broad sectors of the population against the disappeared, rendering apathy or hostility toward those who mobilise for their search, investigation into their disappearance, and justice for wrongdoing. A form of social silencing surrounds the act. Without the need for overt or official forms of censorship, the silence in the media reflects the social distancing from the disappeared.

Marginalisation of certain sectors of society renders them vulnerable to violent and exploitative labour that has its own logic of disappearance. The ability of certain legal and illegal economic enterprises to avoid redress for, or even to work together with state officials in, violent systems of modern slavery and community control is the result of poverty, inequality, and corruption in democracies or in authoritarian and armed-conflict systems. In this sense, and as developed in various chapters of the book, focusing on the direct responsibility of states and security forces in the act of disappearance is not enough. Acquiescence, illustrated by the failure of state institutions to address victims' and survivors' charge of disappearance as a crime against humanity, also warrants attention in understanding contemporary practice.

The nature of disappearance limits the possibility of mobilisation against this form of violence. Disappearance with impunity results from the economic, social, and political power disparities. In such systems, framing devices are used to stigmatise as deviants the disappeared and those who defend the search for the missing, and negates the right to truth, justice, and guarantees of non-recurrence. That evidence disappears with the individual limits knowledge about the act. The absence of information weakens efforts to denounce the act effectively. The social psychology of ambiguous loss in which relatives do not know what has happened can also defuse mobilisation. The legal system and official discourse are key to the process of creating 'ambiguity' surrounding the nature or even the existence of the crime. This is particularly the case when, as survivors attest, they are stigmatised by their association with the disappeared person, and they are seen as social deviants because of their class, race, and geographic location. Who will listen to them?

Overcoming the myths of the disappeared, the silence and invisibility of the act, and constraints on mobilisation, requires strength, creativity, and resonance. The strength to mobilise against all hope of a response appears to emerge out of despair. Mothers, wives, sisters, and other family members remark that they would do anything to recover their loved one. These are not new struggles; recognition of the resolve and extreme measures family members will take in such situations has existed since Sophocles' *Antigone* in 441 BCE (Sophocles 1990). But the testimonies provided in this book, and the historical knowledge garnered from other experiences, show that strength is also a result of collective mobilisation. Those who feel too powerless, are too timid, or are too fearful to act on their own find strength through numbers and through solidarity. There is, in other words, a way to overcome ambiguous loss through mobilisation. But as the works by Mara Loveman (1998) and by Kristina Thalhammer (2001) show, this form of high-risk mobilisation is not attempted by all. Some families are certain that mobilising will lead to the disappearance of more of their family members or friends. Others act even in the recognition of this knowledge or expectation.

Creativity may help overcome the fear of mobilisation in violent contexts. Engaging civil society actors in public processes of raising attention may begin to reduce fear. Associations with a range of actors – human rights activists and advocates, religious leaders, scholars, etc. – assure victims and their families that they are not alone. When they engage in artful and disruptive processes, they break the silence and they generate attention. In each of the cases examined in this book, survivors find each other in the search for the disappeared. In that search they discover that together they have strength. They also find a nexus with groups of relatives to work in unison to generate the evidence that a disappearance happened, that it was not an isolated event, that it could happen to others, that the tragedy has to stop, and that the disappeared need to be found and justice served to prevent future atrocities. In doing so, they tend to garner attention from the local media, and sometimes from international media. Such efforts further reduce the fear associated with mobilisation.

Yet resonance, both within and outside the country, is part of the process of reducing fear and increasing pressure on the state. When mobilisation resonates with communities, nations, and internationally, states are forced to respond in some way. They may try denial. But increasing demand from civil society groups will probably encourage advocates to pursue innovative strategies to challenge such denials.

As a result of heightened pressure, state agents are forced to acknowledge the situation. They begin to develop programmes and policies to address it. These state efforts tend to be partial, poorly designed and implemented, and underfinanced, thus failing to address effectively the right to life, justice, and reparations for victims.

What we have shown in this chapter is that the logics of disappearances in the historical and contemporary periods are not identical, but they are very similar. We have also shown that the responses to them – the dynamic of collective mobilisation, pressure, adaptation to the political and legal framework – are essential to drawing attention to the invisible phenomenon of disappearance and the absence of effective state attention to the crime. This depends on the mobilisation of victims and their relatives from below, because these disappearances often occur at the margins of society. To address this form of wrongdoing, however, domestic and international advocates and their creative legal and media strategies have always been key. One of the primary differences we see among the cases examined in this book is not, then, the logics of disappearance, the method of mobilisation around them, and the response from the state across time, but rather what is taking place within countries. What seems to explain the relatively low level of disappearances in contemporary Argentina compared to the cases in Mexico, El Salvador, and Brazil is not the history of disappearances, but rather the historical mobilisation within Argentina to address disappearances when they occurred under democracy. The use of advocacy networks to raise attention, and institutions to pursue official responses to disappearance, may explain the difference between the massive number of disappearances in Brazil, El Salvador, and Mexico, and the extraordinary and isolated cases in Argentina. While one, two, or three cases are too many, such a situation is enviable for those victims and survivors in countries experiencing tens of thousands of such cases. This should serve as encouragement to advocates, that their mobilisation against disappearances now will also lay the foundation for prevention of those crimes in the future.

## References

Aguilar, P., and I. Kovras (2019), 'Explaining Disappearances as a Tool of Political Terror', *International Political Science Review*, 40:3, 437–52.

Aprea, G. (2015), *Documental, testimonios y memorias: el pasado militante* (Buenos Aires, Manantial).

Arditti, R. (1999), *Searching for Life: The Grandmothers of the Plaza de Mayo and the Disappeared Children of Argentina* (Berkeley, University of California Press).

Auyero, J. (2010), 'Clandestine Connections: The Political and Relational Makings of Collective Violence', in *Violent Democracies in Latin America*, ed. D. M. Goldstein and E. D. Arias (Durham, NC, Duke University Press), pp. 108–32.

Bales, K. (1999), *Disposable People: New Slavery in the Global Economy* (Berkeley, University of California Press).

Boss, P. (1999), *Ambiguous Loss: Learning to Live with Unresolved Grief* (Cambridge, MA, Harvard University Press).

Bozkurt H., and Ö. Kaya (2014), 'Holding Up the Photograph: Experiences of the Women whose Husbands Were Forcibly Disappeared' (Istanbul, Hakikat Adalet Hafıza Merkezi – Truth Justice Memory Center), https://dealingwiththepast.org/wp-content/uploads/2015/03/Holding_Up_the_Photograph-Hafiza_Merkezi_2014.pdf (accessed 25 March 2020).

Burt, J.-M. (2017), 'Judge Sends Five High-Ranking Military Officers to Trial in Molina Theissen Case', *International Justice Monitor* (6 March), www.ijmonitor.org/2017/03/judge-sends-five-high-ranking-military-officers-to-trial-in-molina-theissen-case/ (accessed 1 April 2020).

Butler, J. (2015), *Precariousness and Grievability: When Is Life Grievable?* (London, Verso).

Crankshaw, E. (2011), *Gestapo* (London, Bloomsbury Reader).

Fontes P., and L. R. Corrêa (2018), 'Labor and Dictatorship in Brazil: A Historiographical Review', *International Labor and Working-Class History*, 93 (Spring), 27–51.

Goffman, E. (1963), *Stigma: Notes on the Management of Spoiled Identity* (New York, Simon & Schuster).

Loveman, M. (1998), 'High Risk Collective Action: Defending Human Rights in Chile, Uruguay, and Argentina', *American Journal of Sociology*, 104:2, 477–525.

O'Donnell, G. A. (1973), *Modernization and Bureaucratic-Authoritarianism* (Berkeley, Institute for International Studies, University of California).

Payne, L. A., G. Pereira, and L. Bernal-Bermúdez (2020), *Corporate Accountability and Transitional Justice: Deploying Archimedes' Lever* (Cambridge and New York, Cambridge University Press).

Sanford, V. (2008), 'From Genocide to Feminicide: Impunity and Human Rights in Twenty-First Century Guatemala', *Journal of Human Rights*, 7:2, 104–22.

Sophocles (1990), *Antigone* (Oxford, Oxford University Press).
Thalhammer, K. E. (2001), 'I'll Take the High Road: Pathways to Human Rights Activism in Authoritarian Argentina', *Political Psychology*, 22:3, 493–520.
Vázquez Valencia, L. D. (2019), *Captura del estado, macrocriminalidad y derechos humanos* (Mexico City, FLACSO-Mexico and Heinrich Böll Stiftung Foundation).
United States Senate (1981), 'Hearings before the Committee on Foreign Relations', Ninety-Seventh Congress, First Session, 18 March and 9 April (Washington, DC, US Government Printing Office).
Willis, G. D. (2015), *The Killing Consensus: The Police, Organized Crime, and the Regulation of Life and Death in Urban Brazil* (Oakland, CA, University of California Press).

# 2

# Conceptualising Disappearances in International Law

BARBARA A. FREY

DESPITE THE ABSOLUTE prohibition of enforced disappearances across several regimes of international law, this volume shows the persistence of this crime as 'a repertoire of political action' (Payne and Ansolabehere, Chapter 1, p. 21) that continues to occur even in states that have had significant political transitions toward democracy. This chapter reconsiders the international legal framework, and especially the concept of state acquiescence, in light of the realities of violence and impunity facing post-transitional societies in Latin America.

Case studies in this volume demonstrate the mutually constitutive character of the legal and social meanings of disappearances, and the need, therefore, to stretch the parameters of the legal definition to align it with the social realities of the crime. States and human rights bodies have resorted to an unsatisfying differentiation between the concepts of 'enforced disappearance'[1] – when there is a state linkage to the crime – and 'disappearance' – a catchall construction of the crime when state involvement cannot be proven (Serrano, Chapter 17). This chapter seeks to end that distinction by demonstrating that state impunity, demonstrated by the systemic failure to search and to investigate, is enough of a linkage to prove legal accountability. In other words, in contexts of known violence, a 'disappearance' without a prompt, independent, and effective investigation should be deemed an 'enforced disappearance'.

Because of the legal threshold of 'acquiescence' needed to hold a state accountable for an enforced disappearance, some post-transitional states are prone to build 'a wall of silence' (Keller and Heri 2014: 742), by failing to investigate disappearances and thus being able to deny their responsibility for the crimes. Such deniability serves the logics of disappearance described in Chapter 1 by Payne

[1] The use of 'forced disappearances' is more prevalent in Latin America, probably because of the Inter-American treaties and case law, while the international community uses the term 'enforced disappearances'. They are conceived as interchangeable for the purposes of this chapter.

*Proceedings of the British Academy*, **237**, 37–62, © The British Academy 2021.

and Ansolabehere, including hiding wrongdoing, eliminating disposable peoples, seeking economic profits, and promoting social control through ambiguous loss. The socio-legal contexts in which generalised and structural violence takes place in post-transitional societies underscore the need to examine how governments 'acquiesce' to substantive human rights violations, even when the crimes themselves are carried out by non-state actors, or when the proof of state involvement in the disappearance also disappears.

Impunity – the impossibility, de jure or de facto, of bringing the perpetrators of violations to account (UN Commission on Human Rights 2005a: 6) – is both the means and the end to the crime of enforced disappearance (Huhle 2019). Perpetrators, whether states or non-state actors, choose to disappear individuals as a way of disappearing evidence of the crime itself. Even when a state is willing to undertake an investigation, a disappearance is an inherently difficult crime to solve. In most cases there is no body, and scarce physical evidence. All too often, however, government officials in democratic states in Latin America do not even attempt to investigate a disappearance or to make even a minimal effort to search for the whereabouts of the disappeared. This may be because of the difficulty of such an investigation, or the fear of undertaking one in a context of violent crime. Alternatively, failure to search or investigate is meant to conceal the involvement of state agents themselves. Whatever the reasons, there are few repercussions for government officials who fail to search or investigate in response to allegations of enforced disappearances. On the contrary, state officials at all levels may have perverse incentives to ignore or to hide evidence connected to the crime in order to deny that there was a human rights violation at all.

Another way to avoid state responsibility for enforced disappearances is to construct a state definition of the crime that requires an evidentiary burden of proof so high that it is almost impossible to meet. In criminalising the act of enforced disappearance as one of the greatest severity, continuity, and imprescriptibility, state legislators may elect to define the crime in a way that heightens the level of proof needed to show the state's role in it. To avoid this result, human rights advocates led by families of the disappeared have pushed to construct new definitions of criminal responsibility, including crimes committed by private actors who take advantage of the state's structural failures and omissions. These social movements and families of victims have also pushed for the codification of new priorities in the face of the changed social realities, inculcating in national law the exigencies of searching for victims and relatives, as well as the demand for collective and individual reparations. None of these domestic reforms, however, has been able to address the underlying problem of impunity in disappearance cases, a problem that needs further attention from the international legal community.

To understand the international legal framework on enforced disappearances in relation to impunity in post-transitional contexts, this chapter first sets out the core elements of the violation, as established in various relevant bodies of international law. It then explores the element of state linkage, or acquiescence, in contexts of systematic violence and widespread impunity, looking specifically at the structural connection between impunity and acquiescence. The chapter argues that the due-diligence standard, a positive duty that has been developed in many areas of human rights jurisprudence, provides a more effective analytical approach for evaluating the accountability of states for enforced disappearances, especially in contexts of generalised violence and impunity. Finally, the chapter comments on trends in international standard-setting concerning the core requirements for adequate searches and investigations, and concludes that those requirements should frame the construction of more resonant legal norms to address enforced disappearances in post-transitional societies.

## International Legal Framework on Enforced Disappearance

As the editors point out in the Introduction to this volume, the enforced disappearance of persons was a tool of repressive governments long before the era of the Latin American dictatorships, from the 1960s through the 1980s. Still, the region's experience had a direct impact on the narrative framing of the crime and the legal elements that formed the basis of the international legal norm prohibiting enforced disappearance (Frey 2009: 69; Dulitzky 2019: 439). The first UN General Assembly resolution to condemn enforced disappearances, adopted in 1978, reflected international concerns about the practice as it was carried out by Argentina's dictatorship at the time. The resolution did not mention Argentina by name, but the disappearances it described came straight from the reports of that country's period of state terrorism (Frey 2009: 61).

Since that foundational 1978 resolution, the core legal elements of the violation of enforced disappearance have been restated in several international legal instruments, building on the narrative framework of disappearances during the period of state terrorism. The elements of an enforced disappearance thus include (1) the deprivation of liberty, by or with (2) the consent or acquiescence of the state or a party to armed conflict, followed by (3) a denial of information about the whereabouts of the person. Despite its specific origins, international courts and other enforcement mechanisms have managed to apply that definition successfully to disappearances in many diverse contexts, including civil war, authoritarian regimes, dictatorships, and democracies (Dulitzky 2019: 475). It is time, however, to stretch the definition further.

The crime of enforced disappearance is condemned universally in treaties and jurisprudence. Whether in wartime or peacetime, the act of 'disappearing' a human being is recognised as among the cruellest of violations, a crime that victimises families and communities as well as the direct victim. Several scholars argue that the prohibition on enforced disappearance is so well accepted that it has attained the status of *jus cogens*, a non-derogable rule of law even in extreme circumstances such as states of emergency (Citroni 2009; ALI 1987). International law does not distinguish among victims; the enforced disappearance of a 'disposable person' (Chapter 1) should carry the same criminal disapprobation as when the victim is from an elite social class.

An enforced disappearance consists of multiple violations of human rights (Inter-American Court of Human Rights 1988: para. 5; UN Human Rights Committee 2018: para. 58; UN General Assembly 1992, article 1.2), and each of these constituent rights has a legal significance of its own, providing opportune strategic approaches for holding states accountable. Among the civil and political rights violated by disappearances are the right to life, the right to be free from torture, the right to be free from arbitrary detention, the right to recognition before the law, and the right to a fair trial (UN Office of the High Commissioner for Human Rights 2009: 3). Less prominent in the jurisprudence but of equal importance to the victims, disappearances also result in severe economic and social rights violations for direct and indirect victims. These crimes completely undermine the victims' rights to work; to care for their families; and to live healthy, sustainable lives (UN Office of the High Commissioner for Human Rights 2009: 3–4).

Enforced disappearance is a continuing human rights violation, and states have not met their obligations with regard to these violations until the whereabouts of the disappeared person are determined (UN General Assembly 1992: article 17; UN Working Group on Enforced or Involuntary Disappearances 2010: para. 1). Because of this, many post-transitional states find themselves in the position of addressing at least two categories of enforced disappearances: historical disappearances from past regimes and current disappearances taking place in a different socio-legal context. These distinct yet related categories of enforced disappearances call for states to establish different processes for truth and accountability, animated by the demands of varying protagonists. The investigation of historical crimes may call for different priorities, processes, standards of proof, and measures of success than the search and investigation into current violations. As Payne and Ansolabehere note in Chapter 1, the logics of disappearance may have their roots in historical crimes, such as the need to construct the victims as disposable, but the different contexts result in variations in the crime, and its perpetrators and victims, that call for different approaches to the truth (see also Federman *et al.*, Chapter 10).

## The Threshold of Acquiescence in Definitions of Enforced Disappearance

The term 'acquiescence' consistently appears in international legal definitions of enforced disappearance, as the lowest rung on the ladder of state responsibility for the violation. The 2006 International Convention for the Protection of All Persons from Enforced Disappearance (hereafter Convention, or ICED) is the most recent binding treaty to define and outlaw the crime. The Convention contains, in article 2, the following definition:

> 'enforced disappearance' is considered to be the arrest, detention, abduction or any other form of deprivation of liberty by agents of the State or by persons or groups of persons acting with the authorization, support or acquiescence of the State, followed by a refusal to acknowledge the deprivation of liberty or by concealment of the fate or whereabouts of the disappeared person, which place such a person outside the protection of the law.

The ICED's definition contains the same core elements as previous instruments of international law: (1) deprivation of liberty, by or with (2) the support or acquiescence of the state, and (3) concealment of the whereabouts of the victim. These same operative elements are found in other human rights instruments, including the 1992 UN Declaration on the Protection of All Persons from Enforced Disappearances[2] and the 1994 Inter-American Convention on Forced Disappearance of Persons (Organization of American States 1994),[3] as well as in the 1998 Rome Statute of the International Criminal Court (UN General Assembly 1998).[4]

In every treaty definition of enforced disappearance, the term acquiescence appears at the end of a sequence of elements for proving state linkage, including 'consent or acquiescence' in the Declaration, or 'authorization, support or acquiescence' in the ICED, the Inter-American Convention, and the Rome Statute. According to the rule of non-redundancy in treaty interpretation, each word in these treaty definitions should be interpreted as distinct and non-superfluous (Linderfalk 2007: 109–10). It follows, given its placement in every one of these definitions, that the term acquiescence should be interpreted as the least possible standard of proof needed to demonstrate the state's responsibility for an enforced disappearance.

The question arises whether, and in what circumstances, the state's lack of investigation into a disappearance is itself a form of acquiescence to the underlying

[2] The Declaration on Disappearances states that an enforced disappearance is when 'persons are arrested, detained or abducted against their will or otherwise deprived of their liberty by officials of different branches or levels of Government, or by organized groups or private individuals acting on behalf of, or with the support, direct or indirect, consent or acquiescence of the Government, followed by a refusal to disclose the fate or whereabouts of the persons concerned or a refusal to acknowledge the deprivation of their liberty, which places such persons outside the protection of the law.'

[3] The Convention defines a forced disappearance as 'the act of depriving a person or persons of his or their freedom, in whatever way, perpetrated by agents of the state or by persons or groups of persons acting with the authorization, support, or acquiescence of the state, followed by an absence of information or a refusal to acknowledge that deprivation of freedom or to give information on the whereabouts of that person, thereby impeding his or her recourse to the applicable legal remedies and procedural guarantees'.

[4] Article 7(2)(i) of the Rome Statute provides, '"Enforced disappearance of persons" means the arrest, detention or abduction of persons by, or with the authorization, support or acquiescence of, a State or a political organization, followed by a refusal to acknowledge that deprivation of freedom or to give information on the fate or whereabouts of those persons, with the intention of removing them from the protection of the law for a prolonged period of time.'

violation. Various articles in the ICED commit the State Party to investigate, but the treaty is silent on whether violations of these articles constitute violations of the underlying crime itself. Article 3, for instance, addresses crimes by non-state actors, imposing only the obligation for the State Party to 'take appropriate measures to investigate acts' and 'to bring those responsible to justice'. Article 3 does not suggest what standard states must meet in investigating or prosecuting disappearances, nor whether failure to 'take appropriate measures' would result in state accountability for the crime itself. Article 6 requires States Parties to impose criminal responsibility upon a superior who 'failed to take all necessary and reasonable measures within his or her power to prevent or repress the commission of an enforced disappearance or to submit the matter to the competent authorities for investigation and prosecution'. Similarly, ICED Article 12 requires that, upon receiving a report of a disappearance from any individual, the competent state authorities must 'examine the allegation promptly and impartially and, where necessary, undertake without delay a thorough and impartial investigation'. The Convention, however, does not set forth consequences for not doing so.

These silences in the law are the result of the concern that states not be held accountable for private-sphere crimes. During the drafting of the Convention, several state delegations supported the inclusion of language asserting the state's responsibility to prevent and combat enforced disappearances by non-state actors, acknowledging that states were no longer the sole subjects of international law (UN Commission on Human Rights 2005b: para. 30). Other delegations, however, opposed the inclusion of state responsibility for the crimes of non-state actors because it would be 'too broad' and might cover acts such as abduction that were already punishable under national law (para. 31). Another proposal excluded from the final draft was language on 'due diligence', specifically that 'States parties would undertake, if enforced disappearances were committed by non-State actors, to take any steps that might reasonably be expected of them in the circumstances to prevent the occurrence of such disappearances, punish the perpetrators under criminal law and offer reparation to the victims' (para. 34). In the end, the Convention did not contain any reference to due diligence.

The Convention does not enjoy robust support by states; there are only 63 States Parties to the treaty – representing less than a third of UN Member States. While most Latin American states have signed or ratified the ICED, El Salvador and Suriname have not taken action (UN Commission on Human Rights 2005b, para. 30).[5] Even states that have not joined the treaty, however, are bound by custom to prevent and punish the multiple violations that result from a disappearance, including violations of the right to life, freedom from torture, and the right to recognition under law. Jurisprudence on enforced disappearances from many

[5] Similarly, only 15 of 34 member states of the Organization of American States (OAS) have ratified the Inter-American Convention against Forced Disappearances, including Argentina, Brazil, and Mexico. El Salvador is not a party.

international bodies is also binding on states, including general comments and case law from the United Nations Human Rights Committee (HRC), the Inter-American Court of Human Rights, and the European Court of Human Rights (ECtHR) (Vermeulen 2012, 27).

### Definitions of Disappearance in Other Legal Settings

The drafters of the ICED had the benefit of decades of experience in the UN and regional systems addressing the problem of enforced disappearances, including the very first thematic procedure established, the UN Working Group on Enforced and Involuntary Disappearances (hereafter WGEID or Working Group), which grew out of concern about the practice of disappearances in Argentina and Chile (Frey 2009: 62). The Working Group is authorised to respond to disappearances in any state, regardless of their record of treaty ratifications, and applies the definition of enforced disappearances found in the Declaration on the Protection of all Persons from Enforced Disappearance, which has the same operative elements as the ICED definition (Frey 2009: 62).

The Inter-American Human Rights System also prohibits forced disappearances in its treaties and case law. The Inter-American Commission on Human Rights (IACHR) was an early leader on the issue of disappearances, denouncing the problem as early as 1974, and prompting the international community to address the problem in the United Nations (Dulitzky 2019: 440–2). The IACHR's 1979–80 site visit and report on human rights violations in Argentina was foundational for the international understanding of the practice of enforced disappearance (Dulitzky 2019: 440; Farer 2016: 868). Two Honduran disappearance cases, *Velásquez Rodríguez* (Inter-American Court of Human Rights 1988) and *Godínez Cruz* (Inter-American Court of Human Rights 1989), were the first contested cases before the Inter-American Court of Human Rights (See Serrano, Chapter 17). The OAS adopted the Inter-American Convention on the Forced Disappearance of Persons in 1994; its drafting was carried out in tandem with the UN Declaration, resulting in similar construction (Brody and González 1997: 371; Serrano, Chapter 17).

Other bodies of law also address disappearances. International humanitarian law, or the Law of Armed Conflict, prohibits the practice of disappearances in wartime, whether international or non-international armed conflict. While humanitarian law treaties do not use the term 'enforced disappearance', the International Committee of the Red Cross, which has the authority to define the rules of armed conflict, has identified enforced disappearances as a violation of customary humanitarian law (Rule 98) (Henckaerts and Doswald-Beck 2009: 340). Disappearances are compound violations of humanitarian law, comprising arbitrary deprivations of liberty, torture, and murder (Rule 98) (Henckaerts and Doswald-Beck 2009: 340). The Law of Armed Conflict also imposes the duty to investigate, requiring that each party to the armed conflict 'take all feasible measures to account for persons reported missing as a result of armed conflict and to provide their family members with information it has on their fate' (Rule 117) (Henckaerts and Doswald-Beck 2009: 341).

International criminal law also outlaws the systematic practice of enforced disappearance as a crime against humanity. The inclusion of enforced disappearance as a crime in the Rome Statute has given advocates an additional and arguably more punitive route for bringing international attention to these crimes (see, e.g., Chapters 8 and 16 in this volume) when they are 'committed as part of a widespread or systematic attack directed against any civilian population, with knowledge of the attack' (article 7). The Rome Statute defines enforced disappearance as:

> the arrest, detention or abduction of persons by, or with the authorization, support or acquiescence of, a State or a political organisation, followed by a refusal to acknowledge that deprivation of freedom or to give information on the fate or whereabouts of those persons, with the intention of removing them from the protection of the law for a prolonged period of time. (article 7(2)(i))

The final element of this definition, intent to remove victims for a prolonged period, adds an additional level of proof for complainants.

## Reconceptualising Acquiescence in Disappearance Cases

While the universal legal prohibition on enforced disappearances is clear, the socio-political determinants of the crime in post-transitional societies require a rethinking of the state's responsibility for disappearances, especially in contexts of generalised violence. How does international law account for democratic states that have, at a minimum, performative systems of justice, including model laws, but achieve almost no results when it comes to their obligations to prevent, investigate, or punish disappearances? To answer this question requires an assessment of the concept of acquiescence in contexts of historical repression, generalised violence, and structural impunity that characterise many post-transitional Latin American states.

Many enforced disappearances described in this volume easily meet the threshold of state linkage because they are carried out (1) directly by state agents or (2) by other persons acting with the consent and support of the state. For example, in the case of the direct police violations in Brazil (Weichert, Chapter 8), or when the police disappear persons in El Salvador as part of their 'death squad' activities (Mendez, Chapter 12), there is clear evidence of state linkage. Similarly, in cases involving collusion between state agents and organised crime in northeastern Mexico (Ansolabehere and Martos, Chapter 4), the disappearances are carried out with the requisite consent and support of the state to fall squarely within the international law definition of an enforced disappearance.

The broader puzzle addressed here involves a third category of disappearances in post-transitional states, encompassing those carried out by organised crime or other private actors without a verifiable connection to the state. In their reporting, states have been eager to differentiate various crimes that are 'in the nature of enforced disappearance' but that instead take place 'without the authorization, support or acquiescence of the State, such as kidnapping, human-trafficking and procuring prostitution' (UN Committee on Enforced Disappearances 2014a: paras 94ff.; UN Committee on Enforced Disappearances 2019b: para. 27). States can easily sidestep their legal responsibility for crimes by private actors by ignoring or hiding evidence, simulating an investigation without finding culpable state actors, or merely delaying their actions for long enough to endanger the life and personal integrity of the victim. This matter is addressed in the chapters on Argentina, Brazil, El Salvador, and Mexico in this volume. These examples of wilful omission could be the result of organised crime involvement in a disappearance (the Ayotzinapa case in Mexico), or of 'accidental' death and bureaucratic incompetence in identifying the person (the Arruga case in Argentina), or of finding the person too late (the Maldonado case in Argentina).

This chapter argues that, in various circumstances, the state's failure to investigate crimes by private actors is itself a form of acquiescence to the underlying crime. These circumstances include situations of systematic violence and impunity, as shown in the cases from Brazil, El Salvador, and Mexico in this volume. Yet, as Federman *et al.* (Chapter 10) further argue, in contexts of historical state repression, acquiescence might also be presumed when the state fails to rule out its involvement in a disappearance. The objective of such an approach is to reduce the space within which the state can use a strategy of deniability in a systematic manner negate its own responsibility for human rights atrocities. Those who seek to expand the scope of acquiescence to hold states accountable for enforced disappearances can borrow conceptually from the jurisprudence on the duty of due diligence. The conceptual gap between these two legal formulas for state linkage is addressed next.

## How Due Diligence Is Used to Hold States Accountable

The legal principle of due diligence has been used effectively to hold states accountable for their failure to take positive steps to prevent or remedy human rights violations. Due diligence is a general principle of international law for evaluating the conduct of a state in relation to its legal obligations. Historically, due diligence related to the responsibility of states for private actors, and to what preventive measures were required by the state in its sphere of exclusive control when international law was breached by private persons (Koivurova 2010). In the sphere of human rights law, due diligence is a two-pronged obligation, measuring the state's conduct in both pre-abuse and post-abuse settings (Edwards 2006: 374). Due diligence requires states to take steps to prevent or minimise foreseeable human rights violations by private actors, and they can be held responsible for those violations for failing to do so. Due diligence also requires states to investigate, prosecute, punish, and provide reparations for victims of violations. In assessing state responsibility for enforced disappearances, therefore, due diligence provides an important standard for measuring the state's efforts to carry out a timely search for the victims as well as to investigate criminal responsibility effectively.

In a series of contested cases, the Inter-American Court elaborated a due-diligence framework that remains potent in examining the actions of states, especially in the context of post-transitional disappearances described in this volume. In the seminal Inter-American Court decision, *Velásquez Rodríguez* (Inter-American Court of Human Rights 1988), the Court found the state of Honduras responsible for the disappearances of Manfredo Velásquez – a student at the National Autonomous University of Honduras – and others, allegedly at the hands of the armed forces of Honduras. The state denied its involvement and the Court was not able to establish that state actors carried out or consented to the crime. Instead, the Court held the state responsible because it failed to take reasonable steps to prevent the violations or to carry out a serious investigation of the violations. The Court defined the state's *duty to prevent* broadly, as including the use of 'all those means of a legal, political, administrative and cultural nature that promote the protection of human rights and ensure that any violations are considered and treated as illegal acts, which, as such, may lead to the punishment of those responsible and the obligation to indemnify the victims for damages' (para. 175). The Court's conception shows a multifaceted understanding of the socio-legal institutions required to prevent a context of generalised violence.

The *Velásquez* Court then delineated the *duty to investigate*:

> The State is obligated to investigate every situation involving a violation of the rights protected by the Convention. If the State apparatus acts in such a way that the violation goes unpunished and the victim's full enjoyment of such rights is not restored as soon as possible, the State has failed to comply with its duty to ensure the free and full exercise of those rights to the persons within its jurisdiction. The same is true when the State allows private persons or groups to act freely and with impunity to the detriment of the rights recognized by the Convention. (Para. 176).

The Court thus set out clear standards for measuring the adequacy of the state's investigation in cases of enforced disappearance. States must (1) investigate every violation, (2) ensure that violators are punished, and (3) restore the full enjoyment of the victim's rights in (4) a timely manner. The Court confirmed that the same standards of investigation apply if disappearances are carried out by private persons or groups in a context of impunity.

Importantly for this analysis, the *Velásquez Rodríguez* case pre-dated the definition of forced disappearance set forth in the 1994 Inter-American Convention on Forced Disappearance of Persons, and the complainants therefore did not need to prove state acquiescence to hold Honduras responsible for the violation. Instead, the Court based its ruling on the American Convention on Human Rights (OAS 1969), identifying the crime as a disappearance, but specifically holding the state accountable for violations of the Convention's article 1 (free and full exercise of rights), as well as other substantive rights violated in a disappearance: article 4 (right to life), article 5 (freedom from torture), and article 7 (personal liberty).

Building on the reasoning of *Velásquez Rodríguez*, the Inter-American Court further clarified the state's responsibility to carry out an immediate search and investigation in a context of generalised violence in the case of *González v. Mexico*, otherwise known as the *'Cotton Field'* case.[6] In the case, three young females, including two minors, were disappeared in October 2001 after leaving their workplaces in Ciudad Juárez. Despite their families' repeated contacts with law enforcement, state and local officials did virtually nothing to investigate the disappearances, refusing to act for 72 hours after the disappearance, except to take the statements of those who reported the missing girls. Clues were overlooked and evidence lost in law enforcement's so-called investigation of the disappearances. One mother testified that she had received several telephone calls in the days following her daughter's disappearance; during one of the calls she could actually hear her daughter arguing with someone. Yet, when the mother took this information to the state Attorney General's Office, she was told that they could not trace the phone calls (para. 188). The mother of another girl reported that officials did not enquire at her daughter's school or interview her friends (para. 188). A third mother reported that she informed the authorities that, two weeks before her disappearance, the young woman had been harassed by two police agents. Again, government authorities did not investigate (para. 190).

The *'Cotton Field'* Court found that Mexico had violated its general obligation to guarantee rights (American Convention, article 1(1)) and the obligation to adopt domestic legal provisions (article 2), as well as the due-diligence obligations established in article 7(b) of the Convention of Belém do Pará.[7] The Court noted the significance of the context of 'a powerful wave of violence against women' in Ciudad Juárez at the time the women disappeared.

> [I]n this context, an obligation of strict due diligence arises in regard to reports of missing women, with respect to search operations during the first hours and days ... Above all, it is essential that police authorities, prosecutors and judicial officials take prompt immediate action by ordering, without delay, the necessary measures to determine the whereabouts of the victims or the place where they may have been retained. Adequate procedures should exist for reporting disappearances, which should result in an immediate effective investigation. The authorities should presume that the disappeared person has been deprived of liberty and is still alive until there is no longer any uncertainty about her fate. (Inter-American Court of Human Rights 2009: para. 278)

[6] The complainants brought the cases as violations of the right to life, but the facts demonstrate that the women were disappeared before their bodies were discovered in the cotton field. See Inter-American Court of Human Rights (2009).

[7] The Inter-American Convention on the Prevention, Punishment, and Eradication of Violence against Women (known as the Convention Belém do Pará), 33 I.L.M. 1534 (1994), *entered into force* 5 March 1995, provides in article 7: 'The States Parties condemn all forms of violence against women and agree to pursue, by all appropriate means and without delay, policies to prevent, punish and eradicate such violence and undertake to ... (b) apply due diligence to prevent, investigate and impose penalties for violence against women.'

In a later case, *Alvarado Espinoza* (Inter-American Court of Human Rights 2018), the Court again faulted the investigative steps taken by the state in the disappearance of three cousins in Mexico, which, while clearly numerous, were ineffective, insufficient, and dilatory. Despite many witness statements; documentary pieces of evidence; inspections; and expert reports, provided as proof of the state's efforts, the Court found that the state had violated its duty to realise a serious, impartial, and exhaustive investigation. The *Alvarado Espinoza* Court found the 'context of generalised violence' (para. 216) to be significant, creating a situation of constructive knowledge that heightened the state's responsibility for the excessive period of time it took to conduct a search and investigate the disappearance (para. 225).

In the line of Inter-American Court cases that descend from *Velásquez Rodríguez*, the Court has delineated quite clearly the due-diligence obligations of states to carry out immediate and effective searches and investigations of alleged disappearances, especially in contexts of generalised violations.[8] The Court has concluded that these violations by omission are not merely procedural problems, but constitute violations of the underlying rights of the victims and their families – violations of the rights to life and to personal integrity under the American Convention on Human Rights.

The Inter-American Court's due-diligence analysis has been incorporated into the UN HRC case law and commentary. The HRC is a treaty body that interprets and oversees the enforcement of the International Covenant on Civil and Political Rights. The Covenant pre-dated the legal definition of enforced disappearance. Its engagement with disappearance cases is therefore based on the constituent rights found in the Covenant: article 6 (right to life), article 7 (prohibition of torture or cruel, inhuman, or degrading treatment or punishment), article 9 (liberty and security of persons), and article 16 (right to recognition of a person before the law) (UN Human Rights Committee 2018: para. 58).

The HRC's jurisprudence on due diligence is based on the general legal obligations 'to respect and ensure', guaranteed by article 2(1) of the International Covenant on Civil and Political Rights. States Parties must exercise due diligence to prevent, punish, investigate, or redress the harm caused by state actors, as well as by private persons or entities (UN Human Rights Committee 2004: para. 8). In its General Comment 36, the Committee reiterated that obligation with a specific focus on the right to life, guaranteed by article 6 of the Covenant. General Comment 36

[8] The Court has also applied the state's due-diligence responsibility to prevent and investigate other *erga omnes* violations by private actors, including slavery. Cf. the case of *Masacres de Rio Negro* v. *Guatemala* (2012), Judgment of 4 September 2012 ('When States have knowledge of an act that constitutes slavery or forced labor … they should initiate ex officio the pertinent investigation to establish corresponding individual responsiblities') (Inter-American Court of Human Rights 2012: para. 225); and the case of *Workers of 'La Hacienda Brasil Verde'* v. *Brazil* (2016), Judgment of 20 October 2016 ('[T]he due diligence requirement has been shown to be implicit in all cases, but when the possibility exists of rescuing persons from the denounced situation, the investigation should be carried out with urgency') (Inter-American Court of Human Rights 2016: paras 362–4).

asserted that due diligence gave rise to 'the duty to protect life, which 'includes an obligation for States Parties to take appropriate legal measures in order to protect life from all foreseeable threats, including from threats emanating from private persons or entities' (UN Human Rights Committee 2018: para. 22). The duty to protect life also requires states to use their public authority in a way most consistent with respecting the right to life, including the establishment of adequate institutions and procedures for preventing deprivation of life, investigating and prosecuting violations, punishing perpetrators, and providing reparations to victims (para. 23).

In General Comment 36 (UN Human Rights Committee 2018), the Committee also addressed the state's obligations regarding enforced disappearance as 'a unique and integrated series of acts and omissions representing a grave threat to life' (para. 58). The Committee specifically identified the due-diligence responsibilities to prevent and investigate disappearances:

> States parties must take adequate measures to prevent the enforced disappearance of individuals, and conduct an effective and speedy inquiry to establish the fate and whereabouts of persons who may have been subject to enforced disappearance. States parties should also ensure that the enforced disappearance of persons is punished with appropriate criminal sanctions and introduce prompt and effective procedures to investigate cases of disappearances thoroughly, by independent and impartial bodies that operate, as a rule, within the ordinary criminal justice system. (UN Human Rights Committee 2018: para. 58).

Under this standard, the Human Rights Committee has held states responsible for the underlying rights violations in enforced disappearance cases if they failed to act with due diligence to prevent or to investigate violations (see, e.g., *El Boathi* v. *Algeria* (UN Human Rights Committee (2014): para. 7.5)). In the case of *Téllez Padilla* v. *Mexico* (UN Human Rights Committee 2019), the Human Rights Committee's decision turned on its assessment of the government of Mexico's lack of due diligence in investigating the detention and subsequent disappearance of Christian Téllez in the state of Veracruz. The victim's family documented its exhaustive efforts requesting that federal, state, and local officials search for their relative. They also noted the state's failure to undertake critical steps in investigating the disappearance, such as failing to test for fingerprints or DNA on the victim's car, failing to request data from security cameras and telephone records before they were erased, and failing to take statements from police suspects identified by eyewitnesses until four years after the disappearance.

The state argued that due diligence is an obligation of process, not result, and that obligations under the Covenant should be interpreted in a way that does not impose a disproportionate burden on states. The HRC took note of the state's arguments but found that its untimely and ineffective investigation into Mr. Téllez's disappearance resulted in the loss of important evidence, especially in light of the context of generalised violence and disappearances in the country (UN Human Rights Committee 2019: paras 9.4, 9.10). Based on those findings, the Committee decided that the state had violated the victims' right to a remedy under article 2(3), as read in conjunction with other substantive violations in the Covenant: articles 6(1) (right to life), 7 (freedom from torture), 9 (freedom from arbitrary detention), and 16 (recognition before the law).

The due-diligence standard has thus been a constructive conceptual pathway toward international legal accountability for states that fail to take the steps within their power to prevent foreseeable harm in disappearance cases and to investigate promptly and effectively. Due diligence, however, is a measure that has been applied in relation to the state's duty to protect the right to life, freedom from torture, and freedom from slavery. In cases of enforced disappearance, the analysis turns on a different assessment: whether the state acquiesced in the crime.

## How Acquiescence Is Used to Minimise State Accountability

The principle of acquiescence is defined in international law as 'consent inferred from a juridically relevant silence or inaction' (Nuno 2006: para 2). It descends from the common law principle 'Qui tacit consentire videtur si loqui debuisset ac potuisset', or '[H]e who keeps silent is held to consent if he must and can speak' (para 2. The principle is commonly used in the area of interstate relations in international law, where unilateral consent is tacitly conveyed by a state, through silence or inaction, if an objection or protest related to the conduct of another state would be called for.

The principle of acquiescence entered the vocabulary of international human rights law in legal definitions of violations: initially, in the treaty definition of torture (UN General Assembly 1984: art. 1)[9] and then the declaration and treaty definitions of enforced disappearance.[10] With regard to these two grave violations, the burden of proof is on the complainants to demonstrate, at a minimum, the 'consent and acquiescence' of state actors if the state is to be held accountable. The concern is that, given the lack of treaty interpretation on the question of acquiescence,[11] states may benefit from the absence of specific proof of state involvement

[9] Article 1 defined torture as 'when such pain or suffering is inflicted by or at the instigation of or with the consent or acquiescence of a public official or other person acting in an official capacity'.

[10] Declaration on Disappearances, preambular para. 3; Inter-American Convention on Forced Disappearance of Persons, article II; International Convention for the Protection of All Persons from Enforced Disappearance, article 2. See also Rome Statute of the International Criminal Court, article 7(2)(i).

[11] The ECtHR has the most developed jurisprudence on 'acquiescence or connivance', which is an '[ECtHR]-specific theory of state complicity' adopted by the Court itself and not an interpretation of a treaty (Milanovich 2019). See European Court of Human Rights (2001: para. 81): 'the acquiescence or connivance of the authorities of a Contracting State in the acts of private individuals which violate the Convention rights of other individuals within its jurisdiction may engage that State's responsibility under the Convention'. The UN Committee on Enforced Disappearances does not as yet have any case law on acquiescence.

in disappearances. Nuno has noted that, in the area of human rights, 'a cautious approach to findings of acquiescence continues to be warranted, the burden of proof lying on the party invoking it'. There is a lack of uniformity in the discretion states enjoy, and 'silence or inaction is seldom an adequate manifestation of consent' (Nuno 2006: para. 28).

The burden has thus remained on the victims to show that the state knew or should have known of the illegal conduct and conveyed silence and inaction in the face of that knowledge. This has been the approach of the UN Committee against Torture (UNCAT) with regard to similar language on acquiescence. According to Alice Edwards (2006: 374), UNCAT interpreted the 'consent or acquiescence' element of the Convention against Torture's definition of torture as requiring actual knowledge of a particular incident and actual refusal to act. Evaluating the jurisprudence of UNCAT in relation to private-sphere crimes against women, Edwards notes that, because of the acquiescence threshold, 'What these cases demonstrate is that the definition of "torture" has been interpreted more restrictively by UNCAT than by other international treaty bodies' (373).[12] Edwards also notes that the acquiescence element in the Convention against Torture 'does not seem to create obligations on a state to take any pre-abuse preventive measures' (374), meaning that the States Party's failure to prevent an act of violence against a victim would not necessarily meet the threshold of acquiescence in the torture treaty definition. Despite UNCAT's reluctance to impose obligations for failure to prevent torture, jurisprudence on disappearances under the American Convention on Human Rights and the International Covenant on Civil and Political Rights has found states responsible for torture when they failed to use due diligence to prevent or investigate disappearances.[13] This discrepancy illuminates the conceptual legal gap that allows states to avoid responsibility for their role in disappearances under the standard of due diligence, but not under the other, acquiescence.

While the CED has yet to decide a contentious case involving a question of state acquiescence, its submission forms for complainants reflect the same approach as UNCAT, requiring proof of actual state knowledge of disappearances. The CED's model complaint form asks complainants to provide the following information: 'If the persons presumed to be responsible for the events in question cannot be identified as agents of the State, explain why you believe that government authorities or persons associated with them are responsible for those events (for example, if you believe that they acted with the authorization, support or acquiescence/approval of

[12] Citing *S. V. et al.* v. *Canada*, CAT 49/1996, *Elmi* v. *Australia*, CAT49/1996, and *Dzemajl et al.* v. *Yugoslavia*, CAT161/2000.

[13] See discussion of Inter-American Court of Human Rights cases *Velásquez Rodríguez* (Inter-American Court of Human Rights 1988) and *Alvarado Espinoza* (Inter-American Court of Human Rights 2018), and the HRC decision in *Téllez Padilla* (UN Human Rights Committee 2019).

the State).'[14] By connecting acquiescence with approval – an element not included in the ICED definition – this particular form signals the need to show actual and not constructive knowledge of the crime. The Committee's practice with regard to urgent actions (Huhle 2019), however, indicates that it does not intend to place such a high burden on the victims.

The UN Working Group on Enforced or Involuntary Disappearances has been cautious about limiting its mandate to consider only those cases in which 'the act in question is perpetrated by state actors or by private individuals or organised groups (e.g. paramilitary groups) acting on behalf of, or with the support, direct or indirect, consent or acquiescence of the Government' (UN Working Group on Enforced or Involuntary Disappearances 2008: 10). The Working Group specifically distinguishes enforced disappearances from 'related offenses such as abduction and kidnapping' (10). The form provided to victims who wish to submit communications to the Working Group requires evidence of a state linkage, requesting the following information: 'If identification as State agents is not possible, why do you believe that Government authorities, or persons linked to them, are responsible for the incident?' (UN Committee on Enforced Disappearances (2014b: para. 4(b)).[15]

This burden placed on the complainants to show actual knowledge of state actors in enforced disappearance cases runs contrary to the due-diligence jurisprudence in cases involving disappearances. Such a discrepancy raises the question as to why the state can be held accountable for the violations that underlie disappearances – such as right to life and personal integrity – while not held equally accountable for the composite crime of enforced disappearance? The resulting accountability gap suggests the need for new jurisprudence on acquiescence recognising that the failure to search and investigate constitutes acquiescence to the underlying crime of enforced disappearance, especially in the context of generalised violence and impunity, when the state knew or should have known the risks to the victim. This analysis would be a more fitting legal response to the realities of disappearances in post-transitional societies marked by widespread violence, whether at the hands of state or of non-state actors.

[14] Despite this language in its model form, the former Chair of the CED reported that the Committee had never rejected an urgent action where the responsibility for the enforced disappearance was uncertain, precisely because (a) it considers that it is the state's obligation to investigate all disappearances and (b) it is the state that has to prove who is the perpetrator, not the victim (Huhle 2019).

[15] It is not that these bodies do not recognise the obligation of states to search and investigate, but this omission does not manifest itself as a violation of the underlying crime of enforced disappearance. States may be called out for the failure to investigate, while avoiding condemnation for particular disappearances and patterns of disappearance – which would be a much more serious allegation legally, politically, and socially.

## Reconceptualising Acquiescence as the State Failure to Search or Investigate

This chapter has identified a gap in two lines of legal analysis concerning state responsibility for the crime of enforced disappearance under international law. The analysis that flows from the definition of enforced disappearance under the 2006 Convention on Enforced Disappearance and the 1994 Inter-American Convention on Forced Disappearance of Persons, requiring proof of acquiescence, places the burden on the victims to provide evidence that the state actually knew about the disappearance and kept silent about the crime. A parallel due-diligence analysis is used in disappearance cases in which the decision-makers are interpreting the rights to life, prohibition against torture, and recognition of the person – rights that are also violated by enforced disappearances. The due-diligence analysis has been used effectively to hold states responsible for disappearances, even when actual knowledge of the crime by state actors cannot be demonstrated.

State officials who fail to investigate disappearance cases should not be held to a lesser standard than those in cases involving other substantive rights. Yet democratic states – even those experiencing dramatic levels of disappearances – have relied on the higher level of proof regarding acquiescence to shield themselves from responsibility, and to avoid being charged with potential crimes against humanity (see, e.g., Saenz 2017). As noted by Federman *et al.* in Chapter 10, a country such as Argentina, with its past record of state involvement in enforced disappearances, may have an even greater responsibility to investigate the crime or its cover-up, even regarding a singular case of disappearance.

The ECtHR has taken steps to prevent States Parties to the European Convention on Human Rights (Council of Europe 1953) from shielding themselves from responsibility for enforced disappearance by failing to investigate the crime (Keller and Heri 2014: 745). Helen Keller (a judge on the Court) and Corina Heri describe the troubling state practice by which national authorities maintain a 'wall of silence', denying the very facts that 'a definitional element of enforced disappearance' comprises (745). The ECtHR has used several procedural strategies to address these denials. For instance, it has 'relied on inferences and presumptions and has redistributed the burden of proof based on the severity of the allegations, the lack of clarity about the factual situation, and the nature of the rights in question' (738). In place of carrying out missions to conduct its own de novo fact-finding in cases of sparse evidence, the Court has shifted the burden to the state, requiring it 'to disprove a prima facie case as established by the applicants' (738).[16] The Court has

[16] The HRC used the same burden-shifting practice in the *Téllez Padilla* finding of enforced disappearance (UN Human Rights Committee 2019: para. 9.3).

also accepted specific and contextual evidence from a variety of sources, including reports of independent experts, international and domestic non-governmental organisations, third-party states, and academic researchers to explain the context in which the specific crime occurred (Keller and Heri 2014: 740). The ECtHR has used these procedural and evidentiary practices to hold states accountable for hundreds of enforced disappearances in the region (737).

As decision-makers address disappearance cases under the ICED and Inter-American Convention, they will have to respond to a similar 'wall of silence' posed by states, including democratic states, that seek to avoid human rights responsibility. Based on the experience of the ECtHR, these bodies may employ burden-shifting procedures to balance the evidentiary playing field when states impair access to information. Analytically, the Inter-American Court and the UN treaty bodies should also draw upon relevant due-diligence jurisprudence to assess whether states have acquiesced in enforced disappearances by failing to take necessary positive steps to search for the disappeared or to investigate the crime.

An effective legal framework for post-transitional disappearances requires that the analysis of state linkage take into consideration the broader socio-political circumstances in which the crimes occur. In the contexts of impunity and generalised violence found in many post-transitional states in Latin America, including Brazil, El Salvador, and Mexico, governments have constructive knowledge of the patterns of violence, including disappearances. The Inter-American Court – in the *'Cotton Field'* (Inter-American Court of Human Rights 2009)[17] and *Alvarado* (Inter-American Court of Human Rights 2018)[18] cases, among others – has found the context of known violence to be of central importance in its due-diligence analysis. Similarly, the HRC held the state responsible for enforced disappearance in the Téllez Padilla (UN Human Rights Committee 2019) case, 'in light of the general context of human rights violations – in particular, the practice of enforced disappearances – prevalent at the time and place at which the events occurred' (para. 9.4).

In contexts of generalised violations, the positive responsibilities of states require an effective legal framework for preventing and prosecuting disappearances. At a minimum, states must carry out prompt and adequate *searches* for the victims as well as *investigations* of the crimes. In situations characterised by life-threatening circumstances, failure to search or to investigate is tantamount to tacit consent by the state, arising to the threshold of acquiescence. This legal approach would tie impunity to responsibility for the underlying crime of enforced disappearance, eliminating the jurisprudential gap between acquiescence and the due-diligence responsibilities of the state called for under other treaties.

[17] Para. 368 (finding that investigating with due diligence requires taking into consideration the context of violations).

[18] Para. 225 (finding excessive a period of nine days before searching for the victims in the military installation given the context).

In contexts of generalised violations, the Inter-American Court and the HRC have found the following (non-exhaustive) list of state acts or omissions to violate their positive obligations in disappearance cases:

- delaying the search and investigation in a manner that exacerbated the risk to the victim (Inter-American Court of Human Rights 2018: para. 225);
- pursuing an investigation as a mere formality pre-ordained to be ineffective (Inter-American Court of Human Rights 1988: para. 177);
- depending solely upon the initiative of the victim or their family, or upon their offer of proof, without an effective search for the truth by the government (Inter-American Court of Human Rights 1988: para. 177);
- refusing to investigate military or state agents despite evidence of their involvement (Inter-American Court of Human Rights 2018: para. 216);
- failing to secure the crime scene or to collect evidence near the crime scene (Inter-American Court of Human Rights 2018: para. 221; United Nations Human Rights Committee 2019: paras 9, 10);
- failing to handle evidence properly and to preserve chain of custody regarding crime scene evidence (Inter-American Court of Human Rights 2009: para. 309);
- irregularities and deficiencies in autopsies, in identification of bodies, and in their proper return to the families (Inter-American Court of Human Rights 2009: para. 333).

Contexts of generalised violations may include the sheer number of violations in a particular country as well as disproportionate violations against differentiated sectors of society such as women, indigenous communities, migrants, Afro-descendants, and pronouncements by international organisations.

Recently adopted UN guidelines addressing search and investigation in disappearance cases demonstrate the movement of international law and policy toward strict positive responsibility for core human rights violations. In addition to the jurisprudence on due diligence in the Inter-American system and the UN treaty bodies, these two sets of guiding principles on search and investigation provide relevant standards against which to measure state acquiescence for enforced disappearances. The sections below briefly explain the significance of the Minnesota Protocol (see further explanation in Chapter 14) – a set of internationally recognised guidelines for how to carry out an adequate investigation in a disappearance case – and the UN Guiding Principles on Search (further explained in Chapter 15) – similar guidelines regarding the search for the whereabouts of disappeared persons.

## Minnesota Protocol

The 2016 revision of the Minnesota Protocol on Potentially Unlawful Death (UN Office of the High Commissioner for Human Rights 2017) is a restatement of the obligations of states to investigate deaths and disappearances (Frey, Chapter 14). The revision reflected the dramatic advances in international law regarding the duty to investigate since the initial version of the manual was adopted in 1991. Potentially unlawful deaths fall into three categories: (1) deaths that may have been caused by acts or omissions of the state, (2) deaths in custody, and (3) deaths in which the state may have failed to meet its obligations to protect life. The enforced disappearances taking place in the post-transitional Latin American states fall into either the first or third categories.

The Minnesota Protocol sets forth the elements of the state's actions to investigate. It must be prompt, effective and thorough, independent and impartial, and transparent (UN High Commissioner 2017: para. 22). It further explains each of these four elements as follows.

### *Prompt*

Authorities must conduct an investigation as soon as possible and proceed without unreasonable delays. Investigations not carried out in this manner violate the right to life and the right to an effective remedy.

### *Effective and Thorough*

Investigators should collect and confirm all testimonial, documentary and physical evidence. At a minimum they must: (1) identify the victim(s); (2) recover and preserve all probative materials; (3) identify possible witnesses and obtain their testimony and evidence; (4) in the event of death, determine the cause, manner, place and time of death, and all surrounding circumstances; and (5) determine who was involved in the death or disappearance and their individual responsibility for the crime. '[I]n the case of an enforced disappearance, an investigation must seek to determine the fate of the disappeared and, if applicable, the location of their remains' (para. 25).

### *Independent and Impartial*

Investigators and investigative mechanisms 'must be independent institutionally and formally, as well as in practice and perception, at all stages' (para. 28). Investigators must be able to perform their professional functions 'without intimidation, hindrance, harassment or improper interference' (para. 30). Furthermore, investigators must 'consider and appropriately pursue exculpatory as well as inculpatory evidence' (para. 31).

### *Transparent*

Investigations must be open to the scrutiny of the victims' families as well as the general public. At a minimum, states should make public the existence of an investigation, and its procedures and findings (para. 32). Limitations on transparency may only be justified by the privacy and safety of affected persons, and in no circumstances may a state 'restrict transparency in a way that would conceal the fate or whereabouts of any victim of an enforced disappearance or unlawful killing, or would result in impunity for those responsible' (para. 33).

**UN Guiding Principles on Search**

Complementary to the Minnesota Protocol, the 2019 UN CED adopted its Guiding Principles for the Search for Disappeared Persons to put forward best practices 'arising from States' obligation to search' (UN Committee on Enforced Disappearances 2019a: introductory para. 2). The Guiding Principles emphasised the search for living disappeared persons (Huhle, Chapter 15). While the Guiding Principles are soft law, they flow from article 24 of ICED: 'Each victim has the right to know the truth regarding the circumstances of the enforced disappearance, the progress and results of the investigation and the fate of the disappeared person' (UN General Assembly 2006). The Convention is the first international human rights treaty expressly to provide for the right to the truth (UN Office of the High Commissioner for Human Rights 2009). The Guiding Principles respond to the primary concern expressed by most families of disappeared persons – the desire to know the whereabouts and the fate of their loved ones.

The Guiding Principles contain several standards for measuring the adequacy of the state's search. For instance, the principles require authorities to begin the search immediately after they have knowledge of the disappearance, by whatever means, even when no formal complaint or request has been made (UN Committee on Enforced Disappearances 2019a: paras 6.1, 6.2). The state must demonstrate a comprehensive strategy that explores every reasonable hypothesis and is based on all available information, including that provided by the relatives or accusers (paras 8.1, 8.2). The Guiding Principles address the tendency for authorities to criminalise the victims in disappearances by insisting that the search 'should not be based on preconceptions regarding the individual circumstances and characteristics of the disappeared person' (para. 8.2).

The Principles recommend the use of well-established forensic methods by experienced professionals, including 'persons with specialist and technical knowledge, forensic experts and other scientists, and civil society organisations to come up with the hypothesis for the disappearance' (para. 8.4). The search strategy should include a contextual analysis to determine patterns, and clarify motives and modus operandi of the perpetrators (para. 8.6). The authorities responsible for the search should have adequate resources and expertise to carry out the work (para. 10.2). With no prior permission they should have unrestricted access to places and to information necessary for the search, including those deemed to pertain to national security (paras 10.3, 10.4). The Guiding Principles recommend that the search be coordinated by a competent body having the authority to call for cooperation by all government entities that have material information in the case, including authorities responsible for criminal investigation of the case (para. 12).

## Conclusion

Enforced disappearance is one of the most serious crimes, prohibited across several regimes of international law, including human rights, humanitarian, and criminal law. Despite this, disappearances occur with alarming regularity even in democratic states, such as those described in this volume, with almost no legal repercussions for the perpetrators or the state. The violation of enforced disappearance is notoriously difficult to prove, whether state actors are involved directly or indirectly. While the modus operandi may have shifted since the crime was defined in the era of the Latin American authoritarian regimes and armed conflicts, many of the logics behind it remain the same (Payne and Ansolabehere, Chapter 1). Because of the difficulty of proving the crime under the existing legal framework, states have evaded responsibility from the failure to expose, prevent, or punish disappearances. Consquently, they are able to hide wrongdoing, to eliminate disposable peoples, and to promote social control through ambiguous loss.

This chapter proposes a legal framework that meets the challenge of state accountability for enforced disappearances in post-transition societies. A relevant and effective framework must embrace contextual analysis and foreground the positive obligations of states to search and to investigate these crimes, using generally accepted principles to measure the adequacy of the state's responses to reported disappearances. While the international community has been hesitant to impose state responsibility in contexts dominated by organised crime, stretching the legal framework is necessary to disrupt the incentives for states to use dilatory and inadequate searches and investigations in disappearance cases. These omissions amount to systematic impunity that violates the rights of victims, families, and societies and creates the context in which horrific patterns of enforced disappearances thrive and families suffer.

Courts and human rights bodies must overcome the state-constructed silences in situations of historic repression or generalised human rights atrocities, holding states accountable for acquiescing to the underlying crime of enforced disappearances when they fail to take adequate steps to search for the victims and to investigate the crimes against them. This chapter has attempted to expand the legal means by which advocates can advance human rights by promoting states' positive responsibilities in cases of enforced disappearance.

## References

American Law Institute [ALI] (1987), Restatement Third of Foreign Relations Law, sec. 702.

Brody R., and F. González (1997), 'Nunca Más: An Analysis of International Instruments on "Disappearances"', *Human Rights Quarterly*, 19, 365–405.

Citroni, G. (2009), 'Recent Developments in International Law to Combat Enforced Disappearances', *Revista internacional de direito e cidadania*, 89–111, https://boa.unimib.it/retrieve/handle/10281/7274/8504/Citroni_Recent_Developments.pdf (accessed 18 January 2021).

Council of Europe (1953), 'Convention for the Protection of Human Rights and Fundamental Freedoms', ETS 5, 213 UNTS 222, *entered into force* 3 September 1953, as amended by Protocols nos 3, 5, and 8, which *entered into force* on 21 September 1970, 20 December 1971, and 1 January 1990 respectively.

Dulitzky, A. (2019), 'The Latin American Flavor of Enforced Disappearances', *Chicago Journal of International Law*, 19 (Winter), 423–89.

Edwards, A. (2006), 'The "Feminizing" of Torture under International Human Rights Law', *Leiden Journal of International Law*, 19, 349–91.

European Court of Human Rights (2001), *Case of Cyprus* v. *Turkey*, no. 25781/94 (10 May).

Farer, T. (2016), 'I Cried for You, Argentina', *Human Rights Quarterly*, 38, 851–927.

Frey, B. (2009), '*Los Desaparecidos*: The Latin American Experience as a Narrative Framework for the International Norm against Forced Disappearances', *Hispanic Issues Online*, 12, 52–72.

Henckaerts, J., and L. Doswald-Beck (2009), *International Committee of the Red Cross, Customary International Humanitarian Law*, Vol. I (Cambridge and New York, Cambridge University Press).

Huhle, R. (2019), personal correspondence, available from the author.

Inter-American Court of Human Rights (1988), *Velásquez Rodríguez Case*, Judgment of 29 July, Inter-American Court of Human Rights (Ser. C), no. 4.

Inter-American Court of Human Rights (1989), *Case of Godinez Cruz*, Judgment of 20 January, Inter-American Court of Human Rights (Ser. C), no. 5.

Inter-American Court of Human Rights (2009), *Gonzalez et al. ('Cotton Field')* v. *Mexico*, Judgment of 16 November, Inter-American Court of Human Rights.

Inter-American Court of Human Rights (2012), *Case of Masacres de Rio Negro* v. *Guatemala*, Judgment of 4 September, Inter-American Court of Human Rights.

Inter-American Court of Human Rights (2016), *Case of Workers of 'La Hacienda Brasil Verde'* v. *Brazil*, Judgment of 20 October, Inter-American Court of Human Rights.

Inter-American Court of Human Rights (2018), *Case of Alvarado Espinoza*, Sentence of 28 November (funds, reparations and costs), www.gob.mx/cms/uploads/attachment/file/427946/Sentencia_CoIDH_-_Caso_Alvarado_Espinoza_y_otros_vs._M_xco.pdf (accessed 11 October 2019).

Keller, H., and C. Heri (2014), 'Enforced Disappearance and the European Court of Human Rights: A Wall of Silence, Fact-Finding Difficulties and States as Subversive Objectors', *Journal of International Criminal Justice*, 12, 735–50.

Koivurova, T. (2010), 'Due Diligence', in *Max Planck Encyclopedia of Public International Law*, https://opil.ouplaw.com/view/10.1093/law:epil/9780199231690/law-9780199231690-e1034?prd=EPIL (accessed 11 October 2019).

Linderfalk, U. (2007), *On the Interpretation of Treaties: The Modern International Law as Expressed in the 1969 Vienna Convention on the Law of Treaties* (Dordrecht, Springer).

Milanovich, M. (2019), 'State Acquiescence or Connivance in the Wrongful Conduct of Third Parties in the Jurisprudence of the European Court of Human Rights', https://papers.ssrn.com/sol3/papers.cfm?abstract_id=3454007 (accessed 7 October 2019).

Nuno, S. (2006), 'Acquiescence', in *Max Planck Encyclopedia of Public International Law*, https://opil.ouplaw.com/view/10.1093/law:epil/9780199231690/law-9780199231690-e1373 (accessed 11 October 2019).

Organization of American States [OAS] (1969), American Convention on Human Rights. Organization of American States, Treaty Series no. 36, 1144 UNTS 123, *entered into force* 18 July 1978.

Organization of American States (1994), Inter-American Convention on Forced Disappearance of Persons, 33 ILM 1429, *entered into force* 28 March 1996.

Saenz, R. (2017), 'Confronting Mexico's Enforced Disappearance Monsters: How the ICC Can Contribute to the Process of Realizing Criminal Justice Reform in Mexico', *Vanderbilt Journal of Transnational Law*, 50:1, 45–112.

United Nations [UN] Commission on Human Rights (2005a), Set of Principles for the Protection and Promotion of Human Rights through Action to Combat Impunity, UN Document E/CN.4/2005/102/Add.1.

United Nations [UN] Commission on Human Rights (2005b), Report of the Intersessional Open-Ended Working Group to Elaborate a Draft Legally Binding Normative Instrument for the Protection of All Persons from Enforced Disappearance, UN Document E/CN.4/2005/66.

United Nations [UN] Committee on Enforced Disappearances (2014a), Consideration of reports submitted by States parties, Mexico (17 April), United Nations Document CED/C/MEX/1.

United Nations [UN] Committee on Enforced Disappearances (2014b), Guide for Presenting a Communication or Individual Complaint to the Committee, UN Document CED/5, Q. 4.6 (b), https://undocs.org/sp/CED/C/5 (accessed 23 June 2020).

United Nations [UN] Committee on Enforced Disappearances (2019a), Guiding Principles for the Search for Disappeared Persons, United Nations Document CED/C/7, 8 May 2019.

United Nations [UN] Committee on Enforced Disappearances (2019b), Report submitted by Brazil under article 29(1) of the Convention (3 October), United Nations Document CED/C/BRA/.

United Nations [UN] General Assembly (1984), Convention against Torture and Other Cruel, Inhuman or Degrading Treatment or Punishment, General Assembly Resolution 39/46 (annex 39 UN GAOR Supp. (no. 51) at 197, United Nations Document A/39/51 (1984)), *entered into force* 26 June 1987.

United Nations [UN] General Assembly (1992), Declaration on the Protection of All Persons from Enforced Disappearances, General Assembly Resolution 47/133, 47 UN GAOR Supp. (no. 49) at 207, UN Document A/47/49 (1992).

United Nations [UN] General Assembly (1998), *Rome Statute of the International Criminal Court (Last Amended 2010)*, 17 July 1998, www.refworld.org/docid/3ae6b3a84.html (accessed 23 June, 2020).

United Nations [UN] General Assembly (2006), International Convention for the Protection of All Persons from Enforced Disappearance, General Assembly Resolution 61/177, United Nations Document A/RES/61/177, *entered into force* 23 December 2010.

United Nations [UN] Human Rights Committee (2004), General Comment 31, Nature of the General Legal Obligation on States Parties to the Covenant, United Nations Document CCPR/C/21/Rev.1/Add.13.

United Nations [UN] Human Rights Committee (2014), *El Boathi* v. *Algeria*, Communication no. 2398/2014, United Nations Document CCPR/C/122/D/2398/2014.

United Nations [UN] Human Rights Committee (2018), General Comment no. 36 on article 6 of the International Covenant on Civil and Political Rights, On the Right to Life, United Nations Document CCPR/C/GC/36.

United Nations [UN] Human Rights Committee (2019), *Téllez-Padilla* v. *Mexico*, Communication no. 2750/2016, United Nations Document CCPR/C/126/D/2750/2016.

United Nations [UN] Office of the High Commissioner for Human Rights (2009), Fact Sheet no. 6, rev. 3, Enforced or Involuntary Disappearances.

United Nations [UN] Office of the High Commissioner for Human Rights (2017), *Minnesota Protocol on Potentially Unlawful Death*, United Nations Document HR/PUB/17/4, www.ohchr.org/Documents/Publications/MinnesotaProtocol.pdf (accessed 15 October 2019).

United Nations [UN] Working Group on Enforced or Involuntary Disappearances (2008), General Comment on Definition, para. 1, in UN Human Rights Council, Report of the Working Group on Enforced or Involuntary Disappearances, United Nations Document A/HRC/7/2, 10 January 2008.

United Nations [UN] Working Group on Enforced or Involuntary Disappearances (2010), General Comment on Enforced Disappearance as a Continuous Crime, United Nations Document A/HRC/16/48.

Vermeulen, M. (2012), *Enforced Disappearance: Determining State Responsibility under the International Convention for the Protection of All Persons from Enforced Disappearance* (Cambridge, Intersentia).

# Part II

# Country Case Studies

# Mexico

# 3

# My Promise to Look for You

LULÚ HERRERA WITH PAULA CUELLAR CUELLAR

## Introduction

MEXICO HAS NEVER been recognised as a country facing armed conflict. Nonetheless, President Felipe Calderón Hinojosa (2006–12) declared a 'War on Drugs' in December 2006, and the administration of Enrique Peña Nieto (2012–18) continued the war. The unprecedented levels of violence that ensued were marked by the phenomenon of disappearance; more than 60,000 disappearances were officially registered by January 2020. During this era, an unknown number of families in Mexico have faced the tragedy of not knowing what happened to, or the whereabouts of, their loved ones. As a consequence, thousands of mothers, wives, and daughters have abandoned their former lives and occupations to assume the tasks normally undertaken by lawyers, forensic anthropologists, private investigators, and detectives. They have had to put aside their fears in order to sit down and converse with governmental authorities as equals. It was while she was undertaking this kind of arduous effort to search for relatives that I met Lulú Herrera.

Lulú Herrera is Brandon Esteban Acosta Herrera's mother and Esteban Acosta Rodríguez's wife. She has been trying to find these two disappeared loved ones for over 10 years. Since 2009, her life has been torn apart by this painful experience. Her testimony sheds light on the struggle that so many women in Mexico have faced. What follows is her story.

Paula Cuellar Cuellar

## My Story

Our tragedy began on Saturday 29 August 2009. On that day, my eight-year-old child, Brandon Esteban Acosta Herrera; my husband, Esteban Acosta Rodríguez; and my two brothers-in-law, Gualberto Acosta Rodríguez and Gerardo Acosta Rodríguez, were disappeared. The last two – Gualberto Acosta Rodríguez and

Gerardo Acosta Rodríguez – are US citizens who are married with children and live in Los Angeles, California. The disappearance occurred at about 7.30 a.m., near the Plan de Guadalupe airport in the city of Ramos Arizpe, Coahuila (Mexico), a city next to Saltillo, Coahuila. We know this because of calls that were made by those passing by in their vehicles where the event took place on the Saltillo–Monterrey highway. My husband and my child were taking my brothers-in-law to the Monterrey airport so that they could return to Los Angeles for work.

That very morning different drivers called the state's emergency services to report that armed men in various vehicles had blocked a tan Malibu car – which was ours – and forced those in the car to get out. This is how the authorities learned what had happened.

On the Friday night my husband had called in to work saying that he would return from Monterrey at 12 p.m. He is the head of security and custody in the Centro de Reinserción Social (CERESO; Centre for Social Reintegration) in Saltillo, the municipal men's prison. By this time in 2009, he had been working about 17 years in the state's public security services as a government employee.

That day I had gone to the hospital because my mother-in-law was hospitalised. I didn't try to communicate with my husband until about 12 or 12.30 p.m., when he hadn't called me. At that time, I tried to reach him by calling his two mobile phones. My calls went to voicemail. I didn't think anything was unusual, however. I assumed they were driving on the highway, or that the flight was delayed, or that they were in a communication dead zone. So, I was in the hospital until about 2 p.m., when I went to my mother's house to eat before returning to the hospital to take care of my mother-in-law.

That afternoon, I went home – our house is very close to my mother's – to bathe and put on more comfortable clothing. When I entered the house, my mother called saying that the wife of Gualberto – the brother-in-law who was traveling to Los Angeles – had phoned. She said that the flight had arrived but my brother-in-law was not on board. I then went back to my mother's house and I spoke to Gualberto's wife to say that they should keep looking for him, and that I couldn't reach them. She gave me all of the information on the flight and I called the airlines in Monterrey to check. For privacy reasons, they could not tell me the names of the passengers on the flight. Nonetheless, the airline's representative told me that of the 82 passengers meant to board, only 81 had done so. I thus deduced that Gualberto had not boarded the plane.

At this point my mom and I went to the state prosecutor's office. Because it was Saturday, and not a normal work day, only two guards were on duty. I explained what had happened: that my husband, my son, and my brothers-in-law had left the house very early; that I had tried to reach them on all four mobile phones – two for my husband and one for each of my brothers-in-law – and that my calls had gone to voicemail. The authorities asked me for their full names and ages, descriptions of the clothing that they had been wearing, physical characteristics, distinguishing features – moles, scars – and a description of the car.

By this time I was getting nervous, and I asked to use the bathroom. They showed me where it was, and just outside I saw an Escalade SUV with flat tyres and that day's date (29 August 2009) on a sticker, dusted with the grey-black powder that is used in criminal investigations. That seemed strange to me. I was looking at the SUV while waiting for my mom. I then said to her, 'Hey, this SUV has today's date on it', but I never imagined that it had anything to do with us.

When we returned to the desk, the guards asked me to repeat all of the information: their names, their particular characteristics, the details of the car. They said that the chief commander was on his way to speak to me and I had the sense that they were speaking in code. I understood some of what they were saying because I knew the codes that my husband uses in his work. I got very nervous at that moment and I began to cry.

The chief commander arrived and asked me how I had travelled to the station. I told him that we had taken a taxi, since we didn't have our car. He said that their agents were going to take me and my mom in one of their cars to the anti-kidnapping unit. I was not feeling well and I didn't understand what he meant by the anti-kidnapping unit, but my mom immediately understood that a kidnapping had occurred. It seemed to take a very long time to get from the office where we were to the building of the anti-kidnapping unit.

When we arrived, I started crying even more. Three agents of the state prosecutor's office had accompanied us on the trip. When I entered the office of the anti-kidnapping unit, the Public Minister was waiting for us because the state prosecutor had told him we were coming. When I arrived at the door, the first thing I saw on the desk was my husband Esteban's tennis shoe and also my brother-in-law Gerardo's tennis shoe. I began to feel sick, thinking that they had had a car accident. Drops of blood stained my husband's shoe. I thought they had been harmed in the accident. Above all, I began to think about my child.

The agent from the Public Ministry asked them to take me out of the office, but outside I lost control. I started rolling all over the ground. I asked the agents from the Public Ministry not to go, to stay and help me. I yelled, asking help from everyone. My mom tried to calm me down and called my house to see if one of our relatives would accompany me. She told me that I had to pull myself together because I was the only one who knew the information that they needed. I then calmed down, and when I felt a little less nervous and calmer they let me go back into the Public Ministry.

There they asked a lot of questions. They explained to me that they had received four different calls from emergency services to request help at the place on the highway near the Plan de Guadalupe airport in Ramos Arizpe. One person reported a car accident. Another reported a crash. Another reported a kidnapping. And another reported that various armed men had surrounded a Malibu. The agent then moved my husband and brother-in-law's tennis shoes into sight. I identified them as theirs, that they were the ones they had worn that day. They showed me other objects that I did not recognise. All of these objects had been taken from the Escalade SUV that

I had seen when I went to the bathroom at the state prosecutor's office. That SUV had been involved in the disappearance, but it had been abandoned, with flat tyres, about 600 metres from the airport. They abandoned it and fled, in their own cars and in ours. My husband's tennis shoe had been found on the highway and my brother-in-law's was found inside the Escalade along with other objects that I could not identify as ours. That day we left very late at night from the anti-kidnapping unit.

The next day they asked me to bring recent photographs of my son, my husband, and my two brothers-in-law. I took the photographs very early the next morning. The day before, when we had left after making the preliminary investigation application, we went to the CERESO, my husband's workplace, to see if any of his colleagues knew anything, or had received any news or calls, but they didn't know any more than I did. They told me that the director of the CERESO had been trying all day to reach my husband, but he never made contact. The next day, the director of the CERESO, my husband's boss, quit his job.

## The Fight to Find a Life

From that moment I began my pilgrimage. I went to many agencies. I went to the Sixth Military Zone, to the Navy, to the local headquarters of the General Prosecutor's Office. I knocked on every door that I could find to ask for help. I still do. Now, after nearly eight years without any news of my child and my husband, I am still active in the group that we formed in Fuerzas Unidas por Nuestros Desaparecidos en Coahuila/Fuerzas Unidas por Nuestros Desaparecidos/as en México (United Forces for Our Disappeared in Cuahuila/United Forces for Our Disappeared in Mexico; FUUNDEC/FUNDEM) to search for every one of the disappeared, and to make demands on the government to search for the living. As a mother, my hope will stay alive until I find my child.

I am one of the FUUNDEC founding families. Sometime between September and October of 2009, the priest in my church visited me and explained that he too had a brother who had disappeared in Coahuila. He told me that in the Saltillo Diocese a group of families of the disappeared had begun to meet. I went to the Fray Juan de Larios Diocesan Centre for Human Rights in October 2009. I had an interview with the Director, Blanca Isabel Martínez Bustos, to put together a case file. At that time they asked if I might want to join other families of the disappeared in Coahuila.

When my child and my husband were disappeared, I was very distant from the phenomenon. I didn't know what a disappearance was and I had no idea that it was happening so nearby. I knew about kidnappings, but only those of businessmen, people with a lot of money, and those kidnappings occurred in Mexico City, Guadalajara, or Monterrey – that is, in big cities and never here in Saltillo. And not disappearances of regular civilians, family people.

This is how I began to meet with other families. This is how I met those from Parras de la Fuente. They experienced the disappearance of two people who were father and son. Others were from Mexico City. They had experienced the disappearance of 12 people. They had come to work in Coahuila, selling paintings door to door, and the 12 of them disappeared in Allende, Coahuila. Another family was from Barca, Jalisco. They had three disappeared boys who had been in Coahuila for work. They were working in the jewellery business.

In October 2009, a small group had formed to search for 21 people in Coahuila. This did a lot for me. To speak of a disappeared person is significant. To speak of 21, well, it is a very big crime. We didn't realise at that time that we were going to be searching for many, many more. We continued to get together periodically but we felt a lot of fear, fear of going public because of the consequences that we could face in our lives, for our families, in our homes, and for our disappeared relatives – a sense that more harm could come to them than they already faced as victims.

Nevertheless, on 19 December 2009, feeling a bit stronger than before, we decided to undertake a public action regarding disappearances in the State of Coahuila and to call a press conference. It took place at the offices of the bishop, with the support from the Fray Juan de Larios Diocesan Centre for Human Rights. This was news, a bomb that hit society. This same day we had a meeting with administrators in the governor's office. Our demand was to establish a direct dialogue with the governor. At the time, the governor of Coahuila was Professor Humberto Moreira Valdez, the brother of Rubén Moreira Valdez, who later himself succeeded him as governor. Our demand was not met very quickly; it was not until September 2010 that, for the first time, we were received by the governor. By that time, there were more families. The group had grown because, through our making disappearances public, more people who had lived through the same tragedy began to approach us and ask for information, to join, and to begin the search for the disappeared.

On 10 May 2010 we organised our first march to Mexico City. We were a small group but we nonetheless made news. It was on that day that FUUNDEC was born. Although, as a movement, we had emerged on 19 December 2009, we recorded the name of our group on 10 May 2010.

From there we decided to look into contacts with different federal authorities when we could not gain direct contact with the governor of Coahuila. This is how we began our dialogue with the Mexican government. In September 2010, when the governor finally received us, we demanded a commitment from him to meet every month, and to create working groups to design strategies for the search for and investigation into the disappeared.

It was difficult in the beginning because all of the families wanted the governor to hear their stories. These were very long meetings. Some didn't end until dawn. From 2010 on we began our dialogue with the Coahuila government. Our demand – and our ongoing strategy, which we still have today – is for the active search for our loved ones and to find them alive.

As a group we have achieved many things. Although many people might think or say 'What is the purpose of spending so many years in the struggle without finding your son or your husband?', we know ourselves that we have not achieved our principal objective because we have not found even one of our disappeared. On the other hand, the work that we have done on behalf of the disappeared and their families, principally to protect them, to protect their rights and their legal status, has advanced, and we continue to hope for the active search and location of the disappeared alive.

At the same time, we have had to work in other areas. In legislation, for example, we have achieved a victory in Coahuila: a law that prohibits disappearances and a law on the declaration of absence by disappearance. Another achievement is the creation of the Programa de Atención Integral a Familiares de Personas Desaparecidas en Coahuila (Programme for Families of the Disappeared; PROFADE). This programme guarantees the protection of the right to health, housing, education, and work. It is principally a recognition that many of the disappeared are young men and the heads of their families, and that for this reason, when they are disappeared, the family, the children, and the wife find themselves without defence. Usually, the wife has to find work and there are problems with feeding the family, paying bills, covering rent, and paying for housing without Instituto del Fondo Nacional de la Vivienda para los Trabajadores (Institute of the National Housing Fund for Workers; INFONAVIT). The children have problems in their studies; in school there is a high degree of truancy because they don't have car fare, lunch money, bus fare, school supplies, or money to buy uniforms. There are not only the emotional problems of losing a loved one to disappearance; families are also affected by the secondary issues of health, housing, education, nutrition, and work. For these reasons, it was necessary to demand that the government create this programme, to attend to the basic needs of families; to allow for their survival; and, at the same time, to search for the disappeared.

In addition, we have worked on raising sensitivity and visibility in society because, essentially, our disappeared and we, the families, face revictimisation. For society, it is very easy to condemn and judge us and them (the disappeared) by saying 'there must have been some reason they were taken away', or 'they went to the dark side', or 'they were in bad company', or 'they were involved in illegal activities'. Some official authorities even intimidated us and revictimised us and our family members. It has not been easy to raise the consciousness of people and to make disappearance visible. It is the responsibility not only of the families to do this, but of all of us – all of society, whether we are at work or at school, those with a job and with a profession, in all of those spaces, including in our homes. In this space of visibility, the government has collaborated in some publicity campaigns in the state of Coahuila through spots and reports on radio, television, and in the print media, and through the photographs of our disappeared. But it has not been enough.

# 4

# Disappearances in Mexico: An Analysis Based on the Northeast Region

KARINA ANSOLABEHERE AND ALVARO MARTOS

## Introduction

MEXICO HAS OFFICIALLY recorded over 61,637 disappeared and/or unlocated persons.[1] A tragedy of this magnitude led family members to organise numerous groups for the purpose of looking for their loved ones, and gave rise to the formation of a national movement to coordinate diverse demands regarding truth, justice, reparation for victims, and guarantees of non-repetition. This tragedy also animated cooperation and dialogue among families of disappeared persons, organisations, and academic groups, which in turn broadened the debate and made the issue more visible. The analysis presented here is the result of a similar collaborative effort.

Because Mexico does not have an authoritarian regime or a declared internal armed conflict, but rather has an electoral democracy with high levels of violence, it allows us to reflect on how the logics of disappearance persist in different types of post-transitional contexts. This chapter demonstrates that the logics of disappearance described in Chapter 1 are not only present, but are indeed especially acute, given the particularities of Mexico's northeast region, i.e. the states of Coahuila, Nuevo León, and Tamaulipas.

The analysis presented here is based on research carried out by the Observatorio sobre Desaparición e Impunidad en México (Observatory on Disappearances and Impunity in Mexico, hereafter 'Observatorio') in the states of Coahuila, Nuevo

[1] As of January 2020, the most recent exact figures were 61,637 persons disappeared and unaccounted for, and 85,396 persons located, giving a total of 147,033 persons who experienced at least one direct disappearance (Comisión Nacional de Búsqueda, 2020). However, we note that there is currently no active registry of reliable data on this type of crime. As this chapter was being prepared, the number of disappeared persons in Mexico was unknown.

*Proceedings of the British Academy*, **237**, 73–96, © The British Academy 2021.

León, and Tamaulipas. The sources of data are cases of disappearance documented by civil society organisations and groups of family members. The analysis of those cases is complemented by examination of the political, economic, and social contexts in which they occurred.[2]

This chapter is organised as follows. First, we present the questions initially driving the project and the framework underpinning the analysis. Second, we discuss the methodology used. The third section provides an overview of the findings on the timing and location of disappearances in northeastern Mexico. Fourth, we present our findings on the logics of disappearance evident in northeastern Mexico. We draw our conclusions at the end of the chapter.

## Analytical Framework: The Logics of Disappearances in Violent Democracies

Chapter 1 of this volume discusses four logics of disappearances: its clandestine nature, the notion of 'disposable peoples', political economy, and ambiguous loss. In this chapter, we analyse the main features of each of these logics in northeastern Mexico between 2007 and 2017, in the context of the so-called 'war on drugs'. In this region of the country, all four logics are present in an environment characterised by a convergence of multiple forms of violence that use disappearance as a specific repertoire of action.

In Coahuila, Nuevo León, and Tamaulipas, we identified a set of circumstances that have led to disappearances. The circumstances align with the concept of violent pluralism (Arias and Goldstein 2010), aimed at control over specific populations and territories within a framework of electoral democracy. The dynamics of criminal violence and its relationship with state violence constitute a regime of violence with specific patterns and rules that includes the disappearance of people.

Each of the logics of disappearances focuses on different aspects of the phenomenon: the victims, the perpetrators, and the socioeconomic systems in which disappearances are made possible. Each of these logics, and the aspects they illuminate, account for facets of the phenomenon that attempt to answer the question: Why do people disappear in certain places, at certain times? By taking into consideration these logics in a single analysis, we were able to put together a scenario that not only makes visible and contrasts their rationales and dynamics, but also reveals their different levels of interconnection. Furthermore, these multiple approaches demonstrate the complex web in which disappearances are woven.

[2] This chapter would not have been possible without the generous support of Ciudadanos en Apoyo a los Derechos Humanos (CADHAC) in Nuevo León; Centro Diocesano Fray Juan de Larios (CDFJL) in Coahuila; I(dh)eas; and the collectives of relatives AMORES, FUUNDEC/FUNDEM, Grupo VIDA, Alas de Esperanza, and Familias Unidas de Piedras Negras, which allowed us access to case-file documents. The project was funded by Open Society Foundations; University of Minnesota Human Rights Initiative; British Academy Newton Advance Fellowship; and CONACYT, Convocatoria Problemas Nacionales.

In what follows, we situate each logic of disappearance within a broader context of those actors who articulate it.

The logics of disposable peoples and ambiguous loss express a victim-centred point of view. They explain disappearances based on the victims' characteristics or actions that make them a target for disappearance. A common view holds that those who are disappeared typically represent sectors that were marginalised prior to the act of disappearance (Hilgers and Macdonald 2017; Willis 2015); as such, the victims of disappearance constitute sectors considered to be dangerous or ostracised. For this reason, they can disappear without consequences, at least for some time. The chance of being a victim of disappearance, therefore, is not random. These risks increase in relation to a person's association with groups considered dangerous in that specific context, such as guerrilla, political opposition, indigenous, non-traditional gender, religious or ethnic minority, criminal. Thus, different groups of people may be targeted and disappear if they are considered 'dangerous' or 'undesirable' in different political, social, or economic environments.

A victims' perspective also demands attention to the consequences of disappearances on the most immediate relatives and communities. Ambiguous loss (Boss 1999) has been recognised as a potential form of social control. Disappearance generates a duality in which the person is absent but what happened to him/her is not known. This places relatives in a situation of uncertainty and ambiguity that can prove paralysing. Family members may refrain from taking action involving authorities for fear of provoking reprisals against their missing relative whom they want to protect. These family members also face uncertainty vis-à-vis the authorities resulting from the legal status of the disappeared person. Wives, for example, are unable to collect their working husbands' pensions because they do not have a death certificate, or to access to their family member's life insurance, or even the ability to register their children at school because of the uncertain juridical status of the disappeared person. Likewise, ambiguous loss reflects on the construction of social meaning related to the disappeared. To the extent that socially they are classified as 'dangerous', the families of disposable persons (the subversives, the criminals) are also stigmatised, weakening the legitimacy of their claims. In many cases, resolving this situation hinges on recognising that it is not an individual problem; it also happens to other people, and acknowledging this fact helps to overcome fear and disorientation, as relatives join together with other families of the disappeared to look for their loved ones or demand that authorities locate them (Kovras 2017). The testimonies of relatives of disappeared persons in Mexico attest to how this control mechanism works (Antillón 2018; Veráztegui 2018).

Some approaches to disappearance emphasise the motives of the perpetrators to generate terror and impose order (Calveiro, 1998). They also stress that this strategy is used because it has been employed before, and thus constitutes a known repertoire, or it is utilised to avoid internal or international scorn and accusations. In circumstances where the act of disappearance generates international responsibility for the state, this strategy of concealment and clandestine acts makes accountability for these acts difficult, and thus becomes a viable option for state actors, at least in the short term. Furthermore, the perpetrators use disappearances at certain times, generally at the beginning of periods of violence, and abandon this practice when international pressure increases, or when this type of repression is no longer necessary (Aguilar and Kovras 2019).

The existing explanations for why disappearance, concealment, and denial are chosen tend to refer to a particular type of perpetrator: state agents. However, our research, and that of other authors in this book, reveals that private agents are also engaged in disappearances. The case of Mexico – and especially the northeastern region – exemplifies this panorama. As we set out below, the perpetrators of violence include officials, unofficial agents, or a combination of official and unofficial agents who collude with each other. In addition, owing to the country's multilevel system of governance (federal, state, and municipal), no single logic exists behind disappearances, and instead various relationships emerge between state agents and non-state actors at each level of government.

Finally, disappearances can be explained because of the social and political conditions that make these types of acts possible, i.e. the distribution of economic, political, and social power between state and non-state actors. A political-economic logic behind disappearances emerges, taking into account corporate responsibility and the economic rationality of disappearances (both in legal and illegal businesses) (Payne *et al.* 2020). People become exchange commodities within a criminal economic system that traffics people; uses slave labour; or eliminates competition, opposition, or other barriers to profit-making. In addition, the families of disappeared persons become poorer as their livelihoods are affected. This logic of disappearances recalls structures of production, circulation and distribution of goods, power, privilege, and money, which produce and reproduce inequalities.

These logics behind disappearances are demonstrated in our research on northeastern Mexico during the context of the 'war on drugs'. To conduct that research, we developed the methodology set out below.

## Methodology

For the analysis of the four logics of disappearances in the northeast of Mexico, our main source was the database assembled by the Observatorio.

To systematise these records, we used the model of *who did what to whom* and *what was the response of the state* developed by Patrick Ball (1996) and the Human Rights Information and Documentation Systems (HURIDOCS) network (Dueck *et al.* 2007). We designed a coding instrument to be used in the construction of a database for analysis. The coding instrument and the implementation of the database were enriched by the participation of a wide range of individuals and organisations working side by side with victims who provided meaningful comments in the process and also helped us to reach a deeper understanding of our major findings. This systematised information provides an overview of five main elements of disappearance: the victims, the perpetrators, the disappearance (i.e. when, how, and where it occurred), the outcome (i.e. whether persons remain missing, found alive, found dead), and the response by the state to relatives' reports or claims. Because, with a disappearance, much information is also lost, the data further determine what is knowable and not (yet) knowable from these events.

The database contains 1,633 cases of disappearances that primarily occurred in the three northeastern states of Coahuila, Nuevo León, and Tamaulipas. These constituted 1,364 (83 per cent) of the cases, with the rest distributed across an additional 15 states.[3]

For our analysis, statistical processing software (R, SPSS, Stata, and Excel) and geographic information systems (QGIS) were used to produce maps and spatial representations of the data. The main parameters were based on counting procedures, calculations of descriptive statistics by variables, and bivariate analysis, taking into account the characteristics of the data used (mostly categorical.)

Furthermore, in order to complement the quantitative information and to understand in depth the dynamics of the disappearances, qualitative techniques were used to collect and analyse information such as interviews, testimonies from families, and documentary analysis of key actors.

There are several limitations to the data that must be acknowledged. We mentioned above the problem of a lack of information on the disappeared and disappearances owing to their clandestine nature. In addition, we recognise reporting bias. We rely on information provided by victims and victim-support organisations and, thus, the analysis does not consider cases that have gone unreported to these organisations. To check general patterns and trends, we were able to compare our data to those gathered by the former National Registry of Missing and Disappeared People (RNPED) and the National Victimisation Survey (ENVIPE). In general, we found that they showed similar trends. Although we cannot claim to have a full data set on the disappeared in northeastern Mexico, we nonetheless contend that these data are valuable owing to their origin and to the patterns they identify about a phenomenon whose main characteristic is the concealment of information.[4]

[3] Disappearance cases that occurred outside the three states mentioned above were included in the database because they came from the same source as the others, but were excluded from the analysis since they took place beyond the boundaries of the selected states. The number of cases in this database used for the analysis is 1,364.

[4] A particularity of the information is that there is considerable asymmetry between the events registered in Nuevo León and Coahuila and those registered in Tamaulipas (which, interestingly, is the state with the highest number of missing persons in the country according to official sources and the National Victimisation Survey). This is because the information on Tamaulipas was accessed from documentation produced by CADHAC (Nuevo León) and the Fray Juan de Larios Diocesan Centre (Coahuila). For security reasons, the project team did not travel to Tamaulipas as it did to the other states. All of this is to say that the lower number of cases in Tamaulipas does not reflect a lower number of actual disappearances, but rather is an expression of the problems of violence that the state faces, and the difficulties inherent in analysing a phenomenon such as this. However, the patterns we find in Tamaulipas are consistent with the findings of case studies of disappearances in the state (OHCHR 2018).

The data allow us to identify certain patterns that indicate evidence of the logics of disappearance: its clandestine nature, disposable peoples, political economy, and ambiguous loss. For the analysis of the logic of clandestine acts, data on state, non-state, or combined perpetrators; evidence of witnesses; and details related to the act of disappearance proved relevant. On the logic of disposable peoples, we drew on victims' socio-demographic data (e.g. educational level, occupation, age, sex). The data on victims' occupations also proved useful for analysis of the political economy logic, as did the location of the disappearance. The logic of ambiguous loss primarily required the complementary qualitative analyses mentioned previously: interviews with organisations and family members, analysis of testimonies, and secondary information on the experiences of families derived from their support organisations and networks.

Before discussing the findings related to the logics of disappearances, we present an overview of the spatial and temporal dynamics of disappearances in the region. In so doing, we combine different scales of analysis (regional, state, and municipal) to highlight continuities and discontinuities. The overview highlights the relevance of this first-of-its-kind regional analysis in exploring the four logics of disappearances. The three states of Mexico's northeast region experienced a concurrent crisis of disappearance. This resulted from joint operations undertaken by the army, the navy, the federal police, and state police forces at the border with the United States, and in a context of territorial disputes among criminal groups themselves.

## The Dynamics of Disappearances in Northeast Mexico

Since they share a number of characteristics, the three states of the northeast region can be considered a geographical, economic, social, political, and also human-rights-violation unit. One of the main features of the region is its border with southern Texas, making it a geostrategic region for trade and exchange, legal and illegal, of people, goods, and services (Schmidt Nederovich *et al.* 2017). Furthermore, 'its location makes it [part of] the shortest route from Central and South America for transporting drugs by land, sea, and air to distribution centres in Texas' (Galán and Corrales 2017: 132). It has an extensive network of road and communications infrastructure. The highway corridors include: Mexico City to Nuevo Laredo, with a branch to Piedras Negras; Veracruz to Monterrey, with a branch to Matamoros (south to north); and Mazatlán to Matamoros (west to east). Two significant companies holding licences to rail routes in the region account for 48 per cent of the total Mexican railway network: Ferrocarril del Noreste and Kansas City Southern de México (KCSM). In addition, the ports of Altamira, Tampico, and Matamoros in Tamaulipas, when factored into its road network, make it the state with the greatest connectivity in the region. Within the region, Tamaulipas has a key portion of the border. Its location gives it a long-shared boundary with the United States. It has

18 international crossing points into the United States, the highest of any border state. And it has a long coastline on the Gulf of Mexico.

One of the characteristics of this region is the high level of criminal violence linked to the trafficking of drugs, people, and weapons along the northern border with the United States, the main transit route for cocaine, marijuana, and heroin. Added to this mix are the failed security policies developed through the 'war on drugs' or 'war on narcotics smugglers', which has persisted over the past 40 years. In its Mexican version, this strategy was implemented during Felipe Calderón's government (2006–12) and was continued by his successor, Enrique Peña Nieto (2012–18). These policies led to a record increase in the rate of homicides, kidnappings, violent robberies, and car hijackings between one presidential term and the next, according to data from the National Security Commissioner.[5] During the period under review, the federal government's predominant strategy involved joint operations in which the armed forces and the federal and state police coordinated with each other. In the region, operations included, among others, the Joint Operation Tamaulipas–Nuevo León in 2008 (Rea Gómez *et al.* 2019), Operation Northeast – Nuevo León–Tamaulipas–Coahuila and San Luis Potosí – in 2010 (Notimex 2011), and Operation Laguna Segura in 2011 (Dávila 2011). Note that these operations coincided with the beginning of the increase in disappearances. The analysis of the data set built by the Observatorio in Mexico showed that a significant proportion of disappearances were attributed to federal agents.

Disappearances in the region became a widespread phenomenon between 2001 and 2017, according to official records, as well as to the organisations that collaborated on this project. Disappearances peaked in 2011, when 408 cases were documented in the three states. Figure 4.1 presents a distribution of disappearances over time that is also reflected in Figure 4.2's presentation of the data from the RNPED data.

In 2011, there were greater numbers of both men and women who disappeared. However, the disappearances of women were concentrated around this year (37 per cent of disappearances of women occurred in 2011), while those of men were distributed throughout the period.[6] Disappearances, however, are not distributed in the same way over time in each of the states as Figure 4.3 shows. In Coahuila, disappearances are more dispersed over the period. In Nuevo León, they are mainly concentrated around 2011. Disappearances in Tamaulipas were recorded from 2009 to 2012, with a concentration in 2011 and 2012, and most of the cases recorded in 2012.

[5] Ejecutivo del Sistema Nacional de Seguridad Pública (SESNSP), www.gob.mx/sesnsp/acciones-y-programas/incidencia-delictiva-87005?idiom=es (accessed 16 February 2021).

[6] This is confirmed if we compare the Kurtosis coefficients that measure the concentration of the data around the central area of the distribution (in our case 2011): 1.4 for men and 3.5 for women (the higher the coefficient, the more concentrated the data).

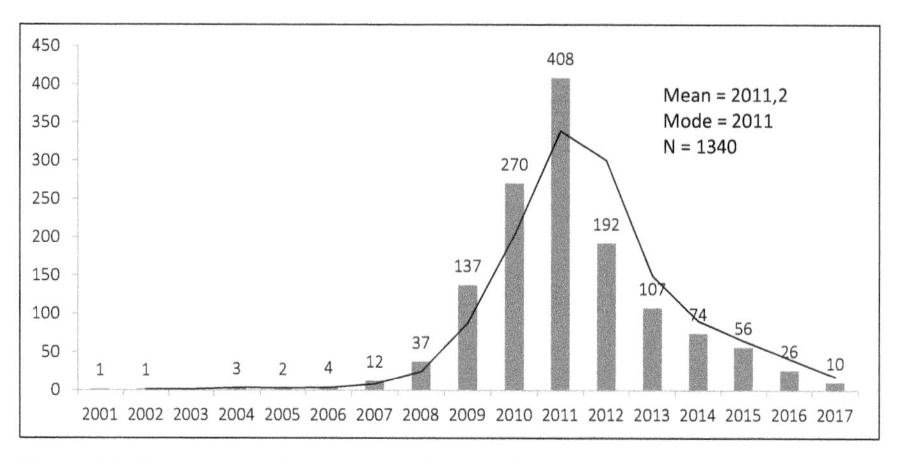


**Figure 4.1** Disappearances by year in Mexico's northeast region.

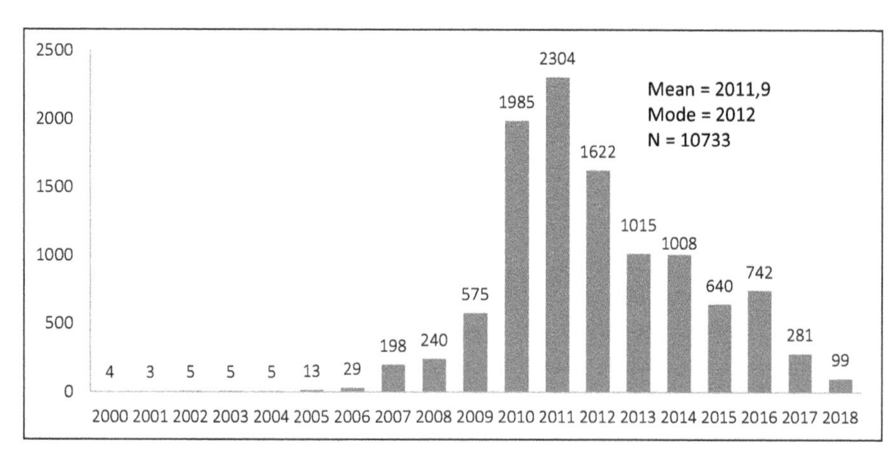


**Figure 4.2** Disappearances by year in the northeast region according to RNPED (2018).

We know that criminal violence tends to be concentrated in large cities because of the convergence of resources, people, and transport channels. The disappearances in Coahuila, Nuevo León, and Tamaulipas follow this logic.[7] The municipality that concentrates the greatest number of disappearances is Piedras Negras, Coahuila, with 20 per cent of the cases (278) and, accordingly, it has a *very high incidence*. It is followed by a second group of municipalities – Monterrey (165), Nuevo León; Saltillo (165) and Torreón (103), Coahuila – with between 8 per cent and 12 per cent of the cases and a *high incidence* rate. The next group, of *medium incidence*,

[7] It is worth noting that, as an example of the biases mentioned previously, the Observatorio's database is influenced by the location of the organisations and groups that document disappearances and accompany relatives.

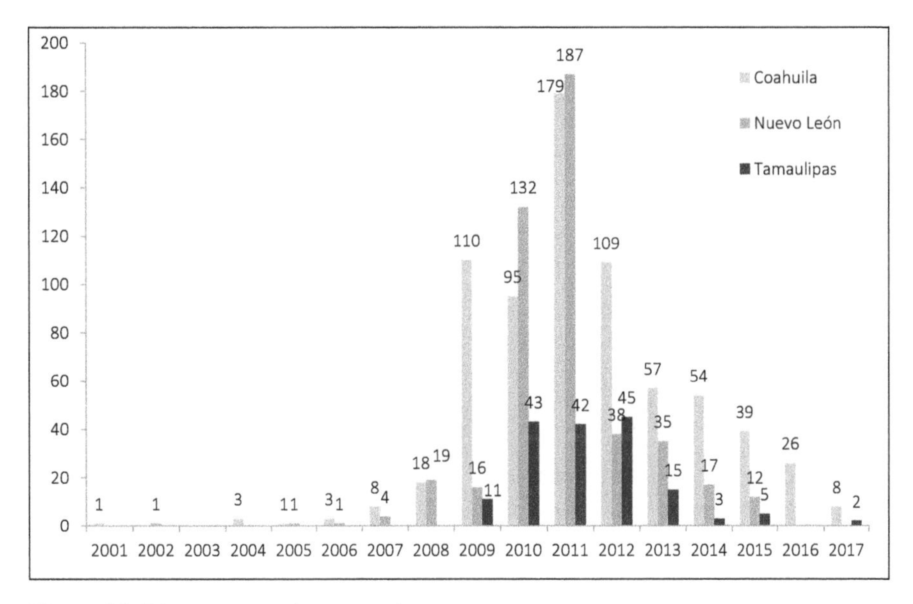


**Figure 4.3** Disappearances by year and state.

covers municipalities with between 2 per cent and 3 per cent of the registered cases (10 municipalities with between 20 and 50 disappearances each.) In this category, Allende (47) and Monclova (32) have the most in Coahuila, Guadalupe (46) and Apodaca (37) have the most in Nuevo León, and Reynosa (43) and Nuevo Laredo (34) have the most in Tamaulipas. The *low incidence* group includes 12 municipalities with between 10 and 20 disappearances and, finally, 33 municipalities have *very low incidence*, with between 1 and 10 disappearances. Figure 4.4 shows the spatial distribution and intensity of disappearances.

Comparing the three states in the region, we see that the three municipalities with the highest number of disappearances have cities that, because of their economic and political characteristics, are important entities within each state. Some are state capitals – seats of executive, legislative, and judicial powers – and the most populated (Saltillo in Coahuila, Monterrey in Nuevo León); others are cities that border with the United States (Nuevo Laredo, Río Bravo, and Reynosa in Tamaulipas, and Piedras Negras in Coahuila) or are within a major metropolitan area (Apodaca and Guadalupe in the metropolitan area of Monterrey; Reynosa-Río Bravo-McAllen in the homonymous metropolitan area).

In terms of the extent of the phenomenon at the local level, of the 132 municipalities within Mexico's northeast region, 61 recorded disappearances, equivalent to 46 per cent of the territorial extension. This percentage is slightly higher in Nuevo León (47 per cent) and Coahuila (55 per cent), but is lower in Tamaulipas (35 per cent). Although disappearances are concentrated in the main urban centres, these percentages demonstrate that disappearances are not exclusive to major cities,

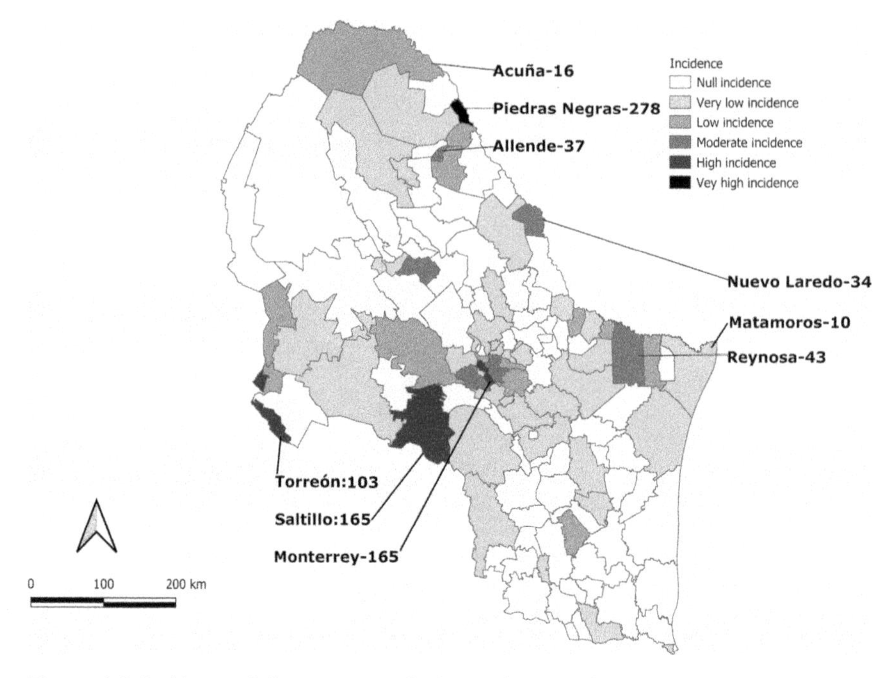


**Figure 4.4** Incidence of disappearances in the northeast region.

**Table 4.1** Main municipalities and number of disappearances by state.

| | Coahuila | Nuevo León | Tamaulipas |
|---|---|---|---|
| Municipality 1 (number and percentage of disappeared in the state) | Piedras Negras (278 [38%]) | Monterrey (165 [35%]) | Reynosa (43 [26%]) |
| Municipality 2 (number and percentage of disappeared in the state) | Saltillo (165 [23%]) | Guadalupe (46 [10%]) | Nuevo Laredo (34 [20%]) |
| Municipality 3 (number and percentage of disappeared in the state) | Torreón (103 [14%]) | Apodaca (37 [8%]) | Río Bravo (14 [8%]) |

Source: Prepared by the authors based on data from the Observatory on Disappearance and Impunity in Mexico, with information documented by CDFJL, CADHAC, Grupo Vida, Alas de Esperanza, and Familias Unidas.

but rather occurred in almost half of the municipalities in the entire region. This territorial extension of disappearances is indicative of the different types of violence, insofar as they are not concentrated solely along drug routes.

In sum, this overview of the data shows that disappearances change over time and with regard to location. In the next section, we use these data, linking them to the logics behind patterns of disappearance in the region.

## The Logics of Disappearance in Northeastern Mexico

The general dynamics of disappearances in northeastern Mexico described in the previous section allow us to identify key features that confirm the logics behind disappearances in the region.

### Clandestine Acts of Disappearance

The analysis of disappearances in Mexico's northeast allowed us to determine that different types of violence converged in the region: violence driven by state agents in order to control criminal groups and the local population, violence implemented among criminal groups themselves and unleashed against state agents and the population, and violence exercised through collusion between state agents and criminal groups. Disappearances in the region are one manifestation of these multiple sources of violence. The clandestine nature of disappearances is interwoven with them.

The types of perpetrators involved in the disappearances indicate reasons behind the acts. Although information on perpetrators is largely missing, given the nature of the act, our data nonetheless shows that in 36 per cent of the cases at least one state agent is involved. In 64 per cent of the cases the perpetrators included non-state actors, seemingly operating without any state authority; see Figure 4.5. The state agents who were identified as perpetrators were not all at the lower levels of authority but were distributed across the local, state, and federal levels, as illustrated in Figure 4.6.

These numbers might appear to suggest that the phenomenon is largely one in which state forces do not tend to be involved. Yet a third of them suggest direct involvement by state actors. Moreover, accounts from the families of disappeared persons, journalistic sources, and the few judicial processes that addressed disappearance reveal the active participation of security forces alone or in collaboration with criminal groups. This coordinated participation was identified in 37 cases. Of these, in one instance federal agents were documented acting with private individuals; there were three documented cases of state officials colluding with individuals, and in 33 documented examples municipal officials acted with private individuals.

In this context of diverse perpetrators, the motivations for dealing clandestinely are varied. For the armed forces, the logic of warfare stipulates that members of

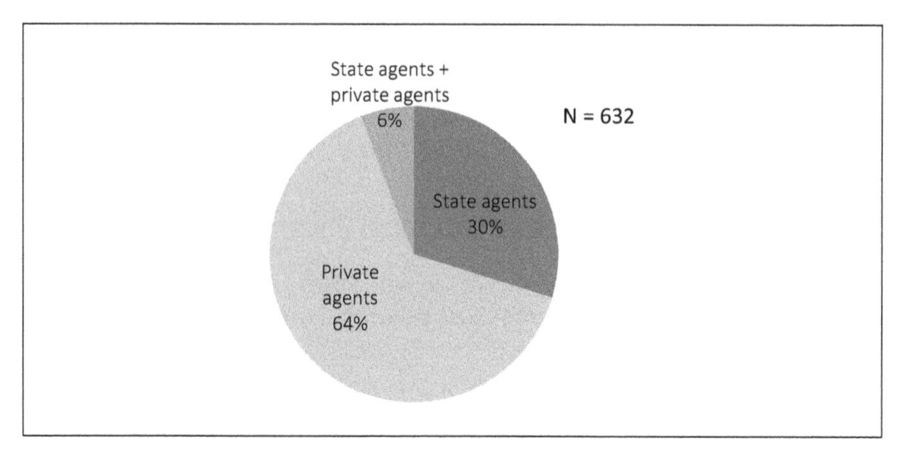


**Figure 4.5** Type of perpetrator in the northeast region.

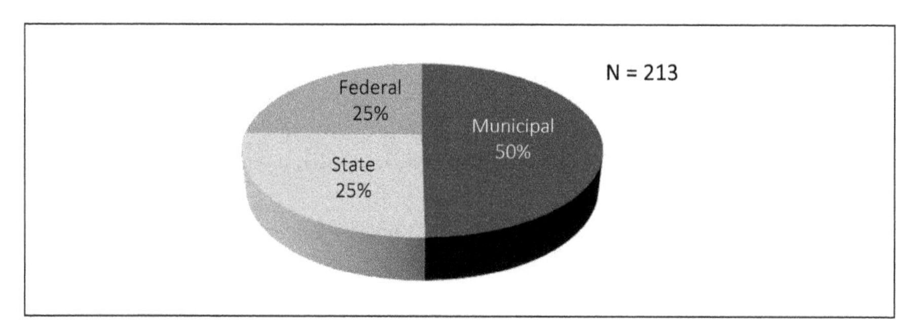


**Figure 4.6** State agents identified as perpetrators according to governmental sector, northeast region.

criminal groups (real, potential, suspected) are enemies. In these cases, clandestine acts are linked to the concealment of human rights violations to avoid being held accountable and to avoid international scorn, at least in the initial years. While sources cannot be specifically identified for security reasons, interviews in the region revealed that, in the early years of the 'war on drugs', the armed forces were ordered not to leave bodies behind.

For criminal groups, different motivations drive the clandestine nature of the disappearances. One of these is to hide evidence of the crime in order to hinder investigations, especially at the beginning of the period when the crime of disappearance by individuals did not exist, or to avoid generating widespread alarm in the population. In addition, according to journalistic investigations, other motivations have to do with exploitation, forced recruitment, and slave labour. In this scenario, relatives lose contact with their disappeared family member, deliberately heightening the state of fear designed to maintain silence and secrecy around the event. A third motivation behind clandestine acts of disappearance by criminal groups is their use as a form of reprisal or the threat of reprisal against those who refuse to cooperate in criminal activity, or defy secrecy or other rules of conduct (Payne *et al.* 2020).

Most cases of collusion between state and non-state agents involve municipal police working with criminal groups. These police tend to ignore acts of violence, or actively facilitate them by handing detained individuals over to the criminal groups. In this logic of clandestine acts of disappearance, the criminal act is hidden. There are rarely outside witnesses. Of the recorded cases, relatives and organisations could only identify the presence of witnesses in 21 per cent of the cases, while in the remaining 79 per cent there is no information about possible witnesses to the events. When there are witnesses, in most cases (52 per cent) relatives or friends themselves provide information, since the events occurred in their homes or while they were accompanying the victims. Other types of witnesses include work colleagues or employees, vendors on public streets, neighbours, and passers-by who by chance witness the events (as exemplified in the case described by Lulú Herrera in Chapter 3). This same pattern at the regional level is repeated in each state analysed: lack of information in more than 75 per cent of the cases, and family and friends as the main witnesses. As mentioned in Chapter 18 by Volga de Pina Ravest, prevailing fear of reprisals for speaking out perpetuates the unwillingness of witnesses to become involved.

The clandestine nature and logic of disappearance is also revealed in the lack of information on how the disappearances occurred; see Figure 4.7. In most of the cases in this regional study (62 per cent), information regarding the capture of the individual is unavailable.

Data on the state's response to claims made from family members further reveal the logic of clandestine acts behind the disappearances. Authorities reacted in a number of ways that undermined the possibility of searching for or finding the individual, as indicated in Chapter 18. They avoided receiving such complaints by maintaining a waiting period, they pretended to investigate when no action was in fact taken, or they cautioned families against jeopardising

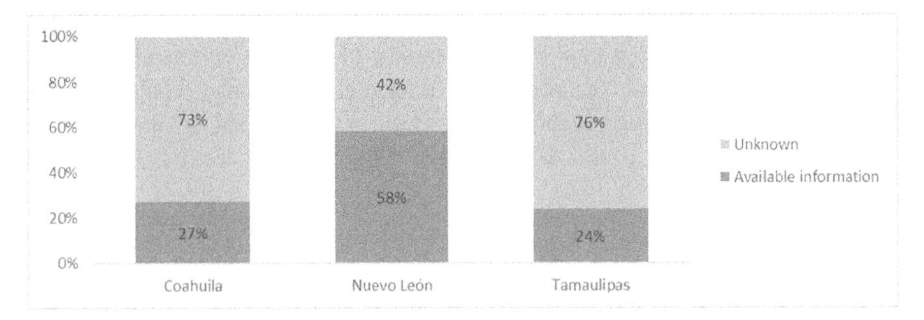


**Figure 4.7** Availability of information on capture method by state.

the security of their disappeared relatives (Observatorio sobre Desaparición e Impunidad 2019b). Some families had to visit more than ten state offices before they were able to file a claim (Observatorio sobre Desaparición e Impunidad 2017). It was not uncommon for families to be told that they needed to return at a later time to receive information only to learn when they did so that no record of their previous visit existed, and thus no search had begun (Observatorio sobre Desaparición e Impunidad 2019a). In another common practice the authorities informally registered the claims instead of opening up an official inquiry or investigation, thus preventing a timely follow-up of cases. Standard practice also included filing 'ex officio searches', in which requests on the whereabouts of persons were issued by authorities, but without the required follow-up search and investigation connected to an official process. In sum, these responses led to long periods of inactivity where the agents failed to carry out any type of investigation and/or search, thus forfeiting the opportunity to pursue the information in a timely manner and effectively trace the person's whereabouts.[8] The logic indicates that these delay tactics are possible because of the clandestine nature of the violence. They suggest deliberate efforts to avoid searching for the person, either to hide state actors' direct involvement in the crime or to protect themselves from reprisals from other non-state actors who carried out the crime.

In sum, the logic of clandestine acts behind disappearances plays out in northeastern Mexico in a variety of ways. There is an array of perpetrators with various motives. Little is known about how people are disappeared. The clandestine nature of disappearance thus acts as a deterrent to investigation, search, and justice, hinting at the logic behind it.

## Disposable Population

The profile of the disappeared in northeastern Mexico fits the logic of disposable peoples described in Chapter 1 of this volume. Those who have disappeared are 'disposable' in two senses, first, because of their marginal social status, and second, because the narratives in the region link disappearances to criminality, thereby rhetorically justifying their disappearance.

The victims of disappearance in northeastern Mexico are not members of the political, social, economic, or cultural elite of the region or country. They tend to be young, primarily male, with secondary education: small vendors, drivers, students, or, in the case of women, domestic workers. Their relatives are thus not part of

[8] This type of situation has been documented on several occasions by families, their groups and accompanying organisations, international bodies specialising in this field, and the National Human Rights Commission in its recommendation 042/2018 and in the Special Report on the Disappearance of Persons and Clandestine Graves in Mexico (Comisión Nacional de Derechos Humanos, 2017).

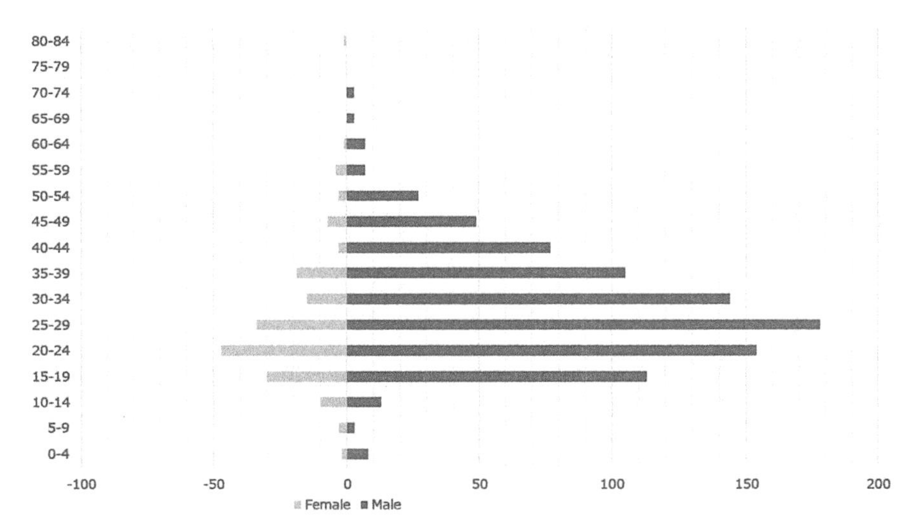


**Figure 4.8** Population pyramid of disappeared persons.

influential groups whose voices are heard in public spaces or by state officials. We set out below the findings from our research.

As Figure 4.8 shows, at the regional level, more men (84 per cent) than women (16 per cent) disappear, and more young people (30 years old, on average) disappear than older people. The population pyramid illustrates this trend. It also shows that disappeared women are even younger than disappeared men. The average age of women is 24 and that of men is 33. In addition to the disappeared being mostly young people, 40 per cent have a secondary education – i.e. a basic educational level. Some 15 per cent have less schooling and a similar proportion have university education (See Table 4.2).

The jobs held by disappeared persons support the idea of their lack of political, social, or economic influence. This information is available for 49 per cent of the disappeared. Of those whose jobs are identified the predominant occupations of men are: vendors and sales employees (21 per cent); drivers of transportation vehicles (passengers and cargo) and movable machinery (13 per cent); students (9 per cent); domestic, care, and cleaning workers (4 per cent); workers in private protection and security services (4 per cent), and police and traffic officers (4 per cent). The rest of the sample is distributed among different jobs, ranging from professional services (lawyers, accountants, engineers, veterinarians, architects, designers, etc.) to manual work in different trades (electricians, carpenters, plasterers, masons, painters, etc.). In none of these cases is there a record of political activism. The majority of women are domestic workers, cleaners, and care workers (35 per cent); students (20 per cent); and vendors and sales employees (14 per cent).

**Table 4.2** Level of education of disappeared people by state.

| | Coahuila | | Nuevo León | | Tamaulipas | |
|---|---|---|---|---|---|---|
| Level of education | No. | % | No. | % | No. | % |
| University | 45 | 24 | 44 | 14 | 6 | 12 |
| High school | 36 | 20 | 61 | 19 | 5 | 10 |
| Secondary | 61 | 33 | 135 | 42 | 24 | 48 |
| Technical studies | 13 | 7 | 25 | 8 | 6 | 12 |
| Primary | 23 | 12 | 48 | 15 | 9 | 18 |
| No formal education | 8 | 4 | 7 | 2 | 0 | 0 |
| Total | 186 | 100 | 320 | 100 | 50 | 100 |

Source: Prepared by the authors based on data from the Observatory on Disappearance and Impunity in Mexico, with information documented by CDFJL, CADHAC, Grupo Vida, Alas de Esperanza, and Familias Unidas.

In a setting characterised by the 'war against criminal groups' and emphasising the disputes among the groups themselves, it is mostly young and lower-income people who disappear and who fit into a public narrative that blames the victims for their disappearance. This narrative categorises people with these specific backgrounds as dangerous to the public and state agents (for supposedly being members of criminal groups), and dangerous to criminal groups (as potential members of a rival group). Thus, the victims in this common narrative become suspects of criminal activity. The testimony presented in Chapter 3 by Lulú Herrera reflects on the criminal stigma attached to the disappeared and their families.

The official narrative within the northeastern states reiterates the characterisation of the victims as disposable populations. Authorities interpret disappearances as a consequence of the activities of criminal groups, and therefore the disappeared are associated with these groups. The idea that people disappear because 'they must have done something' is echoed in a context typified by criminality. The following quote from the governor of Nuevo León referring to the increase in disappearances in his state exemplifies this type of mindset: 'It was a very difficult stage in the country in which the majority of the disappeared have, or had some reason, to be disappeared' (Sinembargo.mx 2015).

In essence, the disappeared and their families are not recognised as victims of structural inequality. Instead, the construction of the disappeared assigns to them the blame for their own fate, hiding the political-economic logic behind disappearances.

**Political Economy**

Disappearances in northeastern Mexico have a specific political economy involving, first, disappeared people's roles in producing and distributing economic and political resources, and, second, their use as exchange commodities in an economic order in which exploitation, enslavement, and forced recruitment are accepted practices.

As we pointed out in the section on the logic of the disposable peoples, those who disappear are economically vulnerable. They are small vendors or transport workers, who cannot pay extortion fees extracted by criminal groups, state agents, or those suspected of being part of criminal groups.

Yet evidence suggests that at times the disappeared include people who are physically exploited or forcibly recruited into new forms of slave labour: tunnel digging, telephone services, construction work, or sex slavery. Once they have exhausted their utility, they are 'thrown away' or disappeared. Although first-hand accounts are scarce, a few testimonies from survivors confirm this logic (Guillén and Petersen 2019; López Marroquín 2019). The absence of the state in investigating these patterns of disappearance contrasts sharply with the response to disappearances of business leaders in the region motivated by extortion. In such cases, the state responds with proactive approaches and immediate intervention. This highlights the selective role the state plays, the networks of cooperation between political and economic elites, and the logic of political economy behind disappearances in the region.

A significant number of disappearances occur in workplaces or private establishments (see Figure 4.9) although the willingness of employers to clarify

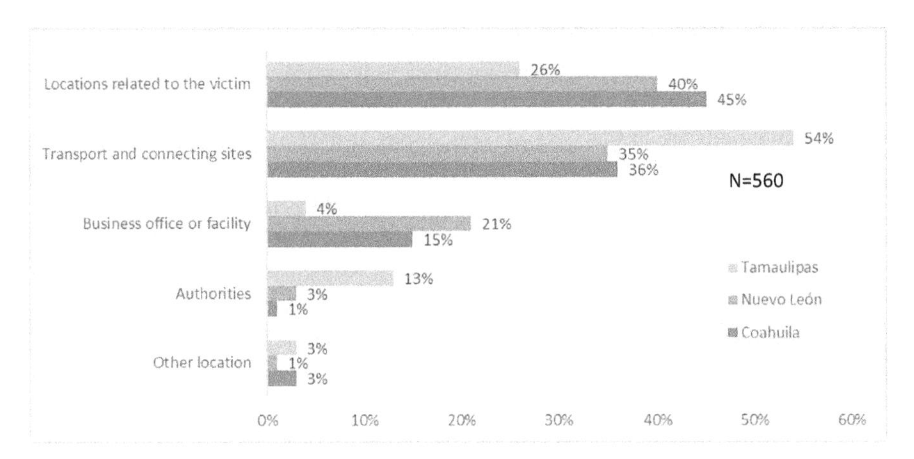


**Figure 4.9** Places of the events of disappearances in Coahuila, Nuevo León, and Tamaulipas.

cases and their own responsibility are aspects that require further attention. Disappearances also generate a series of negative economic impacts that primarily affect the families of the victims. The predominant profile of the disappeared person – young and male – means that these individuals are often the main breadwinner in the family at the time of their disappearance, or are the person upon whom the future income of the family depends.[9] This situation is scaled up when larger populations are subjected to sustained violence, leading to forced internal displacement and the ensuing disruption of economic activities in the region. In turn, as part of the general phenomenon of violence in the 'war on drugs', there is evidence that points to the impact of disappearances on human-capital formation (Brown and Velásquez 2017; Soria Romo 2017), their links to economic inequality (Enamorado *et al.* 2016) and loss of formal jobs, as well as the increase in illegal activities and territorial disputes between cartels for control of shipping routes (Dell *et al.* 2019). However, it is important to note that, because of their comparative advantages in terms of location, infrastructure, and capital, the states discussed in this study are among the least affected by the economic costs of violence in relation to their state-level gross domestic product (Institute for Economics and Peace 2019; Soria Romo 2018).

Finally, disappearances, from the point of view of the family members who search for their loved ones, are followed by uncertainty and fear. This, in turn, is linked to the fourth logic of disappearance: ambiguous loss.

## Ambiguous Loss

The previous section on the logic of clandestine acts highlighted the diversity of official and unofficial perpetrators and the links among them. These links between state actors and criminal groups are not a recent phenomenon in the region. They began in the late 1970s, when the Gulf Cartel began to expand and consolidate its extensive network in the state of Tamaulipas at the municipal, state, and even federal levels, in addition to taking control of the media with the aim of forcing dissident actors to collaborate (Correa-Cabrera 2014; Correa-Cabrera *et al.* 2015; Flores Pérez 2014).

Relatives of disappeared persons and their organisations have denounced the corruption of the authorities as one of the causes of violence in the country. However, it is also true that employers often fail to exercise due diligence when their employees disappear in the course of their work. This fraying of the social fabric is also manifest in the general population's perceptions and experiences.

In this context there are many stories of family members who recount their initial bewilderment and fear, as well as the feeling of misunderstanding and loneliness in the face of their situation. As the director of one organisation that accompanies

[9] There are few studies that examine the specific economic impacts of disappearances. An exception is the case of Veracruz, discussed in IMDHD (2020).

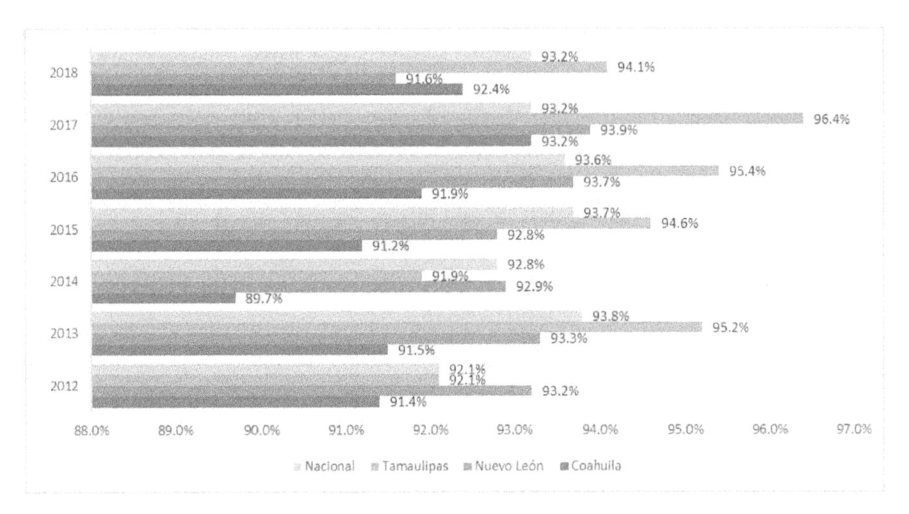


**Figure 4.10** Unregistered figures of the disappeared by state and at the federal level.

relatives of disappeared persons in the region told us, 'when we asked them for their testimony … I can't forget … they all agreed on one thing: they felt as though they had been knocked out, the disappearance of their children literally left them prostrated in bed, took away their will to live'.

Families also recounted state agents' reluctance to become involved in their cases, the officials' indifference adding to their suffering and despair. An example is that, notwithstanding the number of disappeared persons, judicial investigations remain paralysed, and the results of searches for missing people are insignificant. For example, in Coahuila, we found two court sentences for forced disappearance and none for disappearance by private actors; there has not been a single sentence for disappearance rendered at the state level in either Nuevo León or Tamaulipas.

Quantitatively, fear and uncertainty are manifested in the mistrust and culture of silence that led to relatives' decisions not to report crimes to the authorities; see Figure 4.10. At the regional level, the dark figure – or unreported level – of crime in Tamaulipas is not only the highest in the region, it also exceeds the national figure between 2012 and 2017, increasing from 2014 to reach 96.4 per cent in 2017. Tamaulipas and Nuevo Leon are among the states with the highest dark figure of crime, along with Chiapas, Sinaloa, Zacatecas, Nayarit, Guerrero, and the State of Mexico (Instituto Nacional de Estadísticas y Censos, Mexico 2018).[10]

However, some families managed to overcome their fear and scepticism by mobilising. Groups of relatives of the disappeared who work alone or are connected to local and national civil society organisations have sprung up around the country.

[10] ENVIPE is the National Victimisation Survey, organised by the National Institute of Geography and Statistics of Mexico. The dark figure of crime is equal to the percentage of *crimes* that are not reported.

This is not unique to Mexico; in other similar cases where there are numerous disappearances groups of relatives have mobilised in solidarity, for collective action, and to overcome fear and stigma (Kovras 2017). They articulate demands and denounce the state, push for the judicial authorities to take action, or search for their relatives themselves. Today there are more than 10 groups of family members in the northeast region who seek truth and justice for their loved ones.

In sum, the findings from northeastern Mexico present evidence that supports the four logics behind disappearance in violent democracies. In the final section, we explore the interconnections among these logics.

## Final Considerations

In the analysis of the data on disappearances in northeastern Mexico, we have made visible the particularities of these logics in a regime of multidimensional violence. In such a violent setting, disappearances are one of several manifestations of the multifaceted violence that takes place for the control of territory, population, and valuable resources. The logics of disappearances are linked and mutually reinforcing. They persist until public visibility and outcry slowly begin to chip away at the powerful edifice. The violent nature of some contemporary electoral democracies enhances the logics of disappearance, but also the means to resist them, as we can see in the case of the social movement against disappearances in Mexico.

In violent electoral democracies, there are multiple perpetrators of violence. We have shown that both state and non-state actors use disappearance in their repertoire of actions. Disappearance – as a clandestine act – allows this repertoire to persist. The lack of information about how and why people disappear prevails, revealing neither state nor non-state actors' involvement in the acts. Disappearance thus becomes normalised in violent electoral democracies.

Indeed, in 'low-intensity' violent democracies, the need for federal and local authorities to conceal human rights violations is even greater than for an authoritarian government. In post-transition contexts, perpetrators face more monitoring mechanisms, institutional checks, accountability systems, and barriers to freedom of speech that could expose and halt disappearances. International legal instruments, discussed in Chapters 2 and 14–17, further pressure states to align their domestic legislation and institutional practices with human rights standards.[11] With levels of impunity whereby 95 per cent of the crimes never result in sentences, the criminal justice system is essentially ineffectual. Hiding these acts from scrutiny further ensures impunity.

[11] For example, including the crime of forced disappearance in the criminal codes of Mexican states was the result of the mobilisation undertaken by the relatives of disappeared persons who sought truth and justice in their cases.

The clandestine nature of the acts is linked to the profile of the people who disappear. They are not part of the elite. Even before they disappeared, they were invisible and had no public voice. They were part of a disposable population in a neoliberal regime, and continue to be so after their disappearance because of public narratives that blame them for their own plight. With the presumption that they 'were up to something', they are suspected of participation in criminal activities. There is a degrading of the magnitude of the problem because of the disappeared persons' social standing. Their lives are worth less than others. The acts committed against them occur through the combined logics of clandestine operations and disposable peoples. Only after some time does someone dare to speak out on their behalf and make them visible. But this process involves overcoming the logic of ambiguous loss.

From the victims' point of view, the ambiguous loss of the disappearance never ends. Disorientation and fear are common denominators in the testimonies of relatives of disappeared persons. They are afraid to search, to persist in their enquiries, because they believe that this may further harm their loved ones. Families also feel socially isolated, alone. The narrative of the disposable population has an impact on the relatives themselves and on their neighbours. Their acquaintances point at them, blame them, or avoid the issue. Ambiguity of the loss exists because they do not know what happened to their loved ones, but also because of the social stigma placed on the victims themselves, which immediately identifies them as criminals. Ambiguous loss thus acts as a way to stymie claims made on behalf of the disappeared.

One aspect that is clearly highlighted in the case of northeastern Mexico is that this situation is possible because of a history of close ties between state agents and criminal groups through corruption and collusion. This is exemplified, among other things, by the former governors and other officials extradited to the United States or brought to trial in Mexico. This type of scenario heightens the sense of ambiguous loss and mistrust towards the authorities, and generates favourable circumstances for the economic profitability of disappearances. Such a situation increases feelings of powerlessness among relatives, even among those who are organised and mobilised.

In the cycle of disappearances, however, many families come together and mobilise despite the fear. In Nuevo León and Coahuila, there are long-standing civil society organisations that relatives contact for support. When they do so, a different cycle begins, the sequence is broken, the state is denounced, demands are made, and an identity is built from the dignity that arises from searching for loved ones. In this new cycle, it becomes possible for relatives to identify themselves, position themselves, and be heard. In this process characterised by pain and stigmatisation, relatives find and amplify their own voices.

## References

Aguilar, P., and I. Kovras (2019), 'Explaining Disappearances as a Tool of Political Terror', *International Political Science Review*, 40:3, 437–52.

Antillón, X. (ed.) (2018), 'Yo solo quería que amaneciera: impactos psicosociales del caso Ayotzinapa', FUNDAR, Centro de Análisis e Investigación AC, https://fundar.org.mx/impactos-psicosociales-de-casoayotzinapa (accessed 24 January 2021).

Arias, E. D., and D. M. Goldstein (2010), 'Violent Pluralism: Understanding the New Democracies of Latin America', in *Violent Democracies in Latin America*, ed. E. D. Arias and D. M. Goldstein (Durham, NC, Duke University Press), 1–34.

Ball, P. D. (1996), 'Who Did What to Whom? Planning and Implementing a Large Scale Human Rights Data Project', Human Rights Data Analysis Group, https://hrdag.org/publications/who-did-what-to-whom-planning-and-implementing-a-large-scale-human-rights-data-project/ (accessed 24 January 2021).

Boss, P. (1999), *Ambiguous Loss: Learning to Live with Unresolved Grief* (Cambridge, MA, Harvard University Press).

Brown, R., and A. Velásquez (2017), 'The Effect of Violent Crime on the Human Capital Accumulation of Young Adults', *Journal of Development Economics*, 127, 1–12.

Calveiro, P. (1998), *Poder y desaparición: los campos de concentración en Argentina* (Buenos Aires, Ediciones Colihue SRL).

Comisión Nacional de Búsqueda (2020), 'Informe sobre fosas clandestinas y registro nacional de personas desaparecidas o no localizadas', www.alejandroencinas.mx/wp-content/uploads/2020/01/REGISTRODEPERSONASDESAPARECIDAS.pdf (accessed 24 January 2021).

Comisión Nacional de Derechos Humanos (2017), 'Informe especial de la Comisión Nacional de Derechos Humanos sobre desaparición de personas en fosas clandestinas en México', http://informe.cndh.org.mx/uploads/menu/30100/InformeEspecial_Desapariciondepersonasyfosasclandestinas.pdf (accessed 24 January 2021).

Correa-Cabrera, G. (2014), 'Violence on the "Forgotten" Border: Mexico's Drug War, the State, and the Paramilitarization of Organized Crime in Tamaulipas in a "New Democratic Era" ', *Journal of Borderlands Studies*, 29:4, 419–33.

Correa-Cabrera, G., M. Keck, and J. Nava (2015), 'Losing the Monopoly of Violence: The State, a Drug War and the Paramilitarization of Organized Crime in Mexico (2007–10)', *State Crime Journal*, 4:1, 77–95.

Dávila, P. (2011), 'Operativos conjuntos: invasión federal disfrazada', *Proceso*, www.proceso.com.mx/285581/operativos-conjuntos-invasion-federal-disfrazada (accessed 24 January 2021).

Dell, M., B. Feigenberg, and K. Teshima (2019), 'The Violent Consequences of Trade-Induced Worker Displacement in Mexico', *American Economic Review: Insights*, 1:1, 43–58

Dueck, J., M. Guzman, and B. Verstappen (2007), *Formatos estándares de Eventos de HURIDOCS: una herramienta para la documentación de violaciones a los derechos humanos* (Versoix, HURIDOCS).

Enamorado, T., L. F. López-Calva, C. Rodríguez-Castelán, and H. Winkler (2016), 'Income Inequality and Violent Crime: Evidence from Mexico's Drug War', *Journal of Development Economics*, 120, 128–43.

Flores Pérez, C. A. (2014), 'Political Protection and the Origins of the Gulf Cartel', *Crime, Law and Social Change*, 61:5, 517–39.

Galán, B. I. V., and S. C. Corrales (2017), 'Análisis de correlación de la violencia y la criminalidad en el noreste de México entre 2008 y 2014', *Sociedad y Economía*, 32, 127–46.
Guillén, A., and D. Petersen (2019), 'El regreso del infierno: los desaparecidos que están vivos', *A dónde van los desaparecidos*, https://adondevanlosdesaparecidos.org/2019/02/04/los-desaparecidos-que-estan-vivos/ (accessed 24 January 2021).
Hilgers, T., and L. Macdonald (2017), 'Introduction: How violence varies. Subnational place, identity, and embeddedness', in *Violence in Latin America and the Caribbean*, ed. T. Hilgers and L. Macdonald (Cambridge, MA, Cambridge University Press), pp. 1–30.
Institute for Economics and Peace (2019), 'Índice de Paz de México 2019: Identificar y medir los factores que impulsanla paz', https://reliefweb.int/report/mexico/ndice-de-paz-m-xico-2019-identificar-y-medir-los-factores-que-impulsan-la-paz (accessed 16 February 2021).
Instituto Mexicano de Derechos Humanos y Democracia [IMDHD] (2020), 'Una realidad invisibilizada: las vulneraciones a los derechos económicos y sociales de los familiares de las personas desaparecidas en Veracruz', https://imdhd.org/wp-content/uploads/2020/03/UNA-REALIDAD-INVISIVILIZADA.pdf (accessed 24 January 2021).
Instituto Nacional de Estadísticas y Censos, México (2018), 'Encuesta Nacional de Victimización y Percepción sobre Seguridad Pública (ENVIPE) 2018', www.inegi.org.mx/programas/envipe/2018/ (accessed 24 January 2021).
Kovras, I. (2017), *Grassroots Activism and the Evolution of Transitional Justice: The Families of the Disappeared* (Cambridge, Cambridge University Press).
López Marroquín, S. (2019), 'Desaparición, esclavitud y trata de personas: situación de las mujeres en México', *Cuicuilco: Revista de ciencias antropológicas*, 26:74, 163–81.
Notimex (2011), 'Sedena da a conocer resultados de la operación noreste', *El Informador*, 15 June.
Observatorio sobre Desaparición e Impunidad (2017), 'Informe sobre desapariciones en el Estado de Nuevo León con información de Cadhac', FLACSO-Mexico, University of Minnesota, University of Oxford, www.flacso.edu.mx/sites/default/files/observatorio_-_informe_nuevo_leon.pdf (accessed 24 January 2021).
Observatorio sobre Desaparición e Impunidad (2019a), 'Informe comparado sobre eventos de desaparición: Nuevo León, Coahuila y Tamaulipas (región noroeste)', FLACSO-Mexico, University of Minnesota, University of Oxford.
Payne, L. A., G. Pereira, and L. Bernal-Bermúdez (2020), *Transitional Justice and Corporate Accountability from Below: Deploying Archimedes' Lever* (Cambridge, Cambridge University Press).
Rea Gómez, D., P. Ferri, and M. González Islas (2019), *La tropa: por qué mata un soldado* (Madrid, Aguilar).
Schmidt Nederovich, S., L. Cervera Gómez, and A. Botello Mares (2017), 'México: territorialización de los homicidios. Las razones de la violencia en el norte del país, www.academia.edu/34245097/M%C3%A9xico_territorializaci%C3%B3n_de_los_homicidios._Las_razones_de_la_violencia_en_el_norte_del_pa%C3%ADs._Mexico_territorizalization_of_the_murders._The_reasons_for_the_violence_in_the_north_of_the_country (accessed 1 May, 2020).
Sinembargo.mx (2015), '"El Bronco", un mes: ¿se acabó el amor?', 5 November, www.sinembargo.mx/05-11-2015/3041148 (accessed 22 June 2020).
Soria Romo, R. (2017), 'Impacto de la violencia e inseguridad en la competitividad de los estados mexicanos', *Economía sociedad y territorio* (May), 279–307.

Soria Romo, R. (2018), 'Una estimación del costo de la inseguridad y la delincuencia en México: análisis comparativo a nivel de las entidades federativas', *Gestión y política pública*, 27:1, 111–47.

Veráztegui, J. (2018), *Memoria de un corazón ausente: historias de vida*, 1st edn (Berlin, Heinrich Böll).

United Nations Office of the High Commissioner for Human Rights [OHCHR] (2018), 'Zeid urge a México a actuar para poner fin a la ola de desapariciones en Nuevo Laredo', www.ohchr.org/SP/NewsEvents/Pages/DisplayNews.aspx?NewsID=23157&LangID=S (accessed 16 February 2021).

Willis, G. D. (2015), *The Killing Consensus: Police, Organized Crime, and the Regulation of Life and Death in Urban Brazil* (Berkeley, University of California Press).

# 5

# The Legal Framework on Disappearances in Mexico: From Demands to the Law and Back to Demands

SANDRA SERRANO AND VOLGA DE PINA RAVEST

## Introduction

SINCE 2006, MURDERS, disappearances, torture, gender-based violence, and forced displacement have increased significantly and continuously in Mexico. Accordingly, victims' groups, civil society organisations (CSOs), and international organisations have brought increasing pressure on the Mexican government to end these violations, find the disappeared, undertake reparations, and bring the perpetrators to justice. Social mobilisation has taken mainly two paths: the direct search for disappeared persons, and the call for legal reforms and the creation of institutions with the authority to search for persons and investigate and punish those responsible for the disappearance of people. Chapters 3 and 11 of this book discuss examples of the direct search for disappeared persons. This chapter analyses the mobilisations undertaken to bring about legal changes that led to the development of novel normative and institutional structures aimed at addressing the problem of disappeared persons in Mexico.

The General Law on the Forced Disappearance of Persons, Disappearances Committed by Individuals, and the National System for the Search for Persons (hereinafter General Law, or Law), passed in 2017, successfully incorporating the main complaints presented about disappearances in Mexico to international human rights bodies in the years leading up to its adoption. The Law is the result of a complex national and international mobilisation of victims' groups and CSOs that led to a gradual sophistication of demands. These groups advocated for the Law to address various facets of the problem in a setting where disappearances, impunity, and the desperation of families continued to increase, while the weakness

*Proceedings of the British Academy*, **237**, 97–122, © The British Academy 2021.

of existing governmental mechanisms to respond to this type of phenomena was increasingly evident.

Although the General Law incorporates the vast majority of the social demands raised by CSOs and victims' groups, it contains a very complex scheme for prevention, search, and investigation that leaves open certain loopholes that could prevent or hinder its fulfilment. In addition, the Law's normative and institutional innovations coexist with other laws and institutions created to address general human rights problems or other crimes. This chapter argues that while legal mobilisation was able to achieve a prescriptive status for the crime of disappearance (Risse and Sikkink 1999), problems with enforcement remain. The disappearance of persons persists, and new institutions created by the Law must coexist with previous mechanisms that have similar authorities and thus risk neutralising the positive impacts of the General Law. Accordingly, this chapter draws attention to the promotion of legal mobilisation strategies in countries, such as Mexico, that issue calls for normative and institutional changes without giving much concern to their enforcement, since, in practice, new provisions clash with previously created structures that have similar authority, greater decision-making power, and better ability to exercise that authority. We show here that the problem is a matter not even of will, but rather of non-compliance by the government's bureaucracy.

Accordingly, the chapter outlines the activists' demands and the way they were embodied by the Law. It concludes with an analysis of the problems that the resulting structure has for preventing disappearances, searching for persons, and bringing perpetrators to justice.

## The Social Demands that Led to the Law

The institutional development that led to the General Law and the issues it addressed were the result of various milestones regarding problems of public security and human rights violations. These problems led to increasing civic awareness of the seriousness of the disappearance of persons and its growing importance within the public agenda.

From 2009 until the approval of the General Law, victims' groups and civil society organisations articulated demands that were initially local, while disappearances and the Mexican government's attitude towards them triggered various alerts. Given the resistance from government authorities at different levels to accepting and addressing the growing crisis of disappearances, victims' groups found it necessary to resort to networks, first national and then international. This strategy, as Keck and Sikkink (1998) point out, helped modify the terms of the debate on this issue and attracted the attention of authorities with respect to its framing. Civil society networks also exerted 'moral' pressure through strategies that focused on blaming and shaming, which weakened governmental credibility.

These results did not occur immediately. Internally, the complaints of collectives and organisations went unheeded for a long time, since disappearances were not even recognised as such. The first mobilisation strategies were focused on making the problem visible by reinterpreting or reconceptualising different elements of the problem in order to 'frame' it within international definitions of enforced disappearances and thus improve the success of their demands, as analysed by Barbara A. Frey in Chapter 2, since in a post-transitional context the complaints had particular characteristics.

Using strategies that Keck and Sikkink (1998: 31–3) recognise as having a 'boomerang' effect, it was necessary for victims' relatives and domestic activists to reach out to external actors in order to unblock channels that were dysfunctional at the national level, since they lacked enough influence to achieve changes in the policy of attention to victims. Thus, the General Law was shaped by interactions among actors at different levels, in which international organisations played a fundamental role.

The starting point in our review is the militarisation of security, the effects of which (illegal executions, torture, disappearance of persons, among other serious violations) provoked the mobilisation of civil society. In response to the disappearances produced by heightened violence brought about by the militarisation of public security at the end of 2009, as Lulú Herrera and Paula Cuellar Cuellar point out in Chapter 3, the Fuerzas Unidas por Nuestros Desaparecidos (United Forces for Our Disappeared; FUUNDEC) in Coahuila emerged as the first group of families of disappeared persons in Mexico. Since its inception, FUUNDEC has been accompanied by the Centro Diocesano para los Derechos Humanos Fray Juan de Larios (Fray Juan de Larios Diocesan Centre for Human Rights). Other families from various regions of the country would later join these networks. In 2009 in Nuevo León – another state with large numbers of disappearances – a group of families working with the organisation Ciudadanos en Apoyo a los Derechos Humanos (Citizens in Support of Human Rights; CADHAC) also began to gain visibility as it processed initial reports of disappearances (Villarreal Martínez 2016).

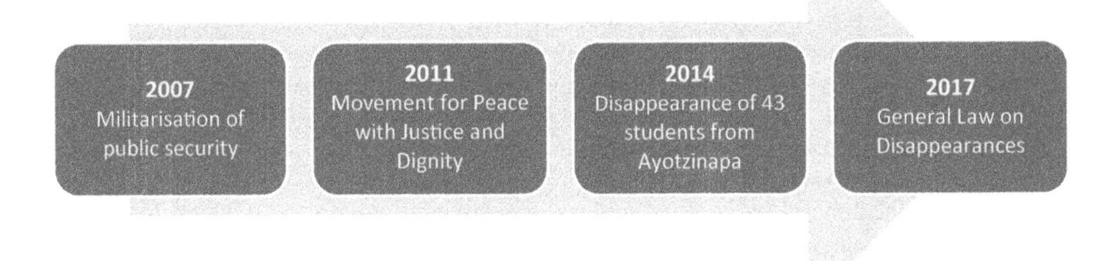


**Figure 5.1** Relevant milestones in the adoption of a legal framework on disappearances in Mexico.

Given that the official narrative denied outright the existence of disappeared persons, these first groups in the north of the country encountered numerous difficulties in making their plight known. When they went public with denunciations, the official response justified disappearances as an accidental, and inevitable, consequence of the strategy to combat organised crime (collateral damage). Officials alleged, as an alternative justification, that victims were involved with organised crime, so that, in essence, victims were blamed for their own disappearance ('they had it coming') or their disappearance was denied ('they're not really missing, they're working for criminals'). As discussed by Leigh A. Payne and Karina Ansolabehere in Chapter 1, public officials treated victims of disappearance as 'disposable people', offering no further response to their families.

Initially, these first groups focused on documenting cases and creating ways for families to exchange information. Later they accused the government of being responsible for the disappearances, emphasising that these were not isolated events and that government agents and criminal groups were perpetrating them jointly and/or with government acquiescence, as Barbara A. Frey discusses in Chapter 2 of this book. Relatives' groups worked diligently to denounce the official discourse publicly, revealing that the disappearances that concerned them had numerous characteristics in common with those that occurred during dictatorships or armed conflicts, also analysed in Chapter 1. In addition, relatives embarked on outreach campaigns to inform the public of the growing problem of the disappearance of persons, at a time when national civil society organisations were not yet working on the issue, prompting relatives to create the first networks of like-minded groups (Aureliani 2019).

The emergence in 2011 of the Movimiento por la Paz con Justicia y Dignidad (Movement for Peace with Justice and Dignity; MPJD)[1] and the 'Caravana del Consuelo' ('Caravan of Consolation')[2] placed victims' experiences of violence in different regions of Mexico on the national agenda, led to greater coordination of organisations and groups of victims, and attained great international visibility.

[1] The MPJD was created in March 2011 after the murder of Juan Francisco Sicilia, son of the poet and activist Javier Sicilia; three friends of the former (Gabriel, Julio, and Luis); and two other adults in the state of Morelos. In response, Javier Sicilia and other social leaders and victims began to mobilise to put forward their main demand, i.e. the cessation of violence. A rally held in Mexico City's central plaza (Zócalo) on 8 May 2011 was well attended. During the rally, a 'national pact' containing six points was announced: (1) truth and justice, (2) an end to the strategy of war and a focus on citizen security, (3) combating corruption and impunity, (4) combating the economic basis and profits of crime, (5) emergency attention for young people and effective actions to strengthen the social fabric, and (6) participatory democracy and democratisation in the media (Azaola 2012).

[2] This was the beginning of three tours that the MPJD undertook in 2011, referred to as peace caravans. The first caravan, in June 2011, travelled mainly to cities in Mexico's northern states, where violence was rife, such as Coahuila, Nuevo León, and Chihuahua. In September 2011, a second caravan travelled to southern Mexico, and later a third toured some cities in the United States. During these journeys, events were held in public squares and behind closed doors, where hundreds of victims' testimonies were heard.

The victims' movement was internationalised and networks were interwoven with CSOs that subsequently helped to promote international litigation.

During 2011, victims' relatives held two meetings with then President Felipe Calderón (who militarised public security) and established working groups with various authorities, where discussion centred on access to justice, attention to victims, and modification of the security strategy. The results of this process were disappointing, since the government unilaterally modified many of the agreed proposals (Azaola 2012: 161). However, both the complaints and the networks of defence and activism around violence were strengthened. Notably, there was a slight but clear shift in the official narrative implying a certain level of public acknowledgement of the victims' demands, although responses did not necessarily ensue. The Mexican government recognised the existence of a problem and the need to make some concessions (Risse & Sikkink 1999).

This MPJD initiative principally helped to highlight the plight of disappeared persons and the search for the disappeared undertaken by their relatives. Relatives demanded an end to an official narrative that justified or denied the disappearances, and were able to place their complaints on the agenda, which reflected a growing and remarkable level of complexity involving the need for formal legal accusations, search, investigation, and attention to victims.

In 2011, the first communications of CSOs and family members were reviewed by international bodies, and the UN Working Group on Disappearances (WGEID) issued its first recommendations on Mexico.[3] These declarations set the tone for what would later become the General Law on Disappearances.

However, the turning point in the legal battle between victims and government actors was the forced disappearance of 43 students from the Ayotzinapa Rural Teachers' College in the Iguala state of Guerrero on 26 September 2014. This was a socially and politically decisive moment. The greater public finally recognised that disappearances were a serious problem and, in light of the strong national and international pressure, the federal government was forced to accept the existence of thousands of disappeared persons. As a result, the first steps were taken to implement constitutional reforms that led to the enactment of the General Law on Disappearances and the fulfilment of pertinent recommendations issued previously by various international bodies.

The disappearance of the 43 students also led to the creation of the Grupo Interdisciplinario de Expertos Independientes (Interdisciplinary Group of Independent Experts; GIEI) by the Inter-American Commission on Human Rights (IACHR), discussed in more detail in Chapter 17, composed of specialists from different countries in the region to investigate the Ayotzinapa case and to help

[3] The WGEID is an extra-conventional UN mechanism mandated by the Human Rights Council to assist relatives of disappeared persons in finding out their fate and whereabouts. Its mandated authorities include analysing case reports, conducting country visits, issuing recommendations, and monitoring the implementation of the Declaration on the Protection of All Persons from Enforced Disappearance.

search for the young people. As part of its reports,[4] the GIEI made a number of recommendations concerning the criminal investigation of those responsible for disappearances and the search for disappeared persons, which later served as inputs for the General Law on Disappearances.

Furthermore, the GIEI made clear that disappearances occur in Mexico with the direct and indirect involvement of government agents, sometimes acting jointly with criminal groups, at times acting alone. The GIEI's investigations revealed for the first time that the disappearance of persons in the country existed within a system of macro-criminality that included a pact of impunity for the perpetrators, be they government agents or members of criminal groups.

## Transplanting International Decisions

Between each of the milestones mentioned heretofore, a process of national and international formal complaints occurred, and a government response ensued. The complaints heard before international organisations were essential in understanding the complexity of the General Law, whose emphasis is on enacting regulations and creating institutions. Table 5.1 summarises the recommendations or measures of non-repetition in the main international bodies that dealt in greater depth with the phenomenon of disappearances in Mexico.

The main bodies that have dealt with disappearances in Mexico are the WGEID and the GIEI. However, the work of the IACHR in this area should also be highlighted. The recommendations issued by these bodies were based on two sources, either the formal complaints of the victims and CSOs and related visits to Mexico, or their own inquiries carried out in the country. The former were the main sources for the WGEID and IACHR, while the latter were, by their nature, the main source for the GIEI. This had an impact on what was recommended and how recommendations were made.

The reports of international organisations were also linked to the milestones mentioned previously. The social discontent that had been building since 2009, and which led to the MPJD, also had an initial and decisive impact on the WGEID. In that year, the WGEID issued a report after its mission to Mexico (WGEID 2011) that contained in its concluding observations recommendations that formed the basis of what would later be the General Law on Disappearances, as seen in Table 5.2.

[4] The GIEI issued two reports (September 2015 and April 2016) before the Mexican government decided to cancel the Group's cooperation on 30 April 2016. In addition to the recommendations issued on disappearances in Mexico, the reports discuss the progress of the inquiries into the fate of the 43 students from the teachers' college. One of the most important findings held that the disappearance was committed by a criminal group, Guerreros Unidos (United Warriors), which is part of a complex and expanding transnational drug trafficking network, alleged to have transported heroin on buses in collusion with municipal, state, and federal governments, and whose inner workings are still unknown (GIEI 2015, 2016).

**Table 5.1** Recommendations on disappearance

| **Recommendations** | **Universal System** | | | | | **Inter-American System** | | |
|---|---|---|---|---|---|---|---|---|
| | **Committee against Forced Disappearances** | **Working Group on Forced or Involuntary Disappearances** | **Council on Human Rights (UPR)**[a] | **CEDAW**[b] | **CAT**[c] | **IACtHR** | **IACHR** | **GIEI** |
| Standardise the crime of enforced disappearance | X | X | X | X | X | X | | X |
| Standardise the crime of disappearance by individuals | X | | | | | | | X |
| Establish search mechanisms | X | X | X | | | | | X |
| Establish urgent-search mechanism | | X | X | X | | X | X | X |
| Acknowledge declaration of absence | X | X | X | | | | | X |
| Establish a forensic institution | X | X | | X | X | | X | X |
| Adopt a General Law | | X | | | X | | X | X |
| Establish a national registry of disappeared persons | X | X | X | X | | X | X | X |
| Establish a Public Prosecutor's Office or Specialised Unit | X | X | | | | | | X |
| Standardise local legislation | X | X | | X | | | X | |

(*continued*)

**Table 5.1** (*Cont.*)

| | | | | | | |
|---|---|---|---|---|---|---|
| Establish mechanisms to facilitate reparations | X | X | X | | | X |
| Establish mechanisms for psychosocial assistance for direct and indirect victims | | X | | | | |
| Enact legislation on the use of force | | X | | | | X |
| Adapt the writ of protection for disappearance | | X | | | | |
| Establish a genetic databank | X | X | | | X | |
| Establish victim and witness protection mechanisms | X | X | | | | |
| Establish a national registry of detentions | | X | | | | X |
| Exclude disappearances from military exemption | | | X | X | X | X |
| Create special human rights courts | | | | | | X |
| Create current-affairs analysis units | | | | | | X |

a Universal Periodic Review
b UN Convention on the Elimination of All Forms of Discrimination against Women
c Committee against Torture

Source: Prepared by the authors on the basis of reports from international organisations. Shading indicates those recommendations shared by international human rights institutions.

**Table 5.2** Recommendations of the WGEID (2011)

| | |
|---|---|
| Revise the regulatory framework | Ensure that the crime of disappearance is included in the criminal codes of all entities and that a comprehensive law on enforced or involuntary disappearances, defining disappearance, is enacted as soon as possible. The law should define disappearance as an autonomous offence; create a specific search procedure with the participation of relatives; establish a national registry of disappeared persons that guarantees that relatives, lawyers, human rights defenders, and any other person have full access; allow declarations of absence as a consequence of disappearance; ensure full protection and support for relatives and witnesses; and guarantee the right to full reparation (para. 86). |
| Investigate to find the responsible party | Guarantee coordination between authorities, adoption, and training in an investigation protocol; assume lines of inquiry according to procedures, and guarantee access and collaboration of the victims' relatives in the inquiries (paras 92–100). |
| Location of victims (search) | The writ of protection should consider the particularities of the disappearance, assure training and resources for the search for the disappeared person, and establish a national program to search for persons with an immediate-action protocol (paras 95, 97, 102). |
| Forensic identification (deceased persons) | Use of and access to all existing databases and highly trained personnel for the exhumation and identification of mortal remains; create and update a database with personal information on victims at the federal and state levels, including genetic information (DNA) and tissue samples obtained from mortal remains and relatives of victims; and guarantee resources for forensic institutions (paras 102–4). |
| Reparations and support measures | Strengthen the figure of the coadjutant and guarantee access by relatives to the inquiry and provide them information. Also, guarantee medical and psychosocial assistance (paras 100, 101, 108). |

Source: Prepared by the authors based on WGEID (2011).

The Working Group proposed the characteristics and the main lines of a comprehensive policy on the disappearance of persons in Mexico, adding recommendations on the withdrawal of the armed forces from public security tasks, given its role in the growing problem of disappearances in the country.

After 2014, various international organisations took a stand regarding disappearances in Mexico. The WGEID followed up on its 2011 report, while the Committee against Enforced Disappearances (CED), the IACHR, and the Human Rights Council issued statements on the situation in Mexico. The CED report reiterated, at times further clarifying, the recommendations of the WGEID report, focusing on the creation of a specialised investigation unit within the prosecutor's office, as well as the ante-mortem/post-mortem database (CED 2015). In its 2016 report, the IACHR also reiterated the core points of a proposed public policy design developed by the Working Group, adding that the lines of investigation on disappearances should involve both the actual perpetrator(s) and the responsibility up the chain of command (IACHR 2016).

The most detailed investigative reports were issued by the GIEI in 2015 and 2016. In these reports, the Group of Experts revealed the most serious problems in the investigation of disappearances, not in isolation but as part of the investigations carried out by prosecutors' offices in general. The GIEI's focus enabled it to go into greater depth and to further specify policy and institutional recommendations, as well as those pertaining to the task of investigating and searching for persons. The GIEI's recommendations were more detailed and differed from those issued by the WGEID, in that they included research into the institutions that should be implementing the proposed reforms, without taking for granted that the public prosecutors' offices, for example, would actually carry out the recommendations. The GIEI's recommendations also identified where capacity existed and how to strengthen it.

The abundance of information described here may derive from the fact that the GIEI had to go into depth in its analysis of a particular case and from there identify institutional strengths and weaknesses, in order to avoid falling into the trap of dichotomising: either lack of capacity or lack of intention. Something similar happened in the judgment of the *'Cotton Field'* case of the Inter-American Court of Human Rights ((IACtHR 2009), where the Court set out precise requirements for the Mexican government regarding the disappearance of women, which would later be a basis for the search mechanism proposed by the UN Working Group, and ultimately included in the General Law on Disappearances. Indeed, the *'Cotton Field'* ruling defined the characteristics of the immediate search mechanism in cases of disappearances of women in Mexico. Ironically, in reports and actions on disappearances that followed, women were left out of the main policies.[5]

[5] In paragraph 506, the IACtHR ruling states: 'The Court considers that the Alba Protocol, or any other similar disposition in Chihuahua, should follow, among others, the following parameters: (i) implement searches *ex officio* and without delay, when cases of disappearance occur, as a measure to protect the life, personal freedom, and personal integrity of the disappeared person; (ii) establish coordinated work between various security forces to find the whereabouts of the person; (iii) removing any *de facto* or *de*

The drafting of the General Law, then, was a true exercise in transplanting international decisions, in which a rather complex normative framework was defined, based on the reinterpretation of concepts, obligations, and entities from the conventional framework, as analysed by Barbara A. Frey in Chapter 2. This exercise both interpreted the law and designed legal and institutional frameworks (Berkowitz *et al.* 2003; Langer 2004), but it was not achieved solely at the initiative of international bodies. Civil society organisations lobbied for the recommendations adopted by the Working Group and later included its report in formulating their demands to other international bodies, so that in successive reviews these policy lines on disappearances became the subject of discussion among the government, CSOs, and international bodies. During the revision of the Law, the advocates used these specific recommendations to add or elaborate additional provisions.

The General Law on Disappearances was finally enacted in 2017, after the impact of the disappearance of the 43 Ayotzinapa students gave the issue wider visibility nationally and internationally, and because of the diligent monitoring of international organisations and CSOs. However, the Mexican government's record in creating and restructuring institutions still resulted in a compliance gap, particularly if we consider the entire institutional context since 2011 with regard to disappearances.

## The General Law on the Disappearance of Persons

The General Law undoubtedly established a novel regulatory and institutional framework, setting as its objectives the search for persons, investigation into perpetrators, and identification of remains found anywhere in the country.

Remarkably, it is a General Law, which implies that it is applicable throughout the country. Since Mexico is a federal entity, each sub-national state has a broad margin of action to create criminal codes on this matter, as well as search mechanisms. Some states, such as Nuevo León or Coahuila, already had strong institutional

---

*jure* obstacles that render the search ineffective or that make it impossible to initiate, such as requiring preliminary investigations or procedures; (iv) allocate the human, financial, logistical, scientific, or other resources necessary for the success of the search; (v) compare the report of disappearance with the database of disappeared persons referred to in section 4.2.4 *infra*; and (vi) prioritize searches in areas where it is reasonably likely that the disappeared person will be found without arbitrarily ruling out other possibilities or areas of search' (IACtHR 2009). For its part, the WGEID pointed out the following characteristics for the search mechanism: (a) implemention of the search *ex officio* and without delay in cases of disappearances; (b) coordination of efforts of the various security agencies to locate the person; (c) elimination of any de jure or de facto obstacles that reduce the effectiveness of the search or prevent it from being initiated; (d) allocation of the human, financial, logistical, scientific, or any other type of resources necessary for the search to be carried out successfully; (e) availability of highly trained personnel for the exhumation and identification of mortal remains; (f) contrasting of the report of the missing person with all existing databases on the subject; (g) prioritisation of the search area where it is reasonably likely that the disappeared person will be found, without arbitrarily ruling out other possibilities or areas; (h) access to and full use of the Mexico Platform; and (i) ensuring that the programme is implemented with full budgetary and operational independence (WGEID 2011).

structures before the Law was passed, but the vast majority did not even sanction disappearance as a specific crime. The advantage of its being a General Law is its ability to standardise legal provisions and institutions, but the concurrent problem is that it is not flexible enough to adapt to different local contexts. Thus, some states have adopted local laws on disappearance, resulting in conflict-of-law questions.[6]

The General Law is governed by a set of general principles that seek to inform its various functions: effectiveness and completeness, due diligence, humanitarian approach, maximum protection, non-revictimisation, joint participation with relatives, presumption of life, and truth. These are principles that have been widely developed in international law, and they generally seek to ensure both the participation of victims and compliance with the rights to truth and justice, as well as activities aimed at searching for the disappeared. As principles, they should inform the interpretation of the Law as a whole, even though the practice in Mexico has been to ignore them.

The Law distinguishes between different types of protected persons: the disappeared person, and the missing person; the scope of these terms is described in Chapter 18. The former is a person whose whereabouts are unknown and whose absence is presumed to be related to the commission of a crime; the latter refers to a person whose location is unknown but where there is no information to suggest that his or her absence is due to a crime. If, over time, there is no news of a person who is missing, he or she will be considered a disappeared person. In both cases, the relevant authorities are obliged to start the search with due diligence. The Law also recognises unidentified deceased persons so that their remains can be treated with dignity, identified, and returned to their families. With regard to the rights of the disappeared, the Law recognises their legal status and interests, as well as the right to be found, have damages repaired, and have their name and honour restored.

A fourth group recognised by the Law are the relatives of the victims, who are by far the most important reason for the existence of these regulations and around whom the entire institutional structure revolves. The Law recognises a robust set of rights to ensure their participation in the search and legal proceedings surrounding the disappearance, as well as access to measures of protection, aid, assistance, and attention. The underlying intention is to avoid leaving the relatives of the victims out of any action undertaken by the various search and protection mechanisms, but also to ensure that they play an active role, through the provision of evidence or experts, among other possibilities. This is one of the most important innovations of

[6] Since it is a general law, it was expected to be applied directly by the states, through executive acts that would enforce obligations by creating secondary initiatives and instruments. However, in different states around the country, legislative procedures have approved their own state disappearance laws, which, although positively adapting to the local institutional context (accounting for local authorities, municipalities, and other aspects), also give rise to modifications in the scope and definitions of the General Law, which were intended to be standardised. This can result in other problems, since a model of differentiated attention to disappearances at the sub-national level could be replicated, with consequences for coordination at the national level.

the Law; however, the way in which relatives and authorities establish their relationship is not regulated by the Law, leaving open the possibility that the objectives set forth will not be implemented, unless organised groups of relatives continue to lodge complaints.

Additionally, the classification of the crime of disappearance in accordance with international standards was one of the international recommendations most consistently issued to the Mexican government. The General Law addresses this concern by establishing two crimes whose classification reflects both the progress of international law on the subject and the need for sanctions in accordance with the current context of disappearances in the country. The first of these is the crime of enforced disappearance, which can be committed by an authority or by an individual with the acquiescence of a public official. This crime encompasses the loss of a person's liberty in any form, as well as the refusal to acknowledge a person's loss of liberty or to provide information about the person's fate or whereabouts. The second offence concerns disappearances committed by private individuals who deprive a person of liberty for the purpose of concealing the victim or his/her fate or whereabouts. The first crime carries a penalty of between 40 and 60 years' imprisonment; the second is punishable by 25 to 50 years.

This distinction between these two classifications follows the intent of article 3 of the International Convention for the Protection of All Persons from Enforced Disappearance. In principle, it does not appear to expand the content or scope of the prohibition of enforced disappearance as a human right to include disappearances committed by individuals. The General Law, however, does not reference the differentiated nature of the two crimes; on the contrary, the Law's general provisions and the institutions in charge of enforcing it apply equally to both. This is particularly relevant for holding a government accountable should its investigation of either crime be deficient, as Barbara A. Frey discusses in Chapter 2 of this book.

The problem that the Law sought to address was that of disappearances in which government intervention (direct or by authorisation, support, or acquiescence) was not patently clear, but where, regardless, a person had been disappeared. Acknowledgement of the problem is relevant because, although the crimes put the emphasis on the perpetrator, the logic of the Law puts the victims at the centre. Thus, broadening the content and scope of protected situations does not lead to a widening of the concept of enforced disappearance, but rather broadens the government's obligations toward the victims of disappearance and their families.

For example, article 3 establishes general obligations to respect, protect, guarantee, and promote human rights, as an overall framework of responsibilities for all authorities in the country. Without distinguishing between the two crimes, article 5 stipulates that the authorities are obliged to act with due diligence in searching for and investigating any disappeared person. The Law combines two mechanisms that can potentially strengthen each other: on the one hand, the differentiated legal responsibility that seeks to cover those cases committed by individuals without clear government participation and, on the other hand, the parameters of protection, investigation, and search within the framework of international human rights law. The Law seems to move indirectly toward the proposal made by Frey in Chapter 2. Furthermore, the Law also establishes other crimes linked to actions following a disappearance, such as concealing evidence or obstructing criminal investigations or search actions.

Apart from these general principles of the Law, one of its most remarkable (and problematic) aspects is the complex institutional structure, which involves several different authorities at the federal and local levels, within both the executive and judicial branches, charged with searching, investigating, and identifying. The sphere of responsibilities developed in the Law is a framework that rests on the willingness of the different authorities to coordinate and that, although valuable, leaves the disappeared and their families in limbo, as we discuss in the following section. The Law mandates, among other aspects, the creation of:

1 National System to Search for Disappeared Persons;
2 National Search Commission and 33 local commissions;
3 specialised prosecutors' offices for disappeared persons in each local and federal prosecutor's office;
4 National Registry of Missing and Disappeared People, a National Registry of Deceased or Unidentified Persons, and a National Registry of Burial Sites;
5 National Forensic Data Bank;
6 Citizens' Council.

The purpose of the National Search System is to establish the general policy for the Mexican government in matters of searching, locating, and identifying, as well as for the prevention, investigation, and sanction of crimes established by the Law. This policy applies to different federal authorities at the highest level, as well as the National Search Commission, the local representations of the prosecutor, the executive secretariat for public security, local search commissions, the federal police, and a Citizens' Council. In accordance with the Law, the Citizens' Council is the body for reaching agreements and coordinating policies, as well as for issuing action guidelines and protocols. However, in its composition, we can see that the political leverage of some members may be greater than others – a power disparity that may affect its decisions.

One of the great achievements of the Law is the separation of search work, carried out by the National Commission and the local commissions, from investigation. The search commissions are created as a non-formalised alternative with the potential to generate greater trust among victims' families. As Volga de Pina Ravest discusses in Chapter 18, the prosecutors' offices never focused on searching for people but rather concentrated on the investigation of those likely to be responsible, leaving aside the main demand of families: to find disappeared persons.

Delaying tactics, lack of due diligence, and the fact that disappearances are often committed by government agents themselves, plus the suspicion (often proven) of links between authorities and criminal groups, have highlighted the need to create a non-judicial mechanism of public servants with no links to the security and justice system.

The search commissions have very diverse legal powers to employ different types of resources and tools to take charge of urgent searches (in the first 24–72 hours), long-standing searches, and historical searches (disappearances that occurred in the 1960s and 1970s). In addition, the National Commission is responsible for creating a National Programme to Search for Persons.

In line with international recommendations, the investigation of crimes is the responsibility of the corresponding authority, i.e., the state or federal prosecutor's office, as appropriate. In addition, in order to create a system directly concerned with prosecuting disappearances, the Law provides for the establishment of specialised prosecutor's offices within each state prosecutor's office and the federal prosecutor's office. These offices have the main responsibility for criminal investigations, as they have been given the necessary authority to conduct them with the utmost due diligence. They are also responsible for forensic identification and, as such, the office of the Prosecutor General of the Republic (FGR) is responsible for implementing the National Exhumation and Forensic Identification Program.

While the criminal investigation is centred on the perpetrator, the search commissions should focus on the disappeared person. However, the very logic of the Search System created by the Law requires the broadest cooperation and coordination between prosecutors' offices and search commissions. As discussed in Chapter 18, there are essential actions involved in the search for persons that can only be carried out by the public prosecutors' offices, in accordance with criminal procedural norms, and also because the information obtained by both commissions and public prosecutors' offices informs both tasks. If information, analysis, and findings are not shared, the task of both will be limited, to the detriment of the victims and their families.

In response to international recommendations, the Law creates different types of national registries, one for disappeared or missing persons, another for deceased or unidentified persons, and a third for burial sites. These national registries are meant to help search for and identify persons and thus depend on the inputs provided by local authorities. In addition, the Law aims to register the greatest possible number of disappeared persons. To accomplish this, there should be accessible and reliable mechanisms so that families can participate in the registration process. Undoubtedly, creating and standardising these registries is one of the great challenges of the Law, since, on the one hand, it must achieve the greatest possible standardisation of local authorities' registries and avoid under-registration, and, on the other, it must standardise the data using information provided by the families. Linked to these registries, the creation of a forensic data bank was also mandated, in accordance with international recommendations, which should help with the tasks of searching, locating, and identifying.

The Law's entire structure must be supervised by and directed by a Citizens' Council, composed of five family members, four specialists, and four representatives of human rights organisations. This Council's responsibilities are very broad and range from proposing actions for how the institutional structures should function to issuing recommendations to authorities who do not fulfil their obligations. However, the Law does not provide the Council with sufficient political strength to enable it to comply fully with the tasks entrusted to it, thus running the risk of becoming just another piece of the institutional jigsaw puzzle without having a real role in decision-making.

In short, the General Law represents a huge step forward in incorporating international recommendations on the problem of disappearances by establishing a far-reaching institutional structure. The structure, however, is dependent on the efforts and willingness of multiple authorities to coordinate, thus limiting the leverage that law-makers sought to give to victims' families. Moreover, as discussed below, the Law calls for a greater dispersal of funds to families but does not grant them sufficient legal recourse to address the difficulties of searching for and identifying their loved ones on their own.

## The Institutional Entanglement in Addressing the Disappearance of Persons

The enactment of the General Law on Disappearances is a major achievement of the human rights movement. It represents both an advocacy tool and the implementation of the highest standards to address the disappearance of persons. However, Mexico's domestic normative and institutional framework for the search, investigation, sanction, and reparation of disappearances itself entails a complex labyrinth that existed before the General Law and has survived its passage. This framework is a fragmented cluster of assorted institutions and processes that carry out tasks that rarely complement each other. This creates various technical, budgetary, and coordination problems, the most serious consequence of which is the gruelling path that the victims (relatives of disappeared persons) must tread to search for answers, involving dozens of different offices where different files are opened, none of which produces real results.

Indeed, the General Law on Disappearances attempted to repurpose some of the existing mechanisms and to create new ones with authority to address newly recognised dimensions of the problem. The Law promoted the obligation of those states that had not already done so, despite having a significant rate of disappearances, to set up specialised mechanisms.

The objective of closing these many legal gaps was only partially achieved, since the General Law also added additional layers to an already complex institutional framework on disappearances. Adding these new procedures generated duplication of tasks, overlapping authorities, and erosion of responsibilities, thus neutralising the effectiveness of each mechanism.

The existing framework was already complex. The oldest precedent of this process is from the demands of relatives of disappeared persons during the so-called 'Dirty War' in Mexico during the 1990s. The demands from that time focused on 'classic' forced disappearances (those committed by government agents against persons considered to be adversaries or subversives) and encompassed other related demands, such as the exclusion of military jurisdiction and some aspects related to the ineffectiveness of the investigations. These demands led to the classification of forced disappearance as crimes in the Federal Criminal Code and in different state codes in the period from 2001 to 2009.

The demands regarding the classification of the crime of disappearance continued for several years, since this aspect was not approved in all of Mexico's states or was not standardised according to conventional definitions. Beginning in 2007, these demands were broadened to recognise recent disappearances as well, whose perpetrators are not only government agents but also individuals who are mainly linked to criminal drug-trafficking groups. Thus, the General Law regulates past and recent disappearances, adding a criminal classification for disappearance committed by individuals,[7] since those that, for various reasons, could not be considered forced disappearances were investigated as kidnappings or other forms of deprivation of liberty.

Since Mexico is a federal state, its institutional and legal framework is diverse. For our analysis we will focus on the federal level, but the decentralisation of rules, authorities, and processes should be considered one of the key factors that affect outcomes – i.e. a lack of compliance (Risse *et al.* 2013).

Many reforms and specialised agencies prior to the General Law were in reaction to the milestones described above, but these had important antecedents. From 2003 to 2013, for example, various mechanisms were set up to search for and locate women and girls in Ciudad Juárez, Chihuahua, in connection with the circumstances that led to the ruling in the *'Cotton Field'* case. These mechanisms were later extended to other parts of Mexico.

As previously indicated, in response to national and international pressure, in 2011 a series of other measures began to be adopted in the country, many of them in line with international recommendations. They were adopted, however, in an uncoordinated and isolated manner. Dozens of reforms and institutions followed one after the other, up until the adoption of the General Law on Disappearances. This type of uncoordinated growth resulted in capacity problems, but also revealed a lack of deliberateness in recognising and addressing the phenomenon of disappearance. Table 5.3 illustrates the large number of institutions and procedures created between 2011 and 2017, which now coexist with the General Law.[8] The

[7] The first time this crime was categorised was in 2014 in the State of Coahuila.

[8] The appendix lists the years they began and links to their websites.

**Table 5.3** Institutions and processes related to the disappearance of persons in Mexico.

| Before 2011 | 2011–13 | 2014–15 | 2017–20 |
|---|---|---|---|
| First penal classification of enforced disappearance | Registry of disappeared women and girls | Special Office for the 'Iguala Case' – National Commission for Human Rights | General Law on Disappearances |
| Coordination mechanism for the search for women and girls in Ciudad Juárez, Chihuahua | Search protocols for women and girls | Office of Investigation 'Iguala Case' – PGR | Specialised investigation in prosecutors' offices<br>• Current-events analysis units<br>• Migrants' Unit and MAE[a] are incorporated in FE[b]-FGR |
| | Genetic database of women and girls | Specialised prosecutor's office for searches – PGR and some states | • Commissions for searches<br>• Current-events analysis units |
| | 'Dar Contigo' ('Find You') Programme: women and girls | Standardised protocol for searches – prosecutors' offices | RNPED |
| | Alba Protocol extension | Migrant Investigation Unit | National Registry of Burial Sites |
| | Amber Alert | External Support Mechanism | National Registry of Deceased and Unidentified Persons |
| | RNPED | 'Have you seen?' Programme | National Forensic Database |
| | Writ of protection for searches | AM/PM Base | Unique Information System |
| | Specialised Search Unit – PGR | | Standardised protocol for searches – commissions |
| | Forensic Commission | | Standardised protocol for searches – prosecutors' offices |
| | General Victims' Law – Executive Commission for the Attention of Victims | | Co-adjuvant commission for the Ayotzinapa case<br>Special prosecutor for the Ayotzinapa case |

a Mecanismo de Apoyo Exterior Mexicano de Búsqueda e Investigación (Mexican Foreign Search and Investigation Support Mechanism)

b Fiscalía Especializada (Specialised prosecutor)

Source: Prepared by the authors.

unhighlighted cells are general mechanisms to deal with disappearances, while the shaded ones correspond to the Ayotzinapa (or 'Iguala') case, the disappearance of women (in compliance with the *'Cotton Field'* ruling), and other specific mechanisms.

In 2011, disappearances began to be addressed at the National Conference on the Procurement of Justice (CNPJ 2011); proposals for protocols, databases, and registries began to emerge, as well as mechanisms for attending to victims, which have always placed special emphasis on victims of disappearance.

These mechanisms were established at the same time as the adoption of the 2011 WGEID Observations, with the crisis of disappearances in Mexico already at one of its highest levels. However, the government's response to the phenomenon was still one of denial. The long road of pressuring for accountability was just beginning, as was the growth of institutions and mechanisms.

From 2011 until the General Law was enacted; the National Registry of Missing and Disappeared People and various genetic databases related to disappeared women and girls, as well as wide-ranging and different programs aimed at searching for and locating people were created, including the start of the Amber Alert (for minors).

In compliance with a constitutional reform (2011), a new writ-of-protection law was enacted in 2013 that, in article 15, included a writ of protection for searches, applicable to cases of forced disappearance. Also in 2013, the Specialised Unit for the Search for Disappeared Persons was created in the then Procuraduría General de la República (Attorney General's Office; PGR (now Fiscalía General de la República; FGR). It acted as a public prosecutor's office, with responsibility for investigating, searching, locating persons, and undertaking forensic identification. It also had the authority to prosecute crimes related to disappearance, which, notably, was never exercised.

The development of institutions also revealed the importance of cases related to disappeared and murdered migrants in Mexico, giving rise to yet more agencies and mechanisms. These included the 'Forensic Commission', a special unit for the identification of remains located in San Fernando in Tamaulipas and Cadereyta in Nuevo León, which arose from an agreement between the PGR, the Argentine Forensic Anthropology Team, and various CSOs.[9]

The General Law on Victims, promoted by the MPJD and enacted in 2013, also included various specific provisions on disappearances, given the important place these crimes already had on the public agenda. The Victims' Law created the Executive Commission for Attention to Victims, which replaced a previous social

[9] The following entities participated in the agreement: Comité de Familiares de Migrantes Fallecidos y Desaparecidos (El Salvador); el Comité de Familiares de Migrantes de El Progreso, Fundación para la Justicia y el Estado Democrático de Derecho; Casa del Migrante (Saltillo, Coahuila); Centro Diocesano de Derechos Humanos Fray Juan de Larios AC; Asociación Civil Voces Mesoamericanas; Mesa Nacional para las Migraciones (Guatemala); Asociación Misioneros de San Carlos Scalabrinianos (Guatemala); Centro de Derechos Humanos Victoria Diez AC; and Foro Nacional para la Migración (Honduras).

prosecutor's office. It also mandated the creation of standardised agencies in the states, in order to include a National System of Attention to Victims, which remains in place, since many states did not create their own commissions for victims.

In 2014, the Ayotzinapa case stimulated the establishment of further agencies and mechanisms that, ironically, were created almost simultaneously with those described above, but that dealt with Ayotzinapa differently from all the other disappearance cases. For instance, in 2014, the National Commission on Human Rights (CNDH) created a special office for the 'Iguala' case (CNDH 2019), and in 2015 the PGR created the Office for the Investigation of the 'Iguala Case' (Ayotzinapa) in the Subprocuraduría de Derechos Humanos, Prevención del Delito y Servicios a la Comunidad (Office of the Deputy Prosecutor for Human Rights, Crime Prevention, and Community Services). The latter office conducted the second stage of the Ayotzinapa investigation; the first was carried out in the national organised crime unit of the PGR.

In December 2018, a further decree was published creating a commission to assist with the PGR's investigations into the Ayotzinapa case and establishing a new special prosecutor's office within the FGR (Centro Prodh 2018). This was ordered by a federal court as an 'alternative' procedure to remedy the shortcomings of the initial investigation.

As previously mentioned, the disappearance of the 43 students also gave impetus to the already growing institutionality around the phenomenon of disappearances in general. Many of the most important reforms in terms of search and investigation began in 2015. This was a crucial year: a constitutional reform granted the national Congress the power to issue the General Law on Disappearances. The Specialised Prosecutor's Office for the Search of Disappeared Persons was also created, replacing the previous unit, but at a higher level in the hierarchy, and the Standardised Protocol for the Search of Disappeared Persons and the Investigation of the Crime of Forced Disappearance was issued, which was adopted by the National Conference of Procurement of Justice and thus became applicable nationwide.

In addition, the Investigation Unit for Crimes against Migrants and the Foreign Support Mechanism for Search and Investigation (MAE) were established to facilitate the coordination of international PGR offices (such as the coordination of international affairs and the attaché offices abroad) to ensure that the families of migrants could report cases; provide information and genetic samples; and, in general, have access to justice and reparation of damages. In addition, the 'Have You Seen?' program was established to disseminate files with data on disappeared persons, and the agreement between the PGR and the International Committee of the Red Cross for the implementation of the ante-mortem/post-mortem database (PGR 2015) was signed.

During this period, various similar mechanisms also emerged at the state level, such as the Grupo Especializado de Busqueda Inmediata (Specialised Group on Immediate Search; GEBI) of the Nuevo León Attorney General's Office and the specialised prosecutor's office for handling complaints regarding 'missing' persons in Veracruz.

Except for the National Registry of Missing and Disappeared People, which was rescinded by the General Law, and the mandate to draw up a new search and investigation protocol, which led to the discontinuation of the previous search protocol, no other agencies or mechanisms were abolished, since the Law only stipulated for their standardisation and coordination and not for their replacement. Thus, all these previously created laws and procedures still coexist with the mechanisms created by the General Law.

Further, since the adoption of the General Law, some of these other agencies and processes have slowly begun to function. In 2018, the PGR created the office of the specialised prosecutor for the investigation of disappearances, which merged with the office for migrants and issued a new investigation protocol. The National Search Commission was also established. In some states, specialised prosecutors' offices and search commissions were also created.

Table 5.4 depicts the institutional structure in place at the beginning of 2020 regarding disappearances. This entire institutional framework for searches, investigations, and reparations, in practice and in design, creates confusion for the victims and allows the government itself to tolerate and sustain (by pointing to the measures taken) its own indifference in failing to comply with rights. A greater number of institutions does not necessarily mean a greater level of compliance with human rights, nor does it mean greater protection of rights. For victims it means more doors to knock on, along with a dilution of resources, weakened jurisdictional authorities, and a neutralisation of existing institutions.

## Final Reflections

Clearly, the General Law was a step forward in the effort to respect and guarantee the rights of victims of disappearance and their families. Its enactment also demonstrates how victims' groups and civil society organisations can make use of international bodies to strengthen national agendas regarding structural problems such as the disappearance of persons in Mexico. However, it also shows how complicated it is to create, implement, and coordinate various institutions with differing political and economic mandates.

Today, the General Law has two major challenges: first, to facilitate families' approaches to overlapping institutions in order to search, identify, and investigate. The task at hand entails organising various existing institutions and phasing out those that lack a clear objective or conflict with others. The second challenge involves achieving consistent and coordinated action among very different authorities. It is the task of the Mexican government, and not that of international organisations, victims' groups, or civil society organisations, to have coordinated institutional structures capable of producing the results for which they were conceived.

**Table 5.4** Federal institutional structure for disappeared persons (2020).

| | Mechanism | Investigation of perpetrators | Search for and location of disappeared persons | Identification of deceased persons | Sanction | Measures of support, attention, and protection for victims | Reparation |
|---|---|---|---|---|---|---|---|
| Penal Justice System | Prosecutors' Offices specialising in disappearances | X | X | X | | X | |
| | Specialised units to trace kidnappings | X | X | X | | X | |
| | Specialised Prosecutors' Offices in trafficking in persons | X | X | X | | | |
| | Prosecutors Offices' areas for victim assistance | | | | | X | |
| | Criminal judges | | | | X | X | X |
| | Expert and forensic services | X | X | X | | | |

| | | | | | | | |
|---|---|---|---|---|---|---|---|
| Public security system | Public security forces | X | X | | | | |
| Federal Judicial Branch | Writ of protection, article 15 | | X | | | | X |
| | Writ of protection | | | | | | X |
| Ombudsman system | National and state commissions on human rights | X | X | | X | X | X |
| Coordination mechanisms | Amber Alert (children and adolescents) | | X | | | | |
| | Alba Protocol (women) | | X | | | | |
| | Other similar protocols | | X | | | | |
| National Search System | Search commissions | | X | | | X | |
| | Registries | X | X | X | | | |

Source: Prepared by the authors.

## References

Aureliani, T. (2019), 'La historia que necesitamos valorar: a 10 años de FUUNDEC-FUNDEM', *A dónde van los desaparecidos*, https://adondevanlosdesaparecidos.org/2019/12/19/la-historia-que-necesitamos-valorar-a-10-anos-de-fuundec-fundem/ (accessed 26 April 2020).

Azaola, E. (2012), 'El movimiento por la Paz con Justicia y Dignidad', *Desacatos*, 40, www.scielo.org.mx/scielo.php?script=sci_arttext&pid=S1607-050X2012000300011 (accessed 15 May 2020).

Berkowitz, D., K. Pistor, and J.-F. Richard (2003), 'The Transplant Effect', *The American Journal of Comparative Law*, 51:1, 163–203.

Centro Prodh (2018), *Histórica sentencia del Poder Judicial de la Federación en el Caso Ayotzinapa*, Centro de Derechos Humanos Miguel Agustín Pro Juárez, https://centroprodh.org.mx/2018/06/04/historica-sentencia-del-poder-judicial-de-la-federacion-en-el-caso-ayotzinapa/ (accessed 10 May 2019).

Comisión Nacional de los Derechos Humanos [CNDH] (2019), *Oficina Especial para el Caso Iguala*, http://informe.cndh.org.mx/menu.aspx?id=40061 (accessed 10 May 2019).

Committee on Enforced Disappearances [CED] (2015), *Observaciones finales sobre el informe presentado por México en virtud del artículo 29, párrafo 1, de la Convención*, CED/C/MEX/CO/1 (United Nations, Geneva).

Conferencia Nacional de Procuración de Justicia [CNPJ] (2011), *Boletín 35 Interprocuradurías*, www.cnpj.gob.mx/publicaciones/Publicaciones/Bolet%C3%ADn%2035.0.pdf (accessed 10 May 2018).

Inter-American Commission on Human Rights [IACHR] (2016), 'Situation on Human Rights in Mexico' (Washington DC, OAS), www.oas.org/en/iachr/reports/pdfs/Mexico2016-en.pdf (accessed 16 February 2021).

Inter-American Court of Human Rights [IACtHR] (2009), *Gonzalez et al. ('Cotton Field') v. Mexico*, Judgment of the Inter-American Court of Human Rights, 16 November 2009.

Grupo Interdisciplinario de Expertos Independientes [GIEI] (2015), 'Informe Ayotzinapa: investigación y primeras conclusiones de las desapariciones y homicidios de los normalistas de Ayotzinapa' (Mexico, GIEI), http://centroprodh.org.mx/GIEI/wp-content/uploads/2016/08/InformeAyotziUNO.jpg (accessed 16 February 2021).

Grupo Interdisciplinario de Expertos Independientes [GIEI] (2016), 'Informe Ayotzinapa II: avances y nuevas conclusiones sobre la investigación, búsqueda y atención a las víctimas' (Mexico, GIEI), www.oas.org/es/cidh/actividades/giei/giei-informeayotzinapa2.pdf (accessed 16 February 2021).

Keck, M., and K. Sikkink (1998), *Activists beyond Borders* (Ithaca, Cornell University Press).

Langer, M. (2004), 'From Legal Transplants to Legal Translations: The Globalization of Plea Bargaining and the Americanization Thesis in Criminal Procedure', *Harvard International Law Journal*, 45:1, 1–64.

Procuraduría General de la República [PGR] (2015), *3er Informe de Labores 2014–2015*, http://gaceta.diputados.gob.mx/Gaceta/63/2015/sep/InfGob/Inf_PGR-20150903.pdf (accessed 31 May 2019).

Risse, T., and K. Sikkink (1999), 'The Socialization of International Human Rights Norms into Domestic Practices: Introduction', in *The Power of Human Rights: International Norms and Domestic Change*, ed. T. Risse, S. Ropp, and K. Sikkink (Cambridge, Cambridge University Press).

Risse, T., S. C. Ropp, and K. Sikkink (2013), *The Persistent Power of Human Rights: From Commitment to Compliance* (New York, Cambridge University Press).

Villarreal Martínez, M. T. (2016), 'Los colectivos de familiares de personas desaparecidas y la procuración de justicia', *Intersticios sociales*, www.scielo.org.mx/scielo.php?script=sci_arttext&pid=S2007-49642016000100007&lng=es&tlng=es (accessed 26 January 2021).

Working Group on Enforced or Involuntary Disappearances [WGEID] (2011), *Informe del Grupo de Trabajo sobre desaparición forzadas o involuntarias: misión a México*, Consejo de Derechos Humanos, A/HRC/19/58/Add.2 (United Nations, Geneva).

# Brazil

# 6

# Woman, Mother, Human Rights Defender

DÉBORA MARIA DA SILVA
WITH RAIANE PATRÍCIA SEVERINO ASSUMPÇÃO

## Background

DÉBORA MARIA DA Silva lost her son Edson on 15 May 2006, during one of the largest massacres since the end of the Brazilian dictatorship (1964–85). More than 500 people were murdered and forcibly disappeared between 12 and 20 May 2006. This was a supposed response by São Paulo state security agents to attacks carried out by a criminal group known as Primeiro Comando da Capital (First Capital Command; PCC). Débora's account of those events, like those of other victims' families, denounces the particular form that state violence takes in Brazil in the post-transition era: the execution of victims (apparent from the location of the killing, the number of shots fired, and the places on the body hit, as presented in Chapter 7); the disappearance of the bodies and the cover-up of the killing; the state's disregard for victims' rights; and the flawed investigation and judicial processes. Her testimony highlights two characteristics of disappearance in Brazil today: first, the disappearance of the bodies in hospitals, morgues, and unmarked graves; second, the disappearance of the evidence of the killing. State authorities claim that their investigations into and trials for crimes cannot be concluded because of insufficient evidence – that is, the disappearance of the evidence. The blatant disregard for victims and their rights is unmistakable in the treatment relatives receive when they seek help from state authorities. They are denied information about the events that occurred and the investigations into them. This is part of a strategy to convince the families that there is no way to determine the responsible parties. As a result, in addition to coping with the pain of losing their sons and daughters, the family members have had to carry out their own investigations to find proof and devise strategies to fight against invisibility and injustice. Débora's experience recounted here shows how a mother, driven by pain and horror, turned into a leader of a movement that aimed to fight so that other mothers would not suffer as she had.

Débora and the other mothers of the movement have transformed their private pain into a public cause, so that the lives of their sons and daughters are not forgotten, so that those responsible for the crimes face justice, and so that killing and disappearance in Brazil are no longer an everyday occurrence ignored by the state.

Raiane Patrícia Severino Assumpção

## May Mothers: Débora da Silva's Story

I coordinate the May Mothers group. Every hour of my day, every day of my week, is dedicated to a cause: to end the killing and disappearance of our sons and daughters. I only understood the extent of the genocide of young, poor, black youths on 15 May 2006, when a bullet was lodged in Edson's cervical spine. Edson was my eldest. At that time, he was 29 years old. He was born before I was 17. I raised this child with all of the care that a mother can give to someone. The shot that went through his heart also destroyed mine. Ten years later, the person who shot him has still not faced any punishment.

I am going to tell you this story from the beginning. It was a Sunday. My family was celebrating my birthday with a lunch at home in Santos, São Paulo. These were sombre times for *Paulistas* (the people of São Paulo state). The state had imposed a curfew. There was not a living soul on the street. I was overcome by a deep despair that settled into my chest. On 12 May, a bloody war had begun that didn't have anything to do with us. It involved the police and the Primeiro Comando da Capital (First Capital Command), a criminal organisation that had taken over the prisons. At the end of that afternoon, Edson kissed me goodbye. He told me to turn off the television because he sensed that I was devastated by the news of so many people being killed. I remember saying to him, 'Be careful with your life.' I didn't want him to leave, to go back to his house. Edson had had a tooth extracted and he still had stitches in his mouth; he was in pain. He decided he needed to leave to go and buy some medication on his way home. I stuck by the radio and the television listening to the names of the dead to see if I knew any of them. One of them turned out to be my Edson. The death of my son drove me crazy from the very moment I found out he was missing.

[Note: The official report states that the Military Police were called in to investigate a murder. When they arrived at the site they found the body of Edson Rogério, Débora's son, on the ground next to a motorcycle. The victim was allegedly rescued by the Military Police, but died in the emergency room. Edson's body had five bullet wounds: three in the chest and abdomen that had entered from the front; two below the waist that had entered from behind. The report stated that forensic physicians tried to remove one of the bullets from the victim's spinal column, but their instruments broke. Edson was buried with that bullet. The case was closed in 2008. The body was subsequently exhumed, and the bullet removed for ballistic identification in June 2012. The ballistic testing still has not occurred.][1]

For many years before his death, Edson had suffered the consequences of a choice he had never made – to live on the periphery. He was identified as a suspect in an armed assault. After being tortured, he signed a confession, was tried and sentenced, and went to prison. I did not rest until I gathered evidence that identified the true criminal. My son was in jail for two years before he received a pardon and was finally able to leave and start work. The pardon wiped his record clean of a criminal past. After he left my house on that terrible Sunday, 15 May, he stopped at a gas station where he was filling up his motorcycle. When he left shortly afterwards he was seized and shot by the Military Police. The police searched through his record 23 times to try to justify his death, to find something that identified him as a criminal.

I began to look for other women in mourning like me. We created the Independent May Mothers Movement. I cry a lot, still. But the tears teach us another way, they teach us a lesson. Pain has taught me to resist, to discover my rights, and to emphasise successes. The first was convincing the press that those murdered – almost all young, poor, black, and from the periphery – were not criminals. Only 2 per cent of those executed in the streets had ever had past run-ins with the police.

There have never been more murders in the country than in that May. The first reports listed 493 dead. The human rights non-governmental organisation Conectas reported an even higher estimate: 532 dead. Five years later, researchers at Harvard University in the United States compiled testimonies – many of them provided by us, the mothers – and lists of names that led them to conclude that the massacre may have had as many as 600 victims. And, still, there was silence in the country. No one wanted to know what had happened to those families, even more invisible after having lost their sons and daughters because of state silence. Many of the victims had been their families' financial support. One girl, Ana Paula Gonzaga, who was 29 years old, would have given birth on that day. She had just packed her suitcase for the hospital trip, had gone to the bakery with her husband, and ended up cravenly slaughtered.

This grief has driven me to speak with a lot of officials, including Dilma Rousseff when she was president of the country. In December 2013, I went to Brasilia to receive a medal from the federal government at the International Forum on Human Rights. She was on the stage. I called on Rousseff to push the congress and the nation to demilitarise the police, the group that kills more than any other, to protect citizens. The world is puzzled by Brazil, where 56,000 people are killed each year; 33,000 of them are between 12 and 18 years old. There is an undeclared death sentence on the periphery. This is what I said to Rousseff: 'Our country produces 56,000 May Mothers every year. This is another dictatorship. A dictatorship led by the Military Police.'

[1] Boletim de Ocorrência no. 2171/2006, 1° DP de Santos; Laudo Necroscópico no. 232/2006, Instituto Médico Legal de Santos.

There is a terrible underlying logic maintained by a corrupt political system that pits the poor against the poor, everyone killing each other. Instead of developing social policies, the state has turned the [urban] periphery into a repository of suspects, to show that it has an effective security policy. But effective in what? Killing our sons and daughters?

To shift the focus from the topic of death to the topic of life, I work with children in the *cortiços* (tenements) of Santos. We create teams to cut hair, give manicures. We provide things such as chocolate eggs or toys during Easter. We put on hip-hop shows, theatre performances, Sunday parties. I am always travelling, meeting with mothers all over the country, participating in discussions, talking with politicians. We made a film and wrote a book. It is crucial to make the mothers visible in society so that we can influence public policies to improve education, health, life, security. My work is not paid. My husband is the breadwinner. I receive funds for travel and meals. And nothing else is important to me. Because my life is not mine any more. It is public. I am going to continue screaming until I lose my voice or I change the cruel reality in my country.

# 7

# State Violence in Brazil: Execution, Slaughter, and Disappearance in the Post-Authoritarian Era

JAVIER AMADEO AND RAIANE PATRÍCIA SEVERINO ASSUMPÇÃO*

## Introduction

ACCORDING TO GLOBONEWS, the Brazilian Public Security Office reports that more than 5,000 people were killed by the Military Police in the State of São Paulo from April 2007 to May 2017.[1] Statistics show that the number of deaths has increased dramatically over time. In the first three months of 2017, 160 people were killed by public security forces compared to 69 people in 2007, an increase of more than 100 per cent.

The alarming data on violence in Brazil are the result of the number of deaths by firearm. The *Mapa da violência 2016* study documented that firearm fatalities reached nearly 1 million between 1980 and 2014, with most of those deaths in recent years: nearly 9,000 registered in 1980 and nearly 45,000 in 2014. The study

*The present text was elaborated from the results of the research project 'State Violence in Brazil: A Study of *Crimes of May* 2006 in the Perspective of Transitional Justice and Forensic Anthropology'. The research was conducted as part of an institutional collaboration project between the Anthropology and Archaeology Forensic Centre (São Paulo Federal University) and the Latin American Centre, School of Interdisciplinary and Area Studies (Oxford University), and was supported by the Newton Fund of the British government. We would like to thank our partners for their support and encouragement. We would like also to thank the other researchers from the Anthropology and Archaeology Forensic Centre who participated in the project, without whom this text would not have been possible: Claudia R. Plens, Maria Elizete Kunkel, Bruno Konder Comparato, Camila Diogo de Souza, Aline Lúcia de Rocco Gomes, Débora Maria da Silva, Valéria Ap. de Oliveira Silva, Marina Figueiredo, Rebeca Padrão Amorim Puccinelli, Edson Barbosa da Rocha, Delphine Denise Lacroix, Lorrane Rodrigues, Bruno Everton Bezerra da Rocha, and Natália Aurora dos Santos. Final Report: Unifesp and CAAF (2019).

[1] http://g1.globo.com/globo-news/jornal-globo-news/videos/t/videos/v/mais-de-cinco-mil-pessoas-foram-mortas-por-policiais-em-sp-nos-ultimos-10-anos/5996574/ (accessed 8 May 2019).

*Proceedings of the British Academy*, **237**, 129–147, © The British Academy 2021.

attributes the cause of most death to homicide (85 per cent). It further places Brazil tenth in the world for the ratio of firearm deaths to population size. The profile of the victims identified in the report is noteworthy: more than 90 per cent of the victims are young – principally between 15 and 29 years old – men of colour (Waiselfisz 2016: 68–72).

Disappearance (enforced or not) is another social phenomenon of enormous significance in the democratic era that has been insufficiently addressed by the government and scholars. According to data from the Brazilian Public Security Forum, based on a study requested by the International Committee of the Red Cross, nearly 700,000 reports of disappearance were registered in Brazil between 2007 and 2016. This first systematic study with concrete data on disappearance shows that over 70,000 disappearances were registered in 2016 alone. As Olaya Hanashiro, senior consultant at the Brazilian Public Security Forum, states, 'No one was looking at this phenomenon beyond the period of the military dictatorship. And yet disappearance did not stop happening in the daily life of the population' with the transition.[2]

The causes of these extreme levels of violence in Brazil, and the means to reduce them, present theoretical and policy challenges. While a single chapter cannot fulfil that goal, we introduce a set of factors underlying the violence that contribute to the development of effective policy proposals for reducing it.[3] The first part of the chapter presents the contours of state violence in Brazil in the post-transition period. It focuses on the legacy of the civil-military dictatorship and underlying structural inequality as the cause of contemporary violence. The second part examines the Crimes of May in 2016, a paradigmatic example of post-transition-era violence in Brazil that features summary execution, killing, and disappearance. In the third part of the chapter, we analyse the legal mechanisms adopted by the May Crimes' victims' families in their struggle for justice for this tragedy. We contend that structural inequality and authoritarian legacies converge to explain the Crimes of May and the ineffective state response to the incident.

## The Deep Roots of Violence in Brazil

Two factors constitute the deep roots of contemporary violence in Brazil: the legacy of the civil-military dictatorship and structural inequality. We argue that the transitional justice mechanisms adopted in the country did not break with the authoritarian past or build a firm foundation for democracy. Long-standing inequality has blocked marginalised social groups from becoming rights-bearing citizens, perpetuating structural violence in the country.

[2] https://g1.globo.com/sao-paulo/noticia/brasil-registra-8-desaparecimentos-por-hora-nos-ultimos-10-anos-diz-estudo-inedito.ghtml (accessed 8 May 2019).

[3] On this issue see also the works published in Amadeo (2019).

## Legacy of the Authoritarian Past

Brazil has made some advances in transitional justice, but enormous challenges remain.[4] In documenting Brazil's transitional justice efforts, Abrão and Torelly (2012) recognise the modest outcomes in the country compared to its neighbours in the region. An ambitious set of reparations, and truth and memory processes, were adopted in the 1988 Constitution and implemented by subsequent governments. The steps taken forward, however, coexist with impunity, reinforced institutionally by the 1979 Amnesty Law (*Lei da Anistia*) recognised legally in the Constitution.[5] Abrão and Torelly suggest that 'amnesty as impunity and oblivion' is not the only way to see Brazil's transitional justice process. They emphasise the compensation made to victims of past abuse as recognition and truth about wrongdoing. They contend that these processes opened up a national dialogue, setting the stage for accountability efforts (Abrão and Torelly 2012: 152–3).

In particular, they highlight two institutional innovations: the Special Commission on Political Deaths and Disappearances (Comissão Especial sobre Mortos e Desaparecidos Políticos) in 1995 and the Amnesty Commission (Comissão de Anistia) of 2001. The Deaths and Disappearance Commission aimed at recognising the state's responsibility for killings and enforced disappearances during the civil-military dictatorship, locating the bodies of the dead and disappeared, and hearing reparation requests from victims.[6] The Amnesty Commission considered petitions from victims for amnesty and symbolic or economic reparations owed to them for their treatment during the dictatorship, such as compensation for loss of employment or educational opportunities resulting from political, worker, or student activism.[7]

In advancing truth and memory and symbolic accountability, the creation of the National Truth Commission (Comissão Nacional da Verdade; CNV) in 2012 was key.[8] The CNV aimed to recover memory and truth about serious human rights violations, fill gaps in the understanding of Brazilian history, and strengthen

[4] Specific transitional justice mechanisms include: individual, collective, material, and symbolic reparations for human rights violations; truth and memory processes; criminal prosecutions for perpetrators of past gross violations of human rights; and reforms of the legal system and public institutions (e.g. public security, judiciary, and intelligence agencies). For a definition of transitional justice, see www.ictj.org/about/transitional-justice (accessed 31 January 2021). For key texts on transitional justice, see Olsen *et al.* (2001); Roht-Arriaza and Mariezcurrena (2006), Lessa and Payne (2012); and Payne *et al.* (2015).

[5] On the question of the transition and the legacy of the dictatorship, see also Teles (2015).

[6] On the question of political disappearance in Brazil during the military period and its link to post-transition violence, see Azevedo (2018). The mobilisation of families of the disappeared is also discussed by Teles (2019).

[7] Abrão and Torelly (2012: 154–5) note that the process in Brazil went beyond economic compensation, and included declarations of political amnesty and particular rights, for example to finish studies in public institutions and to have diplomas from foreign institutions recognised.

[8] The Commission was part of the 2009 National Human Rights Programme. See http://cnv.memoriasreveladas.gov.br (accessed 31 January 2021).

democratic values. While systematising information on human rights violations, the CNV engendered controversy over: the lack of political and budgetary autonomy, the inclusion within the historical period of investigation of the period before (1946–64), during (1964–85), and following (1985–8) the dictatorship; and its inability to advance legal remedies for serious violations of human rights (Paiva and Pomar 2011; Costa and Silva 2017: 168).

Important institutional reforms included closing down the central organs of the regime's repressive apparatus: the National Intelligence Service (Serviço Nacional de Inteligência; SNI), the Information Operations Detachment–Internal Defence Operations Centre (Destacamento de Operações de Informação–Centro de Operações de Defesa Interna; DOI-CODI), and the Department of Political and Social Order (Departamento de Ordem Política e Social; DOPS). Reforms also included the creation of a Ministry of Defence that subordinated the armed forces to civilian control (Abrão and Torelly 2012: 163) and the creation of new human rights agencies, specifically the Special Secretariat for Human Rights (Secretaria Especial de Direitos Humanos). Despite these significant steps toward building democracy and human rights safeguards, the authoritarian legacy permeates state institutions. Examples are the absence of civilian oversight of, and the militarised structure within, the country's armed forces and public security systems.

The 'authoritarian rubbish', in the words of former President Fernando Henrique Cardoso (1985: 8–9), pervades the legal and institutional framework governing the public security apparatus. Paulo Sergio Pinheiro (1999: 56) notes the absence in the 1988 federal constitution of the kinds of rule-of-law provisions that establish democratic control over public security institutions and an effective judicial enforcement system.[9] Marlon Weichert (2019: 395, Chapter 8) also links contemporary violence in Brazil to the authoritarian legacy that hovers over the democratic period. The social and political repression perpetuated by public security and justice sectors during the dictatorship persist after the transition. The democratic state, according to Weichert, has maintained the repressive apparatus of the past; democratic oversight has not emerged to check it.

In sum, the greatest challenge for Brazil's transitional justice efforts is to end impunity for the human rights violations of the authoritarian era. Abrão and Torelly highlight the idea that equality before the law necessarily implies an obligation on the part of the state to investigate and punish human rights violations. In Brazil, unlike other countries in the region, no criminal trials of state perpetrators of past abuses have occurred. As the authors state, the 'culture of impunity prevented the recognition of the victims' right to judicial protection'. Impunity persists even for serious violations of human rights, where evidence of victims, perpetrators, and the acts themselves exist, and when institutional processes have officially acknowledged wrongdoing. Impunity is one of the major obstacles to democratic consolidation in Brazil (Abrão and Torelly 2012: 164–5).

[9] See also Pinheiro (1994).

## Structural Violence in Brazil

The other central element for understanding contemporary state violence in Brazil relates to what Pinheiro calls systemic or structural violence, in which 'the arbitrariness of state institutions is combined with high levels of violent crime, organised crime, great intensity of physical violence in conflicts between citizens and widespread impunity' (Pinheiro 1999: 39). Pinheiro's notion of structural violence emerges from deep-rooted, extremely asymmetric social relations in the country arising in the colonial period and continuing today. It is perpetuated by elites' authoritarian domination over popular sectors and the violent suppression of resistance from those classes (39).

The return to democratic rule of law and the remobilisation of the popular sector requires rights-engendered challenges to authoritarian practices. Pinheiro identifies an important distinction over rights-mobilisation during the authoritarian period and in contemporary Brazil. The Brazilian state today has not created, institutionalised, or legitimised a repressive apparatus; it has nonetheless tolerated state agents' acts, thereby creating a permissive environment for abuses with impunity (Pinheiro 1999: 39; Pinheiro 2002).

A second distinction from the authoritarian period is the target of repression. A political opposition demanding social justice is no longer the main enemy of the state. Instead, those sectors of society that the political opposition once represented – the poor, the residents of the periphery, racial minorities, indigenous people, and subordinate social groups – are the victims of contemporary state violence: the 'disposable peoples' identified in Chapter 1 of this volume. The state as a whole may not be responsible for directly perpetrating violations, but it indirectly does so by failing to prevent or punish state agents when they are involved in violations and by denying the fundamental rights of citizenship to marginalised populations. When violations by state agents are tolerated, violence aimed at particular 'disposable' sectors continues and weakens democracy (Pinheiro 1999: 40). Tolerated acts include those carried out during the Crimes of May: execution of suspected criminals by the Military Police and the slaughter or enforced disappearance by extermination groups in collaboration with the police.

This tolerance persists despite pressure on Brazil from international human rights governmental and non-governmental organisations and the country's own official recognition of its international obligations adopted in domestic legal instruments. For Pinheiro, 'This failure to implement the law weakens the validity of constitutional guarantees, perpetuates an illegal cycle of violence and makes it difficult to strengthen the legitimacy of the democratic government as a promoter of citizenship.' The failure makes evident the continuity of practices from the authoritarian period to the post-transition – what Pinheiro terms 'differentiated expressions of the same structure of domination founded on hierarchy, discrimination, impunity, and social exclusion' (Pinheiro 1999: 42).

The process of democratic consolidation has faced the obstacle of 'structural violations', or a recognition of the political, social, and economic rights of certain citizens, because of their class, colour, location, or age. Pinheiro (1999: 52) thus identifies the paradox in Brazil of building a democratic political regime without corresponding democratic citizenship.

While violence is widespread in Brazil, Pinheiro emphasises that it is also concentrated in the poor urban peripheries of key cities. There is thus an overlap between poverty and victims of violence. According to Pinheiro (1999: 52), there is 'a clear correlation between living conditions, violence, and death rates, between violations of civil and political rights and violations of social and economic rights; violence is clearly a significant part of social deprivation'.

Structural violence takes the form of criminalising poverty, according to Weichert, aimed at limiting the fundamental freedoms and rights guarantees for certain – economically and socially marginalised – sectors of the population and protecting the freedoms and rights of the ruling classes. The rhetoric of drug warfare and fighting crime provides the justification for the repression of certain populations, military encirclement and occupation of poor neighbourhoods, and institutionalising a permanent state of siege in particular urban territories. The young black population in these poor neighbourhoods is the hardest hit. Statistical data and qualitative analyses reveal the systematic persecution of this civilian population through violence or mass incarceration (Weichert 2019: 396–8).

## Social Mobilisation and the Crimes of May

The Crimes of May 2006 represent one of the most important episodes of state violence in Brazil's post-transition period. More than 500 people were murdered between 12 May and 20 May 2006, owing to the response by security force agents from the State of São Paulo to attacks by the criminal faction known as the Capital First Command (Primeiro Comando da Capital; PCC). In the Baixada Santista region alone, 60 murders occurred in those two weeks.[10]

Mothers and relatives of the victims in the Baixada Santista region created the May Mothers Independent Movement (Movimento Independente Mães de Maio), as recounted in Chapter 6, to seek a response to grave human rights violations linked to security forces. The movement sought truth and justice for the crimes committed and, in the absence of an effective state response to the crimes, a serious investigation, or the initiation of legal procedures on behalf of the victims. The mothers organised in a vacuum of knowledge about the events, without official support, and because of a fear that the case would be shelved if they did not act. A renowned lawyer from the city of Santos heard their claims and began to work

[10] The metropolitan region of Baixada Santista comprises nine municipalities: Santos, Cubatão, São Vicente, Guarujá, Bertioga, Praia Grande, Mongaguá, Itanhaém, and Peruíbe.

with them to pressure the federal government legally to recognise the cases and to hear them together. The Public Defender's Office took on the case and filed a complaint against Brazil for violation of the American Convention on Human Rights. Simultaneously mothers pursued private and individual investigations, and publicly denounced state authorities' negligence in investigating the crimes that had victimised their sons and daughters.

The mothers' mobilisation, the media visibility it captured, and broad civil society support for the demand for investigation, provoked the opposite response from the state from the one the mothers had anticipated. They faced intimidation efforts rather than investigation efforts. Nearly a year after the May Crimes, one of the mothers, Ednalva Santos, was falsely accused of drug-trafficking charges. She was arrested and detained for nearly a week before the charges were eventually dropped and she was released.[11] The case against another mother, Vera Lúcia Gonzaga dos Santos, did not end as well. Found guilty on drug-trafficking charges, she was sentenced to four years in jail. During her imprisonment, the deadline for applying for reparations for her daughter and granddaughters' killing lapsed. Vera Lúcia Gonzaga dos Santos was released from prison on good behaviour after only a few months, but the prison experience and the futile struggle for justice for the crime committed against her family caused a deep depression that she did not survive. She passed away in 2018.

State intimidation and pressure tactics notwithstanding, mothers continued to join the movement and actively seek state responses to their demands. Maria Sônia Lins, the mother of Wagner Lins dos Santos, killed in the May Crimes, is an example. Before she contacted the movement, state authorities had ignored her demand for investigation into the crime. The May Mothers put her in touch with the state attorney, who initiated a legal process for reparations. Her story shows that by joining the movement, mothers enhanced their claims rather than weakening them.

The May Mothers sought collective processes as well. They approached the Human Rights Commission of the Santos Municipal Council, the Regional Council of Medicine (CRM), and the São Paulo Council of Defence of the Rights of the Human Person (CONDEPE). While these state agencies mainly put obstacles in the mothers' path to justice and reparations, according to May Mothers' founder and coordinator Débora Maria (Chapter 6), the mothers transformed barriers into motivations to continue the struggle and reaffirm their convictions.

They were able to do so in part because the struggle sometimes led to victories. A meeting at CONDEPE consolidated the movement itself. The president of CONDEPE, Rose Nogueira, invited the group of mothers, then known as Mães da Baixada (Mothers of the Baixada), to share their personal stories about the May Crimes, eventually published in the book *Mães de Maio* (Movimento Mães de Maio 2011). In the conversations leading to the book, Débora Maria expressed the frustrations of failing to reach attention from and solidarity with the wider society.

[11] The false accusation, arrest, and detention no doubt compounded Ednalva Santos' current poor health and depression following the loss of her son and 12 years without justice for the crime.

Rose Nogueira introduced them to the idea of a movement, like the Argentine Mothers of the Plaza de Mayo, to facilitate access to existing resources for the defence of human rights. Débora Maria attributes the birth of the May Mothers movement to that interaction.

Other victories followed. The mothers' persistence resulted in the founding of a Human Rights Centre, at the invitation of the Santos Citizenship Forum. It also created the First Human Rights Conference of Santos, which subsequently developed into the São Paulo State Conference on Human Rights. The mothers gained the public space that they had sought as an outcome of their mobilisation, their struggle, their collective demands, and their solidarity.

Their mobilisation sometimes even achieved positive state responses. In 2010, for example, the mothers won their demand to transfer jurisdiction from the local to the federal level for the investigation and prosecution of the crimes. That year they also succeeded in their civil action for reparations in eight cases previously dismissed in lower courts, but partially reinstated on appeal. The mothers also demanded and won the designation of a May Mothers' Day (12 May) on the São Paulo State official calendar, regulated by Law 14981/2013.[12] The Human Rights Commission of the São Paulo Legislative Assembly in May 2014 formed a subcommittee for a May Mothers' Truth Commission on Democracy, in response to the mothers' demand.[13] On 17 July 2014, Law 15501 established the Week of Victims of Violence in São Paulo State. The Official Gazette of the State of São Paulo declared the annual observation of this week from 12 to 19 May in recognition of the crimes.[14] In 2015 the May Mothers took their case to the Organization of American States (OAS) in an effort to increase international pressure on the Brazilian state to reopen the cases and to investigate them at the federal level to determine state responsibility.

The May Mothers have also expanded their network to include mothers of victims of police violence in other cities in Brazil (São Paulo capital, Salvador, and Rio de Janeiro) and other parts of the world (United States, Colombia, Argentina, Mexico, and Chile). They have become the face of a national and potentially global movement that condemns democratic state violence, specifically state agents' commission of crimes and omission of a response to victims of crimes and their families. Despite this national and international attention, the mothers are steadfast in their pursuit of their immediate goals: the search for truth and justice for the Crimes of May 2006; the recognition of the role of the state in the violence; and the identification, prosecution, and punishment of those responsible, including the direct perpetrators of the crime and the command responsibility of their superiors in the public security system.

[12] Information obtained through the official website: www.al.sp.gov.br/noticia/?id=358315 (accessed 1 February 2021).

[13] According to May Mothers' founder and coordinator, Débora Maria, this Commission was short lived. It was disbanded six months after its creation by parliamentary forces opposed to it.

[14] See www.al.sp.gov.br/noticia/?id=358315.

## The 2006 Crimes of May

The Crimes of May investigations that occurred reveal evidence of the type of killing, the perpetrators, the victims, and the legal procedures and instruments adopted or denied that prevented access to justice. That evidence points to the role played by democratic state agents in violence perpetrated in post-transition Brazil.

The main source of evidence is the report by the Special Committee on the Crimes of May, created in 2010 by the Secretariat of Human Rights. The report recognises the role of the public security force and extermination groups formed by police in the violence. The motive behind the violence is identified as retaliation for attacks by the PCC criminal organisation. This took the form of a 'response wave' that resulted in hundreds of homicides,[15] summary executions,[16] slaughter,[17] and enforced disappearance of civilians.[18]

The São Paulo State Ombudsman's Office had received complaints about extermination groups formed by police, circulating in cars and on motorcycles, wearing hoods, prepared to kill criminals, to avenge the deaths of their colleagues. These were seen as a way for the police to send a message to the PCC to expect retaliation for their acts. Of the 493 murders analysed by the Ombudsman's Office, 89 indicated summary execution at the hands of public security forces. Other evidence points to slaughter and enforced disappearance as a method of social control through violence.

The report makes explicit that multiple types of violence were used in a demonstration of power. As such, direct and indirect forms of violence imposed social control over certain sectors of the population.

### Executions

The evidence raised in the report 'São Paulo sob achaque' ('São Paulo under Threat') suggests that summary executions were a tactic used during the May 2006 events. The report highlights a 'very high level of lethal action by on-duty police

[15] Brazil is the world leader in the number of homicides, according to the Violence Atlas, produced jointly by the Brazilian Forum of Public Security and the Institute of Applied Economic Research (FBSP 2017). In 2014 alone there were almost 60,000 homicides in the country, which means 10 per cent of the total number of cases worldwide.

[16] These are cases in which the authorities or security forces' agents, with the explicit or implicit support of the authorities, kill civilians without justification (such as self-defence).

[17] Slaughter is an extreme use of lethal violence as a form of social control. Mass killing of this type is a public display of power used by criminal organisations and public agents, particularly notable in contexts of institutional weakness and disputes over control of territories and markets (Silva *et al.* 2019).

[18] Enforced disappearance is defined as the deprivation of liberty of a person or persons, in whatever form, by agents of the state or by persons or groups of persons acting with the consent, support, or acquiescence of the state, followed by a lack of information or refusal to acknowledge the deprivation of liberty or information on the location of the person, thus preventing the exercise of legal remedies and procedural safeguards (OAS 1994). See also Chapter 2.

(uniformed) after the first days of the attack'. The timing of the violence contradicts official explanations that the violence was in direct and immediate response to a surprise attack by the PCC (IHRC and Justiça Global 2011: 74).

According to Public Security Office information on 14 May at 7.00 p.m., the police action report registered a ratio of 5.8 imprisonments for every person killed between 12 and 14 May, and 0.5 imprisonments for each death in the days following. The official figures show a 10-fold increase in the violence during several days of the attack (IHRC and Justiça Global 2011: 75).

The report also provides evidence of summary executions, casting doubt on official claims that killings resulted from clashes with police. Forensic evidence provided indications of execution-style killing: entry of fatal bullets at short, rather than distant, range, from above, and in areas of highest fatality on the body (IHRC and Justiça Global 2011: 76). Investigations into particular cases of victims allegedly killed in confrontations with the police further challenge the official explanation. Of the four shots fired by the police that killed Jose Arruda da Silva in Marília on 17 May, for example, one entered his back. Eduardo Braz de Santana was killed by police on 13 May, allegedly in an armed confrontation, yet one of the three bullets entered at his eyebrow from a 50 cm distance, suggesting an execution after surrender rather than a clash (IHRC and Justiça Global 2011: 82 – 4).

## Slaughter

Evidence suggests that in addition to summary execution, a number of incidents of slaughter also occurred. In Bristol Park, in the southern zone of São Paulo capital, on 14 May 2006, one incident involved five victims: Fabio de Lima Andrade (killed, 24 years old), Edivaldo Barbosa de Andrade (killed, 24 years old), Israel Alves de Souza (killed, 25 years old), Fernando Elza (wounded, 22 years old), and Eduardo Barbosa de Andrade (wounded, 23 years old). Eyewitness reports indicated that two men driving a dark-coloured vehicle approached an unarmed group of young people and fired at them several times. The survivors were rescued and taken to the hospital. One of them (Barbosa) was violently removed from the hospital by the military police, held inside the police car for hours, and subsequently presented to the 83rd Police Department in Bristol Park responsible for reporting on the massacre he witnessed. The other survivor (Elza) was murdered by the occupants of a dark-coloured car seven months later, just after being called to testify in the case, and in the same location in Bristol Park (Caramante 2006).

Just over two years after the incident, the authorities decided to close the case, alleging lack of evidence identifying the perpetrators of the slaughter. In the words of the prosecutor, 'despite all the steps taken, it was not possible to identify the perpetrators of the crime' (Conectas Direitos Humanos 2009: 6).

The slaughter at the Bar do Cabeça in Guarujá on 14 May 2006 provides another reference. According to official information, four hooded individuals entered the bar, owned by Francisco de Oliveira, and began shooting before fleeing in a silver car. The slaughter resulted in the death of six people. Despite the violence, the incident appeared in only a small note in the *Expresso Popular* newspaper.[19] Official documents confirmed that no evidence was collected at the time because of the focus on protection of security agents during the Baixada Santista attacks by the PCC. Indeed, of the six victims, only three are identified in the official documents: Daniel Borges dos Santos, Maurílio Melo, and Willian Pereira dos Santos. The others are identified only as 'male'.

Both slaughters are characteristic of similar crimes during the post-transition period. The slaughters were carried out by unidentified people wearing hoods and in cars or on motorcycles without identification plates. The victims in general were young men and residents of the urban peripheries. Witnesses claim that shortly after the killing, police officers arrive and tamper or destroy evidence, eliminating the possibility of fully investigating the crime and identifying perpetrators.

## Disappearance

In addition to summary execution and slaughter, the Crimes of May involved disappearances of young people in the city of São Paulo and the surrounding metropolitan region. The evidence points to the probable involvement of state agents (police officers) in enforced disappearances.

On 13 May, in the southern region of São Paulo, Ronaldo Procópio Alves, 30 years old, disappeared. According to eyewitnesses, Ronaldo was allegedly approached by the military police in the neighbourhood of Parelheiros, and later placed in an official vehicle. On the same day, his family was notified that he was in custody at the 25th police station. When the family arrived at the station, they were told that he had been released. He has been missing without a trace since that day (Fernandes 2011: 85).

On 14 May, in the city of Guarulhos, two young men – Diego Augusto Sant'ana (15) and Everton Pereira dos Santos (26) – were reported missing. According to eyewitnesses, Diego and Everton were together when they were detained by police officers and taken away in an official vehicle. Everton's family members learned of his custody at the police station and his transfer the next day to a temporary detention facility. On the following day, however, the police denied any knowledge of Everton's custody (Fernandes 2011: 85). Both Diego and Everton remain missing.

Also in Guarulhos, on 15 May, Paulo Alexandre Gomes (23) left home at the end of the day and was never seen by his family again. Eyewitnesses saw police approach and attack Paulo, but no other information about the victim exists (Fernandes 2011: 85). His father, Francisco Gomes, compares his son's disappearance with the military dictatorship: 'The impunity of that time is the same today.

[19] 'Rebeliões terminam nos presídios de São Paulo', *Expresso Popular*, 16 May 2006.

The dictatorship is now disguised as democracy. They do whatever they want to do.'[20]

Evidence reveals patterns of how enforced disappearances occurred and who was victimised during the Crimes of May. First, in each case, eyewitnesses recount the presence of police forces during the last moments in which these four individuals were seen alive, increasing the likelihood of official involvement in their disappearance. Despite this police presence, relatives have not received any state assistance in the search for the missing. On the contrary, they felt their requests for information and support were met with disregard at police stations. Second, the profile of victims is similar in all four cases: they were young, black, with low levels of education. Three of them were on parole or had finished their parole at the time of their disappearance. All lived in violent outlying regions of the city characterised by the absence of the state in the provision of public services (Fernandes 2011: 84).

## The Complaint to the Inter-American Human Rights System

In March 2015, the Specialised Centre of Citizenship and Human Rights of the Public Defender's Office (State of São Paulo) filed a complaint with the Inter-American Human Rights system against the Brazilian State for violation of the American Convention on Human Rights. The complaint listed six summary executions that killed nine people in the Baixada Santista region (eight in 2006 and one in 2007) and left one survivor.[21] The 2006 cases, as noted in the complaint, occurred during the 2006 May Crimes. The complaint was filed following the failure of the Brazilian state to respond to requests by victims' relatives for investigation and justice.

In 2010, as a result of pressure from the families, a 'request for competence displacement' was submitted to the Attorney General's Office. This mechanism, established in the Federal Constitution,[22] seeks to ensure compliance with obligations under international human rights treaties in cases of serious human rights violations, transferring jurisdiction to the federal government (DPESP 2015: 54). Ten years after the claim was filed, the case remained pending without a final decision.

The complaint submitted to the Inter-American Commission on Human Rights in 2015 attempted to overcome this stalemate in the Brazilian judiciary by moving the case to an international human rights body. The Public Defender's complaint describes the historical and social context leading to the May 2006 crimes of

[20] www.redebrasilatual.com.br/revistas/64/cidadania (accessed 1 February 2021).

[21] The victims were: Marcos Rebello Filho, Thiago Roberto Soares, Edson Rogério Silva dos Santos, Wagner Lins dos Santos, Diego Viera dos Santos Miranda (survivor), Ana Paula Gonzaga dos Santos, Eddie Joey de Oliveira, Ricardo Porto Noronha, Mateus Andrade de Freitas, and Rogério Monteiro Ferreira.

[22] Federal Constitution, article 109, para. 5.

summary executions; extermination groups formed by military police officers; and the absence of investigations; and, as a consequence, lack of accountability.

The complaint states that at the beginning of May 2006, the government of São Paulo ordered the transfer of prisoners to a maximum-security prison located 620 km from the capital. The goal of the measure was to isolate the leaders of the PCC. A series of attacks followed, according to official sources, initiated by the PCC in retaliation for their prison transfer, isolation, and the control over their organisation (DPESP 2015: 27–8).

The complaint focuses on violent incidents in the Baixada Santista region beginning in the early morning on 12 May through 20 May. Most of the casualties occurred during the night and in the early hours of the morning. The majority (53) of the 60 fatalities were civilians (88 per cent), and 7 (12 per cent) were public security agents (Unifesp and CAAF 2019: 162–5).

These data on Baixada Santista reflect the figures for the entire São Paulo state presented in the study *Análise dos impactos dos ataques do PCC em São Paulo em maio de 2006* (*Analysis of the Impact of the PCC Attacks in São Paulo in May 2006*). That study concurs that the vast majority of killings involved civilian victims: out of a total of 564 victims, 505 (89 per cent) were civilians, and 59 (11 per cent) were public security agents (LAV-UERJ 2008: 10–11).

The complaint also draws attention to the timing of the deaths in order to understand the dynamics of the violence and the role of public security agents in it. Using the data gathered by the Laboratório de Análise da Violência (Laboratory of Violence Analysis; LAV), the complaint highlights the concentration of public security agent deaths in the early days of the events (12–13 May) and civilian deaths later (14–17 May). While the ratio of security-agent-to-civilian deaths was nearly equal in those early days, it rose by between 10 and 20 times after 14 May (LAV-UERJ 2008: 11). The report interprets those findings as 'consistent with a scenario in which attacks on agents in the early days prompted acts of retaliation by police officers in the following days, with a high number of victims' (LAV-UERJ 2008: 11). The data on the dynamics of violence in the Baixada Santista match the broader study on São Paulo state (Unifesp and CAAF 2019: 166).[23]

The complaint further draws on the Military Police Ombudsman's Office report on signs of summary execution and information related to police participation in the activities of extermination groups. It includes reports from civil society organisations that provided further indications of summary execution. These cases are classified in the complaint as 'resistance followed by death' (DPESP 2015: 33).

Further analysis of the 'resistance followed by death' cases was summarised in a report ('Preliminary Report: Cases Presented as Resistance followed by Death'

[23] The cases of the fatal victims presented in the complaint are distributed over the following days: 14 May – Marcos Rebello Filho and Thiago Roberto Soares; 15 May – Edson Rogério Silva dos Santos, Wagner Lins dos Santos, Ana Paula Gonzaga dos Santos, and Eddie Joey de Oliveira; 17 May – Ricardo Porto Noronha and Mateus Andrade de Freitas.

(Figueiredo 2007)). That report challenged police allegations of deaths during armed confrontations. It suggested instead the summary execution of defenceless people in police custody.[24] The 124 deaths included in the report that fall into this category and occurred between 12 and 20 May identify the three patterns we previously mentioned: the location of the shots in highly lethal areas of the body, the concentration of shots in a single small area of the body with little distance between them, and the 'top-down' orientation of those shots. The report draws the conclusion that: 'The combination of these factors points to a situation more compatible with execution than the exchange of shots in a confrontation … In an armed confrontation the three patterns of shots are unlikely, even if considered in isolation. Because they occur in combination in many individual cases, we affirm that they are executions' (CONDEPE 2007: 89–90).

The analysis of the Baixada Santista events generated an analysis of 53 autopsy reports with 255 bullet wounds, or an average of four-and-a-half bullets per individual killed. This number is considered higher than the average number of shots in armed confrontations, and is more consistent with summary executions. The highly lethal location of the bullet wounds is evident from their concentration in the head, followed by the thorax, targeting vulnerable body organs of the brain, heart, and lung. The autopsy reports further point to summary executions of civilian victims (Unifesp and CAAF 2019: 168–70).

The complaint also draws attention to information gathered from the State Council on Human Rights Defence regarding police failure to protect and preserve evidence and to use experts to investigate the crimes, and their premature closure of cases without identifying perpetrators of crimes (CONDEPE 2007).

In response to these findings included in the complaint, Adriana Loche, formerly the executive secretary of the Santo Dias Centre for Human Rights, a non-governmental organisation promoting the protection of human rights, stated: 'Such attitudes reveal the inability, inertia, neglect, partiality or lack of political will of the Brazilian state for its institutions and authorities to carry out criminal prosecution within its reach, especially with regard to policing duties' (CONDEPE 2007: 122).

The complaint addresses this central state failure to undertake serious investigations and the corresponding impunity of the perpetrators. According to the Public Defender's Office, there were significant breaches in standard investigative procedures. As a result, the cases were all filed without identifying the authors of the crime (DPESP 2015: 48).

Police inquiries further ended even when evidence connected the multiple crimes: the modus operandi involving hooded men on motorcycles or cars, the concentration of shots on the body and taken at a short distance, and the timing indicating police retaliation for PCC's attacks. The failure to investigate suggests

[24] See IHRC and Justiça Global (2011: 73–6).

a cover-up. The crime scenes were not protected from tampering, reports were not filed on the evidence gathered, few projectiles were collected, and follow-up with eyewitnesses did not occur to identify criminal suspects (DPESP 2015: 50).

The Public Defender's Office noted an additional pattern in police investigations: 'In all of the police investigations [following the May Crimes], the initial concern involved "investigating" the criminal records of the victims' (DPESP 2015: 50). This statement reinforces the view that the police attempted to criminalise – and thus excuse the killing of – the victims of the crimes. This fitted the narrative of victims' deaths in armed confrontations with the police. By attempting to link victims to drug-trafficking or other forms of criminality, the police denied their innocence in the violent acts, thereby justifying their deaths. The Public Defender's Office report hinted at the absence of political will within the country's police and judicial systems, proving them 'incapable of ascertaining, judging, and punishing the perpetrators of these crimes' (DPESP 2015: 51). Thirteen years since this event, criminal investigations remain closed, the culprits free, and impunity safeguarded. The Public Defender's Office lists these basic procedural failures as follows:

> a lack of systematic investigation into all cases that showed evidence of summary execution per extermination group in the Baixada Santista region; absence of expert reports at crime scenes; absence of testimony by witnesses; not obtaining recordings of security cameras from buildings near the crime scene; absence of testimony of identified witnesses and surviving victims; failure to carry out investigations on seized projectiles and not carrying out comparative ballistic confrontation between all cases; absence of evidence collection in hospitals where the victims were rescued and where military police officers would have arrived carrying hoods rolled over their heads and mini-machine guns; failure to carry out examination of bodies of surviving victims; attempts by the Police Delegates and by the representative of the Public Prosecution Service to allocate to the next of kin the responsibility of finding new evidence and witnesses; and lack of investigation into the activities of the extermination group formed by police officers (DPESP 2015: 51–2).

We should also emphasise the absence of investigation into extermination groups' activities, which could have led to cross-referencing information on the full set of cases to reach full understanding of those involved in the crimes and their association. As the Public Defender's Office points out, the evident negligence in the investigation processes 'prevented relatives from having full access to justice and truth, with the elucidation of the facts and the responsibility of the guilty parties, both in the civil and criminal spheres' (DPESP 2015: 52).

The Public Defender's Office thus reached the conclusion that in the cases analysed there was 'a clear violation of the human rights of victims, their personal integrity, their personal freedom and security, and judicial guarantees and judicial protection, all of which are guaranteed by the American Convention on Human Rights' (DPESP 2015: 52–3).

## Concluding Remarks

As we emphasised previously, the Crimes of May 2006 can be considered an emblematic case of state violence in post-transition Brazil. It shows the authoritarian legacy and structural dynamics behind contemporary violence. Evidence from various sources of data and the cross-referencing of information on the crimes show how state violence is produced and legitimised in the democratic era.[25]

The profile of the victims is consistent with the logic set out in Chapter 1. These are the 'disposable people' in Brazil who are denied their physical integrity rights. Young, black, poor, male individuals are socially constructed as criminals and therefore deserving of the kind of violent policing they encountered in May 2006. The active efforts by the police to investigate not the crimes, but the victims' past run-ins with the law, as shown in Chapter 6, make manifest the attempt to stigmatise them and their families and to justify the violence. Deep structural inequality in Brazil creates a context in which the police transform citizens into disposable peoples.

The logic of clandestine operations (Chapter 1) by the police is evident in the efforts to cover up the violence with a narrative. The narrative of armed confrontation between the police and a criminal organisation (PCC) does not match the evidence of how these individuals were killed (the timing after the confrontations and the type of violence in summary execution, slaughter, and disappearance).

Disappearances in Brazil during the Crimes of May share certain dynamics with other post-transition disappearances covered in this volume. As in the other cases, the tactics used in the authoritarian period had a legacy that carried over into the post-transition. These included targeting certain individuals who threatened the state, branding them 'disposable' through stigma, and using clandestine activities to violate the human rights of those individuals with impunity.

The disappearances that took place in Brazil during the Crimes of May, however, also vary somewhat from the other cases analysed in this book. The involvement of public security agents in the killing of citizens tended to be more overt than in the other cases. What disappeared is the evidence of public security agents' involvement in wrongdoing. They tampered with the crime scene, destroyed evidence that could incriminate those responsible, failed to follow up eyewitness reports to identify the facts, and disappeared bodies in hospitals or morgues where families had to find them. While most families did eventually find their murdered relatives, they continue in many cases to seek official investigations into the killings. Without investigations, the families do not have an official cause of death. They have had to struggle to pursue reparations. And no judicial cases have been opened.

[25] See Unifesp and CAAF (2019).

In this situation, families live with ambiguous loss. The logic set out in Chapter 1 describes how the absence of investigations, truth, and justice has further stigmatised the families. When ambiguous loss has failed to achieve its intended effect of social control, and families have mobilised to seek answers, public security forces have pursued more aggressive acts of intimidation against those relatives.

The Brazilian case shows that the logics behind disappearance are powerful. At times, however, and against all odds, this chapter has shown that relatives resist and persist. The formation of the Independent Mothers of May Movement transformed the deep pain of individual family members (especially the mothers) into collective action. They used their own 'weapons of the weak' (Scott 1987), their own pursuit of the truth, their stories, their pain, to expose the violent action of the Brazilian public security sector and the judiciary. In so doing, those considered 'disposable' – because of the political economy of poverty, inequality, and race in Brazil – asserted their right to have rights (Arendt 1979) in a democracy. They took a stand against the 'authoritarian rubbish' still present in the country's institutional structure despite, or perhaps because of, the limited transitional justice process. They pushed for a democratic order: ensuring the rule of law and ending human rights violations through civil and democratic control over public security institutions and an effective functioning of the judiciary (Pinheiro, 1999: 56). They demanded to be treated like full citizens with the social and economic rights constitutive of a democratic political regime (Pinheiro, 1999: 52).

We close this chapter with a set of recommendations to achieve those goals. These follow the Public Defender's Office demand for remedial measures following the Crimes of May (DPESP 2015: 73–4):

- **obligation to investigate and punish** those directly and indirectly responsible for the assassinations of the victims by the Federal Justice system;
- **reparation of material and non-material damages**, such as medical, hospital, and psychological treatments and costs of legal proceedings caused by the loss of loved ones and the non-punishment of those responsible;
- **reparation of moral damages** through the presentation by the state of a formal and public request for apologies to the victims, through a public act and the mass media, in order to alleviate the feelings of injustice, lack of protection, fear, and shame of these victims before the state responsible for the violence suffered, unrecognised, and unrepaired;
- **guarantees of non-repetition** through the construction of a monument in honour of the victims in the city of Santos, elaboration and approval of administrative and legislative rules, determining that cases of summary executions should be investigated, with priority and precedence, by a specialised police department in compliance with all international standard procedures for investigations of summary executions.

## References


Abrão, P., and M. Torelly (2012), 'Resistance to Change: Brazil's Persistent Amnesty and Its Alternatives for Truth and Justice', in *Amnesty in the Age of Human Rights Accountability*, ed. F. Lessa and L. A. Payne (Cambridge and New York, Cambridge University Press), pp. 152–81.

Amadeo, J. (ed.) (2019), *Violência de estado na América Latina: direitos humanos, justiça de transicão e antropologia forense* (São Paulo, Editora da Unifesp).

Arendt, H. (1979), *The Origins of Totalitarianism* (New York, Harcourt Brace).

Azevedo, D. de L. (2018), 'Our Dead and Disappeared: Reflections on the Construction of the Notion of Political Disappearance in Brazil', *Vibrant: Virtual Brazilian Anthropology*, 15:3. DOI: 10.1590/1809-43412018v15n3d507.

Caramante, A. (2006), 'Testemunha de chacina na zona sul de SP é morta a tiros', *Folha de São Paulo* (10 December), www1.folha.uol.com.br/folha/cotidiano/ult95u129223.shtml (accessed 16 February 2021).

Cardoso, F. H. (1985), 'A agenda da transição', *Lua nova* 2:2, 7–9.

Conectas Direitos Humanos (2009), *Incidente de deslocamento de competência para a Justiça Federal* (São Paulo, Parque Bristol).

Conselho Estadual de Defesa dos Direitos da Pessoa Humana [CONDEPE] (2007), *Crimes de Maio* (São Paulo, CONDEPE).

Costa, A. S. M., and M. A. de C. Silva (2017), 'Novas fontes, novas versões: contribuições do acervo da Comissão Nacional da Verdade', *Revista de administração contemporânea*, 21:2, 163–83.

Defensoria Pública do Estado de São Paulo [DPESP] (2015), *Denuncia do núcleo especializado de cidadania e direitos humanos da Defensoria Pública do Estado de São Paulo contra Brasil por violação da Convenção Americana de Direitos Humanos* (São Paulo, DPESP).

Fernandes, F. G. (2011), 'Barbárie e direitos humanos: as execuções sumárias e desaparecimentos forçados de maio (2006) em São Paulo', master's thesis, Pontifícia Universidade Católica de São Paulo.

Figueiredo, R. M. de (2007), 'Perícia criminal: relatório preliminar. Casos apresentados como resistência seguida de morte', in Conselho Estadual de Defesa dos Direitos da Pessoa Humana (CONDEPE), *Crimes de Maio* (São Paulo).

Fórum Brasileiro de Segurança Pública [FBSP] (2017), (São Paulo, FBSP), www.forumseguranca.org.br/wp-content/uploads/2019/01/ANUARIO_11_2017.pdf (accessed 16 April 2020).

International Human Rights Clinic [IHRC], and Justiça Global (2011), *São Paulo sob achaque: corrupção, crime organizado e violência institucional em maio de 2006* (n.p., IHRC International Human Rights Clinic and Justiça Global).

Laboratório de Análise da Violência-Universidade Estadual do Rio de Janeiro [LAV-UERJ] (2008), *Análise dos impactos dos ataques do PCC em São Paulo em maio de 2006* (Rio de Janeiro, LAV-UERJ).

Lessa, F., and L. A. Payne (eds) (2012), *Amnesty in the Age of Human Rights Accountability* (Cambridge and New York, Cambridge University Press).

Movimento Mães de Maio (2011), *Mães de Maio: do luto à luta* (São Paulo, Giramundo Artes Gráficas).

Olsen, T. D., L. A. Payne, and A. G. Reiter (2001), *Transitional Justice in Balance: Comparing Processes, Weighing Efficacy* (Washington DC, Institute of Peace Press).

Organization of American States [OAS] (1994), Inter-American Convention on Forced Disappearance of Persons, www.oas.org/juridico/english/treaties/a-60.html#:~:text=forced%20disappearance%20is%20considered%20to%20be%20the%20act,or%20a%20refusal%20to%20acknowledge%20that%20deprivation%20of (accessed 16 February 2021).

Paiva, V., and P. E. da Rocha Pomar (2011), 'Se a ditadura acabou, onde está a democracia? Comissão da verdade sem autonomia atesta pacto entre governo e militares', *Revista Adusp*, 47, 112–17.

Payne, L. A., F. Lessa, and G. Pereira (2015), 'Overcoming Barriers to Justice in the Age of Human Rights Accountability', *Human Rights Quarterly*, 37, 728–54.

Pinheiro, P. S. (1994), 'The Legacy of Authoritarianism in Democratic Brazil', in *Latin American Development and Public Policy*, ed. S. S. Nagel (London, Palgrave Macmillan).

Pinheiro, P. S. (1999), 'O passado não está morto nem passado é ainda', in *Continuidade autoritária e construção da democracia*, ed. P. S. Pinheiro, S. Adorno, N. Cardia, *et al.*, integrated project (Fapesp/CNPq/FFord), final report, 4 vols, www.nevusp.org.

Pinheiro, P. S. (2002), 'The Paradox of Democracy in Brazil', *Brown Journal of World Affairs*, 8:1, 113–22.

Roht-Arriaza, N., and J. Mariezcurrena (2006), *Transitional Justice in the Twenty-First Century: Beyond Truth versus Justice* (Cambridge: Cambridge University Press).

Scott, J. C. (1987), *Weapons of the Weak: Everyday Forms of Peasant Resistance* (New Haven and London, Yale University Press).

Silva, U. V., J. L. Santos, and P. C. Ramos (2019), *Chacinas e a politização das mortes no Brasil* (São Paulo, Fundação Perseu Abramo).

Teles, E. (2015), *Democracia e estado de exceção: transição e memória política no Brasil e na África do Sul* (São Paulo, Editora Fap-Unifesp).

Universidade Federal de São Paulo [Unifesp] and Centro de Antropologia e Arqueologia Forense [CAAF] (2019), *Violência de Estado no Brasil: uma análise dos 'Crimes de Maio' de 2006 na perspectiva da antropologia forense e da justiça de transição. Relatório final* (São Paulo, Universidade Federal de São Paulo), www.unifesp.br/reitoria/caaf/images/novo_site/documentos/Relat%C3%B3rio_-_Crimes_de_Maio.pdf (accessed 31 January 2021).

Waiselfisz, J. J. (2016), *Mapa da violência 2016: homicídios por arma de fogo* (Brasília, Flacso).

Weichert, M. A. (2019), 'As diversas dimensões da violência e sua relação com a perseguição social no Brasil', in *Violência de estado na América Latina: direitos humanos, justiça de transicão e antropologia forense*, ed. J. Amadeo (São Paulo, Editora da Unifesp).

# 8

# Systematic Recurrence of Murders and Disappearances in Democratic Brazil

MARLON ALBERTO WEICHERT*

## Introduction

BRAZIL DURING THE last decade has experienced extremely high levels of lethal violence, which has targeted mostly the black, male, young, and poor population. This violence is perpetrated by both criminal groups and public security forces. There is clear and reliable evidence pointing to an unspoken public policy to persecute that population. This policy can be deduced both from the recurrent omission of state action to adopt effective measures to reduce and prevent systematic deaths, and from the failure of the state to investigate and prosecute the homicides that victimise the population. The state not only remains indifferent toward the killings promoted by criminal gangs, but is also responsible for a significant portion of these deaths. Security forces in Brazil, year after year, have been killing more suspects during police operations, with substantial evidence of the use of summary execution (see Chapter 7).

Recently, what had been a disguised policy began to assume the characteristics of an explicit public policy shaped to justify legally the summary execution of any gun-toting person, notably in the *favelas* and shantytowns. The federal, as well as the Rio de Janeiro and São Paulo state level governments, have adopted a public discourse exempting the police from accountability for the preventive killing of suspects. Bolstering these statements, the federal government has, since 2019, repeatedly offered drafts of law that, once approved, would legalise the preventative murder of suspects during police operations.[1]

*This chapter is an adaptation of an earlier work by the author (Weichert 2017), published with permission from *Sur*.

[1] This chapter was finished in April 2020. By this date, the government, or its supporters in the Congress, have offered, since 2019, nine different drafts of law with provisions that would establish some kind of impunity for security forces or military officials involved in killings of suspects (Drafts of Law 941/

The same phenomenon behind systematic killing is probably influencing the rate of disappearances. Although there is still a lack of research and public data about how many of the approximately 80,000 disappearances every year were the result of a criminal offence, it is not hard to conclude that enforced disappearances are one means used by both criminal gangs and public security forces to eliminate opponents or suspects.[2]

In this chapter, I contend that the systematic murder and disappearance of the civilian population in Brazil may be seen conceptually as a crime against humanity. Even taking into account that the legal definition of crimes against humanity was constructed to deal primarily with serious human rights violations perpetrated against a civilian population during war or authoritarian rule, I argue that it is possible to recognise systematic and widespread attacks against a civilian population in a democratic country. I also defend the view that state failure to curb gang violence may be an indirect policy aimed at mass killings of a specific civil population, an act that would meet one of the core elements of a crime against humanity defined by the Rome Statute. In Brazil, such an omission may be turning into an explicit policy, as referred to above, making clear that the state is willing to persecute part of its own population. This is a theoretical argument. I do not have the evidence regarding the personal responsibility of any individual in the state security apparatus for these acts, as this article is not the place for such an endeavour. The aim of this chapter is to explain in conceptual terms that this particular type of state violence can meet the Rome Statute's definition of systematic attacks directed against a civilian population when state policy encourages – either by commission or omission – those attacks.

## Crimes against Humanity

The concept of crimes against humanity was developed in the ambit of international criminal law after the Second World War in response to the grave violations of human rights perpetrated by the Nazi government in Germany.[3] According to the legal framework in place at that time, the persecution of segments of the civilian population in their own country and by their own government was not punishable as an international crime. The concept of a crime against humanity was then developed for the trial of Nazi leaders to prevent the persecution of national citizens

2019, 2599/2019, 4260/2019, 6125/2019, 132/2020, and 456/2020 before the Lower House, and Drafts of Law 2865/2019, 4640/2019, and 375/2020 before the Senate).

[2] According to the Brazilian Forum for Public Security, 786,071 people were registered as missing between 2007 and 2017. In 2017, 82,684 new cases were registered. It is not clear how many of these missing people were subsequently located, or if the reasons for the disappearance were determined. In 2017, 53,000 individuals' names were removed from the registry (FBSP 2017: 38).

[3] The origins of the concept in fact pre-date the Second World War, with the Treaty of Sèvres, signed after the First World War: notably article 230, which anticipated the creation of an international court to try the massacre of the Armenian people by the Turkish government (World War I Document Archive 2010).

from going unpunished (Fenrick 1999). The first international instrument to establish the concept as a crime was the Statute of the Nuremberg Trials.[4]

This definition was gradually refined, with adjustments, over the course of the second half of the 20th century, until its restatement in article 7 of the Rome Statute, the 1998 treaty that established the International Criminal Court, ratified and promulgated by Brazil in 2002 (President of the Republic of Brazil 2002). The Rome Statute establishes:

> For the purpose of this Statute, 'crime against humanity' means any of the following acts when committed as part of a widespread or systematic attack directed against any civilian population, with knowledge of the attack:
>
> (a) Murder;
> (b) Extermination;
> (c) Enslavement;
> (d) Deportation or forcible transfer of population;
> (e) Imprisonment or other severe deprivation of physical liberty in violation of fundamental rules of international law;
> (f) Torture;
> (g) Rape, sexual slavery, enforced prostitution, forced pregnancy, enforced sterilisation, or any other form of sexual violence of comparable gravity;
> (h) Persecution against any identifiable group or collectivity on political, racial, national, ethnic, cultural, religious, gender as defined in paragraph 3, or other grounds that are universally recognised as impermissible under international law, in connection with any act referred to in this paragraph or any crime within the jurisdiction of the Court;
> (i) Enforced disappearance of persons;
> (j) The crime of apartheid;
> (k) Other inhumane acts of a similar character intentionally causing great suffering, or serious injury to body or to mental or physical health.

Both the summary execution and the enforced disappearance of persons, when committed in the context of a widespread or systematic attack directed against a civilian population, may characterise, according to the Rome Statute, a crime against humanity, as stated in the provisions of items (a) and (i). Other forms of violent persecution against the black and poor civilian population in Brazil, such as illegal imprisonment, and torture, may also match the hypotheses defined by the Rome Statute in article 7, quoted above, (e), (f), and (h).

[4] Article 6 provides: 'The Tribunal established by the Agreement referred to in Article 1 hereof for the trial and punishment of the major war criminals of the European Axis countries shall have the power to try and punish persons who, acting in the interests of the European Axis countries, whether as individuals or as members of organisations, committed any of the following crimes: … (c) CRIMES AGAINST HUMANITY: namely, murder, extermination, enslavement, deportation, and other inhumane acts committed against any civilian population, before or during the war; or persecutions on political, racial or religious grounds in execution of or in connection with any crime within the jurisdiction of the Tribunal, whether or not in violation of the domestic law of the country where perpetrated.' Agreement for the prosecution and punishment of the major criminals of the European Axis, signed at London, on 8 August 1945 (UN Office on Genocide Prevention and the Responsibility to Protect 2020).

In this chapter I maintain that, although the concept of crimes against humanity is more easily connected to contexts of armed conflict and authoritarian regimes (dictatorships), notably because both situations entail a substantial failure of the rule of law, crimes against humanity may also be committed in democracies. Whilst there is a prevalence of democratic governance, remaining authoritarian structures and political groups within the state administration may develop conditions to adopt a systematic or generalised pattern of violence against specific segments of the population. I do not doubt that it is unlikely that such grave crimes may take place in consolidated democracies, but even in long-standing democratic states some authoritarian enclaves may resist the rule of law, and use their political power to persecute a specific civilian population. This risk is greater in states that are in the midst of a transition from authoritarianism or have a weak and incomplete democracy, such as Brazil, in which there is a persistent lack of institutional reform and other initiatives of transitional justice (Weichert 2019). I recognise that this statement raises some complex questions whose answers would demand a discussion of various concepts of democracy and would need to address the seeming paradox that a state that perpetrates international crimes could be considered a democratic one. However, I will not discuss these stormy issues here, which would demand the analysis of elements and examples that extend beyond the focus and length of this single chapter.

## Killings of Black Youths in Brazil

Between 2004 and 2007, approximately 206,000 people were victims of homicide in Brazil, the same figure as in 62 armed conflicts around the world and much higher than the Mexican examples referred to in this book (Chapters 4 and 16) and by others (Open Society Justice Initiative 2019).[5]

These rates are particularly alarming in Brazil, 'a country without conflict over religion or ethnicity, colour or race, without territorial or frontier disputes, without civil war or violent political confrontation'(Waiselfisz 2012a). It nonetheless 'manages to slaughter more citizens than most of the armed conflicts in the world' (Waiselfisz 2012a). In fact, according to World Health Organization (WHO) data, in 2012, Brazil was responsible for about 13.5 per cent of all homicides committed in the world (although it represents 2.8 per cent of the world's population) and about 39 per cent of those perpetrated in Latin American countries.[6] The country is the seventh most violent in the world, after El Salvador, Trinidad and Tobago, Colombia,

[5] According to *Map of Violence 2014 – Homicides and Youth in Brazil*, there were 206,005 homicide victims in Brazil and 208,349 deaths in armed conflict (Waiselfisz 2014).

[6] The WHO data for Brazil are different than the Brazilian Forum for Public Security (FBSP) and the *Map of Violence* data, on which the research for this chapter is based. They are included here for comparison with other countries from a single source. The WHO reports 474,000 murders in the world in 2012, and 165,617 in the countries of the Americas classified as having low or average income. Brazil had 64,357 homicides. This figure is higher than the number published by the FBSP (50,241). See World Health Organization (2014: 138).

the Virgin Islands (USA), Guatemala, and Venezuela, all countries located in Latin America and the Caribbean. Brazil is considered the 'champion' of deaths by homicides among the twelve most populous countries (Waiselfisz 2014: 94).

The deaths and disappearances in Brazil are selective. According to the Fórum Brasileiro de Segurança Pública (Brazilian Forum for Public Security; FBSP), in 2015, 54 per cent of victims of violent death were young people (FBSP 2016, 6). The 2015 *Map of Violence* research confirmed this panorama and showed that in 2012, 285 per cent more young people (15–29 years old) were victims of homicide than older groups. In other words, 'for every person who is not young and who dies, around four young people die' (Waiselfisz 2015: 65). It is also selective in terms of skin colour, as 73 per cent of fatal victims are non-whites (*preto* or *pardo*) (FBSP 2016: 6).[7]

In short, poor black youths are overrepresented among deaths; they make up 41 per cent of all cases of violent death (Amnesty International Brazil 2015 – using 2012 data). A non-white (black or brown) youth has approximately 2.5 times more risk of being killed than a white youth (Waiselfisz 2012b),[8] while 51 per cent of the entire population (not only youths) in the country is non-white (Ministry of Justice 2015: 50). The May Crimes of 2006, discussed in the previous two chapters, provide one such example.

State violence is an important component of the lethal violence in the country. In 2017, police killed 5,159 civilians: more than 14 people per day, 8.1 per cent of the total number of deaths (FBSP 2018: 6). Although qualitative analyses of the national scope are not available on the profile of victims of state violence, a recent study carried out in the municipality of São Paulo showed that 64 per cent of deaths in police interventions were of black people,[9] although black people represent only 37 per cent of the municipal population (Sinhoretto *et al.* 2016). Furthermore, 85 per cent of those killed are young people, under 30 years of age. Of every 100,000 young people who lived in the city, 21 were killed by the police in 2014. The rate for those over 30 years old is 2 per 100,000 inhabitants.

These data refer to homicides. But there are many reasons to consider that disappearances are used by both criminal gangs and security force members to disguise killings and summary executions. That is, the bodies of those killed are not always found or identified, preventing investigation into the facts, as described in the chapters about the May Crimes of 2006 in this book. Disappearances are aimed at covering up the crime and, often, the direct involvement or complicity of state agents in the crime.

The most severe violence in Brazil, either resulting from general criminality or from state intervention, therefore, targets practically the same segment

[7] Black (*preto*) and brown (*pardo*) are used by the Brazilian Institute of Geography and Statistics as official categories of race and colour in the Brazilian national census.

[8] 2010 data. The category 'black' used in this report represents a combination of the categories 'black' and 'brown'.

[9] The rate of the black population killed by the police is 11:100,000, while the white population ratio is 4:100,000.

of society – the young, black, poor population. The vulnerability of these youths has been highlighted by a number of social sectors as a silent 'genocide'.[10] The National Congress, by means of the Parliamentary Commission of Inquiry within the Chamber of Deputies and the Federal Senate, have made this reference.

The Parliamentary Commission of Inquiry in the Chamber of Deputies, assigned to ascertain the causes, reasons, consequences, and social and economic costs of violence, death, and disappearance of young, black, poor people in Brazil, known as the 'Parliamentary Commission of Inquiry on Violence against Young, Black, Poor People', concluded in its report published in July 2015, that:

> The statistics and arguments on the myth of institutional racial cordiality, previously presented, provide the context and indicators that poor, black people in this country, particularly its youth, have been victim of a particular, different type of genocide.
>
> The crime as detailed in the 1956 Law, no. 2889, which led to the consolidation of the provisions of the International Convention on the Prevention and Punishment of the Crime of Genocide, established in Paris on 11 December 1948 at the Third Session of the General Assembly of the United Nations (Decree no. 30.822 of 1952) cannot legally be cited. Here follows sociological recognition, testifying to the outrage at the unfettered killing of young, black, poor people in Brazil and the condemnation of this population in the absence of policies to foster their well-being.
>
> [...]
>
> The genocide encountered by this Commission is the symbolic killing of an entire group in the midst of an absurd number of actual deaths. (Chamber of Deputies 2015)

Similarly, the Federal Senate's Parliamentary Commission of Inquiry on 'Youth Murder' concluded in its Final Report, presented in June 2016, that:

> We have verified through the work of the Commission that, although Brazil stands out for the total number of homicides among young people, and that violence has spread to all cities and all social groups, there is a preferred victim, the number of deaths in this group being startling and worrying.
>
> From the outset the Commission encountered a cruel and undeniable reality: the Brazilian state is directly or indirectly provoking the genocide of the young black population. Once the work was completed, all the public hearings had been carried out, and all the specialists had been heard and numerous documents collected, this bleak picture became clear and we could not find any national or regional public policy aimed at analysing and changing it. (Federal Senate 2016: 145–6)

In weighing this grave scenario, it does not seem – in light of international law, the Convention on the Prevention and Punishment of the Crime of Genocide of 1948, and the Rome Statute – that the situation described falls strictly into the legal definition of genocide as action taken 'with the intention to destroy, entirely or in part, one national, ethnic, racial or religious group'. Although the systematic murder of poor people on the city peripheries is evident, it is not clear that these killings

[10] The alarming level of homicide among black youths motivated Amnesty International's Brazilian branch to launch the 'Young, Black, Alive' campaign (Roque 2014).

constitute an 'intention to destroy an ethnic or racial group', thus posing an obstacle to defining these acts as an international crime.

There are, however, serious reasons for concern in terms of the Brazilian authorities' repeated failure to act to prevent an obvious and systematic pattern of violent acts against this civilian population. In this sense, this situation is evolving into one that could be defined as a crime against humanity.

## Brazilian Killings and Disappearances as Crimes against Humanity

As shown, the Rome Statute defines a crime against humanity as any act of homicide or of violent persecution of a group or community that can be identified as for political or racial reasons, or on the basis of other criteria universally recognised as unacceptable in international law, committed as part of a widespread or systematic attack directed against any civilian population. Article 7, para. 2 states that:

> (a) 'Attack directed against any civilian population' means a course of conduct involving the multiple commission of acts referred to in paragraph 1 against any civilian population, pursuant to or in furtherance of a State or organisational policy to commit such attack;
> [...]
> (g) 'Persecution' means the intentional and severe deprivation of fundamental rights contrary to international law by reason of the identity of the group or collectivity[.]
>
> (United Nations General Assembly 1998)

According to the jurisprudence of the International Criminal Court (see Chapter 16), these definitions indicate that the following requirements must be present in order to define a crime against humanity: (a) an attack directed against a civilian population, (b) a state or organisational policy, (c) that the attack is widespread or systematic, (d) a connection between the individual act and the attack, and (e) knowledge of the attack by the agent (International Criminal Court 2010: 32, para. 79).

It is not within the scope of this chapter to carry out an extensive analysis of the definition cited here, or of its relevance to the actual situation of Brazilian state violence. However, it should be noted that the repetition of homicides and other violent acts faced by the poor, predominantly black youth[11] in large Brazilian cities appears to represent a systematic pattern of persecution against that population.[12] In the

[11] According to the Institute of Applied Economic Research (IPEA 2011: 35), in 2009, among the poorest 10 per cent of the Brazilian population, black people constituted 72 per cent.

[12] Note that in defining crime against humanity, attack may be either widespread or systematic. These elements are disjunctive. As affirmed by the ICC, 'the underlying logic of this concept is 'to separate isolated, random acts from the notion of crimes against humanity' (International Criminal Court 2010: 40–1, para. 94).

wording of the International Criminal Court, 'systematic' refers to the 'organised nature of acts of violence and the unlikelihood that they are random occurrences'. It goes on to say that a systematic attack can often be identified in the practice of a pattern of crimes, in the sense that the regular repetition of similar criminal conduct is not accidental (International Criminal Court 2010: 42, para. 96). In the case under examination, the violent deaths of black and brown youths appear to fit the 'systematic' criterion, especially when one considers a figure of approximately 20,000 of these youths dead per year, partially direct victims of the state.

The term 'attack' is not restricted to military operations. The International Criminal Court understands this term to refer to a situation in which the multiple commission of violent acts as described in article 7(1) of the Rome Statute involves, in other words, a campaign or operation carried out against the civilian population. Victims of the attack may be groups that can be identified according to nationality, ethnicity, or some other distinguishing feature (International Criminal Court 2010: 80–1, para. 33), which could include the category of youths who are killed in poor neighbourhoods or on the outskirts of Brazilian cities, which are largely inhabited by black and brown people.

Finally, there is an essential requirement that conduct is in accordance with, or complies with, a state or organisational policy, in committing the attack (International Criminal Court 2010: 34, para. 83). When the International Criminal Court applies this rule, it has been decided that the policy does not necessarily need to be expressed, precisely or clearly. It can be inferred by the occurrence of a series of events, *inter alia* (a) a generic history of circumstances and a wide political context within which the crimes are committed; (b) coordinated military offensives, repeated in a temporal and geographical way; and (c) the scale of acts of violence perpetrated among others (International Criminal Court 2010: 37, para. 87).[13]

In September 2002 the Assembly of States Parties defined the 'Elements of Crimes' of the Rome Statute and, on the topic of the policy to commit an attack, highlighted that this clause requires that the state or an organisation actively promote or encourage such attacks. However, in a footnote the Assembly of States Parties noted that, in exceptional circumstances, this policy may be implemented by omission. The simple omission by the absence of action would not be sufficient but rather would be a deliberate failure to act, which would consciously prompt the said attack. In any case, '[t]he existence of such a policy cannot be inferred solely from the absence of governmental or organisational action' (International Criminal Court 2001).[14]

In the case of Brazil, it is relevant to note that two Parliamentary Commissions of Inquiry in the National Congress point to the failure of the state to curb violence

[13] The report contains 11 different possible definitions of the policy.

[14] As article 7, n. 6 states: 'Such a policy may, in exceptional circumstances, be implemented by a deliberate failure to take action, which is consciously aimed at encouraging such attack. The existence of such a policy cannot be inferred solely from the absence of governmental or organisational action.'

against black youths, as well as the occurrence of the systematic execution of this population by agents of public security forces. The same point was made by the National Council for Human Rights, a collegiate body, created by law to function as a guardian of human rights at a national level.[15] Federal and state governments also receive frequent demands and complaints from civil society on these incidents and on the systematic practice of extermination and imprisonment of this population.

After these inquiries, and also taking into consideration all the data collected regarding the violent death of young black people, state authorities cannot argue ignorance about the occurrence of violent persecution. These authorities have the legal duty to act and have consistently failed to adopt specific measures to curb such situations. This persistent, repeated failure reveals a tolerance toward this violent persecution, or, in the language of the International Criminal Court, a deliberate failure to take action to change this scenario. It is quite clear that this failure, or acquiescence, as discussed by Barbara A. Frey in Chapter 2, produces the effect of encouraging and feeding into the spiral of violence. A policy of non-action exists and is often disguised in the reinforcement of strategies that have proved either to be ineffective or to compound the situation. The death of a black youth, usually poor, seems to be less important to public authorities. Failure to act in the face of such a serious, known situation is a political option.

The continued failure by the authorities to foster changes in policies on crime, public security and justice, or in the way these are carried out, could be seen as representing a deliberate decision to maintain a policy of persecution of the young, poor/black civil population, according to the interpretation of the 'Elements of Crimes' and the jurisprudence of the International Criminal Court. Therefore, this persistent failure to act could qualify – little by little – as a policy to encourage the continuity of violent, systematic attacks on a civil population, approaching the definition in article 7(1) and (2) of the Rome Statute and interpreted by the States Parties in the document 'Elements of Crimes'.

But it may be even more serious. It must be taken into consideration that, since 2019, the federal government – which changed hands in the 2018 election – has argued that police officers should not be accountable for murders and other violent crimes committed on duty. More than one draft law was presented by the president to the Congress proposing that policemen be allowed to shoot and kill a suspect to prevent an imminent crime from occurring. The president himself is very proud of empowering the police to kill any 'bandit' (for him, a 'good bandit is a dead bandit').[16]

Even without this kind of legal provision, it is clear that summary execution is increasing, at least in Rio de Janeiro and São Paulo. In the first three months of

[15] See, for example, the recommendation issued by the National Council of Human Rights, considered at the Third Ordinary Meeting on 12 and 13 March 2015.

[16] 'A policeman who doesn't kill isn't a policeman', Bolsonaro stated in a public event hosted by *Veja* magazine (Galhardo 2017).

2019, the security forces in Rio de Janeiro killed 434 civilians, 20 per cent more than in 2018 for the same period of time. In São Paulo, the police were responsible for 203 deaths in the first three months of 2019, an increase of 5 per cent compared to 2018. Indeed, both governors also defend tough – *mano dura* – policies and violent confrontation to curb criminality. In Rio de Janeiro, the governor has gone further and has determined that the security forces train snipers to eliminate rifle-toting people in the *favelas*.

## Conclusion

Prior to 2019 there was no evidence to prove that the Brazilian state – or organisations tolerated by it – had an active policy systematically to persecute the civilian population or black youths. There was no indication that high-level public agents incited or disseminated this type of state intervention. But, based on the reluctance to investigate the murder of such populations and to develop policies to curb this violence, combined with the overwhelming rate of killings at the hands of state actors, it was already possible to argue that an unspoken policy to persecute the young, black, and poor population was in place. The persistence of such a scenario confirms the conclusion that a deliberate decision not to act was taken to facilitate or stimulate the systematic attack against that sector of the civilian population, under the guise of the inability of the State to prevent the violence. In this case, a pattern of crimes against humanity meets the Elements of Crimes provisions of the Rome Statute, characterised as a 'policy by omission'.

Since 2019, however, there is evidence that government authorities at the federal level, and in some states, such as Rio de Janeiro, are willing to adopt a clear policy of killing suspects of crimes: basically small-scale drug dealers, who are black, young, and inhabitants of the poor periphery of the cities. It is still early to conduct a more precise analysis of this situation, but there are concerns that Brazil may be ostensibly crossing the threshold of crimes against humanity. What had been a masked policy of omission may be taking shape instead as a clear and intentional decision to perpetrate international crimes, at least with regard to the summary execution, combined with enforced disappearance, of criminal suspects. Although this issue is just part of the widespread killings and disappearance of the black, male, poor, and young population, it may suffice to meet the requirement of a state policy to commit a systematic attack against a civil population, as established in the Rome Statute and in the Elements of Crimes.

## References

Amnesty International Brazil (2015), 'Jovem Negro Vivo!' 'Young, Black, Alive' (Rio de Janeiro: Amnesty International Brazil), https://anistia.org.br/campanhas/jovemnegrovivo/ (accessed 29 April 2020).

Chamber of Deputies (2015), 'Final Report of the Parliamentary Commission for the Homicide Inquiry of Young, Black, Poor People', July (Brasília, Chamber of Deputies), https://goo.gl/rS3Wkd (accessed 25 September 2016).

Federal Senate (2016), 'Final Parliamentary Commission for Youth Murder Inquiry' (8 June) (Brasília, Federal Senate), www12.senado.leg.br/noticias/arquivos/2016/06/08/veja-aintegra-do-relatorio-da-cpi-do-assassinato-de-jovens (accessed 25 September 2016).

Fenrick, W. J. (1999), 'Should Crimes against Humanity Replace War Crimes?', *Columbia Journal of Transnational Law*, 37:3, 767–85.

Fórum Brasileiro de Segurança Pública [FBSP] (2016), 'Anuário Brasileiro de Segurança Pública 2016' (São Paulo, Brasilian Forum for Public Security).

Fórum Brasileiro de Segurança Pública [FBSP] (2017), 'Anuário Brasileiro de Segurança Pública 2017' (São Paulo, Brasilian Forum for Public Security).

Fórum Brasileiro de Segurança Pública [FBSP] (2018), 'Anuário Brasileiro de Segurança Pública 2018' (São Paulo, Brasilian Forum for Public Security).

Galhardo, R. (2017), '"Policial que não mata não é policial', diz Bolsonaro"', *Estadão*, 27 November, https://politica.estadao.com.br/noticias/geral,policial-que-nao-mata-nao-e-policial-diz-bolsonaro,70002098866 (accessed 13 May 2019).

Instituto de Pesquisa Econômica [IPEA] (2011), 'Retrato das desigualdades de gênero e raça', 4th edn (Brasília, Instituto de Pesquisa Econômica Aplicada *et al.*).

International Criminal Court (2001), 'Elements of Crimes', 1 February (The Hague, International Criminal Court), www.iccnow.org/documents/ElementsofCrimes_English.pdf (accessed 21 May 2017).

International Criminal Court (2010), 'Decision Pursuant to Article 15 of the Rome Statute on the Authorisation of an Investigation into the Situation in the Republic of Kenya', 31 March (The Hague, International Criminal Court), www.icc-cpi.int/pages/record.aspx?uri=854287 (accessed 21 May 2017).

Ministry of Justice (2015), 'National Research on Penitentiary Information – INFOPEN – June 2014' (Brasilia, Ministry of Justice), www.justica.gov.br/noticias/mj-divulgara-novo-relatoriodo-infopen-nesta-terca-feira/relatorio-depenversao-web.pdf (accessed 21 May 2017).

Open Society Justice Initiative (2019), 'Undeniable Atrocities – Confronting Crimes against Humanity in Mexico', in collaboration with Comisión para la Defensa y Promoción de Derechos Humanos, Centro Diocesano para los Derechos Humanos Fray Juan de Larios, I(dh)eas Litígios Estratégicos en Derechos Humanos, Fundación para la Justicia y el Estado Democrático de Derecho, and Ciudadanos en Apoyo a los Derechos Humanos – CADHAC, www.opensocietyfoundations.org/sites/default/files/undenialble-atrocities-2nd-edition-20160808.pdf (accessed 13 May 2019).

President of the Republic of Brazil (2002), 'Decreto nº 4.388, de 25 de Setembro de 2002', www.planalto.gov.br/ccivil_03/decreto/2002/D4388.htm (accessed 21 May 2017).

Roque, A. (2014), 'Young, Black, Alive: Breaking the Silence on Brazil's Soaring Youth Homicide Rate' Amnesty International Brazil, www.amnesty.org/en/latest/campaigns/2014/11/young-black-alive-breaking-the-silence-on-brazils-soaring-youth-homicide-rate/ (accessed 6 February 2021).

Sinhoretto, J., M. C. Schlittler, and G. Silvestre (2016), 'Juventude e violência policial no município de São Paulo', *Revista Brasileira de Segurança Pública*, 10:1 (February–March), 10–35.

United Nations [UN] General Assembly (1998), Rome Statute of the International Criminal Court (last Amended 2010), 17 July 1998, www.refworld.org/docid/3ae6b3a84.html (accessed 19 March 2021).

UN Office on Genocide Prevention and the Responsibility to Protect (2020), 'Agreement for the Prosecution and Punishment of the Major War Criminals of the Europe Axis (Nuremberg Tribunal Statute)' (New York, UN Office on Genocide Prevention and the Responsibility to Protect), www.un.org/en/genocideprevention/documents/atrocity-crimes/Doc.2_Charter%20of%20IMT%201945.pdf (accessed 29 April 2020).

Waiselfisz, J. J. (2012a), *Map of Violence 2012 – New Patterns of Violent Murder in Brazil* (Brasília, Instituto Sangari), www.mapadaviolencia.net.br/pdf2012/MapaViolencia2012_atual_mulheres.pdf (accessed 21 May 2017).

Waiselfisz, J. J. (2012b), *2012 Map of Violence – The Colour of Homicide in Brazil* (Brasília, CEBELA, FLACSO, Secretary for Policies for the Promotion of Racial Equality for the Presidency of the Republic), www.mapadaviolencia.net.br/pdf2012/mapa2012_cor.pdf (accessed 21 May 2017).

Waiselfisz, J. J. (2014), *Map of Violence 2014 – Homicides and Youth in Brazil* (Brasília, Secretary General of the Presidency of the Republic), www.mapadaviolencia.org.br/pdf2014/Mapa2014_JovensBrasil_Preliminar.pdf (accessed 21 May 2017).

Waiselfisz, J. J. (2015), *2015 Map of Violence – Death by Fire Arms* (Brasília, Secretary General of the Presidency of the Republic), www.mapadaviolencia.org.br/pdf2015/mapaViolencia2015.pdf (accessed 21 May 2017).

Weichert, M. A. (2017), 'Crimes against Humanity in a Democratic Context', *SUR International Journal on Human Rights*, 14:25, 207–17.

Weichert, M. A. (2019), 'The Outcomes of the Brazilian Truth Commission: Successes and Failures in a Lengthy Transitional Justice Process', in *The Brazilian Truth Commission: Local, National and Global Perspectives* (New York and Oxford, Berghahn), ed. N. Schneider, pp. 382–426.

World Health Organization (2014), 'Global Status Report on Violence Prevention 2014' (Geneva, World Health Organization), http://apps.who.int/iris/handle/10665/145086 (accessed 21 May 2017).

World War I Document Archive (2010), The Treaty of Sèvres, 1920 (Provo, Brigham Young University Library), http://wwi.lib.byu.edu/index.php/Section_I%2C_Articles_1_-_260 (accessed 28 April 2020).

# Argentina

# 9

# Letters for Santiago

SERGIO MALDONADO, GERMÁN MALDONADO, STELLA PELOSO, AND ENRIQUE MALDONADO

## Introduction

SANTIAGO MALDONADO DISAPPEARED on 1 August 2017. In the days before his disappearance, Maldonado had been involved in the *Pu Lof en Resistencia* community protests, a Mapuche indigenous peoples' land struggle with the Benetton Company. He disappeared following violence that had erupted during clashes between the protesters and the gendarmerie.

Maldonado's body was found in the Chubut River and identified on 20 October 2017. The court decision on the cause of death remains in dispute. Judge Gustavo Lleral ruled that there was no crime, contending that 'Maldonado drowned due to immersion in water aggravated by hypothermia' (Perez 2019). Although efforts to remove the 'enforced disappearance' claim and redesignate the case as 'suspicious death' failed, the details of Maldonado's drowning, and particularly the role that the gendarmerie may have played, remain undetermined.

The case was filed with international judicial bodies. During Maldonado's disappearance, the UN Committee on Enforced Disappearances called on the Argentine state to carry out an urgent and comprehensive search, to take testimony from the Pu Lof Mapuche community members present at the protests, to remove the gendarmerie from any role in the investigation and search, and to guarantee the protection of all evidence. The Inter-American Commission of Human Rights (IACHR) further called on the government to pursue a rigorous search and to report on all steps taken in the investigation. The UN and the IACHR closed their cases in January 2018 several months after the body was found.

However, the judicial fight to know the truth continues. Santiago Maldonado's family rejected the closure of the case ordered by the federal judge in charge after finding him dead, and appealed this decision to the Commodore Rivadavia Court of Appeals. On 5 September 2019, the Appeals Chamber of Comodoro Rivadavia (Chubut) ordered the reopening of the case in order to establish state responsibility for the events, although the charge of the forced disappearance of Santiago was removed. Sergio Maldonado, Santiago's brother, is in the process of bringing a legal challenge to this decision.

## Open Letter from Sergio Maldonado, Brother

**Santiago,**

Wherever you are, I want you to know that I love you. Each day that passes I miss you more. I need you to appear soon; I can't stop thinking of you. Each day that passes I cry even more for you and I wonder: why it is you who is going through this and not me. The answer is obvious: I never got involved in different causes like you have.

People like you teach us, you open our eyes, you show us the path, but you also show the evidence of human misery. I hope you can hear me and understand the delay in finding you. It is not because I am not looking for you or that there are people who don't care about you. It's the complete opposite. There are a lot of people who love you without ever having known you. Many people are here, in the plaza, and in many plazas in the country and the world, making demands on your behalf.

To see your face everywhere, always with your smile, makes me very proud. But it also makes me feel sad and helpless, because you are not here with us. There are a lot of interests getting in the way, and you would ask: are these interests more important than my life or the life of any other person? And I would answer yes, sadly, for some these interests are more important than the disappearance of a person in the hands of a state [security] force.

For them, we are only a number, a statistic, a data point. But we people, we are sons, we are brothers, we are friends. We are people with rights, people who demand justice. Santiago, I am looking for you. I will continue and keep searching for you. Besides intuiting where they might have you, it is difficult to locate you.

When this nightmare began, our brother Germán wrote a letter titled 'Letter to a Good Gendarme'. And he asked for the gendarmerie to collaborate [in your search]. I have to confess that I was excited, I believed that this could lead to your rapid reappearance. Now I am convinced that there is no good will on the part of the gendarmerie; none of those officials who participated in the repression of the Mapuche community have any good will. Along with the ministers, judges, and prosecutors, they only look after their own interests.

I am not sure how long it is going to take to find you, until we find the truth.

I know it probably would have been different if you had stayed at home and had not gone out making claims on behalf of the unprotected, for just causes, for the original [indigenous] peoples. But I am not going to get stuck in these details. Every day I come back to ask where you are.

Is it so hard to ask for them to return you to us? I want *los viejos* [our parents], our grandmother, and all of our family to stop suffering, for this nightmare to end.

I would like to ask the top authority in our country, Mr President Mauricio Macri and all of his ministers, I want to ask them: where is Santiago Maldonado?

(S. Maldonado 2017)

## Public Statement from Germán Maldonado, Brother

I want to take this moment to make very clear three issues that have us worried and fed up. First is the communication media, which likes to play around with producing fake news. We are up to our eyeballs with this kind of news, which is totally disrespectful of Santiago, his family, his friends, and all of the people involved in legitimate demands. Gentlemen of the news media and social commentators: be a little more professional, investigate, use reliable sources of information. You cannot imagine the harm you cause when you generate false reports that people consume in your newspapers, dailies, newscasts, radio programmes, and internet sites, and then repeat like parrots, all of your *barrabasadas* [absurdities], which have as their only purpose the creation of discord, controversy, and animosity within society, which are then repeated every day in family, workplace, and institutional settings. Have a little more *amor propio* [reverence] for your profession and yourselves, don't let them use you like puppets for a couple of bucks; we ask that you have a little more *gollete* [backbone], respect, and journalistic professionalism.

The second theme: some of those politicians that babble on about democracy, transparency, truth, and honesty, and then go to the communications media, to the Senate, and to other sites of public and political life to say that 'the Maldonado family is politicising Santiago's disappearance', as if some political parties and human rights organisations do not want Santiago to appear. To all of you, *zánganos del Estado* [drones of the state], parasites feeding on the proletariat: first and foremost, the Maldonado family have never been militants of any political party and, second, this has been a political issue since its beginning, from the moment that the gendarmerie took my brother. Because this institution is under government control, that makes you, the politicians in charge, responsible for the disappearance of my brother. This is the real politicisation. This is what should be revealed to Argentine society. Indeed, I ask myself, where are you, I don't see you, the politicians who want Santiago to reappear? Has anyone seen Carrió out there? I haven't seen her. Have you seen Peña? Michetti? Macri? Vidal? Bullrich?[1] Those who say that they want him to appear never come here to give their support, not anywhere; they never call. In these two months I have never seen them at any march lending support. Those who don't want him to appear, you are a *manga de mentirosos* [swarm of liars], *infames políticos de cuarta* [dishonourable politicians], who only get involved to discredit all of the supporters who are asking for a humane response, like all of those who are here and everywhere throughout the country. You are responsible, *caras de piedra* [stone faced ones]: take charge and *dejen de tirar el fardo a los demás* [stop passing the buck]. [Head of National Security, Patricia] Bullrich, you said in the Senate a couple of weeks ago how easy it is to throw a gendarme out of the window. Now, besides throwing the two gendarmes out of the window, they are going to have to throw a couple of squadrons out of the window, and you should also throw yourself out, and this way you do a favour to society by [taking responsibility for] your cover-up of assassins.

[1] These names refer to the following politicians: Elisa Carrió, congresswoman from Buenos Aires; Marcos Peña, the Chief of Staff during President Macri's administration; Vice-President Gabriela Michetti during the Macri administration; President Mauricio Macri (2015–19); María Eugenia Vidal, governor of the Province of Buenos Aires (2015–19); and Patricia Bullrich, Minister of Security in the Macri administration.

And, third, we want Santiago to appear once and for all. It is embarrassing what is happening in this society in relation to human rights, that after forty years we must say 'Santiago Maldonado present, now, and forever'.[2] We are repeating history. If we continue like this we are going to end up on our knees, kissing the hands of the feudal lords. If we want a just society, we are going to have to take the time to reconsider what kind of society we want to build for ourselves and our children.

I want to thank everyone for supporting us, everyone who is here, always supporting us on all sides. Also all the people in different cities of the world. Thank you with all my heart.

(G. Maldonado 2017)

## Open Letter from Sergio Maldonado, Brother

Santiago, yesterday, on 20 October, I was able to say goodbye to you; *me dejaste parte de tu corazón* [you left me a piece of your heart]. Wherever you are with your soul, I hope that you have witnessed everything that has happened in the last 80 days, all of the people who got to know you, who love you, who mobilised for you, and who raised awareness about you.

I feel as if you are gone, but you left behind for me many brothers and sisters, friends, mothers, fathers, grandparents, cousins. In this way, it was all so unjust, but necessary for making all of us reconsider a lot of things.

*Donde quieras que estés, seguí siendo Santiago. Que nada te detenga, que sigas tu camino* [Wherever you are right now, please continue being Santiago. Let nothing stop you, follow your path].

*Siento que esto tengo que compartirlo con toda la gente que nos ayudó a encontrarte y ayudará a que sepamos la verdad y se haga justiciar* [I feel a lot of sorrow, anguish, pain, anger, and pride for being your brother. I don't have any more words, I only want to thank you for being among one of the many we are looking for. I feel that this is what I have to share with everyone who helped us to find you and it will help in knowing the truth and seeking justice].

I hope that all of the guilty pay for what they did to you and that you can rest in peace. For you and with you always,

I love you so much,

Sergio

(*CNN Español* 2017)

## Open Letter from Stella Peloso and Enrique Maldonado, Parents

To all citizens of Argentina and the world, from our deepest pain as parents of Santiago, we want to thank you for every word of strength, every letter, every hug, and your tears that touched our hearts.

[2] This is the chant used ever since the Argentine dictatorship to remember those who have disappeared.

Our days, our life, have been broken, all we have left is the profound pain of having lost our beloved son.

We remember Santiago smiling, singing, drawing, tattooing, because that is what he did in our home, we hold on to the trips he took, his funny stories, his interminable calls despite the distance, always present, always witty, always supportive.

With each passing day we miss not being able to call him and hear his voice.

Our pain is infinite, and infinite is our thanks to all.

Pelos and Maldonado (2017)

## References

CNN Español (2017), 'La emotive carta a Santiago Maldonado de parte de su hermano', *CNN Español* (21 October), https://cnnespanol.cnn.com/2017/10/21/la-emotiva-carta-a-santiago-maldonado-de-parte-de-su-hermano/ (accessed 22 April 2020).

Maldonado, G. (2017), 'Discurso de Germán Maldonado el 1-10-2017', #JUSTICIAPOR-SANTIAGO, www.santiagomaldonado.com/discurso-german-maldonado-1-10-2017/ (accessed 22 April 2017).

Maldonado, S. (2017), 'Carta a Santiago', #JUSTICIAPORSANTIAGO, www.santiagomaldonado.com/carta-a-santiago/ (accessed 22 April 2020).

Peloso, S., and E. Maldonado (2017), 'Carta de agradecimiento de los padres de Santiago', #JUSTICIAPORSANTIAGO, www.santiagomaldonado.com/carta-agradecimiento-los-padres-santiago/ (accessed 22 April 2020).

Perez, L. (2019), 'Two Years On, the Death of Santiago Maldonado Opens Old Wounds for Argentina' *Front Line Defenders* (1 August), www.frontlinedefenders.org/en/blog/post/two-years-death-santiago-maldonado-opens-old-wounds-argentina (accessed 22 April 2020).

# 10

# Disappearances in Post-Transitional Argentina: A Challenge for Human Rights Interventions

NATALIA FEDERMAN, MARCELA PERELMAN, MICHELLE CAÑAS COMAS, AND GASTÓN CHILLIER*

## Introduction

THIS CHAPTER AIMS to evaluate and share the gained knowledge on disappearances in Argentina in a democratic context. The widespread enforced disappearances that took place under state terrorism and the cases of police brutality and disappearances that have occurred since the democratic recovery have prompted us to consider the contrasts and the continuities on this issue, if any, between the last dictatorship (1976–83) and democratic rule.

This knowledge comes from different sources. For almost 40 years, the Centro de Estudios Legales y Sociales (Centre for Legal and Social Studies; CELS) has researched and litigated enforced disappearance and other crimes that involve state officials. It has worked with a network of activists and a wide range of human rights scholars to consider underlying structural inequality related to these crimes and to patterns of impunity. The critical reflections presented here are the result of an ongoing dialogue among the authors, who represent different backgrounds and approaches to the question. Gastón Chillier, Michelle Cañas Comas, and Marcela Perelman are members of CELS, and Natalia Federman has worked in public policy related to enforced disappearances. The primary source material and analysis presented here emerge from her ongoing doctoral research.

The evidence gathered from legal and policy fields reveals that there are disappearances in which the state is involved in some way but that, nevertheless, do not strictly constitute enforced disappearances, according to the narrow legal definition of the convention as set out in Chapter 2. Such cases may have similar

*The authors would like to thank Ximena Tordini for her careful reading and insightful suggestions.

effects to those that are recognised as enforced disappearances: families' mourning process is hindered, their rights to the enjoyment of the highest attainable standard of physical and mental health are affected, the right to the truth cannot be guaranteed, and access to justice is not ensured, amongst other human rights violations. Therefore, the human rights movement faces the challenge of developing an agenda demanding that when a disappearance occurs the response of the state will establish – and not obstruct – the ultimate fate or whereabouts of the missing person swiftly, and ensure an effective investigation, the verification of facts, and the prosecution of those responsible.

This chapter begins by explaining the challenges that disappearances present in the current democratic context in Argentina. We then set out the scenario of everyday police brutality and harassment that builds the framework in which an extraordinary event such as a disappearance may occur. We describe two cases of disappearance: Luciano Arruga in 2009 and Santiago Maldonado in 2017. We have selected these two cases for analysis not because they are the only ones that occurred since 1983 in Argentina or because they fit the strict legal definition of an enforced disappearance. On the contrary, the outcome of both cases has allowed the fate of the victims to be ascertained and their bodies found, though the details that surrounded their deaths remain undetermined. Both experiences allow us to pinpoint the challenges human rights interventions face when the disappearances occur in the current democratic context, despite Argentina's history of systematic enforced disappearances during the dictatorship and the notable performance of the judiciary in investigating and prosecuting those crimes committed during the era of state terrorism. We subsequently present the leading role that the victims' families have played in demanding accountability for the disappearances, and the struggle they face in doing so. Then we review the responses of the state to cases of alleged enforced disappearances and their lack of compliance with human rights standards. We describe institutional flaws that we have identified that enable disappearances. Finally, we conclude with reflections on the proven inability or reluctance of the Argentine political and judicial system to care adequately for victims and their families. Specifically, the state has proved unwilling to, or incapable of, investigating the the victims's allegations and confirming or ruling out the responsibility of state agents to establish the facts using scientific procedures.

## Systematic Enforced Disappearances and the Democratic Transition

### A Brief Contextualisation

It is well known that after the *coup d'état* in 1976 the Argentine dictatorship issued its National Security Doctrine, which implemented the systematic practice of enforced disappearances aimed at political opponents. Kidnappings were carried out by military and security forces; those abducted were held captive in a network of clandestine detention centres without any record of their arrests; they were tortured and in many cases executed; and their bodies were disappeared. They were thrown from military planes into the river or the sea, or buried in clandestine mass graves or in anonymous 'no name' tombs in cemeteries.

Human rights organisations documented disturbing similarities in the accounts of the eyewitnesses to the abductions: people snatched from their homes, usually at night, by heavily armed individuals who identified themselves as members of the security or armed forces, wearing only some or no components of their uniforms, who made searches without any documents authorising them to do so, and took away, without any explanation, individuals, many of whom remain missing to this day. At times, people were swiftly seized in the street or public places with no arrest warrant or any type of identification. The authorities refused to acknowledge the arrests and denied information on the whereabouts of the missing people. This modus operandi, repeated in nearly all cases, provided proof of a systematic plan of enforced disappearances. As such, it was denounced internationally by human rights organisations.

The fact that the kidnappings occurred so frequently became the most plausible theory to explain the fate of the missing. The informed assumption was that when a political militant went missing, he or she had probably been captured by the armed forces, even when there were no eyewitnesses to the abduction (Federman 2018a). Because the pattern repeated itself, when militants or activists failed to hear from colleagues, or if those colleagues missed a meeting, their organisations would assume they had been kidnapped and would often respond by initiating immediate emergency security measures.

When the dictatorship ended in 1983, the clandestine detention centres were closed. The main political and legal demands of human rights organisations included determination of the fate of the disappeared, the lustration (or removal from office) of the armed and security forces involved in those crimes, and the prosecution of those responsible. Investigations conducted by the country's truth commission – the National Commission on the Disappearance of Persons (CONADEP) – between 1983 and 1984, and by its judiciary until it was blocked by impunity laws, partially exposed the dictatorship's system of disappearance of political opponents. The exhumations of anonymous graves and the work developed by the newly established Argentinian Team of Forensic Anthropology produced considerable knowledge on the bureaucratic mechanisms used to dispose of the corpses and hide the fate of the victims.

In January 1989 approximately 46 rebels attempted to take the army's Tablada barracks. The provincial and federal police and the army responded with an extremely violent repression, killing 32 people and disappearing four others. The events made it clear that, even after the secret prisons had been dismantled, enforced disappearances continued as a modus operandi, a useful tool for armed and security forces.

With time, researchers, experts, and activists began to understand that many practices, regulations, and institutions that had enabled the disappearances in the past had barely shifted since then. The state can, and does, deny information on the fate of the missing. Although disappearances are no longer part of a systematic plan of control, existing institutional structures remain indifferent to the phenomenon, and to their responsibilities to victims.

The Argentine democratic transition agenda did not seriously take into account the urgent measures required to restore trust in the judiciary, the police, and the armed forces.[1] Similarly, the Argentine state has not yet sufficiently developed institutional capacity to respond adequately and independently to new cases of disappearance. Episodes of disappearances that have occurred since 1983, and in which police forces were involved, tried, and even sentenced, have contributed to mistrust of the police forces in this matter. In some cases, albeit rare, evidence suggests that a person may have been a victim of enforced disappearance (as prescribed by article 12 of the International Convention for the Protection of All Persons from Enforced Disappearance), or that the possibility of such an occurrence cannot be ruled out. Yet frequent disappearances, whether enforced or not, have not triggered enough public pressure to catalyse policy-makers into promoting long-term reforms that could help solve the uncertainty that disappearances provoke. This relates to ambiguous loss experienced by the families and the phenomenon of 'disposable persons', discussed in Chapter 1 and explored in the Argentine context below.

## Ordinary Events: Police Harassment and Criminalisation of Social Conflicts

Poor areas, particularly in Buenos Aires province, have historically been a differentiated sphere of security policies and police practices. The way in which police officers interact with residents of these neighbourhoods includes abusive attitudes during daily patrolling procedures and when large operations and deployments occur. The treatment that young men living in these neighbourhoods customarily receive involves diverse violent actions, ranging from discriminatory treatment to extreme cases such as arbitrary executions.

In a 2016 research report published by CELS (2016b) 'police harassment' is defined as a set of practices that constitute a common type of relationship between members of the security forces and young residents of poor neighbourhoods. They involve sustained and recurrent abuse, which form part of security forces' routines in certain areas and toward certain groups. Such practices are not observed in middle- or upper-class areas, where they would not be socially or institutionally

[1] The junta trials, a new legislation on national defence that prohibited the armed forces from participating in matters of internal security, and the demands of human rights organisations to oversee the promotions to higher military ranks, did have some impact on the armed forces, but were not enough to rebuild public trust.

tolerated. Some people suffer this conduct repeatedly, which can escalate the levels of violence and lead to situations of severe human rights violations.

These daily repressive attitudes and behaviours of the police are reinforced in the judiciary's approach to criminality. The police and the judiciary tend to frame social conflicts emerging in protests or other episodes of social tension as criminal conduct. The most vulnerable sectors of the population are often targeted by police and judicial action. Although these investigations are not always successful in determining a criminal act and condemning it, the judicial process itself, in which defendants may be deprived of liberty, is an implicit punishment even if conviction is ultimately avoided (CELS 2013a, b; 2016a; 2017).

## Extraordinary Events: Disappearances

Disappearances in the Argentine democratic context do not exactly match the 'narrative framework' elaborated in the 1960s and 1970s in international forums to denounce systematic kidnappings. These earlier processes played a key role in constructing the legal norm that outlawed and punished the practice of enforced disappearances (Frey 2009; and Chapter 2 of this volume). Today, disappearances do not involve either a single modus operandi or a pattern that repeats itself over and over again (Federman 2018a; Ansolabehere *et al.* 2017). Each case has a different set of features. As a result, no unique theory has emerged to explain the fate of the missing. Nonetheless, certain specific characteristics recur in Argentina:

- occurrences are extraordinary, rather than systematic;
- there is no political or social activism by victims that would constitute a probable reason to be targeted;
- the victims are socially and economically vulnerable, meaning that not everyone is equally at risk of disappearing;
- eyewitnesses to the abductions are rare;
- when witnesses exist, there is little likelihood that they will testify, owing to fear of retaliation or other forms of intimidation;
- when evidence points to police participation, the facts do not always meet the strict legal definition of *enforced disappearance*.

When there is no unique pattern identifiable, and details vary from case to case, drawing the conclusion that the fate of a missing person might be explained as an enforced disappearance is, obviously, a serious challenge. A key aspect of this international crime is the persistent refusal of the authorities to acknowledge that they hold the persons in their custody or otherwise to account for them. The lack of information is a trademark. This is particularly relevant when considering that in the early, and most urgent, stages of the investigation some facts and details may be uncertain and the victim may still be alive.

This is the complex and occasionally time-constraining scenario in which it is critical to decide if enough clues exist to assume that the missing person may have been a victim of an enforced disappearance. Some signs that have been useful in the past to identify a possible case of enforced disappearance, and to activate interventions from a human rights perspective, are the details surrounding the account of the disappearance (where, when, and by whom was the victim last seen), and if evidence exists of previous encounters with, or victimisation by, members of security forces.

Argentine police force illegal practices – ranging widely from mistreatment to torture and even executions – constitute background information that cannot be ignored when disappearances occur. Given these practices, the possibility of an extreme form of institutional violence and cover-up – an enforced disappearance – is a hypothesis that cannot be automatically ruled out.

This is relevant to the cases of Luciano Arruga and Santiago Maldonado. Luciano Arruga was a 16-year-old boy who was last seen on the night of 30 January 2009, when he was on his way to his sister's house. Similar to many youths in his neighbourhood, he had been a victim of police violence many times; he had even been tortured while he was under arrest a few months earlier.[2] Because of this history, when he went missing his family and friends assumed he had been arrested once again and that police agents were refusing to acknowledge his arrest.

Almost six years passed before his remains were found, along with some partial discovery of what had happened the night of his disappearance. Luciano was run over by a car on the highway a few blocks away from where he was last seen, under circumstances that are still unclear. He died a day later in a public hospital and his unidentified body was buried in a Buenos Aires public cemetery. Although his family and friends claimed from day one that his disappearance was not a voluntary one and that he had been subject to police brutality by the local precinct, the judiciary failed to take into account the seriousness of the allegations.

His remains were found in 2014. Identifying him involved a process used previously to match fingerprints of victims of enforced disappearance during the Argentine dictatorship with those of unidentified corpses buried in anonymous graves. When applied to Luciano's search, his fingerprints matched those of 'John Doe', buried a few weeks after Luciano had last been seen (Federman 2018b). This information identified the place where he was buried. His remains were exhumed, re-autopsied, and given to his family.

Almost six years after his disappearance the family received a partial truth about the death and disappearance of Luciano Arruga. The treatment of the family, the police response, and the time it took for them to locate their loved one, suggest a pattern of poor practices by the judicial and police authorities. The systematic unwillingness to attend to the needs of certain populations was reinforced by the political authorities' failure to supervise police actions and listen to the families'

[2] In 2015 the policeman Diego Torales was sentenced to 10 years in prison for torturing Luciano Arruga.

demands. The case exposes the way the state treats certain people – the 'disposable people' discussed in Chapter 1 – with little regard for their dignity and the human rights of their next of kin. Through this kind of response, people disappear within the bureaucracy of the state itself.

Santiago Maldonado (see Chapter 9) was last seen alive on 1 August 2017. At that time, he was attempting to escape from a repressive deployment of the Argentine gendarmerie in the territory of the Mapuche indigenous community known as Pu Lof Cushamen. This repression followed a protest in which Santiago had participated. The first reports stated that he was last seen on the banks on the River Chubut before he disappeared without a trace.

The Pu Lof Mapuche community in Patagonia were locked in a bitter struggle over land that they claimed as their ancestral right. Their protests were often subject to violent repression by local police forces and the national gendarmerie. Thus, when Santiago was not found after the gendarmerie had left the premises and acknowledged no arrests, the reasonable assumption was that he had been the victim of an unlawful detention.

Seventy-seven days later his body was found in the Chubut River. This long time period was the result of several weeks' delay in initiating any significant search efforts. Because of the time that elapsed, many time-sensitive measures were not taken. The gendarmerie, for example, was not removed from the investigation. In addition, the initial search procedures and crime scene processing were carried out without sufficient regard to forensic science protocols, such as the Minnesota Protocol (OHCHR 2017; this volume: Chapter 14). They lacked the professionalism that an enforced disappearance investigation demands (Federman 2017).

A few months after Santiago's remains were found, and an autopsy determined no evidence of foul play (beatings or gunfire injuries), the judge ruled that Santiago had died without intervention from a third party. The judiciary dodged its responsibilities in determining the link between Santiago's death and the unlawful repression carried out by the gendarmerie. The judge closed the investigation of Santiago's death and acquitted all the public officials involved. No further judicial inquiries were conducted into the crimes committed by the gendarmerie deployed in the Pu Lof Cushamen territory. A Court of Appeals later reopened the investigation. Several judges have recused themselves, thereby preventing the judicial inquiry from moving forward. Internal investigations of the gendarmerie have not advanced. Authorities have not yet acknowledged their responsibility for the 77 days of uncertainty produced by search efforts that were a fiasco. They have not apologised for the public attacks they made on Santiago's family members when they demanded answers regarding his fate.

In the disappearance cases of both Luciano Arruga and Santiago Maldonado traditional human rights litigation strategies such as the writ of *habeas corpus* were used to denounce and demand the investigation of the disappearances as they had been during the dictatorship. The outcome of both cases reveals the limitations of these techniques alone. They expose the structural deficits, severe institutional flaws, and a pattern of state responses that have a differential impact on the impoverished and excluded sectors of Argentine society. These may be the underlying explanations for the occurrence and recurrence of some disappearances.

The fact that the discovery of Luciano's and Santiago's remains did not conform exactly to the initial hypothesis of what had happened in each case has presented a paradox: when the cases were investigated as enforced disappearances the bodies were finally found, but after that the initial investigative impulse vanished.

On the one hand, only when the cases were investigated within the framework of enforced disappearances were appropriate investigative measures taken that allowed for the bodies to be found. The cases occurred at different moments and experienced different intensities of social response as a result (Eilbaum and Medeiros 2017). While the Maldonado case provoked a much stronger and immediate social mobilisation and investigative complexities, in both cases civil society pressure was key to triggering the search to find the missing. It is unlikely that steps to find them would have been taken without pressure from their families and the wider public.

On the other hand, once their fate was established, aspects of the initial evidence became subject to other interpretations. The judiciary ruled that the evidence gathered was insufficient to meet the strict legal definition of an enforced disappearance. Severe political and legal challenges blocked the probe into other types of criminal responsibility in these cases. In this sense, steering the investigations from the criminal behaviours initially framed under the legal definition of enforced disappearance to other forms of criminal conduct by state authorities presented an obstacle that has yet to be overcome.

We hope that by examining these two disappearances, and other cases where the facts surrounding the fate of the missing are less clear, will draw out lessons that will prove useful in the future. Some preliminary ideas and steps to do so are set forth in the following sections of the chapter.

## Families' Extraordinary Challenges

In both cases, the victims' relatives were indispensable for getting answers from the state. Both Vanesa Orieta and Sergio Maldonado, the siblings of Luciano and Santiago, along with their friends and families, suffered the uncertainty of not knowing what happened. They refused to give up despite mounting adversity. They faced a system that made access to the investigation difficult, and denied their rights as victims of the process and their right to be heard by political and judicial authorities. They also suffered attacks from both senior government officials and the media (Federman 2017). Sergio's and Germán's public letters in Chapter 9 are an eloquent testimony of this struggle.

When a disappearance occurs, relatives bear a large part of the burden of the leadership in the investigation. The strong involvement of victims' relatives has been essential to making progress on investigations. In the absence of an effective prosecution that rises to the challenge of investigating by carrying out an effective probe, it is the relatives who, faced with no other choice, exercise the role of investigators and the promoters of action in the criminal justice system. This is true for human rights violations in general, not only in cases of disappearances (Pita 2010; Perelman and Pita 2020).

In many cases, victims' relatives work in alliance with – or as part of – the human rights movement to denounce the case publicly and channel the investigation. These alliances are one of the ways in which the knowledge and legitimacy acquired during the fight against impunity for crimes against humanity intersect with the fight to obtain justice for those disappeared after democratic transitions.

## Denial as an Automatic Response by the State: An Old Pattern

When an absence is categorised as an 'enforced disappearance', given Argentine history it obviously strikes a nerve. Nevertheless, experience has proved that the state frequently fails to respond to such cases by adopting urgent measures to confirm or rule out the responsibility of its agents and take into account the human rights of victims and their families.

Framing the case using the legal definition of an enforced disappearance allows family members and human rights activists to present the events taking into account a longer-term horizon, and to detail the wide range of abuses that the victims and others like them endured regularly before they went missing. It also allows those advocating on behalf of the victim to identify the disappearance as an extraordinary event that requires all available resources to be put into motion. Argentina's history of systematic enforced disappearance, and the enormous political significance of such an occurrence in a democracy, leads to the expectation that democratic state institutions will thus respond effectively to these crimes. Yet, the national political and judicial system remain unable to initiate urgent and immediate measures to confirm or rule out the responsibility of state agents in these egregious human rights violations.

A methodical analysis of the responses of the state to the cases of disappearance in which police participation could not be disproved should start by looking into three aspects: the response of political authorities, the reaction of the police agency alleged to have been involved, and the performance of the judiciary. The rationalities and behaviours of these agencies set up a scenario in which human rights organisations and activists deploy their demands. This pattern of responses repeats itself not only in enforced disappearance cases but also in other cases of human rights violations where police officers are involved, as the work of CELS can corroborate. Each aspect is discussed in detail below.

## The Response of Political Authorities

Frequently, the automatic response is denial, and the families' allegations are disregarded. In the cases in which CELS has intervened, as in many others, the response of political authorities has included strategies centred on floating hypotheses that are not backed by any evidence, denying the police force's participation, mistreating family members, and seeking to discredit the eyewitnesses. High-ranking government officials have antagonised the victim's families, questioning their political motivations through offensive public statements. Attempts to create stable liaison mechanisms with the families and their representatives, as required by international standards such as the Minnesota Protocol (Chapter 14), that could ensure relationships of trust and understanding with state authorities have been scarce. Furthermore, leaks of sensitive information to the media have been a frequent ploy.

The unwillingness to supervise a serious internal investigation has sometimes been the least of the failures to comply with international human rights standards. On some occasions, government officials have hidden information that was relevant to understanding what had occurred in an operation, or have released it in a disorganised and incomplete fashion. This strategy of speculating with information is not innocuous: defending the performance of a security force before having even investigated it, and then hiding information or misinforming society, is a way of sending a strong message of political and corporate support to the agents and the security force involved.

## The Reaction of Police Agencies

As in many other criminal procedures in which police members are investigated, the institutional response to the inquiries amounts to corporate cover-up. Instead of promptly and transparently providing the details needed in any investigation (who was on duty, who participated in the operations, which patrol cars were involved, the weapons that were deployed, police communications, etc.), the police agencies usually respond as if they have something to hide. The internal/administrative investigation of the security force may function as the instrument responsible for cover-ups, rather than one that investigates its members. These practices are obviously viewed with suspicion by families and their representatives, and therefore fuel the initial hypothesis of foul play.

Moreover, as we have mentioned, the common response by political officials is to support and defend police versions of events. Thus, the conditions enabling a police cover-up may be reinforced by this type of political response. In other words, with no, or scarce, political monitoring and control over agencies, a police cover-up operation is unlikely to be dismantled by those who have responsibilities to do so.

## The Performance of the Judiciary

The responses previously mentioned are further exacerbated by the judiciary's performance in cases of human rights violations. In enforced disappearances, and in other grave human rights violations, the judiciary more often than not relies on the official version provided by police officers, rather than conducting an independent investigation. One example is that the investigation and safeguarding of evidence are frequently assigned to the same force that was denounced for the crimes under investigation. We mention this in the Maldonado case discussed in this chapter. This type of practice ensures that inquiries will avoid investigating involvement by the police in the crime.

In addition, rather than cross-checking evidence regarding the potential responsibility of police officers, there is a tendency toward tunnel vision, in which the initial case theory is confirmed. Investigation into evidence that seems to contradict that theory is overlooked. Many times, inquiries persist in the assumption that missing people voluntarily left their homes and families or the place where they were last seen. They disregard objective evidence that indicates that these people may have been victims of a crime or may have been harmed in some way.

Another example of irregular practices is the tapping of the families' telephones, impinging on their right to privacy and providing police agencies and judicial officials with an early warning regarding any political or legal strategies families and human rights activists might plan. While other lines of investigation are not being pursued, the criminalisation of victims or witnesses is used to deflect attention away from the possible police perpetrators and shift it onto the victims. The facts are distorted and suspicions are shifted onto the aggrieved persons.

These features, however, are not exclusive to cases of disappearance, and do not happen only in Argentina. We see them repeated in other Latin American countries too. Many of the problems identified by the Interdisciplinary Group of Independent Experts (GIEI) appointed by the Inter-American Commission of Human Rights (see Serrano, Chapter 17) in the investigation of the enforced disappearance of the 43 students in Ayotzinapa are fully applicable: the formality and bureaucracy in the criminal justice system, preponderance of testimonial evidence and confessions, lack of capacity to analyse evidence, absence of contextual analysis in order to be able to investigate criminal patterns and liability, fragmentation of investigations, failure to satisfy the victims' right to truth and to information, investigation leaks by the prosecutors, limits and obstructions to the investigations, failure to investigate potential liability of superiors and not only the actual perpetrators, lack of use of technology in the search for the disappeared, inadequate victim care and management, revictimisation and criminalisation of victims (GIEI 2015, 2016). The chapters on Mexico, Brazil, and El Salvador in this volume recount similar failures to conduct adequate investigation into potentially grave human rights violations.

## Institutional Flaws that Enable Disappearances

The way in which bureaucratic offices in charge of identity documents, birth certifications, and death registration work; the inadequate handling of human remains; and the failure to identify deceased persons contribute to a significant number of persons unaccounted for, as Luciano Arruga's case has taught us. In Argentina, as in most states, the documentation of individual identity has been deeply related in its origin to the modern state's security needs and, hence, to its repressive aspects.

Consequently, the police are involved in most of these bureaucratic processes, or have been until very recently. For example, until 2011, the Federal Police issued some identity cards and all passports under the presumption that no person should remain unknown to the police. In the same vein, morgues and procedures to identify the deceased are still in the hands of, or intimately related to, local police agencies. As in many other aspects of the security forces, these areas have been impervious to reform from a human rights perspective.

On the other hand, the inability of state policies to provide a dynamic, comprehensive, and fully responsive system of identification results in certain socioeconomic groups becoming especially vulnerable owing to their inability to obtain identity documents. Consequently, if they die due to either criminal or natural causes, the chances their body will be identified and their families notified are low. Technological innovation in systems of identification should be accompanied by a broadened awareness of the importance that the determination of the identity of the deceased has in the explanation of the whereabouts of the missing and in families' right to mourn their loved ones. Moreover, crime scene investigation and forensic services' impacts on human rights are matters that Argentine policy-makers, judicial officials, and activists should take into deeper consideration in the near future.

The advanced forensic knowledge of the well-known Argentine Team of Forensic Anthropology, born shortly after the dictatorship ended to recover information on the victims of the dictatorship, enabled human rights organisations to disrupt the processes of concealment during the period of state terrorism. The technical capacity developed as a response to the dictatorship is applied in contemporary cases. The expertise of the Argentine Team of Forensic Anthropology has been sought in cases such as the Ayotzinapa case in Mexico and, more recently, the disappearance of Santiago Maldonado in Argentina. Fully incorporating the work of the Argentine Team into contemporary disappearance cases would attend to the needs of the families of missing persons.

The legitimacy of the forensic team is key in granting relief to family members. Exhausted from their mistreatment by state agencies – either political or judicial – in the search for their loved ones, they find in these experts the opposite: people they trust, who have helped them clear up some uncertainties that the absence of their relatives has produced. Their involvement has, without a doubt, helped family members ease the burden they have carried.

This high standard of performance and professional and ethical values are rarely found in state offices. In general terms, Argentina's judiciary system has not yet capitalised on the enormous amount of forensic knowledge built by the Argentine Team, and still has unprofessional or outdated procedures to search for and collect evidence in crime scene investigations, DNA analysis, and autopsies.

## Final Comments

Enforced disappearances have an enormous political and social significance in Argentina and throughout Latin America. Indeed, the narrative of the human rights violations committed by the military dictatorships in the 1960s and 1970s has shaped both American and international norms outlawing, preventing, and punishing the use of enforced disappearances (Frey 2009). Nevertheless, most Latin American states have proved unable to build institutional capacity to respond adequately to such cases when they occur under democratic rule.

The unexplained absence of someone who is especially vulnerable to unlawful police practices strikes a sensitive chord because it echoes the systematic plan of disappearances carried out during the last dictatorship. The Argentine political and judicial system has proved unable or unwilling to respond adequately to such events, and particularly incapable of investigating the facts alleged by the victims' families, confirming or ruling out the responsibility of state agents, and establishing the facts using scientific procedures. Therefore, the persistent belief that police agencies may be responsible for the unexplained absence is fed by the rationalities and behaviours of the agencies that manage disappearances, whether enforced or not.

With the reflections shared in this chapter, we hope to have contributed to the shedding of light on the pre-conditions that enable disappearances in democracies, and the challenges victims and human rights advocates face in seeking truth and justice when they occur.

The recurrent unexplained absences that occur because of the inability of the state to account for those missing, but that, nonetheless, do not meet the strict legal definition of enforced disappearances are not exclusively an Argentine problem. This leads us to the question of how human rights advocates can demand effective responses from the state even without sufficient proof to allege that the facts meet the strict legal definition of an enforced disappearance, and particularly when state parties deny they fall into that category of crime. A paradoxical situation arises, as we mentioned earlier, in which public scrutiny pressures authorities to adopt the measures to determine the fate of the missing, but if these crimes are immediately determined not to be 'enforced disappearances', subsequent investigations become stuck, and other types of criminal conduct are not properly investigated.

Disappearances in democratic systems, as outlined in Chapter 1, respond to logics and dynamics that vary from those authoritarian state-driven strategies designed to eliminate political opponents and the consequent narrative that led to the normative prohibition. However, they are enabled by the lack of extensive institutional reforms and the same bureaucratic designs that have remained unchanged (such as the systems of identification of people and bodies or the management of the bodies of people who die without proper identification).

In this sense, we want to shed light on disappearances in which state agencies are involved, even though they do not conform to a narrow definition in international law regarding enforced disappearance. The questions that we raise probe whether, as Frey asserts in Chapter 2, the international human rights framework must revise its responses to these types of disappearances, and the legal tools available to address them. These disappearances have similar human rights implications and effects as those internationally condemned. Yet because the crimes do not strictly fit the legal definition of 'enforced disappearances', the responsibility of the state and its agents in these cases is overlooked and minimised, and investigations and prosecutions are hindered.

## References

Ansolabehere, K., B. Frey, and L. A. Payne, L.A. (2017), '"La constitución" de la desaparición forzada: vínculos entre los significados legales y sociales de la desaparición', in *Desde y frente al Estado: pensar, atender y resistir la desaparición de personas en México*, ed. J. Yankelevich (Mexico City, Suprema Corte de Justicia de la Nación), pp. 1–26.

Centre de Estudios Legales y Sociales [CELS] (2013a), *Derechos humanos en Argentina: informe 2013*, 1st edn (Buenos Aires, Siglo XXI Editores).

Centre de Estudios Legales y Sociales [CELS] (2013b), 'Informe alternativo del Centro de Estudios Legales y Sociales al Comité contra la Desaparición Forzada', www.cels.org.ar/web/wp-content/uploads/2017/08/CELS_Informe_Alternativo_CED2013.pdf (accessed 6 February 2021).

Centre de Estudios Legales y Sociales [CELS] (2016a), *Derechos humanos en Argentina: informe 2016*, 1st edn (Buenos Aires, Siglo XXI Editores).

Centre de Estudios Legales y Sociales [CELS] (2016b), *Hostigados: violencia y arbitrariedad policial en los barrios populares*, 1st edn (Buenos Aires, Centro de Estudios Legales y Sociales).

Centre de Estudios Legales y Sociales [CELS] (2017), *El derecho a la protesta social en la Argentina* (Buenos Aires, Centro de Estudios Legales y Sociales).

Eilbaum, L., and F. Medeiros (2017), 'Entre rotinas, temporalidades e moralidades: a construção de processos de repercussão em dois casos etnográficos', in *Casos de repercussão: perspectivas antropológicas sobre rotinas burocráticas e moralidades*, ed. R. Kant de Lima, L. Eilbaum, and F. Medeiros (Rio de Janeiro, Consequência), pp. 15–42.

Federman, N. (2017), 'Santiago Maldonado y Luciano Arruga: un mismo día', *Cosecha Roja* (21 October), http://cosecharoja.org/santiago-maldonado-y-luciano-arruga-un-mismo-dia/ (accessed 22 October, 2017).

Federman, N. (2018a), 'Desapariciones: la negación del derecho a la propia muerte', *Revista voces en el Fénix* (May), www.vocesenelfenix.com/content/desapariciones-la-negaci%C3%B3n-del-derecho-la-propia-muerte (accessed 6 February 2021).
Federman, N. (2018b), 'Tras los rastros de las huellas', *Relatos de archivos* (June), http://tecmered.com/ (accessed 6 February 2021).
Frey, B. (2009), '*Los Desaparecidos*: The Latin American Experience as a Narrative Framework for the International Norm against Enforced Disappearances', Hispanic Issues Series, retrieved from the University of Minnesota Digital Conservancy, http://hdl.handle.net/11299/182852 (accessed 24 January 2021).
Interdisciplinary Group of Independent Experts [GIEI] (2015), *Ayotzinapa Report: Research and Initial Conclusions of the Disappearances and Homicides of the Normalistas from Ayotzinapa* (6 September) (Mexico, GIEI).
Interdisciplinary Group of Independent Experts [GIEI] (2016), *Ayotzinapa Report II: Forward Steps and New Conclusions on the Investigation, Search and Care for Victims* (24 April) (Mexico, GIEI).
Office of the United Nations High Commissioner for Human Rights [OHCHR] (2017), *The Minnesota Protocol on the Investigation of Potentially Unlawful Death (2016)* (New York and Geneva, United Nations).
Perelman, M., and M. V. Pita (2020), 'Hermanes: trayectorias militantes y generación política como claves para pensar el activismo', in *Movilización de víctimas y demandas de justicia en la Argentina contemporánea*, ed. M. V. Pita and S. Pereyra (Buenos Aires, Teseo Press), www.teseopress.com/movilizacion (accessed 6 February 2021).
Pita, M. V. (2010), *Formas de morir y formas de vivir: el activismo contra la violencia policial*, 1st edn (Buenos Aires, Editores del Puerto).

# El Salvador

# 11

# Wilson's Testimony: Abuse of Authority

'WILSON'*

My lifetime companion has – had – a son, Yovani, who worked with a man who was a butcher. My stepson didn't live with us anymore; he had his own life companion. Yovani was 10 when I got together with my partner; his brother Javier was eight, and the youngest was seven.

One day in 2014, Yovani's boss sent him to buy some things at the market. Along the way, he met up with his friend Samuel, and they went together to carry out his duties. That day, Yovani and Samuel disappeared. Yovani was about to turn 17. A woman who works at the market told us at 6 or 7 p.m. what had happened: that at around 11 a.m. some soldiers wearing red-ochre berets [part of the Salvadoran armed forces uniform] had detained them. She couldn't tell us before then because she couldn't leave her stall in the market. Various witnesses told us that they were hit, their telephones were taken from them, and they were tied up with their shoelaces. Then they were moved some five blocks away and put into a white all-terrain Toyota. From there they were taken to another neighbourhood controlled by the Mara Salvatrucha (MS) [gang]. Our neighbourhood is controlled by the Barrio 18 [gang]. After this happened, a friend of Javier's saw soldiers turning Samuel and Yovani over to the MS. We never had any reason to believe that Yovani was involved in gang activity. Maybe he was a friend of theirs, but not a member.

That same night, several of us went to the local police station to look for Yovani and Samuel and to file a police report. At the station they told us that the boys were not there and that they did not know anything about the soldiers who had taken them. They said that possibly they were gang members dressed up as soldiers. They also repeated the usual responses when someone disappears, that maybe they were with a girl or they had left the country. We filed a report and we also went to protest at the military base. My partner, Samuel's parents, and some of the people who had witnessed the abduction were there. We even called on a reporter to record us. We arrived at the base and spoke first to a lieutenant, who would not give us any

*All of the names in this testimonial have been changed to protect the identities of those involved.

*Proceedings of the British Academy*, **237**, 185–188, © The British Academy 2021.

information. A few went into the base and recognised the soldiers who had taken Yovani and Samuel. They had replaced their red-ochre berets with camouflage caps to avoid recognition. I went in after the others – with some fear – and I saw the soldiers pointing their guns at them. This is an abuse of authority. I have been harassed like this before.

One time the police were beating up my stepson, Javier. I ran toward the three policemen who were hitting him and they took aim at me with their guns, yelling 'You, what do you want?'. I answered 'It's my son, he lives here, why are you hitting him?'. They just said 'Go away. You don't belong here. If you don't leave we will take you away also.' They tied up Javier from behind and they took him away one night to the station. His mother immediately went to look for him because if you do nothing and don't look for the boys, they will disappear them. This has happened many times in our neighbourhood. They beat up Javier for pleasure. He was at his sister's house and they started hitting him just because they found him standing there in front of the door. That is not the first time they beat him up. About seven years ago, soldiers and police intensified their abuse against people in our neighbourhood. I know stories of soldiers who have grabbed people and beaten them up. I have a friend who, after they hit him in the back, had kidney- and other internal pain. The man was a senior, with a limp, and still they beat him up. What they are looking for is to get the truth out of you; they want to find out who the gang members are.

In the neighbourhood, the gangs leave us alone. They don't want us to go around talking about them. This is how we live in peace. They don't try to extort from us or help us; they only ask that we don't 'finger [identify] them', as they say, or go around talking about them. There are places where they do bother people. The police and soldiers come into the neighbourhood at times to chase them down and shoot at them, because now the armed forces and the police are allowed to shoot at anyone who attempts to flee. If you're not a gang member but they see you running, they will shoot you. In the report they claim that you, the gang member, fired first.

After going to the military base and to the local police station, we also went to the police stations in Soyapango, Monserrat, Santa Ana, Usulután, San Miguel, and other places to ask for information. After realising that they would not tell us anything, we began to look for them in the hills and in the clandestine graves in the neighbourhood where they had last been seen. We did this for three days because the police wait 72 hours to activate the search process. Supposedly they send an investigator accompanied by two police. In our case, they did not want to help. We had to beg the commander of the local station to help us. In the end, they did, unwillingly.

In one of the searches, I saw a corn field on a hill with a trail that looked like something had slid down through it. I said to Samuel's dad 'Look over there. It looks like something slid down along the ground.' When I stopped and pointed out the place where you could see the trail, the two policemen who were with us turned around and aimed their guns at us. I thought 'This is where we will die.' The good thing is that there were a lot of us, because if it had been only the two of us they would have killed us. They kill people all the time and everything goes on like nothing happened. They will even make the scene out like it was an armed confrontation.

We pursued the leads that we had received from people who had heard of clandestine graves in that neighbourhood. Just below where they had aimed their guns at us, at the edge of a river with black water, there was an MS 'destroyer' [gang] house. That is where there are some very deep wells into which they say that the disappeared have been thrown. A lot of people say that those wells are full of cadavers, but no one can go there. My question is why, when we were getting close to a 'destroyer' house and to the well, the police did not want to keep walking. My curiosity is this: each of the three times that we got close to there, we couldn't go further, and the police said 'They have told me from headquarters that we must return.' They pretended, got out the telephone, and said that we had to go back. People have disappeared there, and at times they have taken kids from other areas and thrown them there. We searched for three days. After that we did not continue because they would not accompany us. The commander came out to say to us very angrily that 'we went along with you and now we're not [going to]'.

The majority of the police have links with the MS gang. At times they are themselves gang members. For example, in my neighbourhood there was a policeman who put a lot of youths in jail. When he captured them, they say that he showed them the inside of his lips, where he had tattooed the letters 'MS'. This is how he let them know that he was a gang member. They are trained as police institutionally, but because they live in gang zones they collaborate. Soldiers also have links to MS or Barrio 18. They give them information; turn over youths to them; traffic in arms, drugs, etc. At times when the police and armed forces want to get rid of someone but they don't want to be linked to killing kids that they pick up, they hand them over to the gangs.

In addition to looking for them in the neighbourhoods, we looked for them in the prisons; we went to the Institute of Legal Medicine, and the morgue. I went several times to the Institute of Legal Medicine, but then I had to stop helping out in this way because to go through photos of dead people is upsetting. You get to the Institute, provide the information on the person that you are looking for, and your family relationship, and then they hand over to you the names and photos of people who appear decapitated, dismembered, skinned, with holes in their bodies. I had to stop going because I began to be traumatised. I am not even the biological father, and still I felt traumatised. We also worked with the Asociación Salvadoreña por los Derechos Humanos (Salvadoran Association of Human Rights; ASDEHU). We made a *habeas corpus* petition at the Constitutional Court. There were 34 soldiers outside the Court. I imagine that they were there to intimidate us, to keep us from saying anything.

I think that Yovani is dead. We have looked everywhere for him. His mother continues to believe he is alive. She cannot forget. Maybe those of us who are fathers can forget more quickly. Mothers don't forget. She feels the pain and the hope always. I say to her yes, maybe he is alive, because citizens can be very judgemental. When you are talking about the case, they say to you 'What are you thinking? Your son is dead.' This is a death sentence; it destroys hope. As a member of the Comité de Familiares de Personas Desaparecidas por la Violencia en El Salvador (Committee of Relatives of People Disappeared by Violence in El Salvador; COFADEVI) what I hope for is that there is an investigation into the truth and that the soldiers tell us what happened to the boys. We know that this investigation is dangerous for us.

12

# A New Generation of Disappearances: Gangs and the State in El Salvador

MARÍA JOSÉ MÉNDEZ

TWO COMPETING PERSPECTIVES emerge in El Salvador regarding disappearances. From the top-down perspective held by Salvadoran authorities, the arbitrary arrest and disappearance of Yovani and Samuel by soldiers – captured in Wilson's narrative testimony (Chapter 11) – is an exception rather than the norm.[1] Those authorities claim that most disappearances are carried out by gang members who have learned that 'without a body there is no crime', the logic of the clandestine act examined in Chapter 1.[2] A bottom-up perspective arises from the everyday lived experience on the peripheries of El Salvador. From this experience, Yovani and Samuel's disappearance is not viewed as an isolated case. It instead reflects the patterns of state abuse of authority leading to disappearances and posing obstacles to families searching for their disappeared relatives. These two perspectives are set out in this chapter.[3]

[1] All names of relatives of the disappeared have been changed to protect the anonymity of individuals. The narrative is based on an interview I conducted with 'Wilson' on 7 May 2018, in San Salvador, El Salvador. I received oral permission from Wilson to publish this interview on the condition of anonymity on 7 May 2018.

[2] According to Carcach and Artola (2016: 3), the Mara Salvatrucha and Barrio 18 (which consists of two factions: Sureños and Revolucionarios) turned to the clandestine burial of their victims in response to the Salvadoran government's crime control policy. They also suggest that gangs use disappearances for the purpose of social control and to demand political concessions for incarcerated gang members. The use of disappearances as a political strategy became the most evident in 2012 when Mara Salvatrucha and Barrio 18 reached a government-backed truce that led to a drastic reduction in homicides in exchange for government concessions such as prison transfers. Investigations revealed that the drop in homicides was partly the result of the gangs' decision to conceal bodies (Cruz and Durán-Martínez 2016).

[3] This chapter draws upon qualitative research involving 25 semi-structured interviews with relatives of the disappeared, government officials, journalists, human rights defenders, and NGO practitioners. These interviews took place in San Salvador, El Salvador, in 2018. Beyond these interviews, the study draws on institutional information about disappearances obtained from the National Civil Police (PNC), Institute of Legal Medicine (IML), and the General Prosecutor's Office (FGR), through the Salvadoran

*Proceedings of the British Academy*, **237**, 189–202, © The British Academy 2021.

## The Bottom-Up View of Disappearances

Yovani and Samuel are (or were) two of many young men swept up by state security forces in anti-gang operations. Their disappearances point to patterns of human rights violations that have been aggravated by the government's *mano dura* ('iron fist') crackdown on violent crime. In his testimonial, Wilson registers the disappearance of his stepson Yovani and that of his stepson's friend Samuel in relation to state violations through abuse of authority – physical harassment, inhumane treatment, the falsification of evidence, arbitrary detention, extra-judicial killings, and disappearances – as well as through patterns of state–criminal cooperation, or clandestine linkages (Chapter 1). His testimonial also gives us a sense of the innumerable obstacles that Salvadorans face in searching for their missing relatives.

## Abuse of Authority

Since its first introduction in 2003, a zero-tolerance policy toward gangs in El Salvador, modelled on anti-crime tactics in the USA such as 'broken windows' policing, has been accompanied by serious abuses of power.[4] *Mano dura* authorised the armed forces to patrol the streets and work with the National Civil Police (PNC) to 'free' poor neighbourhoods of gang violence. Enabled by legislation that criminalised gang affiliation based on ambiguous criteria and provided ample powers of discretion to persecute and capture alleged gang members, state security forces engaged in dozens of round-ups of youths in poor neighbourhoods (Creedon 2007). Just in the first 13 months that *mano dura* took effect, the police arrested 19,275 alleged gang members. Because of lack of evidence, 17,540 (91 per cent) of those arrested were freed (Reyna 2017: 14). *Mano dura* policies, widely denounced by human rights defenders and inhabitants of impoverished communities for waging a 'war on young people', have also led to overcrowded prisons where inmates live in inhumane conditions (Callamard 2018).[5] Legislative changes that softened the penalties for police conduct in anti-gang operations, as well as the government's adoption of 'Extraordinary Measures' in 2016 to hold imprisoned gang members in lockdown, have further exacerbated human rights violations (Reyna 2017: 31–2).

Unit of Access to Public Information. The data were collected in the course of a 2018 Human Rights Lab research project entitled 'Forced Disappearances and Mass Violence in El Salvador'. The collaborative research project with Professor Patrick McNamara was funded by a Grand Challenges Grant from the University of Minnesota.

[4] This model of policing is based on the theory that cracking down on petty crimes such as graffiti and loitering can prevent more serious ones.

[5] In addition to reporting on severe health concerns such as the spread of tuberculosis in prisons, Callamard documents how most men in *bartolinas* – pre-trial detention centres intended to be for 72-hour periods – have been held there for months.

By highlighting the gruesome turn that *mano dura* has taken in the past few years in his neighbourhood, Wilson's account compels an analysis of his stepson's disappearance that takes the reality of state violence seriously. The social and political pressure to deliver results in the government's war on gangs increased after the collapse of the 2012–14 'gang truce', and has led to indiscriminate security raids in poor neighbourhoods controlled by gangs. As Wilson observes, it is common for youths, particularly boys, to be hassled, beaten up, and imprisoned by security forces who consider them gang suspects (International Crisis Group 2018).

Like Wilson, many of those I interviewed also reported the arbitrary detention of their relatives on trumped-up charges that involved security personnel planting evidence such as drugs and weapons.[6] The falsification of evidence extended to tampered scenes where state security forces claim to have responded to attacks by gang members. In his account, Wilson emphasised how security forces could shoot without fear of consequences, and easily transform scenes of extra-judicial killings into scenes of armed confrontation. The disproportionate and rising death toll of alleged gang members in so-called armed confrontations with security personnel has raised alarms about extra-judicial executions.[7]

Wilson refers to the San Blas massacre, in which eight alleged members of a criminal structure were killed during a shootout with police officers on a farm in 2015, an emblematic case of the abusive use of force. A thorough investigation by the news outlet *El Faro* revealed the summary execution by the police of the eight, and the subsequent staging of the incident to appear as if they had died in a shootout. In this case, eight Salvadoran police officers were accused of executing 20-year-old Dennis Martínez Hernández, who was only an employee at the farm (Amaya and Thale 2017). They were later acquitted, confirming Wilson's sense of the widespread impunity that state security forces enjoy in El Salvador, a sense that he expresses in his words 'They kill people all the time and everything goes on like nothing happened' (p. 187).

In 2014, the year Yovani and Samuel went missing, the Fiscalía General de la República (General Prosecutor's Office; FGR) registered several other cases of enforced disappearance. Out of these, only one case presented by the Asociación Salvadoreña por los Derechos Humanos (Salvadoran Association of Human Rights; ASDEHU) resulted in criminal charges (Kiernan 2017). The facts in this sole prosecuted case resembled the case of Yovani and Samuel. Three young men went missing after an army sergeant and five soldiers arrested them in the municipality of Armenia, Sonsonate. Similarly, the men were arrested in a neighbourhood with Barrio 18 presence and taken to a Mara Salvatrucha-controlled area. The case ended in an eight-year conviction for the army sergeant and four-year convictions for the soldiers under his command (Villeda 2018). This was the first time in Salvadoran

[6] 'Wilson', interview with the author, San Salvador, El Salvador, 7 May 2018.

[7] According to official figures from the Ministry of Justice and Public Security, killings of alleged gang members in armed confrontations rose from 103 in 2014 to 591 in 2016. The mortality ratio between civilians and security personnel also jumped from 15 to 112.5. See Callamard (2018).

legal history that military officers were convicted for committing the crime of enforced disappearance (ASDEHU 2017), which is sanctioned in Article 290 of the Salvadoran Criminal Code.[8] On 16 March 2016, Marina Ortiz, the Salvadoran lawyer who took this case, declared in a presentation at the American University in Washington DC that at least 10 per cent of total disappearances in El Salvador can be attributed to the security apparatus of the country, including the armed forces and the PNC (Eldridge and Silva 2016). Although there are not enough data or research that confirm the trend of enforced disappearances within the state security apparatus, these cases point to patterns of state violence.

State harassment in gang-controlled neighbourhoods is so permanent that the population sometimes fears police and military officers as much as or even more than they fear Mara Salvatrucha and Barrio 18. Wilson, for instance, speaks about Barrio 18, the gang that controls his neighbourhood, in less predatory terms than he uses to describe state activity there. He notes that in contrast to state security forces, Barrio 18 does not disturb residents as long as they respect the 'see, hear, and be silent' rule and do not share information about gang activity. According to Verónica Reyna, director of the Human Rights Programme at the Servicio Social Pasionista (Passionist Social Services; SSPAS), in San Salvador, some heavily policed communities now see the security forces as a new criminal group that they do not trust, especially given evidence of 'death squads' operating within the police.[9] The source of this distrust is not only the hostility of security forces and their strong assumption that those who inhabit gang-controlled territories are gang-collaborators but also the blurry line between state and criminal operations.

In his account, Wilson draws attention to the role of state security forces in the illicit underworld. He talks about state agents handing subjects over to gangs, sharing information with them, and aiding in the logistics of drugs- and arms-trafficking. The infiltration of organised crime into security institutions and political parties has been extensively documented since the end of the civil war, particularly in relation to the PNC (Silva 2014). According to data from the Defence Ministry, between 2010 and 2015, 480 gang members and collaborators infiltrated El Salvador's armed forces and police (Yagoub 2016). Although these data might inflate the actual level of gang influence within the security apparatus so as to justify the increasing allocation of resources toward anti-gang operations, it still points

[8] Under Title XIV of the Criminal Code (Offences against the Fundamental Rights and Guarantees of the Individual), article 290 (Offence of Deprivation of Liberty by Public Officials or Employees, Law Enforcement Officers or Public Authorities) stipulates: 'Public officials or employees, law enforcement officers or public authorities who, except where provided by law, impose, agree, order or permit any deprivation of a person's liberty, shall be sentenced to three to six years' imprisonment and barred from their functions or post during that time. If the deprivation of liberty exceeds 48 hours, or where an individual detained in flagrante delicto is not immediately brought before the competent authority, the prison sentence and disqualification shall be increased by up to a third of the maximum' (United Nations Convention against Torture and Other Cruel, Inhuman, or Degrading Treatment or Punishment 2007: 25).

[9] Verónica Reyna, interview with the author, San Salvador, El Salvador, 26 April 2018.

to complex state–criminal relations in El Salvador that might be shaping the phenomenon of disappearance (McNamara 2017: 16–17).

In addition to linking contemporary disappearances to generalised state violence in El Salvador, relatives of the disappeared draw parallels between the disappearances of the civil war (1980–92) and those of the present. For the mother of Oscar Leyva, one of the three men detained in Armenia, who is still deeply marked by the unknown fate of relatives who were disappeared by military officers during the civil war, the most palpable connection is the sense of unresolved grief resulting from disappearance (Arauz 2015). This lack of closure and experience of uncertainty related to the whereabouts of relatives corresponds to the 'ambiguous loss' that Payne and Ansolabehere identify in Chapter 1. Today, many families are reliving the extreme fear they experienced during the war as a result of not knowing whether their relatives are alive or dead. Although these crimes are no longer happening in the context of a counterinsurgency war against Communism, social control through ambiguous loss persists in El Salvador. Relatives are governed by the same norm of silence and terror that death squads imposed through disappearances during the armed conflict (Brigida and Sheridan 2019). Contemporary disappearances are also haunted by other spectres of the past. One major element that characterised them during the conflict is present in the new cases: the state construction of the disappeared and their families as 'internal enemies'. Verónica Reyna elaborates on this construction:

> People who looked for traces of their missing relatives during the war were heavily stigmatised. They were accused of being Communists or guerrilla fighters just like their relatives. It was difficult for them to search in that context. The same happens today, with different characteristics nonetheless, since now it's the gang stigma that marks the disappeared and their families.[10]

Like the stigma of being a Communist during the war, the stigma of being associated with gangs also translates into impunity for perpetrators because the disappeared and their relatives are held to be at fault for the harm that befell them. Their alleged subversion of the dominant order justifies the fate of the disappeared and the failure of the state to investigate wrongdoing. This stigmatisation resonates with another logic that, according to Payne and Ansolabehere (Chapter 1), underlies disappearances in the conflict and post-conflict periods: the social construction of victims and their relatives as enemies of the nation and 'disposable people'.

## Looking for the Missing

Testimonies from inhabitants of gang-controlled communities reveal deep distrust of public authorities (Callamard 2018; International Crisis Group 2017). Relatives

[10] Verónica Reyna, interview, 2018.

of the disappeared must nonetheless turn to those authorities when searching for the missing. Seven out of the eight family members of disappeared relatives whom I interviewed in El Salvador went to their local police stations right after their relatives went missing. Like Wilson, most had to wait 72 hours either to file a police report or to activate the search process. They were told this amount of time must pass before a person could be classified as 'disappeared', even though police officials in San Salvador insist that expecting families to wait is not their policy. Moreover, the families I interviewed experienced a similar response from the authorities in their cases: dismissal. The severity of their loss was diminished through what Wilson calls the usual responses given when someone disappears: 'maybe they were with a girl or they had left the country' (p. 185). When Claudia's brother went missing in 2014, the police told her 'Your relative is probably drunk at a party and that's why he hasn't returned.'[11] Sara, whose nephew went missing in 2017, got a similar response from the police: 'We can't file a report because he might be drunk or staying with someone. Just wait for him; he will be back.'[12] However, relatives did not wait. They went to emergency rooms, local jails, the morgue, and the FGR. They circulated photographs of their missing loved ones on television and Facebook, and plastered them on public walls and lamp posts. They lodged reports at either or all of the following institutions: the PNC, the Institute of Legal Medicine (IML), the FGR), and the Attorney General's Human Rights Division (PDDH).

A common complaint made by relatives of the disappeared is that the government ignores their plight and 'no hace nada' (does nothing) to follow or resolve their cases. Disappointed with government institutions that provide little help and are slow to search for the missing, many of the families become de facto detectives and carry out their own investigations despite the tremendous financial burden that this work puts on them (Valencia 2013). As also shown in the testimony by Lulú Herrera in Mexico (Chapter 3), Salvadoran families of the disappeared also go out of their way to gather evidence and uncover new leads that might help investigators with their case. Those who know that gang members were possibly involved in the disappearance of their relatives also search for their missing in the areas where they were last seen. These areas tend to be gang-controlled territories. Like Wilson, many people search for their relatives' remains in places known to have secret graves. But access to these burial sites is difficult, as Sara observes: 'It is not easy to gain access to clandestine cemeteries [to find relatives] because gangs keep close watch over them.'[13] In spite of the severe risks that entering territories controlled by rival gangs entails, those who cannot convince security personnel to accompany them organise themselves instead to go with their families and neighbours.

It is common knowledge that El Salvador is replete with clandestine cemeteries. At least 158 of them have been found since 2014, with more than 216 victims

[11] 'Claudia', interview with the author, San Salvador, El Salvador, 12 February 2018.
[12] 'Sara', interview with the author, San Salvador, El Salvador, 10 May 2018.
[13] 'Sara', interview, 2018.

hidden inside (EFE 2016). Clandestine cemeteries are usually found in hills, cliffs, meadows, vacant lots, backyards, septic pits, and wells. The fact that many Salvadorans search for their missing at these sites reveals their understanding of the systematic burial of victims in secret graves as part of the modus operandi of disappearances in El Salvador (Rivera 2014).

Besides organising collective efforts in their communities to look for the disappeared, relatives go to non-governmental organisations such as Foundation Cristosal, the International Committee of the Red Cross (ICRC), Cruz Roja Salvadoreña (Salvadoran Red Cross; CRS), Instituto de Derechos Humanos de la UCA (Central American University's Human Rights Institute; IDHUCA), SSPAS, and ASDEHU for mental-health support and for legal guidance and representation. According to representatives of these organisations, not all family members who request help have filed reports at state institutions, partly because they do not trust them. Until now, there is only one collective of relatives of the 'new disappeared' that has publicly denounced the current phenomenon of disappearances. The Comité de Familiares de Personas Desaparecidas por la Violencia en El Salvador (Committee of Relatives of People Disappeared by Violence in El Salvador; CODADEVI) was formed with ASDEHU's assistance and includes dozens of families who are demanding that the government search for their missing loved ones (Terre des hommes 2018).

## The Top-Down View of Disappearances

Although the Salvadoran government has devoted some attention to civil war disappearances, most recently through the launching of the National Commission for the Search for Adults Disappeared in the Context of the Armed Conflict in 2017, it has given less consideration to the current wave of disappearances. Similarly to how the Salvadoran government has not fully recognised the problem of internal displacement, the severity of post-war disappearances has yet to be fully acknowledged (Reuters 2017). According to Amanda Castro, coordinator of the CRS's Psychosocial Attention Unit for Victims of Violence, who has actively participated in meetings hosted by the Victims Attention Division of the Ministry of Justice and Public Security:

> The state has closed its doors to a discussion on the issue of missing persons … Recognising the problem implies that security policies are not working. A decree was announced to search for those who disappeared during the armed conflict. There have been superficial efforts to say that something is being done on the subject. The state does not want to talk about current disappearances because it has to do with the great monster of social violence that the state associates with organised crime.[14]

[14] Amanda Castro, interview with the author, San Salvador, El Salvador, 12 February 2018.

The sense of abandonment felt by family members of disappeared relatives reflects the failure of the government to address the issue. Guadalupe Echeverría, chief of the Homicide and Anti-Gang Unit at the FGR, admits as much: 'As a government we owe a debt to our citizens because we have not yet established a uniform system to investigate the cases brought to us by family members with missing relatives.'[15]

For a phenomenon of violence to generate a comprehensive policy of attention to victims, there needs to be some shared understanding about its nature and magnitude. Government representatives at the four institutions that file missing persons reports (FGR, PDDH, IML, and PNC) identify at least two main problems in naming and quantifying the phenomenon at a national level: confusion regarding the appropriate category for disappearances, and the lack of a consolidated missing persons registry. For statistical purposes, missing persons are recorded under three different categories across the four registries: 'personas desaparecidas' (disappeared persons) at the PNC and IML, 'víctimas de desaparecimiento forzado' (victims of enforced disappearance) at the FGR and PDDH, and 'víctimas de privación de libertad' (victims of deprivation of liberty) at the FGR. Only the last two categories are legally recognised by the Salvadoran penal code. Not only are the categories used to name the phenomenon inconsistent, they also gather different types of cases under the same name. Even though institutions may be using the same legal categories to file reports, they may not be registering the same types of cases. For instance, whereas the FGR does not consider disappearances carried out by gangs as cases of enforced disappearance, the PDDH does. Gerardo Alegría, Deputy Attorney for Vulnerable Populations at the PDDH, explains the decision to classify gang-related disappearances as enforced disappearance as follows:

> Recently, about five years ago, it began to be established that not only state agents could carry out enforced disappearances but also non-state agents. Between 2010 and 2012, we started receiving more reports about the latter type of disappearance. This does not mean that the phenomenon began in those years, it's just that the prosecutor began to record them as enforced disappearances. Before, our operators did not record cases of disappearance by non-state agents. When people reported a disappearance carried out by gangs, we registered those cases as deprivations of liberty, and we sent the complainant to the FGR. Based on the increasing number of cases we began to receive and our assessment about the power that gangs have in the country, we started registering those cases as enforced disappearances. The PDDH had an intense debate over the identification of gangs as actors responsible for human rights violations.[16]

The PDDH's dilemma of how to categorise gang-related disappearances illustrates the conceptual legal hurdles that post-transitional states face in framing crimes as enforced disappearance, and it also points to how legal and social meanings of disappearance constitute each other (Chapter 2). For the PDDH, it is the state-like quality of gangs, their ability to 'halt the state and generate systematic human rights violations', that merits 'stretching' the legal definition of enforced disappearances

[15] Guadalupe Echeverría, interview with the author, San Salvador, El Salvador, 9 May 2018.

[16] Gerardo Alegría, interview with the author, San Salvador, El Salvador, 14 February 2018.

to include cases where there is no evidence of direct or indirect state participation in the crime.[17] Implicit in the decision to expand the legal framework of disappearances is the recognition that it is difficult to investigate and conduct searches within a framework that requires robust evidence of state participation. As a result of the many challenges involved in establishing the state's linkage to the crime within the current legal framework, the Salvadoran state has foregone its obligations to search for victims. As Frey observes (Chapter 2), other states dominated by organised crime have also taken advantage of these legal difficulties to evade their duty to investigate.

The different categories used to register the disappeared not only affect the state's responsibility to search for the missing but also make the process of data standardisation difficult. Except for information shared between the PNC and the FGR, data on the disappeared are not shared between institutions.[18] Currently, there is no consolidated registry of disappeared people; as IML describes, 'Each database is different, that is, some records may be included in a database and excluded in another one because the interested party never went to that institution.'[19] In sum, as the PNC states, 'The lack of data standardisation and refinement between institutions that actively participate in the cases of disappeared people does not allow for a single and consistent figure.'[20]

In addition to acknowledging the difficulties of categorising and quantifying the phenomenon of disappearances, government representatives point to other limitations when investigating cases of disappeared people. The lack of expediency stands out amongst these limitations. Douglas Edenilson Zometa, subcommissioner and chief of the Central Research Division at the PNC, confirmed victims' complaints that security personnel sometimes make them wait for more than a day before reporting the missing and activating a search mechanism:

> Many have the habit – perhaps they learn it from movies – of saying, 'Look, we cannot do anything until 48 hours have passed; if after 48 hours you cannot find your relative then you can come back.' But we want to change that behaviour in our staff so that they learn that no matter how much time has elapsed, our obligation is to assist the relatives of the disappeared and take immediate action … This applies to all cases, including those where someone left voluntarily with their boyfriend, went out with friends, or fell asleep somewhere else.[21]

Zometa inadvertently points to another habit that security personnel have, and that very much influences the idea that relatives should wait for a state response: suggesting that the missing person left voluntarily.

[17] Gerardo Alegría, interview, 2018.

[18] The PNC has up to eight hours to share with the FGR any police reports filed at their station.

[19] Information received on 23 August 2018 through the Unidad de Acceso a la Información Pública del Órgano Judicial (Unit of Access to Public Information, Judiciary).

[20] Information received on 20 August 2018 through the Unidad de Acceso a la Información Pública de la PNC (Unit of Access to Public Information, PNC).

[21] Douglas Edenilson Zometa, interview with the author, San Salvador, El Salvador, 8 May 2018.

The suggestion that the missing left home to be with friends, lovers, or to start a new life in the United States, which Wilson and other relatives of the disappeared in El Salvador, Mexico (Chapter 3), and other democratic countries perceive as a problematic response to their desperation, pervades official narratives about the disappeared. The state representatives I interviewed from the IML, FGR, and PNC all shared the same view that individuals went missing because of their own personal choices. Some provided examples of cases they had received as evidence to support their conjecture. For instance, according to Alvarenga Martínez (2018), head of the IML's Attention Unit for Relatives of Disappeared Persons and Cadaver Recovery, 'Sometimes relatives file a missing person report for a family member who went out partying. Recently, there was a mother who came and reported her son as missing and it turns out he was at a beach party.'[22] People also disappear during migration from El Salvador to the United States, as the Comité de Familiares de Migrantes Fallecidos y Desaparecidos (Committee of Relatives of Dead and Disappeared Migrants; COFAMIDE) has documented for more than a decade. However, the ubiquitous narrative that people leave voluntarily diminishes the forced nature of contemporary disappearances and implies that victims' families are naive or ignorant.

Regarding the lack of expediency in activating search mechanisms, it is important to note that this is not a universal problem. As Gerardo Alegría argues, 'Response mechanisms exist but the problem is that they do not apply to cases that involve ordinary people.'[23] The PNC has a Disappeared Persons Unit (Unidad de Búsqueda de Personas Desaparecidas) that operates under the Special Crimes Unit, and which attends to special cases of the disappeared. According to the manual *El instructivo de investigaciones de personas desaparecidas y extraviadas de la policía* (*Police Instructions for Investigations of Disappeared and Missing Persons*), which was approved in 2012 by the PNC Directive, the cases prioritised include the disappearance of public authority figures, public officers, foreigners on diplomatic missions, and police or military officers. Special cases also include those that cause alarm and national commotion (Valencia 2013). This unit has been quite effective in finding 'important' individuals who have gone missing, confirming Alegría's point that expediency has a differentiated character.[24] This differentiation is evidence of the logic of the social construction of a 'disposable people' identified by Payne and Ansolabehere in Chapter 1. On account of the multiple limitations that government institutions face, an inter-institutional platform conformed by the PDDH, FGR, PNC, IML, Ministry of Justice and Public Security, and Judiciary has been created by the United Nations Office on Drugs and Crime (UNODC) with financial support from the Canadian government to address the

[22] Alvarenga Martínez, interview with the author, San Salvador, El Salvador, 7 May 2018.

[23] Alegría, interview with the author, 14 February 2018.

[24] See the case of Karla Turcios, journalist for the *El Economista* magazine, or the case of the family members of Omar Pintel (physical trainer of Sonsonate Fútbol Club).

phenomenon of disappearances. The Urgent Action Protocol and Search Strategy for Disappeared Persons in El Salvador, within the framework of the project 'Institutional Strengthening in Cases of Disappearances Related to Organised Crime to Reduce Impunity in El Salvador', was launched on 18 December 2018, by UNODC. Although the results of the protocol's implementation remain to be seen, it constitutes an important effort toward assisting family members of the disappeared in a timely and coordinated manner. This inter-institutional protocol is the first comprehensive response for cases of disappeared persons in El Salvador. The protocol is described by UNODC as follows:

> It will allow a unified treatment of disappearance reports, the establishment of a prioritisation system based on the protection of rights, the timely and coordinated response of state institutions, and the identification of criminal patterns and trends. The Protocol guarantees the right of victims to access to justice, through the early and urgent search of disappeared persons without justifications or delays. In this regard, a campaign for 'Urgent Action' was also launched, which enhances the immediate reception of reports[25] and highlights the national institutions' commitment to act in these cases. Other institutions that are in favour of the Urgent Action mechanism can be integrated into this campaign. (UNODC n.d.-b)

The protocol's objectives, to generate a standardised database and identify criminal patterns, constitute an important step toward solving the problem of data inconsistency and providing a better understanding of the nature of disappearances. Echoing government representatives who situate the phenomenon of disappearances within the broader context of criminal violence, the protocol specifies that within the Central American region, 'The phenomenon of disappearances is a reality linked to various crimes in the countries of the Northern Triangle and has presented in recent years the emergence of new actors such as gangs, cartels, and criminal organisations' (UNODC n.d.-a: 17). In El Salvador, the protocol links disappearances with a high number of homicides, deprivation of liberty, femicides, sexual violence, and human trafficking, the carrying out of which may begin with a person's disappearance (UNODC n.d.-a: 17). However, missing from the protocol's framing of the phenomenon of disappearances are the patterns of state violence that Wilson registers in his testimonial and that complicate the implicit attribution of disappearances only to gangs.

## Conclusion

Based on the lowest reported number of disappearances from the PNC (approximately 17,000), more people have disappeared during the post-conflict period than

[25] According to the protocol, 'immediate reception of reports' refers to the institutional need to register all those reported missing regardless of the nature of the disappearance. This means that reports should be filed whether or not elements that traditionally constitute a crime (i.e. details about the perpetrator) are provided. See UNODC (n.d.-a: 38–9).

during the Salvadoran Civil War (at least 8,000).[26] Those who have been forcibly disappeared since 2010 are mostly teenagers and young adults aged between 18 and 30 from low-income households in gang-controlled territories. Despite its astounding scale, the phenomenon of disappearances in El Salvador has garnered little attention from the international community and has yet to be fully examined. This chapter has sought to redress this invisibility by contrasting a top-down and a bottom-up view of the phenomenon.

According to state government officials, disappearances in El Salvador primarily happen at the hands of the Mara Salvatrucha and Barrio 18 gangs. Those inhabiting the peripheries of El Salvador, and suffering the deep psychological impact of having a missing relative, often hold gangs responsible. However, they also connect the phenomenon to abuses by state forces and to complex entanglements between state agents and gangs. This bottom-up view registers patterns of human rights violations that need to be considered when analysing the new generation of disappearances in El Salvador. Given a tendency across Salvadoran official discourses and media accounts to view gangs 'as death messengers par excellence' (Méndez 2018: 2) and as a-priori perpetrators of violence, analysts of the phenomenon should be wary of accepting the claim that gangs are responsible for all disappearances. While gangs play an enormous part in shaping violent dynamics in El Salvador, a bottom-up view of the phenomenon compels a more nuanced analysis that places the issue in a broader continuum of state violations and state–criminal relations. Thus, listening to relatives of the disappeared is crucial for making fuller sense of a phenomenon whose devastating consequences the Salvadoran state and the international community have just begun to consider.

## References

Amaya, K., and G. Thale (2017), 'Amid Rising Violence, El Salvador Fails to Address Reports of Extrajudicial Killings', Washington Office on Latin America [WOLA] (3 November), www.wola.org/analysis/amid-rising-violence-el-salvador-fails-address-reports-extrajudicial-killings/ (accessed 23 April 2020).

Arauz, S. (2015), 'El día en que los militares volvieron a desaparecer personas', *El Faro* (1 June), www.elfaro.net/es/201505/noticias/17030/El-d%C3%ADa-en-que-los-militares-volvieron-a-desaparecer-personas.htm (accessed 23 April 2020).

Asociación Salvadoreña por los Derechos Humanos [ASDEHU] (2017), 'Atención jurídica con familiares de las víctimas de la desaparición actual' (15 May), http://asdehu.com/index.php/2017/05/15/atencion-juridica-con-familiares-de-las-victimas-de-la-desaparicion-actual/ (accessed 23 April 2020).

[26] From January 2010 to December 2019, the PNC reports 17,077 disappeared people (police data received on 21 August 2018 and 6 April 2020).

Brigida, A. C., and M. B. Sheridan (2019), 'Disappeared in El Salvador: The Return of a Cold War Nightmare', *Washington Post* (19 October), www.washingtonpost.com/world/the_americas/disappeared-in-el-salvador-amid-a-cold-war-nightmares-return-a-tale-of-one-body-and-three-grieving-families/2019/10/19/d806d19a-e09d-11e9-be7f-4cc85017c36f_story.html (accessed 13 November 2020).

Callamard, A. (2018), 'El Salvador End of Mission Statement', United Nations Human Rights Office of the High Commissioner (5 February), www.ohchr.org/en/NewsEvents/Pages/DisplayNews.aspx?NewsID=22634&LangID=E (accessed 13 November 2020).

Carcach, C., and E. Artola (2016), 'Disappeared Persons and Homicide in El Salvador', *Crime Science* 5:13, 1–11.

Creedon, K. (2007), 'El Salvador: War on Gangs', North American Congress on Latin America [NACLA] (25 September), https://nacla.org/article/el-salvador-war-gangs (accessed 23 April 2020).

Cruz, J. M., and A. Durán-Martínez (2016), 'Hiding Violence to Deal with the State: Criminal Pacts in El Salvador and Medellin', *Journal of Peace Research*, 53:2, 197–210.

EFE (2016), '¿Cuál es el departamento de El Salvador que registra más cementerios clandestinos?' Elsalvador.com (8 December), www.elsalvador.com/noticias/nacional/211379/cual-es-el-departamento-de-el-salvador-que-registra-mas-cementerios-clandestinos/ (accessed 23 April 2020).

Elridge, J., and H. Silva (2016), 'President Obama and the Disappeared', Washington Office on Latin America [WOLA] (25 March), www.wola.org/analysis/president-obama-and-the-disappeared/ (accessed 23 April 2020).

International Crisis Group (2017), 'El Salvador's Politics of Perpetual Violence' (19 December), www.crisisgroup.org/latin-america-caribbean/central-america/el-salvador/64-el-salvadors-politics-perpetual-violence (accessed 23 April 2020).

International Crisis Group (2018), 'Life under Gang Rule in El Salvador' (26 November), www.crisisgroup.org/latin-america-caribbean/central-america/el-salvador/life-under-gang-rule-el-salvador (accessed 23 April 2020).

Kiernan, M. (2017), 'La Fuerza Armada desapareció a tres jóvenes en tiempos de paz', *Factum* (17 January), www.revistafactum.com/la-fuerza-armada-desaparecio-a-tres-jovenes-en-tiempos-de-paz/ (accessed 13 November 2020).

McNamara, P. J. (2017), 'Political Refugees from El Salvador: Gang Politics, the State, and Asylum Claims', *Refugee Survey Quarterly*, 36:4, 1–24.

Méndez, M. J. (2018), 'The Violence Work of Transnational Gangs in Central America', *Third World Quarterly*, 40:2, 373–88.

Reuters (2017), 'El Salvador Launches Commission to Find Those Missing from Civil War' (27 September), www.reuters.com/article/us-elsalvador-missing/el-salvador-launches-commission-to-find-those-missing-from-civil-war-idUSKCN1C305R (accessed 23 April 2020).

Reyna, V. (2017), 'Estudio sobre las políticas de abordaje al fenómeno de las pandillas en El Salvador (1994–2016)', Friedrich Ebert Stiftung (October), http://library.fes.de/pdf-files/bueros/fesamcentral/13897.pdf (accessed 23 April 2020).

Rivera, J. de J. (2014), 'Pandillas, desaparición de personas y derechos humanos en El Salvador', master's thesis, FLACSO-Mexico.

Silva, H. (2014), *Infiltrados: crónica de la corrupción de la PNC (1992–2013)* (San Salvador, UCA Editores).

Terre des Hommes (2018), 'El Salvador: visibilizar la problemática de las desapariciones actuales por violencia' (19 September), https://tdh-latinoamerica.de/?p=2488 (accessed 13 November 2020).

United Nations Convention against Torture and Other Cruel, Inhuman, or Degrading Treatment or Punishment (2007), 'Consideration of Reports Submitted by States Parties under Article 19 of the Convention: Second Periodic Report Due in 2001. Addendum, El Salvador', United Nations Document CAT/C/SLV/2 (12 December).

United Nations Office on Drugs and Crime [UNODC] (n.d.-a), 'Protocolo de Acción Urgente y Estrategia de Búsqueda de Personas Desaparecidas en El Salvador', http://escuela.fgr.gob.sv/wp-content/uploads/pdf-files/PROTOCOLO-DE-ACCION-URGENTE-Y-ESTRATEGIA-CF.pdf (accessed 23 April 2020).

United Nations Office on Drugs and Crime (UNODC) (n.d.-b), 'UNODC Launches Urgent Action Protocol and Search Strategy for Disappeared Persons in El Salvador', www.unodc.org/ropan/en/unodc-launches-urgent-action-protocol-and-search-strategy-for-disappeared-persons-in-el-salvador.html (accessed 23 April 2020),

Valencia, D. (2013), 'Los desaparecidos que no importan', *El Faro* (21 January), www.salanegra.elfaro.net/es/201301/cronicas/10773/Los-desaparecidos-que-no-importan.htm?st-full_text=0 (accessed 23 April 2020).

Villeda, A. (2018), 'Exmilitares son condenados por la desaparición forzada de tres jóvenes en Armenia, Sonsonate', Fiscalía General de la República (30 November), www.fiscalia.gob.sv/ex-militares-son-condenados-por-la-desaparicion-forzada-de-tres-jovenes-en-armenia-sonsonate/ (accessed 23 April 2020).

Yagoub, M. (2016), '480 Gang Members Infiltrated El Salvador Security Forces: Report', InSight Crime (22 February), www.insightcrime.org/news/brief/did-480-gang-members-infiltrate-el-salvador-security-forces/ (accessed 23 April 2020).

# Part III

# Tools for Advocacy and Mobilisation

13

# The Visual Image as a Tool of Power

LEIGH A. PAYNE AND HUNTER JOHNSON

ANYONE WHO HAS been to a rally or march, a site of memory, a meeting of the families of the disappeared, knows the central role that photographs play. The visual image of the disappeared is not only a ubiquitous, common, and iconic expression used by relatives and their advocates; we contend, following Susan Sontag (1977: 8), that it is 'a tool of power'. In this chapter we explore why the visual image is a tool of power, how it is used, by whom, and with what results.

The visual image functions as a tool of power. It creates 'a grammar … an ethics of seeing … that feels like knowledge – and therefore, like power' (Sontag 1977: 3–4). In this way, it fits the notion that *the medium is the message* (Marshall McLuhan, quoted in LeBourdais (1967)), the chapter's first section. The message of the photo – its tool of power – is how it is used as a call to action.

The photograph is used to furnish evidence of what happened: 'Something we hear about, but doubt, seems proven when we're shown a photograph of it … A photograph passes for incontrovertible proof' (Sontag 1977: 5). *Seeing is believing*; it is used as a form of truth-telling that we explore in the second section of the chapter. A photo is a tool used to make the hidden – the disappeared – visible and understandable.

Visual images are also used to disturb complacency over disappearances. They confront the observer with a social reality that compels knowledge and demands attention. Photos are a tool used to expose *the rupture and emptiness*, the profound personal and societal loss disappearance creates, examined in the third section of the chapter.

For all of the reasons set out above, the visual image in the hands of survivors – the friends and families of those who have disappeared – is a powerful tool, but also one of the only tools available to achieve certain objectives. The photograph is 'lightweight, cheap to produce, easy to carry about, accumulate, store' (Sontag 1977: 3) and 'infinitely reproducible' (Berger 1972a: 291). It thus becomes a

*Proceedings of the British Academy*, **237**, 205–224, © The British Academy 2021.

*weapon of the weak* (Scott 1985), a powerful tool to mobilise, to build solidarity, and to pressure for social change, as we explore in the fourth section of the chapter.

The visual image is therefore a tool of power used to combat one of the primary logics that underlie disappearances, the social construction of the disappeared as 'disposable people' (Chapter 1); 'To photograph is to confer importance' (Sontag 1977: 28). This chapter sets out those four key aspects of the visual image as a tool of power – the medium is the message, seeing is believing, rupture and emptiness, and a weapon of the weak – with illustrations for how this tool has been used and can be used to make disappearances visible, to build solidarity with the families, and to mobilise the search for the missing with the aim of ending the violation.

## The Medium is the Message

The visual image works as a tool of power by allowing for 'fast seeing' (Sontag 1977: 124), creating a transformative story in a single gaze.[1] It thus fits Marshall McLuhan's notion that the medium is the message. In his words, 'a medium is not something neutral – it does something to people. It takes hold of them. It rubs them off, it massages them and bumps them around … and the general roughing up … is what is intended' (LeBourdais 1967).

Relatives intuitively grasp – and put into use – the photograph as a tool, a medium, to transform the message. 'A photograph is already a message about the event it records … At its simplest the message, decoded, means: *I have decided that seeing this is worth recording*' (Berger 1972a: 292). The photographs communicate a message from the survivors: 'This is a person, a missing person, they proclaim. Here is my sister, my husband, my son, my friend. Here they are: *I did not just imagine them*. They have not come home, but they must be somewhere. "Please help!" ' (Edkins 2011: 16–17). Photographs can thus be used by survivors as tools to bear witness to a living person, an important life, one that touched the lives of others, someone who is missing. Together they also emphasise that this is not an isolated event that happened to a single family. Survivors use photographs to say 'This could happen to you. You too could lose someone you love. This has to stop.'

The photograph is a tool of power in producing an alternative story, one that attempts to undermine the prevailing view of the disappeared person as disposable. An early example of this use and the power of the tool occurred in 1988 in Argentina. Estela Carlotto submitted a 'recordatorio' to the *Página/12* newspaper, a photographic remembrance of her missing daughter and grandchild, accompanied with words.

[1] Sontag is quoting Alvin Langdon Coburn's statement about photography from 1918.

SOLICITADA

**LAURA ESTELA CARLOTTO**

**A diez años de su asesinato por la dictadura militar**

Diez años es demasiado tiempo para no verte. Diez años es demasiado tiempo para que no vivas, amando y sufriendo entre nosotros, envejeciendo como es la ley de Dios.
Diez años de búsqueda de tu justicia (con memoria para la historia) es demasiado tiempo para no haberla obtenido.
Diez años buscando el hijito que te robaron es demasiado tiempo para que aún no nos acompañe el clamor general en la demanda.
Diez años no son demasiados para seguir tu ejemplo.

**Tus padres, tus hermanos, tu familia, tus amigos y los demás (aunque no lo sepan) no te olvidamos.**

25-8-88

**Figure 13.1** Remembrance of the disappeared from *Página/12* (Argentina).

> **LAURA ESTELA CARLOTTO**
>
> Ten years after her assassination by the military dictatorship
>
> Ten years is too long to go without seeing you. Ten years is too long to go without you alive, loving, and suffering among us, getting old as is the law of God. Ten years looking for justice (and memory for history) is too long to wait and not receive it. Ten years looking for the little son that they took from you is too long even if there is widespread support for our demand. Ten years is not too long to follow your example. Your parents, your siblings, your family, your friends, and others (even if they don't know it), will never forget you.

*Página/12* director Carlos González (aka Gandhi) remembers the day Estela Carlotto approached him to include her remembrance, the first one of many to come that confronted the dictatorship's disappearances. Two days later, another grandmother did the same. She too had a photo and words of remembrance. More and more arrived, reaching a peak of three or four per day. Sometimes these remembrances spoke only of individual loss, but at other times they told the story of 30,000 disappeared, and openly condemned impunity. According to Gandhi, the newspaper never made a conscious decision to publish the remembrances. They appeared naturally from the relatives' requests. Eventually the newspaper established the 8 cm format that exists still, even in the digital age, and a policy to include remembrances alongside current events.[2] The families used the photographs to challenge the notion that those the security forces had disappeared deserved their fate. They used the photographic medium to show loved ones and to tell a story of atrocity.

Nearly 45 years since the 1976 coup and the installation of authoritarian rule, these remembrances and their power persist. A photo alone, or accompanied by a poem, a note, a call to action, keep the disappeared and the disappearance alive on the pages of the daily. The disappeared remain a physical and material part of our lives. The photographs make the absence present. They tell a truth about the dignity and worth of the person; the loss and injustice are palpable and visible. There is a bond created, a solidarity among the families, with the press, and within society. This medium of the photographic remembrances is used still today to send the message of 'never again'.

The remembrances are 'photographs [that] fill in blanks in our mental pictures of the present and the past' (Sontag 1977: 23). Instead of a number – even a very high number such as the 30,000 disappeared – in Argentina, we sense the depth of the loss and the wrongdoing to the families and to society. The photographs tell a story about a generation who were disappeared not because they were disposable, but because they did not conform. By looking into their eyes, we know that they did not deserve to disappear. That is the message of these remembrances.

The powerful tool of photographs, especially looking into the eyes of the disappeared, is the creation of an emotional bond, an intimacy, the sense of knowing. It has been analysed in psychological and advertising research. As Murphy (2014) states, 'The magnetic and mesmeric nature of eye contact' activates 'parts of the brain that allow us to more acutely and accurately process another person's feelings and intentions'.

The emotional bond made by looking into the eyes of the missing also creates the power behind mobilisation. French artist JR (2008) pastes enormous photographs of eyes in various parts of the world, most famously the Morro da Providência *favela* in Rio de Janeiro. The project *Women Are Heroes* captures, through powerful, watchful eyes, women's social protagonism, rescuing them from an identity that consigns to them only the role of victims. When JR created placards of Eric Garner's eyes as part of the protest against his killing by New York City police, the eyes were seen as

> piercing, looking for justice … to confuse the mediated images of black men as criminals with the actual humanity of a man full of laughter, joy, and sadness. The eyes that marched across the city said something about people needing to be heard and needing the global community to march with them. These eyes said everything about photography … about the cities we all live in and, ultimately, about humanity …

[2] A full set of the remembrances can be found at www.recordatorios.com.ar (accessed 7 February 2021). See also Sosa (2007). A similar effort in Spain, called *guerras de esquelas*, remembers those lost in the Civil War and during the Franco dictatorship (Fernández de Mata 2009).

> [I]mages show the intricate ways in which communities coalesce around a subject. (Thompson 2019: 40)

A bond of solidarity with the disappeared, with the families of those who have disappeared, is the powerful tool and message created by the photographic medium.

Artists working with visual image to reflect on the absence caused by disappearance have deployed the truth-telling and solidarity tool. In 2009, Laura Reuter curated 'The Disappeared', an art exhibit at the North Dakota Museum of Art (North Dakota Museum of Art 2009) featuring the work of twenty-seven South American artists. The catalogue highlights the power of visual image to 'fight amnesia ... as a stay against such atrocities happening again' and even in discovering 'long-hidden identities'. One of the artists featured in the exhibit is Marcelo Brodsky (1997), whose brother is among those disappeared by the Argentine dictatorship. One of his signature works, purchased by the Tate Modern, is the blow-up of his high school class at the Colegio Nacional de Buenos Aires, identifying those disappeared by the state. Juan Manuel Echavarría's photographic collection 'NN' (no name) was also featured: mangled mannequins discarded in an abandoned factory represent the mutilation and disappearance of countless people during Colombia's history of armed conflict. They remain unnamed, unfound, disposed of. The medium of the visual image shows the horror of transforming disappeared people into disposable people. In the hands of artists, these images extend beyond local and national communities. The visual image is used as a powerful tool to extend awareness, solidarity, mobilisation, and pressure for change across borders.

The visual image works as a tool through face-to-face, eye-to-eye contact, by telling a story that challenges common and mistaken assumptions about those who disappeared. It makes the observer aware of a reality they could otherwise ignore. Photographer Edward Weston saw in the visual image the power to '[reveal] to others the living world around them ... showing to them what their own unseeing eyes had missed' (Sontag 1977: 96). We add that the visual image also has the power to create a human connection with those who disappeared and their relatives. This connection, this understanding, is a kind of truth-telling used by families, by communities, by advocates, and by artists as a tool for change, to transform the reality of the living world.

## Seeing Is Believing

'Photography is commonly regarded as an instrument for knowing things', says Sontag (1977: 93). We could apply Sontag's view to contend that the disappeared and disappearances are 'made real by photographs' (161). As proof of this power, Sontag and others reflect on how photographs are used to validate, to give information, to make an inventory, in official documents (22). Indeed, relatives sometimes use photographs replicated from official documents, such as national identification cards, to verify, to register, to produce the evidence of the disappearance.

At other times, relatives imitate, rather than reproduce, official documentation. The use of a type of official missing persons poster, asking for help in finding them, is one such tool. These photographs have a very poignant twist. An example of a poster of missing children, one that might appear in a police station or other locale seeking help in finding them, is instead pasted to a telephone pole in Mexico City. It accuses and provokes the observer, saying 'If they were from your family, would you just stand there and look? David and Miguel were kidnapped more than three years ago. Support us!'.

The photograph of missing people is thus used as a tool to ask for support. The poster appears in a public space – pasted on to a pole – to increase the chances of being seen; it gains visibility. The quality of the medium, its homemade feel, the use of a family snapshot, an image of boys who could be related to you, the attachment to a neighbourhood, the creation of an email for any information that could allow the family to rescue David and Miguel (restatemosadavidymiguel@rescatemosDM), make the loss to this family real. They also appeal to society, suggesting that this is not an isolated case; it could happen to you, and what would you do? The poster that reflects a family tragedy is linked to a wider social phenomenon. It is calling on members of that society to react before it happens to them.

A particular twist on using official documentation techniques as a tool to make the observer see and believe was taken up by the *Madre Terra* (*Mother Earth*) photography project involving the Mothers of Soacha in Colombia. The Mothers formed because their missing children were among the 'false positives' in the Colombian armed conflict, a process described by Sebastián Ramírez Hernández (2019) as '[i]ncited by a government directive which offered soldiers about US$2,000 for each enemy killed in combat', with the result that 'army personnel conspired to kill and murder thousands of civilians'. The *Madre Terra* photography project, originally initiated by the Colombia government's Victims Unit, aimed to represent the mothers' losses.[3] Carlos Saavedra photographed the mothers, who had had themselves buried in the soil, assuming the position that they chose to represent their connection to the land and the disappearance of their family members. The photographs are used as a tool by the families to demand visibility: to see these photographs is to believe, to understand maybe for the first time, the impact of false positives; that the government committed an atrocity; and that any of us, or our children, could be falsely identified as the enemy, killed, and disappeared in a mass grave.

The *Madre Terra* photography project was a powerful tool to show the impact of false positives on 15 families in a very personal way. In the process it connected these families' losses to a broader social phenomenon. The images thus created

[3] The photographs can be found on Carlos Saavedra's website: saavedravisual.com (accessed 7 February 2021). A book exploring the project is forthcoming by Sebastián Ramírez and Carlos Saavedra, titled *Madres terra*. See also articles on the public exhibition of the photographs in 2018: www.eltiempo.com/cultura/arte-y-teatro/exposicion-de-las-madres-de-soacha-en-el-centro-de-memoria-historica-228254; www.semana.com/nacion/articulo/en-video-familias-desaparecidos-falsos-positivos-militares-farc/574471 (both accessed 7 February 2021).

**Figure 13.2** A missing person's poster on a telephone pole in Villa Olímpica, Mexico City.

another take on the notion that the 'personal is political'. They suggest that such a concept not only explains the motivation of certain women to mobilise when their personal lives are affected by political events (Hanisch 1970; Navarro 2001), but also that photographs can make visible that disappearances and the personal

**Figure 13.3** Six mothers pose in burial portraits to safeguard the memory of their disappeared sons in the *Madre Terra* photography project (Colombia).

loss experienced by the families of the disappeared are also political. The visual images used by families attempt to overcome the efforts in society to explain away disappearance with expressions such as 'por algo será' ('there must be a reason'). The powerful tool of the photograph is aimed at overcoming a natural tendency to believe that bad things happen to others, and not to us: the message that a traumatic experience that struck normal people, normal families, could strike you next. How this tool is used stems from what is represented in the photograph: a public space, an everyday image, that represents loss. It stems also from who holds the images: mothers – who could be anyone's mother – and how they hold those images – tenderly for all to see, or worn around their necks like the arms of a child, close to their hearts and breasts. The powerful tool of the photographic image is used by families to make clear to an unconscious or unconcerned public that their children were taken from them.

Such a technique, or tool – to make the loss hit home, quite literally – has been used in different ways by families searching for their missing loved ones in a range of situations. The 'Milk Carton Kids' were images and details of missing children that appeared on milk cartons in the USA in the early 1980s. These images replaced advertisements that had once appeared on those cartons.[4] The idea of the campaign

[4] One of the first 'Milk Carton Kids' was six-year-old Etan Patz, who left his Manhattan home one morning in 1979, but never made it to his school bus. Owing to the tireless efforts of his parents, he became one of the best-known cases of missing children. President Ronald Reagan in 1983 designated

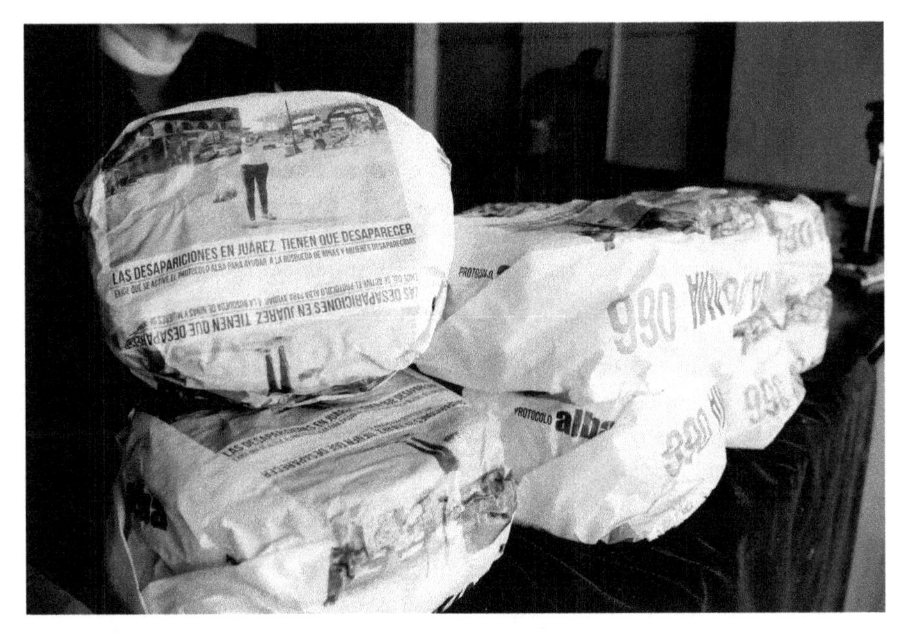


**Figure 13.4** Tortilla wrappers pictured women and children, and bore the words 'Disappearances in Juárez must disappear' (Mexico).

was to use the kind of platform that would enter the homes of every American to make visible the phenomenon of missing children. As Americans poured milk onto their breakfast cereal, they looked into the faces of these missing children. Explicitly referencing the milk carton idea, in 2012 a group in Ciudad Juárez in Mexico used tortilla wrappers as a way to bring images of missing women and children into every home to make them visible and to demand that 'Disappearances in Juárez must Disappear.'

Another campaign used visual images of celebrities as a tool to raise awareness and mobilise support. These celebrities are obviously not among the disappeared. By taking on the personality of the disappeared, therefore, they suggest that this could happen to anyone, even them. They call on the public to see them and believe them as a disappeared person undeserving of wrongdoing, not a disposable person. They recognise the dignity of the disappeared by visually representing their life stories and demanding state response. The Brazilian Bar Association (OAB) initiated a

25 May, the date of Patz's disappearance, as 'National Missing Children's Day'. The non-profit National Child Safety Council, which began the 'Missing Children Milk Carton Program', eventually linked 700 (of 1,600) dairies across the United States in the effort to make these children visible and thus traceable. The milk carton strategy prompted criticism because of the emphasis on white children, who are proportionally much less likely to be disappeared than non-white children. The programme was replaced with the Amber Alert system. For an image of this milk carton strategy, see https://99percentinvisible.org/episode/milk-carton-kids/ (accessed 19 May 2020).

campaign for truth and memory by asking well-known actors to represent those disappeared during the dictatorship. They take on the personality, tell their story, and end each representation with the same words: 'My family never found out what happened to me. Will this torture never end?'. The campaign ends by calling on viewers to participate in the project for finding the truth about the disappeared.[5]

Having famous people take on the roles of the disappeared is a tool aimed at dignifying the lives and stories of victims. Those who disappeared are important because celebrities make them and their lives important. The tool also works by drawing attention to the atrocity of those who may not otherwise be aware of it: followers of popular culture. As a tool of power it makes clear that the disappeared are not known, but the people willing to represent them are household names. Those celebrities bring the people who disappeared, and their stories, into our lives and our living rooms. They raise awareness of the phenomenon of disappearance. By representing normal people with normal lives who are disappeared, celebrity projects challenge viewers to rethink their assumptions that these individuals must have been involved in something to be among the disappeared.

Fashion- and portrait-photographer Richard Avedon once remarked 'It is through the photographs that I know' (Sontag 1977: 121). This is perhaps the intuitive function and power of the visual-image tool: by seeing the faces and looking into the eyes of the disappeared, the public will know what happened. Disappearance is thus a personal tragedy that affected a family, but also a societal one. The visual image as a tool assaults ignorance by bringing the phenomenon of disappearance into everyday life, making it visible, raising awareness, and calling for action and change.

## Rupture and Emptiness

Visual images of the disappeared function as a powerful tool through the familiar, in the literal meaning of the word. We relate to those depicted in the photographs like a family; like someone close; like our own children, sisters, brothers. The connection through seeing makes understanding what happened – the disappearance – so powerful. The visual image of the disappeared creates in an instant a profound story of loss. A *Paris-Match* advertisement suggested this power: 'The weight of words. The shock of photos' (Sontag 1977: 206). The use of the visual image – whether intended or not by the families of the disappeared – is a tool to shock. The images represent those who were so much a part of everyday – family – life, and enable the viewer to understand the profound loss experienced by their absence.

[5] These spots can be found in the Núcleo de Preservação da Memória Política, 'Campanha pela Memória e pela Verdade OAB', YouTube (accessed 30 May 2020). For some examples, see: www.youtube.com/watch?v=B_f21AtnG2w; www.youtube.com/watch?v=reAPWKcLqcM; www.youtube.com/watch?v=q9TQO_fmELg; www.youtube.com/watch?v=WA5jYLI9LuE; www.youtube.com/watch?v=Fi_phyehvE8.

Some of the visual images used as tools of power depict not the presence of the loved ones, but rather their absence. The mother without her child is one such image. Noemí Escandell's *Disappeared* sculpture 'presents a Pietà with the Virgin Mary's empty arms. On her head, she wears one of the kerchiefs of the Mothers of the Plaza de Mayo' from Argentina (Bilbija *et al.* 2005: 26). Similarly, but in the post-transition era, an enormous mural appears on a wall in downtown Monterrey in Mexico, portraying a mother's loving embrace of her missing child.

Mothers with missing sons and daughters reflect one of the deepest, most primordial, forms of loss. The visual image functions as a powerful tool by representing the loss through absence, the missing child. It further represents the rupture of a social bond, along with a personal and family bond. Everyone has a mother. Everyone understands the meaning of such a loss. Disappearance, therefore, is not only a profound loss to individuals' daily, family, and social life, but is also a rupture represented by a mother's inability to fulfil a primordial role of keeping her child safe from violence. Mothers thus become powerful symbolic actors with legitimacy and agency to mobilise. They take to the streets, to the public squares and parks, to the city's walls and poles – they use the powerful tool of the visual image of their loss – to cry out for help, for something to be done, for the search for their children, for their return, for repair, for justice for wrongdoing, and for never again.

Mothers have used the visual image of absence as a powerful tool to represent loss; but they are not the only social actors who have used it. A visual image emerged from the inauguration of the first democratically elected president after

**Figure 13.5** Mural of a mother with her missing child (Mexico).

**Figure 13.6** Benches in remembrance of *los degollados* (Chile).

the Chilean dictatorship, symbolically held in the National Football Stadium – a detention centre that held many political prisoners who never again appeared alive. President Alywin provided a moment for women to perform the *cueca* – a traditional couples dance – alone, demonstrating their loss, a tool aimed at overcoming the national tragedy of disappearance and the need for truth, justice, reparations, and guarantees of non-repetition.[6]

Students and their teachers have also used visual representations of absence as a powerful tool. In Chile, three giant empty school chairs loom over the highway near the Santiago airport to symbolise the place where *los degollados* (the slit-throated) were found after being abducted by the state security forces in front of the Colegio Latinoamericano high school. Three decades later, a movement in solidarity assembled in front of where the school had once stood to witness the installation of empty benches with the names of the three disappeared-murdered. In this symbolic burial, those gathered held close the photos of the loved members of the community who had been murdered and disappeared. So many years later, the visual image of the names of those no longer with us continues to serve as a powerful tool to remember, to never forget.

Chairs have been used as a visual tool to depict the disappearance of students and their teachers elsewhere in Latin America. Every year since 2004, on Guatemala's National Day against Forced Disappearance (21 June), activists place in public 450 chairs – empty except for photographs of the 45,000 who disappeared during the armed conflict (1960–96). The date is connected to the anniversary of the disappearance by state security agents of 27 students' and union leaders.[7] Remembering the disappearance of 43 students from the Normal Rural School of Ayotzinapa in Iguala, Mexico, in 2014 has at times also involved chairs, in what Ileana Diéguez has described as 'a phantasmagoric scene that intends to shape absence' (Diéguez

[6] The *cueca sola* inspired the Sting song 'They Dance Alone' on the *Nothing Like the Sun* album (1987), A&M Records.

[7] 'Con sillas vacías recuerdan a 45.000 desaparecidos de la Guerra en Guatemala', *La Nación* (21 June 2017), www.nacion.com/el-mundo/politica/con-sillas-vacias-recuerdan-a-45-000-desaparecidos-de-la-guerra-en-guatemala/U7WBN4EUVFGEFDJKPSPRGPEJ7Q/story/ (accessed 19 May 2020).

**Figure: 13.7** The *Empty Bicycles* of Rosario, Argentina.

2016: 51). Diéguez describes an installation of 43 school chairs, each empty except for the photograph and name of a disappeared student. The chairs were arranged behind a large banner stating, 'LOS 43 NOS FALTAN A TODOS' ('We are all missing the 43' (Diéguez 2016: 52)). The visual image of loss is a powerful tool for remembering and continuing to search for the missing, for truth, and for justice.

In Rosario in Argentina, a symbolic visual representation of the missing is used as a tool for truth-telling, the struggle against forgetting, and the demand for 'never again'. The *Bicicletas vacias* project involves stencils of bicycles without riders throughout the city. These bicycles do not include the names or faces of the disappeared riders. A number – 350 – identifies the number of disappearances in that city during the dictatorship.[8] The bicycles represent the everydayness of the disappeared. A person leaves home, work, or school on their bicycle and never

[8] A story about the bicycles without riders can be found at '"Memoria y Resistencia en Bicicleta": un homenaje a los desaparecidos', Centediario.com (25 March 2015), http://www.centediario.com/memoria-y-resistencia-en-bicicleta-un-homenaje-a-los-desaparecidos/ (accessed 19 May 2020). See images at https://054.travel/bicicletas-rosario/350-bicicletas-rosario-desaparecidos-dictadura-stencil-street-art-santa-fe-argentina-054-054online/ (accessed 7 February 2021).

**Figure 13.8** *Silueteando V. El Siluetazo* (Argentina).

returns. The bicycle is found, but not the rider. The empty bicycles represent the rupture of everyday life, the disappearance of ordinary people, the emptiness that remains.

A silhouette project (*El Siluetazo)* initiated in Argentina in 1983, during the dictatorship, by three artists working with the Mothers of the Plaza de Mayo, was used as a tool to capture the shocking everydayness of disappearances.[9] People would lie down on paper and have their silhouettes traced. They would paint, spray-paint, and write on the silhouettes. The phrases that were written evoked the loss of disappearance and a call to action: 'aparición con vida' ('return alive'), 'dónde está' ('where are you?'), 'cárcel a los genocidas' ('imprison the genocidaires'), 'ni olvido ni perdón' ('never forget, never forgive'), and '30,000 disappeared'. The silhouettes were attached to walls of buildings close to the Plaza de Mayo. They were not the bodies, shapes, faces of the actual disappeared, but of people who were not (yet) disappeared. In this sense they acted as a tool to reflect on the generalised use of disappearance by the dictatorship; to acknowledge wrongdoing behind the act of disappearance; to make visible that it could be you or someone you love who is disappeared; and thus to demand visibility, understanding, and action to end the violence.

Empty chairs, bicycles without riders, and silhouettes are powerful visual images used as a tool to cast specific individual acts of disappearance within a

[9] See also https://arteymemoriaslatinoamericanas.wordpress.com/2016/05/23/el-siluetazo/ (accessed 7 February 2021).

broader social phenomenon. By not showing faces, these visual images represent the generalised phenomenon. The gaze is oriented toward the perpetration of the crime, the disappearance, as much as the individuals and the families who were victimised by it. As a tool, the visual representation of absence raises awareness that the traumas of single families are a national tragedy. As Berger (1972b: 8) notes, 'We only see what we look at. To look is an act of choice. As a result of this act, what we see is brought within our reach.' The visual image cannot force people to look, but it is a powerful tool to move those who do.

## Weapons of the Weak

'Photographed images do not seem to be statements about the world so much as pieces of it, miniatures of reality that anyone can make or acquire' (Sontag 1977: 4). In that statement Sontag encapsulates how the medium of visual images is used as a tool to capture reality, to make it possible for those not directly affected to see, to believe, to disrupt complacency, to mobilise in solidarity with the families. The power of the tool of the visual image is its universalising potential, to make what is experienced by some, felt by others: 'a promise inherent in photography from its very beginning: to democratise all experiences by translating them into images' (Sontag 1977: 7). Photographs – snapshots from the daily life of the disappeared person, or official identification documents – remain in the family's possession, or can be acquired, even after a disappearance. Images can be inexpensively reproduced and distributed; posted on telephone poles, on city walls, on empty chairs; carried or worn on marches – to reach a broad public, to try to force people to see. They thus have powerful potential as a tool to break the silence about disappearance, to expose wrongdoing, and to catalyse solidarity and mobilisation to pressure for change.

The visual image tool can be used by an individual to highlight a personal and familial trauma. It is also a tool to be used by movements and groups to embed individual events in a broader context: one of 30,000 disappeared in Argentina, one of the 43 students in Ayotzinapa, one of 450 who disappeared on a single day in a single event in Guatemala. In this way the visual image is used as a tool to undermine the claim that the disappeared 'must have been involved in something'. It is a powerful tool that can be used by anyone, even those who are marginalised in society. It is, as such, the weapon of the weak (Scott 1985). Nato Thompson (2019: 32) seems to apply this idea when he states 'The image itself is, in fact, a weapon.'

The visual image is a tool that has the potential to move outside national borders and build international solidarity. A poster in London of one of the disappeared students from Ayotzinapa in Mexico provides an example. An image of one young man is in the photograph. The poster refers (in English), however, to the 43 disappeared Mexican students claiming they were 'disappeared by the state'.

No official investigations or trials have conclusively linked the disappearance to state forces or anyone else. The placement of the poster on a major public and tourist thoroughfare in London, the use of English, and the assignation of blame to Mexican authorities, indicate an effort to bring international solidarity behind the search for truth and justice in the disappearance. It is an example of Keck and Sikkink's (1998) boomerang model, in which local actors, through their mobilisation, attempt to gain attention internationally to name and shame the Mexican state to investigate and stop human rights abuses. Indeed, by using the English translation of the phrase 'They took them alive, we want them alive', used by the Argentine Mothers of the Plaza de Mayo, the Mexican mobilisation may have hoped to catalyse in relation to the 43 students a similar international outcry the Argentine dictatorship experienced over its '30,000' disappeared. Without a doubt, international pressure erupted over the 43 disappearances in Ayotzinapa. Yet the case remains unsolved. And little attention has been brought internationally to the 60,000 others disappeared in the country. The visual-image tool, nonetheless, has the power to build solidarity across borders, to mobilise pressure on the state from outside and inside the country.

The visual image tool also works within groups of victims. Through images, a bond is created among families. Indeed, the images themselves are sometimes linked together reflecting the alliance that has formed out of a shared loss and a shared commitment to struggle for the search of the missing and the quest for justice for wrongdoing. The Mothers of the Plaza de Mayo created a kind of quilt of photographs that is used especially on the anniversary of the coup that put in place the authoritarian regime and its disappearance atrocities. Putting together all of those images in a single banner, a quilt, makes evident the enormity of the loss, the need to act.[10] But it also means that no family is alone. It is a collective struggle.

There are limits to the use of the visual image as a tool or weapon of the weak to end disappearances. Sontag sees this limit in the existing recognition of the social problem, stating 'some unsuspected zone of misery cannot make a dent in public opinion unless there is an appropriate context of feeling and attitude' (Sontag 1977: 17). She goes on to say that 'Photographs cannot create a moral position, but they can reinforce one – and can help build a nascent one' (17) depending on the existence of 'relevant political consciousness' (19). Even in those cases, she contends, 'most photographs do not keep their emotional charge' (21). The emphasis that the families of the disappeared put on the photographs cannot depend only on a pre-existing political consciousness, although that helps. Instead, they attempt – with visual images – to reach out to those who may be unaware of the disappearances, to help them understand, to undermine the accepted logic of

[10] To see an image of the photos in a banner, used on the day of national protest against the authoritarian regime and its disappearances, see '"En unidad y con memoria", Marcha del 24 de marzo: el documento completo leído en la Plaza de Mayo', *Página/12* (24 March 2019), www.pagina12.com.ar/183043-marcha-del-24-de-marzo-el-documento-completo-leido-en-la-pla (accessed 25 May 2020).

**Figure 13.9** Poster of the 43 disappeared students of Ayotzinapa (London).

disappearance, and to build a moral position and political consciousness that aims to end it.

Another potential limitation of the tool is the numbing effect that may result from the assault of visual imagery of the disappeared (Jelin 2003). That emotional shut-down can backfire and work against mobilisation. The editors of the *Photographer's Project*, while recognising these potential weaknesses, defend the use of the visual-image tool as powerful enough to overcome numbing and inertia:

> The term 'compassion fatigue' has been coined for the shameful state many of us arrive at in the face of such a barrage [of a continuous dispatch of news of violence]. And yet, even in this maelstrom, the artist's response to atrocity can be powerfully affecting. The artist – the painter, the photographer, the writer – has the capability to translate the far-away drone of horror into something real and immediate, something so very tangible that we may be moved to act upon our response to it. (Peress and Berger 2008)

As a weapon of the weak, moreover, the visual image is one of the few tools accessible to anyone. It is a powerful tool for creating knowledge, through evidence, and compassion, through emotional connection. It is 'one of the principal devices for experiencing something' (Sontag 1977: 10); that something is the loss of someone who was important to a family, to a society; to challenge the notion that this person was 'disposable'. In this way visual images operate as a tool to undermine the narratives that attempt to blame disappeared persons themselves for the act. It weakens one of the foundational logics of the disappearances. In the process, it builds solidarity to mobilise for change.

## Conclusion: 'We Want Them Back Alive'

The visual images of the missing are not mere photographs and are not only instrumental tools. They are the person. 'Simple snapshots ... insist that this is a person, a person who exists ... They make the missing visible' (Edkins 2011: 1). They are sometimes all that the families have, all that remains, of that person. Clinging to the photographs is also clinging to the hope that the person is still alive and will return. That hope is inherent in the message 'we want them back alive'.

The photographs offer the means to communicate that message. In this sense they are a powerful tool for mobilisation within the community of victims and survivors, providing the unity and numbers necessary for the search for the missing. Sontag refers to 'talismanic uses of photographs [that] express a feeling both sentimental and implicitly magical: they are attempts to contact or lay claim to another reality' (Sontag 1977: 16). Those uses of the tool are not only intended for the directly affected, to generate the internal strength, commitment, and persistence to struggle. Visual images are also intended for those not directly affected, in society and abroad; they are a tool with the potential to raise understanding and consciousness, increase solidarity, mobilise, and pressure states for change.

The use of the visual-images tool has tended to evolve organically, as a natural response by families to the disappearances. It has not necessarily emerged out of a conscious decision or concerted strategy. The observations made in this chapter, however, reflect on the set of goals that visual images have the potential to achieve, and how those images have been, and can be, used to increase the likelihood of their having that effect.

Visual images are, in essence, the tool used to erode the underlying logic of disappearance – the disappeared person as a disposable person. Presenting the disappeared person in photographs challenges the notion that a person deserved to disappear because of connections to violent criminal or politically or economically subversive activity. To look into the eyes of disappeared people is to see them as their family does: as someone who is loved, to be held close, who demands protection, who should return home alive. The images provide the evidence that no one deserves to be disappeared. Each photograph thus presents the story of humanity. To operate as a powerful tool, photographs need to be widely visible, on city streets, in public squares, pasted on walls and poles, made impossible to ignore.

Visual images are a tool to reflect on the deep personal story of loss, and to link that intimate story to a broader social phenomenon: 'This happened to that person, but it could just as easily have happened to me or someone I know.' When the personal is made political, it becomes much harder to dismiss or deny the stories as isolated events. In that way, visual images can challenge the complacency that leads to victim-blaming. Through truly seeing the victims, and situating them within a generalised set of events, negation of the facts becomes much more difficult. That each image tells an individual story linked to a wider social phenomenon increases the understanding that the families are not alone in their struggle. It is also a recognition that this did not happen to some people because of who they were and what they did; it could happen to you. The visual image acts as a tool to make the observer think, often by shocking them with arresting images: why are the chairs empty, the bicycles without riders, the mothers embracing no one, the images only silhouettes without faces? The visual-image tool has the power to present not only the presence but also the absence, and the trauma of loss.

Visual images constitute a tool that can be used by anyone, the marginalised as well as political elites and celebrities in the community, the country, and abroad, to catalyse mobilisation through the understanding of the injustice, generalised phenomenon, and trauma of disappearance. Particularly when these images reach an international audience through the shock of wrongdoing, the mobilisation can pressure the state to search for the missing, to investigate the perpetrators, pursue justice, and mitigate harm. The mobilisation is not only about past and ongoing disappearances, but is a demand that no other families should have to face this sort of atrocity. Visual images thus serve as a tool behind the claim for 'never again'.

## References

Berger, J. (1972a), 'Understanding a Photograph', in *Selected Essays and Articles: The Look of Things*, pp. 291–4, available at https://pdfs.semanticscholar.org/eba5/ba39439def4cd9bf3b29133b9bb5cdaa991d.pdf?_ga=2.200079214.1750842027.1590144739-381869628.1590144739 (accessed 22 May 2020).

Berger, J. (1972b), *Ways of Seeing* (London, Penguin).

Bilbija, K., J. E. Fair, C. E. Milton, and L. A. Payne, L.A. (2005), *The Art of Truth-Telling about Authoritarian Rule* (Madison, University of Wisconsin Press).

Brodsky, M. (1997), *Buena memoria: un ensayo fotográfico de Marcelo Brodsky* (Buenos Aires, La Marca Fotografía).

Contra la Impunidad (2010), 'Justicia para las víctimas de la dictadura genocida franquista', video project (14 June), www.youtube.com/watch?v=xsyEMAjCDbo (accessed 19 May 2020).

Diéguez Caballero, I. (2016), *Cuerpos sin duelo: iconografías y teatralidades del dolor* (Monterrey, Universidad Autónoma de Nuevo León).
Edkins, J. (2011), *Missing: Persons and Politics* (Ithaca, Cornell University Press).
Fernández de Mata, I. (2009), 'In memoriam … esquelas, contra-esquelas y duelos inconclusos de la Guerra Civil Española', *HAFO* I:42, https://politicasdelamemoria.org/wp-content/uploads/2009/01/In-memoriamSmall.pdf-1170.compressed.pdf (accessed 23 May 2020).
Hanisch, C. (1970), 'The Personal Is Political', in *Notes from the Second Year: Women's Liberation*, www.carolhanisch.org/CHwritings/PIP.html (accessed 25 May 2020).
Jelin, E. (2003), *State Repression and the Labors of Memory* (Minneapolis, University of Minnesota Press).
JR (2008), *Women Are Heroes, Brazil*, video and still photographs of the art installation, www.jr-art.net/projects/rio-de-janeiro (accessed 30 May 2020).
Keck, M. E., and K. Sikkink, K. (1998), *Activists beyond Borders: Advocacy Networks in International Politics* (Ithaca, Cornell University Press).
LeBourdais, J. (1967), 'McLuhan: Now the Medium Is the Massage', *New York Times* (19 March), https://timesmachine.nytimes.com/timesmachine/1967/03/19/107185353.html?action=click&contentCollection=Archives&module=LedeAsset®ion=ArchiveBody&pgtype=article&pageNumber=179 (accessed 18 May 2020).
Murphy, K. (2014), 'Psst. Look over Here', *New York Times* (16 May), www.nytimes.com/2014/05/17/sunday-review/the-eyes-have-it.html?_r=1 (accessed 16 May 2020).
Navarro, M. (2001), 'The Personal Is Political: Las Madres de Plaza de Mayo' in *Power and Popular Protest: Latin American Social Movements*, ed. S. Eckstein (Berkeley, University of California Press), pp. 241–58.
North Dakota Museum of Art (2009), *Past Exhibitions: The Disappeared*, www.ndmoa.com/past-2009-the-disappeared (accessed 30 May 2020).
Payne, L. A. (2019a), 'Como hacer una historia transformadora: siete desafios', paper presented at FLACSO-Mexico seminar 'Desaparición de personas en México: documentación, análisis y comunicación, 5 December.
Payne, L. A. (2019b), 'Silence and Memory Politics', in *Rethinking Peace: Discourse, Memory, Translation, and Dialogue*, ed. A. L. Hinton, G. Shani, and J. Alberg (London, Rowman & Littlefield), pp. 109–22.
Peress, G., and J. Berger (2008), 'How Silent Images Can Break the Silence', *Aperture*, 191 (Summer): 44–9.
Ramírez Hernández, S. (2019), 'False Wars', Visual and New Media Review, *Fieldsights* (5 August), https://culanth.org/fieldsights/false-wars (accessed 7 February 2021).
Scott, J. C. (1985), *Weapons of the Weak: Everyday Forms of Peasant Resistance* (New Haven, Yale University Press).
Sontag, S. (1977), *On Photography* (New York, Picador).
Sosa, C. (2007), 'Nomeolvides', *Página/12* (16 September), www.pagina12.com.ar/diario/suplementos/radar/9-4115-2007-09-16.html (accessed 23 May 2020).
Thompson, N. (2019), 'If a Smile Is a Weapon: The Art of JR', in *JR: Can Art Change the World?* (London, Phaidon), pp. 30–41.

# 14

# Using the Minnesota Protocol to Investigate Disappearance Cases

BARBARA A. FREY

## Introduction

THE GUIDELINES ON criminal and forensic investigation found in *The Minnesota Protocol on the Investigation of Potentially Unlawful Death (2016)* (OHCHR 2017) are a source of practical assistance in disappearance cases. They also serve as a standard by which families and advocates can measure the adequacy of the state's efforts to search for the disappeared and to investigate the crime. Although the Protocol's frame is unlawful death, the standards are designed to investigate disappearances as well.

The Minnesota Protocol is a practical guide that supports the implementation of the 1989 UN Principles on the Effective Prevention and Investigation of Extra-Legal, Arbitrary and Summary Executions (United Nations 1991).[1] The Minnesota Protocol establishes 'a common standard of performance in investigating potentially unlawful death or suspected enforced disappearance' (OHCHR 2017: para. 1). The manual sets forth internationally accepted principles and practical guidelines for governments, institutions, and individuals to carry out effective and transparent investigations in cases of death and/or disappearance.[2]

The United Nations published the first version of the Minnesota Protocol in 1991 (United Nations 1991) to address human rights crimes that not only were unpunished, but also had not been investigated. At the time, there were no international legal requirements regarding death investigations. The drafters sought to create a practical guide for investigators and a set of criteria for evaluating the adequacy of the state's investigations of deaths – which pertained to disappearances

[1] The 1989 Principles were endorsed by UN General Assembly Resolution 44/162 of 15 December 1989.
[2] The term investigation refers to the broad set of activities to explain a human rights crime, including the activity of searching for the missing or for evidence regarding their disappearance.

*Proceedings of the British Academy*, **237**, 225–233, © The British Academy 2021.

as well. The original UN Manual made an impact on law and practice, by establishing state responsibilities for investigating disappearances and killings. Regional courts relied on it in a series of seminal judgments (see European Court of Human Rights (1998, 2005); Inter-American Court of Human Rights (2009); and African Commission on Human and Peoples' Rights (2006)). International organisations and non-governmental organisations used it in documentation of cases (UNSREASK 2015). Human rights organisations recognised the Protocol's utility in autopsies and exhumations, but updates were needed to include new technologies, such as DNA analysis (UNSREASK 2015: 9). After a year-long drafting process involving stakeholders representing a wide range of experience and expertise, the UN published the updated Minnesota Protocol in 2016 to reflect best practices distilled from two decades of international criminal investigations. The revised standards are available in all official UN languages and were launched visibly in various regional and national fora to encourage states and civil society to employ them.

The UN High Commissioner for Human Rights, Zeid Ra'ad Al Hussein, explained in the Foreward to the Protocol: 'A suspicious death occurring anywhere in the world is potentially a violation of the right to life, often described as the supreme human right, and therefore a prompt, impartial and effective investigation is key to ensuring that a culture of accountability – rather than impunity – prevails. The same applies to enforced disappearances' (OHCHR 2017: v).

The revised Minnesota Protocol summarises international legal norms on the state's duty to investigate disappearances. The manual also sets out principles and details guidelines on witness interviews, crime scene investigations, interviews, excavation of graves, and autopsy procedures. The Protocol offers best practices for investigating cases in which bodies are missing, as well as considerations for dealing with family members in these cases.[3]

## Legal Responsibility to Investigate Disappearances

The Minnesota Protocol explains when the state is obliged to investigate a disappearance. When the disappearance is caused by acts or omissions of state agents, such as law enforcement personnel, or by non-state actors acting with the consent or acquiescence of the state (OHCHR 2017: para. 2.a), the state clearly must investigate the case in compliance with the Minnesota Protocol. The Protocol also applies when a state fails to meet its obligations to protect human life, including failing to prevent foreseeable threats by non-state actors (OHCHR 2017: para. 2.c). Even if state agents did not evidently cause the disappearance, the state is under a general duty to investigate the case (OHCHR 2017: para. 2.c).

[3] For further details on any aspect of search and investigation, readers are encouraged to consult the Protocol directly, at www.ohchr.org/Documents/Publications/MinnesotaProtocol_SP.pdf (accessed 9 February 2021).

The Protocol explains that the state has a duty to investigate when it knows or should have known that a disappearance has occurred (OHCHR 2017: para. 15). This duty to investigate applies to suspected disappearances even when the state cannot be held responsible for failing to prevent them (OHCHR 2017: para. 18).[4] The Protocol makes clear that, even in times of generalised violence, a state must investigate suspected disappearances. The European Court of Human Rights, in *Jaloud* v. *The Netherlands*, observed, 'It is clear that where the death to be investigated occurs in circumstances of generalised violence, armed conflict or insurgency, obstacles may be placed in the way of investigators ... Nonetheless, even in difficult security conditions, all reasonable steps must be taken to ensure that an effective, independent investigation is conducted into alleged breaches of the right to life' (European Court of Human Rights, Grand Chamber 2014: para. 164).

The duty to investigate applies whether or not the state receives a formal complaint. Instead, the mere knowledge of a disappearance gives rise to an obligation to carry out an effective investigation into the circumstances surrounding the case (European Court of Human Rights 1998: para. b.ii).

## Requirements of an Investigation

The state must carry out prompt, thorough, independent, and transparent investigations of suspected disappearances. The adequacy of each investigation is measured against four criteria explained in the Minnesota Protocol:

> **Prompt**. Authorities must conduct an investigation as soon as possible and proceed without unreasonable delays. The duty of promptness, however, does not justify a rushed investigation (OHCHR 2017: para. 23).
>
> **Effective and Thorough**. Investigators should, to the extent possible, collect and confirm (for example by triangulation) all testimonial, documentary and physical evidence (OHCHR 2017: para. 24). At a minimum, searchers should identify the victims, recover all material probative of the disappearance, identify possible witnesses, and obtain their statements in relation to the disappearance (OHCHR 2017: para. 25).
>
> **Independent and Impartial**. Searchers and their supervisors must be, and be seen to be, independent of undue influence of any political parties, powerful social actors, or suspected perpetrators (OHCHR 2017: paras 28–9). Searchers must analyse all evidence objectively. They must consider and appropriately pursue exculpatory as well as inculpatory evidence (OHCHR 2017: para. 31).

[4] See also article 3, Convention on Enforced Disappearances.

**Transparent**. Search processes and outcomes must be open to the scrutiny of the general public and of victims' families. According to the Minnesota Protocol, 'Transparency promotes the rule of law and public accountability, and enables the efficacy of investigations to be monitored externally.' It also enables the families, human rights defenders, and the general public to assist with the investigation. Searchers should, at a minimum, be transparent about the existence of an investigation, the procedures followed in an investigation, and its findings, including their factual and legal basis (OHCHR 2017: para. 32).

## Conducting an Effective Investigation

The Minnesota Protocol discusses the strategies and practical steps for investigating a suspected disappearance. Section IV of the Protocol provides general guidance, followed by detailed guidelines in Section V on crime-scene investigation, the conduct of interviews, the excavation of graves, the conduct of an autopsy, and the analysis of skeletal remains.

Each investigation should be risk-assessed, to ensure that neither the searchers nor the general public are put in harm's way. Every investigation should be methodical and transparent, and investigators should pursue all legitimate lines of enquiry to avoid overlooking relevant evidence (see e.g. Federman *et al.*, Chapter 10). All materials and observations relevant to the search and investigation should be secured, recorded, and logged. This includes all decisions taken, information gathered, and witness statements. The source, date, and time of collection of all material must also be logged (OHCHR 2017: paras 47–9).

The search and/or investigation team should conduct an initial investigation to identify lines of enquiry. The team should identify all sources of potential evidence and prioritise the collection and preservation of that evidence. The investigators should collect relevant witness statements. The team should plan activities and allocate resources allocated in order to manage:

- the collection, analysis, and management of evidence, data, and materials;
- the forensic examination of important physical locations, including the death/crime scene;
- family liaison;
- the development of a victim profile;
- the finding, interview, and protection of witnesses;
- international technical assistance;
- telecommunications and other digital evidence;
- financial issues;
- the chronology of events.

(OHCHR 2017: para. 52)

In the search for a disappeared person, the searchers should gather any direct or circumstantial evidence that may explain the crime. This includes locating and identifying every important physical location, such as the site of encounters between the victim(s) and any identified suspects, the location of the disappearance, and possible burial sites. The search should take global positioning system (GPS) coordinates at these sites (OHCHR 2017: para. 56).

Searchers and investigators should learn about the victim(s); document their lifestyle, routines, and activities; and their political, religious, or economic background. Missing person reports, family witness statements, and dental and other reliable physical records, as well as fingerprints and DNA, can be used in the search and investigation process (OHCHR 2017: para. 56).

Investigators should examine the crime scene in each case. A crime scene is any physical scene where investigators may locate, record, and recover physical evidence. It may be a place where a person's body or skeletal remains or other personal items of the victim can be found (OHCHR 2017: para. 58). Each crime scene should be secured to protect and gather evidence effectively and to minimise the contamination or loss of relevant material (OHCHR 2017: para. 59). Investigators should keep a record of all personnel entering the scene, with the corresponding date and time of their visits. Individuals interacting with evidence should provide DNA and fingerprints as reference samples. To minimise forensic contamination and to protect the health and safety of personnel, searchers should wear suitable protective clothing, including gloves and masks. Correct packaging for each type of evidence will preserve evidence (OHCHR 2017: para. 59).

All material located at a crime scene is potentially relevant to the investigation, including but not limited to the following:

- documentary evidence, such as maps, photographs, staffing records, interrogation records, administrative records, financial papers, currency receipts, identity documents, phone records, letters of correspondence, and passports;
- physical evidence, such as tools, weapons, fragments of clothing and fibres, keys, paint, glass used in an attack, ligatures, and jewellery;
- biological evidence, such as blood, hair, sexual fluids, urine, fingernails, body parts, bones, teeth, and fingerprints;
- digital evidence, such as mobile phones, computers, tablets, satellite phones, digital storage devices, digital recording devices, digital cameras, and closed-circuit television footage (OHCHR 2017: para. 61).

To ensure the protection of the evidence, investigators must establish a 'chain of custody' by recording every stage of evidence recovery, storage, transportation, and forensic analysis, from crime scene to the end of the judicial processes. Chain of custody is a legal, evidentiary concept requiring that any prospective item of evidence be conclusively documented in order to be eligible for admission as evidence in a legal proceeding (OHCHR 2017: para. 65).

Investigators should keep evidentiary material in a clean and secure facility throughout the process. The storage site should protect against unauthorised entry and cross-contamination. Digital evidence should be collected, preserved, and analysed in accordance with international best practice (OHCHR 2017: para. 66).

## Working with Family Members

The Minnesota Protocol emphasises that the participation of the family members – broadly understood to include relatives of the disappeared person – is an important element of an effective investigation. As such, close relatives must be invited to participate in the investigation, though without compromising its integrity. The search team should seek out relatives of the disappeared and inform them of the investigation and the progress of the investigation, during all its phases. Family members must be invited to propose investigative steps, to provide evidence, and to assert their interests and rights throughout the process. They should be notified of and allowed access to any hearing relevant to the investigation (OHCHR 2017: para. 35).

Family members should be protected from ill-treatment, intimidation, or sanction from their participation in an investigation or their search for information about a disappeared person. The search team should take steps to ensure their safety, physical and psychological well-being, and privacy (OHCHR 2017: para. 36).

Family members have specific rights in relation to human remains. When the identity of a deceased person is determined, family members must be informed immediately and a notification of death posted in an easily accessible way. Family members should also be consulted prior to an autopsy and are entitled to have a representative present during the autopsy. Upon completion of the necessary investigative procedures, human remains should be returned to family members, allowing them to dispose of the deceased according to their beliefs (OHCHR 2017: para. 37).

When feasible, the search team should appoint an experienced family liaison expert to offer the family of the disappeared information and support as well as to collect the information needed to identify a disappeared person. The expert should provide regular updates about the investigation, its progress, and results, and should address any concerns the family may have as the investigation progresses (OHCHR 2017: para. 67).

## Interviews and Witness Protection

The Minnesota Protocol contains guidance on how to obtain accurate, reliable, and complete information from victims, witnesses, suspects, and others. Interviewees should be informed about the potential uses of the interview, and special care should be taken when interviewing grieving family members or those who have witnessed a crime, in order to prevent their re-traumatisation (OHCHR 2017: para. 85).

The security of interviewees and interviewers is paramount and the search team should carry out risk assessments before engaging with any witness. When necessary, the search team should take steps to protect an interviewee and others from ill-treatment or intimidation that might result from providing information. Suggested measures include protecting the identity of the interviewee (within the parameters of the law and the rights of the defence guaranteed under international fair trial standards), physical protection, relocation, and placement in an effective witness-protection program (OHCHR 2017: para. 86).

All interviews should be recorded in written form, audio, or video. The best recording method will depend on the preference of the interviewee, the interview setting, and concerns about privacy and security (OHCHR 2017: paras 88–9).

Detailed guidelines on interviews are in Section V.B. of the Minnesota Protocol. They look in detail at the conduct of an interview: how to prepare, how to begin, how to elicit facts, and how to conclude. The guidelines also address how to interview a suspect, the role of interpreters, and ways to record an interview.

## Recovery of Human Remains

The Minnesota Protocol provides guidance on the recovery and handling of human remains, which require special attention and care, including respect for the dignity of the deceased and compliance with forensic best practices. When human remains are recovered by individuals without training in human biology, it may result in challenges in identifying body parts and/or skeletal elements. The recovery of human remains should, preferably, be under the supervision of a trained forensic anthropologist (if skeletonised) and/or a forensic doctor (if fleshed). Knowledge of forensic archaeology may also assist in the recovery of burnt, fragmented, or buried remains (OHCHR 2017: para. 90).

The recovery process includes labelling, packaging, security (including chain-of-custody documentation), transport, and storage (OHCHR 2017: para. 90). Investigators should not automatically assume that separate body parts belong to the same body; a determination should be made only by a forensic expert (OHCHR 2017: para. 91).

Investigators should take photographs of human remains, whether of a complete body, scattered skeletal remains, or buried bodies. All photographs should include a reference number, a scale, and a direction indicator. Investigators should also make scene sketches and diagrams, supplemented by GPS readings and other notations (OHCHR 2017: para. 92).

The labelling of remains should use unique designator codes, based on:

- location – the geographical location from where the remains are recovered;
- site – to distinguish between different sites (e.g. graves) in a particular location;
- individual – human remains identified as belonging to one unique individual.

The date on which the remains are discovered should be reflected in the designator code. The numbering system may be used for all evidence recovered from the same site (OHCHR 2017: para. 96). If there are multiple human remains, the searchers should consult Interpol's Disaster Victim Identification protocols (e.g. Interpol 2018).

Detailed guidelines on recovery of human remains are in Section V of the Minnesota Protocol, including the process to follow in exhumation of graves, autopsy, and analysis of skeletal remains.

## Identification of Dead Bodies

The identification of the disappeared person is a central objective of the search process. The viewing of the dead body and its recognition by family or friends is a universally used form of ante-mortem and post-mortem comparison that is often reliable in identification. However, visual recognition can be mistaken (OHCHR 2017: para. 116). Because of this, investigators should carefully control the circumstances for such viewings, by protecting the viewer's privacy and minimising distractions. The Minnesota Protocol recommends the presence of trained professionals, such as a forensic doctor, a trained mortuary technician, and a social worker (OHCHR 2017: para 117). Forensic experts should first assess if the dead body is capable of being recognised by visual inspection. The person being asked to make the visual identification should always be informed of the condition of the remains and given the choice whether to proceed (OHCHR 2017: para. 118). Visual recognition alone should not be relied upon in cases of multiple deaths (OHCHR 2017: para. 125). More scientifically reliable methods of identification include fingerprints, dental examination, and DNA analysis (OHCHR 2017: para. 125).

## Conclusion

The Minnesota Protocol is a valuable resource for those who carry out searches and investigations regarding disappearances. It explains the legal standards for states' investigations, as well as strategic and practical guidance. Detailed guidelines on various topics can assist searchers, including steps to follow in crime-scene investigation, the conduct of interviews, the excavation of graves, the conduct of an autopsy, and the analysis of skeletal remains. The Protocol also serves as the authoritative standard for measuring the adequacy of governmental investigations in disappearance cases.

## References

African Commission on Human and Peoples' Rights (2006). *Zimbabwe Human Rights NGO Forum* v. *Zimbabwe*, no. 245/02 (adopted at 39th Ordinary Session, May 2002).

European Court of Human Rights (1998), *Ergi* v. *Turkey*, no. 40/1993/435/514.

European Court of Human Rights (2005), *Nachova* v. *Bulgaria*, nos 43577/98 and 43579/98.

European Court of Human Rights, Grand Chamber (2014), *Case of Jaloud* v. *the Netherlands*, application no. 47708/08 (20 November), Judgment (Merits and Just Satisfaction).

Inter-American Court of Human Rights (2009). *Gonzalez* v. *Mexico*.

Interpol (2018), *Disaster Victim Identification Guide*, www.interpol.int/content/download/589/file/18Y1344%20E%20DVI_Guide.pdf (accessed 6 July 2020).

Office of the United Nations High Commissioner for Human Rights [OHCHR] (2017), *The Minnesota Protocol on the Investigation of Potentially Unlawful Death (2016)*, rev. edn (Geneva and New York, OHCHR).

Office of the United Nations Special Rapporteur on Extrajudicial, Arbitrary and Summary Killings [UNSREASK] (2015), 'Proposal for Revision' (Geneva) (in author's files).

United Nations (1991), *UN Manual on the Effective Prevention and Investigation of Extra-Legal, Arbitrary and Summary Executions*, 12th edn, United Nations Document E/ST/CSDHA/ (Geneva, United Nations).

# 15

# 'Urgent Actions' for the Search for Disappeared Persons in the Specialised Bodies of the United Nations

RAINER HUHLE

## The Pioneering Work of the Working Group on Enforced or Involuntary Disappearances (WGEID)

ENFORCED DISAPPEARANCE IS a crime that marks a very special moment in the history of human rights. When, after the 1973 coup in Chile, people were not only killed without any legal procedure but also arbitrarily detained without leaving a trace for the families who searched for them, and when the same practice was even more common after the 1976 coup in Argentina, people began to name that specific crime: detention/disappearance, or (en)forced disappearance. Mothers and other relatives started demanding information on the whereabouts of their loved ones, defying the repression of the regimes.

The families asked for the help of the international organisations that had been created to protect human rights. As a result, this newly defined crime of enforced disappearance became the object of the first thematic monitoring mechanism within the United Nations Commission on Human Rights, growing out of a national investigation of the situation in Chile. The constitution, in 1980, of the Working Group on Enforced or Involuntary Disappearances (WGEID) was the first example of what today is known as a 'Special Procedure' under the UN Charter, under the authority of the Commission on Human Rights and its successor, the Human Rights Council. This step marked the transition from an exclusively confidential (and therefore invisible) human rights monitoring mechanism to a public monitoring procedure in the UN that named the responsible states and actors. It was a conflictive process that, among other things, cost the director of the UN Human Rights Division, Dutch diplomat and law professor Theo van Boven, his job (Guest 1990: 323). Still, the establishment of the

*Proceedings of the British Academy*, **237**, 234–241, © The British Academy 2021.

Working Group opened a space for the victims of gross human rights violations within the UN human rights protection system. For the first time they could address their complaints directly to an organ of the United Nations.

Without precedent, the WGEID had to construct, step by step, its rules and working methods.[1] In its first year, the WGEID received nearly 2,100 communications on cases of disappeared persons. It concluded that even this number was low, since the Group did not receive information from every country known to have disappearances. Even in those countries, especially in South America, which was the source of most of the WGEID's cases, there were probably more (UN Commission on Human Rights 1981: paras 32–3). The WGEID received case information directly from the concerned families and from witnesses, but also from human rights organisations, intergovernmental organisations, and even from governments (UN Commission on Human Rights 1981: para. 29).

The Commission's resolution (UN Commission on Human Rights 1980) establishing the Working Group, called upon it 'to respond effectively to information that comes before it'. From its beginning, therefore, the WGEID established a channel of communication to the respective governments, transmitting to them the cases it received. The WGEID emphasised that it was 'motivated by the purely humanitarian objective of helping to clarify the whereabouts of persons reported to be missing' (UN Commission on Human Rights 1981: para. 13). In this perspective, the WGEID established different formats of action, according to the degree of reliable information available about the disappearance, including 'immediate action' or 'emergency procedure' when it received information it considered as 'urgent reports'.

In recent years, the WGEID has established several procedures for its intervention on behalf of victims of enforced disappearance. The most immediate procedure is called an 'urgent appeal'. The Group defines it as follows:

> When credible allegations are received that a person has been arrested, detained, abducted, or otherwise deprived of his liberty and has been enforcedly disappeared or is at risk of being disappeared, the Working Group will transmit those allegations to the Minister for Foreign Affairs of the Government concerned by the most direct and rapid means requesting said Government to carry out investigations to clarify the fate or whereabouts of the person(s) concerned and to inform the Working Group about the results. (WGEID 2020)

The procedure that corresponds to the next degree of urgency in the Group's interventions is the 'urgent procedure', which applies to 'cases of enforced disappearances that occurred within the three months preceding receipt of the report by the Working Group' (WGEID 2020). Here, again, the chairperson transmits a letter 'by the most direct and rapid means' to the Minister of Foreign Affairs of the country concerned. At the same time, the WGEID informs the author, or the relatives of the disappeared person, or the source of the communication about this

[1] For an overview of the WGEID's experience see Frouville (2017: 223–60).

action, enabling them to 'enter into communication with the relevant authorities' (UN Human Rights Council 2014: para. 10).

All other cases are considered as 'standard procedures' and are reviewed during one of the three yearly sessions of the Working Group. Like the urgent cases, standard cases are transmitted 'to the Governments concerned with the request that they carry out investigations in order to clarify the fate or whereabouts of the disappeared person, and inform the Working Group of the results' (WGEID 2020).

In addition to these modalities of handling communications about individual cases of enforced disappearances, the WGEID has developed procedures to intervene in cases of intimidation or reprisals ('prompt interventions'), and for allegations that refer to more general situations ('general allegations') (WGEID 2020).

With these, and some occasional exceptions, all the cases of enforced disappearance received by the WGEID have been dealt with on an individual case-by-case basis. According to its July 2019 report, since the beginning of its activities in 1980, the Group has transmitted a total of 57,891 cases to 108 states. Out of these, 45,811 cases in 92 states have not yet been 'clarified, closed or discontinued' (UN Human Rights Council 2019). What could a body of five experts, working on an honorary basis and supported by a minimum staff in the Office of the UN High Commissioner for Human Rights (OHCHR) Secretariat, accomplish with such an enormous number of cases (which still does not nearly represent the total number of forcibly disappeared persons worldwide during these decades)?

The WGEID uses three possible modalities of meeting a request to locate a disappeared person (UN Human Rights Council 2014). First, a case is closed when it is 'clarified', meaning that 'well-documented information' is provided by a source (understanding the families or senders of the information) that 'clearly establishes the fate or whereabouts of a disappeared person' (para. 24). In the more difficult (and probably more frequent) case, it is the state that declares a case as 'clarified'. In such circumstances, the WGEID gives six months to the authors of the request to accept or contest the state's position before closing the case and listing it as 'clarified' (para. 24).

A second modality of closing a case is 'archiving' it. The WGEID archives a case 'when the competent authority … issues a declaration of absence as a result of enforced disappearance and the relatives or other interested parties have manifested, freely and indisputably, their desire not to pursue the case any further' (para. 27).

Finally, there is the possibility to 'discontinue' a case 'where the families have manifested, freely and indisputably, their desire not to pursue the case any further, or when the source is no longer in existence or is unable to follow up the case, and the steps taken by the Working Group to establish communication with other sources have proven unsuccessful' (para. 28).

In all three scenarios, the working methods allow the WGEID to reopen a case when extraordinary circumstances call for it. It is less clear, from its reports, procedures, and working methods, how the WGEID organises its follow-up in order to evaluate the response of states to its actions and to measure their effect.

## The Urgent Actions under the Committee on Enforced Disappearance (CED)

In spite of the considerable achievements since the 1970s in making the crime of enforced disappearance visible, and converting it to an important item in international human rights law, many victims and human rights defenders felt that the existing instruments were not sufficient. The constitution of the WGEID in 1980 and the adoption of the 'Declaration on the Protection of All Persons from Enforced Disappearance' by the General Assembly in 1992 marked decisive steps in combating and outlawing enforced disappearance. The Declaration provided the WGEID with a more solid framework than the piecemeal legal approach on which it initially had to develop its work. As a resolution based on the UN Charter, the Declaration gave the WGEID competence to address the issue of enforced disappearances in all UN member states. Many felt, however, that a resolution was not a sufficiently strong instrument. At the beginning of the 21st century, there was adequate support in the UN to initiate the drafting process of a binding Convention against Enforced Disappearances, a process also supported by the WGEID. In 2006, the Convention was adopted and, by the end of 2010, it had the necessary number of ratifications to enter into force. As of April 2020, 62 states had ratified the Convention.

The Convention establishes a Treaty Body, the Committee on Enforced Disappearances (CED), to monitor the compliance of states with their conventional obligations. Article 30 of the Convention entrusts the CED with the task of receiving 'requests that a disappeared person should be sought and found' and treating it 'as a matter of urgency' (United Nations General Assembly 2006: article 30.1). As in the case of the urgent actions of the WGEID, the Committee examines the issues related to the admissibility of such a 'request of urgent action' (article 30.2) and, if it is admitted, transmits the information received to the concerned State Party, together with recommendations referring to the 'necessary measures, including interim measures, to locate and protect' the disappeared person. In compliance with article 30.3, the Committee also requests the State Party to report, within a 'specified period of time', on the measures it has taken to search for the disappeared person and investigate his or her disappearance, and to implement the Committee's recommendations in that regard. According to article 30.4, the Committee must 'continue its efforts to work with the State Party concerned for as long as the fate of the person sought remains unresolved' and keep the authors of the request informed about this procedure.

When, in March 2012, the CED sent its first 'urgent action' (UA) under article 30 to the government of Mexico, it was still in the process of developing its working methods on the procedure and it still could not foresee the many activities that the ample competences – but also obligations – provided in article 30 would entail. A careful analysis of the language of article 30 convinced the CED that it should not copy the concept of urgency that the WGEID had adopted. The urgency, as defined in article 30.1, is not related to the date the disappearance occurred but to the necessity of searching for the disappeared person. The Committee therefore decided not to establish for its acceptance of a UA a deadline of three months, as the WGEID does, or of any other fixed term. Apart from the temporal restriction that article 35 of the Convention establishes – restricting the CED's competence to cases of enforced disappearance that commenced after the entry into force of the Convention in the state concerned – the CED admits all UA requests it receives.

In close collaboration with the OHCHR Secretariat, the Committee established working methods for the treatment of UA requests. The CED appointed a Rapporteur for UA (with their number rapidly growing, it would soon be a group of Rapporteurs) who would receive the incoming UA requests via email within the shortest time possible from the Geneva-based Secretariat, together with a preliminary examination of its admissibility and a first-draft *note verbale* for the state. This *note verbale* typically contains a summary of the facts of the case, together with basic data regarding the identity of the disappeared person, as well as requests for the competent authorities of the State Party to take immediate action to search for the disappeared person in light of the state's obligations under the Convention. The Rapporteurs then check the conditions of admissibility and revise the reliability of the facts transmitted and the draft note. As a matter of protection, the identity of the source of the information is never revealed to the State Party. Respecting the urgency of any search for a disappeared person, the Committee, thanks to the close cooperation between the Rapporteurs and the Secretariat, is generally able to send the first letter to the state between 24 and 48 hours after receiving the request for urgent action. The time given to the state for its response has varied over time and, also, according to the complexity of the issue and the authorities involved, but usually varies from two to four weeks. When the CED sends the *note verbale* to the State Party, it also sends a letter to the authors informing them about the registration of the UA request and about the Committee's recommendations to the State Party.

In compliance with its obligation to continue to work with the state until the fate of the disappeared person is resolved (article 30.4), the CED established a set of internal guidelines for the actions to be taken after the first letter has been sent. The state's response to the initial *note verbale* is immediately transmitted to the authors of the UA for comment. In most cases, the authors express their concern with regard to the state's lack of action or its failures in terms of the actions taken. It is common for the authors to transmit to the Committee specific requests about actions that they consider necessary, and to ask the Committee to relay these requests for action to the State Party. After having analysed the reliability of the information provided by the State Party and the authors, the Committee sends a follow-up note to the State Party with recommended actions to comply with the obligations of the Convention regarding the search for the disappeared person and the investigation of the disappearance. If the state does not answer the first letter in due time, the Committee sends a reminder. If no reply is received after three reminders, the Committee requests a meeting with the respective Permanent Mission in Geneva for a consultation, explaining the general obligations of the state under article 30 of the Convention and the specific obligations of this procedure. If no reply is received after this meeting, a 'final reminder' is sent to the State Party, informing them that if no reply is received, the Committee may decide to bring the lack of cooperation of the State Party to the attention of the UN General Assembly.

From the first UA in March 2012 until March 2020, the Committee received 885 UAs relating to 18 member states, reaching a peak of 250 cases in 2019. However, more than 90 per cent of these cases related to only two countries: Mexico and Iraq. Rather than the distribution of cases of enforced disappearances in the 62 member states of the Convention, these figures show the growing but uneven ability of victims and civil society organisations to make use of the UA procedure offered by the Convention.

In comparison with the tens of thousands of cases recorded by the WGEID, the number of UAs registered with the CED in its first eight years seems unimpressive. In consequence of the follow-up procedure described, however, the close-to-900 UAs carry with them an enormous amount of continuous correspondence in a triangular exchange of letters among the Committee, the states, and the authors. This workload has to be shouldered by the Rapporteurs together with the Petitions and Urgent Action section of the OHCHR, in addition to the other responsibilities of this section. Those responsibilities include support for the individual complaints procedures of eight of the 10 Treaty Bodies, including the CED. The follow-up correspondence in disappearance cases, which ends only when a case is clarified, can lead to piles of more than 50 follow-up letters in certain cases.

The continuity of the follow-up to UA is not only a demonstration of respect for the victims; it is a duty of the Committee directly and literally prescribed in article 30.4 of the Convention. Under this article, the CED, like the WGEID, closes a case when it is 'resolved'. Since the Convention does not specify the exact meaning of 'as long as the fate of the person sought remains unresolved', the CED designed its procedures for closing cases based on a solid and victim-friendly interpretation of the Convention. Its first years of experience led the Committee to use three different categories of closure when it is informed that a disappeared person is found. It declares a case as definitely 'closed' when the person is found alive and in liberty, and when they are found dead and identified beyond doubt (which normally implies recognition by the family). When a person is located in a detention facility where (s)he had been retained without knowledge of the family, the UA is not closed but is 'discontinued', because of the danger that the illegal situation may be renewed. 'Discontinuation' means that the Committee does not actively follow up on the case by sending more reminders, but can reactivate the UA at any given moment if necessary.[2]

In certain cases, the Committee does not close or discontinue a UA file even when a person is found. According to article 30.3, the CED can request the state

[2] For a detailed exposition of the conditions under which a search can be terminated, see Principle 7 of the 'Guiding Principles for the Search of Disappeared Persons' (CED 2019).

to take interim measures to protect the victims. In fact, many authors of UAs have asked the CED to request such measures of protection, since families, relatives, and representatives suffer threats, persecution, or even danger to their lives while searching for the disappeared person, or investigating the circumstances of the disappearance. The danger, as the Committee noticed, can be even more acute once the body of a disappeared person is found, since the forensic analysis can then feed more data to an ongoing criminal investigation. When such danger is apparent and interim measures remain necessary, the Committee may keep the UA open to follow up on the implementation of measures of protection.

After four years of experience, resulting in hundreds of UAs and very few cases resolved, the Committee saw the opportunity and the necessity of describing in more detail the recurring flaws and failures in the usual practice of searching for the disappeared.[3] Frequently, such failures appeared clearly in the answers received from States Parties, be it in their replies to the UA requests, or during the constructive dialogues carried out for the examination of States Parties' reports, or during workshops or in other spaces of communication. Recognising this pattern, the Committee decided to draft guidelines on good practices in the search for disappeared persons. As a result, 16 'Guiding Principles for the Search for Disappeared Persons' were adopted by the Committee at its 16th session in April 2019. These Principles reflect the accumulated experience of the Committee in its UAs, complemented by a series of oral and written consultations with states; intergovernmental organisations; non-governmental organisations; and, not least, victims. The Principles spell out the States Parties' obligations under the Convention in the search for disappeared persons and set out a general normative framework for compliance with these duties. They make clear that the search for disappeared persons, being an eminently humanitarian task, is at the same time a clearly established legal duty for every state where disappearances occur (CED 2019: para. 1).

## References

Frouville, O. (2017), 'Working Out a Working Group: A View from a Former Working Group Member', in *The United Nations Special Procedures System*, ed. A. Nolan, R. Freedman, and T. Murphy (Leiden, Brill), pp. 223–60.

Guest, I. (1990), *Behind the Disappearances: Argentina's Dirty War against Human Rights and the United Nations* (Philadelphia, University of Pennsylvania Press).

United Nations Commission on Human Rights (1980), 'Question of Missing and Disappeared Persons', Resolution 20 (XXXVI).

United Nations Commission on Human Rights (1981), *Report of the Working Group on Enforced or Involuntary Disappearances*. United Nations Document E/CN.4/1492.

United Nations Committee on Enforced Disappearances [CED] (2019), 'Guiding Principles for the Search of Disappeared Persons', United Nations Document CED/C/7.

[3] At the time of writing (March 2020) 75 cases had been resolved by the Committee.

United Nations General Assembly (2006), 'International Convention for the Protection of All Persons from Enforced Disappearance, General Assembly, 5 Resolution 61/177 (entered into 23 December 2010), UN Document A/RES/61/177.
United Nations Human Rights Council (2014), 'Methods of Work of the Working Group on Enforced or Involuntary Disappearances', United Nations Document A/HRC/WGEID/102/2.
United Nations Human Rights Council (2019), 'Report of the Working Group on Enforced or Involuntary Disappearances', United Nations Document A/HRC/42/40.
United Nations Working Group on Enforced or Involuntary Disappearances [WGEID] (2020), 'Procedures', www.ohchr.org/EN/Issues/Disappearances/Pages/Procedures.aspx (accessed November 13, 2020).

# 16

# Using the International Criminal Court to Denounce Disappearances: Crimes against Humanity in Coahuila, Mexico

MICHAEL W. CHAMBERLIN

## Introduction

SEVERAL OBSERVERS, INCLUDING authors in this volume (Frey, Chapter 2; Weichert, Chapter 8), have argued that the generalised patterns of enforced disappearances in post-transitional Latin American countries may rise to the level of crimes against humanity and, therefore, could be grounds for investigation and prosecution by the International Criminal Court (ICC). With the exception of Cuba and Nicaragua, every Latin American government has ratified the Rome Statute. The ICC therefore has jurisdiction over crimes against humanity committed on the territory of these States Parties or carried out by a national of the States Parties (ICC 1998: article 12, para. 2).

In 2017, the International Federation of Human Rights (FIDH), supported by 100 other organisations, submitted a communication to the ICC detailing crimes committed against the civilian population from 2009 to 2016 in the state of Coahuila de Zaragoza in Mexico, including murder, illegal imprisonment, enforced disappearance, torture, and sexual violence. This chapter explains the procedural and substantive basis of their complaint as a model for others who may seek the ICC's involvement in the investigation and prosecution of a pattern of enforced disappearances.

## Threshold for an ICC Complaint

The ICC has jurisdiction 'over persons for the most serious crimes of international concern' (ICC 1998: article 1), including genocide, crimes against humanity, war

*Proceedings of the British Academy*, **237**, 242–250, © The British Academy 2021.

crimes, and aggression. The Court's jurisdiction is complementary to national criminal jurisdictions. Enforced disappearance is among the prosecutable acts that constitute a crime against humanity, under article 7 of the Rome Statute. Enforced disappearance of persons is defined in the ICC statute as:

> the arrest, detention or abduction of persons by, or with the authorization, support or acquiescence of, a State or a political organisation, followed by a refusal to acknowledge that deprivation of freedom or to give information on the fate or whereabouts of those persons, with the intention of removing them from the protection of the law for a prolonged period of time. (ICC 1998: article 7 (2)(i))

In addition to information about enforced disappearances, communications submitted to the Court typically provide evidence of many different categories of violent acts, such as killings, deprivation of liberty, and torture, to support an allegation of crime against humanity.

With the approval of the Pre-Trial Chamber (PTC) of the ICC, the prosecutor may initiate a preliminary investigation into crimes against humanity based on information sent by reliable sources, including individuals, groups, or non-governmental organisations (ICC 1998: article 15(2)). In order to open an investigation into potential crimes, the ICC prosecutor must determine that the crimes fall within the Court's jurisdiction and are sufficiently serious that they require the attention of the Court. Under the principle of complementarity (article 17), the prosecutor may not proceed with an investigation if there are genuine national proceedings in the case.

To support a prosecution for crimes against humanity, the information provided to the ICC must demonstrate that enforced disappearances were committed 'as part of a widespread or systematic attack directed against any civilian population, with knowledge of the attack' (ICC 1998: article 7). Submissions alleging crimes against humanity must demonstrate that the criminal actions were:

- directed against a civilian population;
- carried out with knowledge of the attack;
- widespread or systematic (ICC 1998: article 7.1); and
- committed pursuant to, or in furtherance of, a state or organisational policy (article 7.2.a).

Submissions to the ICC prosecutor must offer proof of these elements, which are briefly discussed here.

When there is no internationally recognised armed conflict, a 'civilian population' includes 'all persons except those who have the duty to maintain public order and have the legitimate means to exercise force' (Kayieshma in Saenz (2017): 82). To prove this element, the communication must show that individuals targeted for disappearance were not members of security forces or internationally recognised combatants.

Submissions must provide evidence that accused perpetrators of the enforced disappearances must have known that their actions were part of a larger attack upon a civilian population, even if they did not share the purpose or goal behind the larger attack (International Criminal Tribunal for Yugoslavia 2002). A generalised context of violence that includes a well-known pattern of disappearances may be used to demonstrate knowledge of a larger attack (Saenz 2017).

To prove that the attack against the civilian population is widespread, the submission must show a high number of victims and the large-scale nature of the attack (ICC 2010). The ICC explained in the Bemba case that a widespread attack must be 'carried out over a wide geographical area or… in a small geographical area directed against a large number of civilians' (ICC 2009).[1] While the ICC has not designated a minimum number of victims, in *Prosecutor* v. *Ruto*, the PTC found that an attack in four locations with 230 victims was widespread (Saenz 2017; ICC 2012).

Finally, the complainants must demonstrate that the enforced disappearances furthered a state or organisational policy. Such a policy must have been planned and directed by an organisation or state actor; it cannot have been merely a spontaneous crime, and the actual aim of the policy must have been to attack a civilian population (ICC 2012). According to Saenz, a well-documented pattern of enforced disappearances may support an inference of such a policy (Saenz 2017: 86).

As described below, in their communication to the ICC, the FIDH set out to establish the necessary facts to demonstrate that crimes against humanity had been committed in Coahuila, Mexico (FIDH 2017: 43).

## The Communication on Coahuila to the ICC

In July 2017, advocates presented a communication to the ICC soliciting the prosecutor to open a preliminary investigation for crimes against humanity committed in Coahuila, Mexico, in the framework of the national security strategy (FIDH 2017). The communication detailed how, between 2009 and 2016, various crimes against humanity were carried out in Coahuila that were within the competence of the ICC, including grave deprivations of physical liberty, torture, and enforced disappearances, as part of a systematic attack against the civilian population of that state. The material authors of those crimes were the criminal organisation Los Zetas, as well as the government's Special Forces responsible for security in Coahuila.

[1] Jean-Pierre Bemba Gombo, President and Commander-in-Chief of the Movement for the Liberation of the Congo, was charged in 2008 in the ICC with crimes against humanity and war crimes allegedly committed in 2002–3 in the Central African Republic. In 2010, the Pre-Trial Chamber found substantial grounds to proceed with the charges against Bemba, and that the attack he had directed against the civilian population was widespread and systematic. On 8 June 2018, the ICC Appeals Chamber decided, by majority, to acquit Bemba.

The FIDH communication described the context in which the crimes of disappearance were carried out in Mexico and, specifically, in the state of Coahuila. In 2006, former President Felipe de Jesús Calderón Hinojosa (2006–12) of the National Action Party (PAN) declared his 'Security Strategy', initiating a war against narco-trafficking by militarising national security functions.[2] This approach was replicated by the administration of President Enrique Peña Nieto in 2012, and again by the administration of current President Andres Manuel López Obrador (2018–24), with no real substantive variation.

The FIDH communication explained that the Security Strategy resulted in an exponential increase in the number of armed forces engaged in public security functions, from 45,850 active duty forces in 2007 to 96,261 in 2011 (INSYDE, CMDPDH, and CCDH 2014). Additionally, the government transferred military officials to serve as Federal Police (Astorga 2015), replacing multiple officeholders from the public, municipal, and state security forces with military personnel who had been on leave or retired (FIDH, CMDPDH, and CCDH 2014). The government also deployed armed forces to the states through operations or joint operations (Ordorica 2011).

Intentional homicides in Mexico increased dramatically after the initiation of the Security Strategy, reaching a peak of 22,852 homicides in the year 2011. For 2015, officials calculated a total of 20,525 homicides, or 17 for every 100,000 inhabitants at the national level (INEGI 2016). By 2017, the official numbers added up to more than 200,000 homicides between 2006 and 2017,[3] and more than 33,482 persons disappeared during the same period.[4]

The ICC communication alleged facts from two different periods. First, from 2009 to 2011/12, the state security forces were responsible for crimes against humanity in a context of undeniable collusion with Los Zetas. Second, from 2011/12 to 2016, the state security forces committed crimes against humanity directly through the involvement of a variety of Special Forces (FIDH 2017).

The communication presented 32 cases and 73 victims, as well as two databases including 195 and 367 disappeared persons and cases respectively, derived from more than 60 case recommendations published by the Commission of Human Rights of the State of Coahuila for grave violations of human rights, from interviews with victims and non-governmental organisations. All of this occurred within the framework of the official figure at the time, confirming 1,791 complaints by relatives concerning 1,830 persons disappeared in Coahuila between 2006 and 2016.

[2] The PAN political party, considered to be more right-wing, held two consecutive presidential mandates, before the presidency returned to the Institutional Revolutionary Party in 2012.

[3] The dates are collected statistically, by month and by accumulated total, by the Executive Secretariat of the National System of Public Security, www.gob.mx/sesnsp/acciones-y-programas/incidencia-delictiva-87005?idiom=es (accessed 29 June 2020).

[4] The National Registry of Disappeared and Missing Persons (RNPED) may be consulted at https://rnped.segob.gob.mx/ (accessed 29 June 2020). It was replaced by activities put in place by the General Law on Enforced Disappearance of 2018 and ultimately discontinued.

## Crimes against Humanity from 2009 to 2011/2012

During the period 2009–11, Los Zetas consolidated their territorial control over a large zone of operation in Coahuila and maintained a goal of controlling and expanding their territory through fear.[5] Their military methods and the indiscriminate use of violence as a means of control reinforced the cartel's capacity to carry out an attack against the civilian population. During that period, 2009–11, the different public security forces, under the command of the government of Coahuila, acted in collaboration with Los Zetas. Through collusion and corruption, carried out at the highest levels of the state government, Coahuila's security forces supported and committed crimes with Los Zetas, while simultaneously communicating their supposed fight against those same criminal groups.

The ICC communication included information obtained from an analysis of witness statements given in criminal trials against members of Los Zetas carried out in San Antonio and Austin, Texas (Human Rights Clinic 2017). These statements referred to, among other acts, alleged homicides, disappearances, kidnappings, death threats, and forced recruitment by the Zetas cartel in Coahuila. The witnesses also described possible connections between the Mexican authorities and institutions and Los Zetas, which demonstrated the complicity, tolerance, consent, and acquiescence of the Coahuila government with the Zetas cartel.

Through legal reforms put in place in 2009, the hierarchical structure succeeded in concentrating in the hands of one person, Jesús Torres Charles, the functions of the prosecutor's office, the police, and the jails, which facilitated through impunity grave deprivations of physical liberty, torture, and disappearances, among other crimes against the civilian population.

A clear pattern of activities among documented cases during the 2009–12 period revealed that the municipal police carried out detentions and subsequently turned those detained over to members of organised crime units to be disappeared. The report *En el desamparo* (Aguayo Quezada *et al.* 2016) documented how the municipal police were on two payrolls, that of the municipality and that of Los Zetas.

An important example documented in the ICC communication is the 'Massacre of Allende'. At the beginning of March 2011, in the municipality of Allende and adjoining areas, Los Zetas looted and destroyed all the homes in their path. This resulted in an undetermined number of persons being killed and disappeared, a figure that ranges between 42 and 300 disappeared persons. All these crimes took place in public view and while the police and authorities stood by and did nothing.

[5] The cartel Los Zetas originated as the armed enforcement branch of the Gulf Cartel, and was known for extreme violence. It consisted, principally, of deserters from the special forces of the Mexican and Guatemalan armies. In 1998, Los Zetas were established to protect the Gulf Cartel, then under the control of Osiel Cárdenas Guillen, in its actions against the Sinaloa Cartel. In the following years, Los Zetas gained more importance for the Gulf Cartel and, eventually, were responsible for securing cocaine operations and trafficking routes for drugs and money (Human Rights Clinic 2017).

Other testimony shows the collaboration of the security forces in the Allende Massacre. Some facts indicate that the mayor of Allende, but also the governor of Coahuila, must have had knowledge of these facts, and that their acts of omission were not from lack of knowledge, but from their actual collusion with the criminal group (FIDH 2017).

Similarly, between 2008 and 2012, the prison in the city of Piedras Negras, under the responsibility of the government of the state of Coahuila, was converted into a centre of operations for Los Zetas. The inmates belonging to this criminal organisation came and went as they pleased from this state prison, hiding there each time they were pursued by federal forces. Inside the prison premises, they manufactured the material necessary for their criminal activities (among other things, bulletproof vests, uniforms, modified bodywork, etc.), and at the same time they transferred persons to the prison where they killed them with acid or burnt them in steel tanks. It is estimated that at least 150 persons were victims of these crimes, which could be committed because they had the support of Coahuila's authorities (FIDH 2017).

## Crimes against Humanity in 2011/2012 to 2016

The next governor of Coahuila, Rubén Moreira, in spite of being the brother of the previous governor, Humberto Moreira, recognised from the start of his administration in 2011 that 'We have reached the point – if it has not already been passed – where the monopoly of authority does not lie with the government, but with organised crime' (FIDH 2017). He declared that he wanted to distance himself from these practices. He created three security forces: the Specialised Weapons and Tactics Groups (known by its initials in Spanish, GATE) in December 2011, and the Municipal Specialised Weapons and Tactics Group (GATEM) and Response and Mixed Operations Group (GROM) in 2012, supposedly to fight against narco-trafficking. In 2012, federal military forces attacked Los Zetas, resulting in their deconstruction and dispersal.

Starting in 2011, a large number of violations were reported to have been directly carried out by security forces, including grave deprivations of physical liberty, torture, killings, and forced disappearances. The security forces of Coahuila involved in these crimes included the GATE and the Accredited State Police. In 2012, similar crimes began to be reported at the hands of GATEM and/or elite forces and the GROM, and later by a newly named security unit, 'Force Coahuila', in 2016. More than 50 per cent of the cases analysed showed crimes committed by one of these special forces units.

The ICC communication formulated two hypotheses for this phase of the violations. First, the perpetrators considered that those who were presumed guilty of narco-trafficking could be disappeared or killed immediately to regain territorial control from the criminal organisations, while in reality these actions did not touch those who were actually presumed guilty, focusing instead on those who were innocent or who were merely street dealers. Second, the perpetrators carried out deprivations of liberty, torture, or disappearances against innocent victims, street dealers, or members of other narco groups, terrorising the civilian population to protect drug trafficking and to control border territory.

The cases analysed formed a clear and systematic pattern of criminal activity: they began with the search of homes, the interception of vehicles, or the harassment of persons in the streets, which then escalated into grave deprivations of the physical liberty of civilians, without any judicial warrant. The torture techniques used in the described cases were always similar: blows using the hands, or with boards or vehicles; suffocation by covering the victim's head with a bag; electric shocks to different parts of the body, including the genitals; drowning; sexual torture; and death threats arising to psychological torture.

Following along the lines set out in Chapter 1 of this volume, the victims constituted what could be referred to as 'disposable peoples': middle- and lower-class men and women, without university degrees, who are unemployed or, failing that, are engaged in technical work activities, the informal economy, or commerce, and who live or work in humble neighbourhoods.

## Analysis of Post-Transition Disappearances in Mexico

Los Zetas began these new forms of criminality by using terror and state capture. As Valdez (2017) describes:

> behind the assassination of the 43 normal school students of Ayotzinapa, which occurred in Guerrero in September 2014 … were the capture and reconfiguration of the municipalities of Iguala and Cocula. The municipal police obeyed the orders of the murderous organisation the Guerreros Unidos, without hesitation … With less visibility, in 2011, the police of San Fernando, Tamaulipas, helped Los Zetas to transfer kidnapped youths from Michoacan in buses that they directed to Morelia and Matamoros to a ranch where they were killed.

This is precisely the criminal scheme described in Coahuila.

Two data points explain these findings, the nature of the cartels, and the involvement of the political class in the cartels. The National Conference of Governors, in a document titled 'Toward a New Integrated System to Combat Organised Crime: Strategy and Action Plan', explained how 'the phenomenon of narco-trafficking had led to the formation of a kind of anti-state or anti-government, which resulted in a population that operates across a territory and exercises its power through money, the use of physical and armed violence, or the threat of its use' (Valdez 2017).

The crimes did not stop in 2016. The patterns of criminality documented in the communication to the ICC provide an example of what was occurring throughout the country, and with other criminal groups as well. The constant in these patterns is the presence of networks of macro-criminality consisting of criminals, businesses, and state authorities through which legal and illicit business activities are intermixed, and a double discourse that justifies an armed territorial deployment to fight against drug trafficking while, at the same time, ensuring a high index of impunity for these groups (Vázquez Valencia 2019).

## Conclusion

The communication on crimes against humanity in Coahuila sent to the ICC is one of several that have been filed and that describe similar contexts in various regions of the country in a highly complex plot of corruption, impunity, and lack of a rule of law under the dominance of macro-criminal networks. These contexts perhaps represent a new type of unconventional actor, perhaps a new kind of armed conflict.

The crimes, while in considerable decline in Coahuila after the period here reviewed, continue to occur in other regions of the country. The elements of corruption and impunity in macro-criminality schemes persist.

In response, the ICC prosecutor's office has so far been silent. Nevertheless, investigations such as the one described here promote understanding within the general public, particularly about the victims, the crimes, and their perpetrators, to establish a context in which the struggle for truth and justice unfolds. In the long run, this effort is expected to be an important piece in a larger puzzle for establishing justice, either through the ICC or through a special mechanism for transitional justice in Mexico in the near future.

## References

Aguayo Quezada, S., *et al.* (2016), *En el desamparo: Los Zetas, el Estado, la sociedad y las víctimas de San Fernando, Tamaulipas (2010) y Allende, Coahuila (2011)*, El Colegio de México, http://eneldesamparo.colmex.mx/images/documentos/en-el-desamparo.pdf (accessed 23 September 2017).

Astorga, L. (2015), *¿Qué querían que hiciera? Inseguridad y delincuencia organizada en el gobierno de Felipe Calderón* (Mexico City, Grijalbo).

Federation for Human Rights (FIDH), Mexican Commission of Defense and Human Rights Promotion (CMDPDH), and Citizens' Commission of Human Rights of the Northeast (CCDH) (2014), *Report on the Alleged Commission of Crimes against Humanity in Baja California between 2006 and 2012*, www.fidh.org/IMG/pdf/mexique642ang2014web.pdf (accessed 8 June 2020).

Federation of Human Rights (FIDH) *et al.* (2017). *México: Killings, Disappearances and Torture in Coahuila de Zaragoza Constitute Crimes against Humanity: Communication in Accordance with Article 15 of the Rome Statute of the International Criminal Court* (June), www.fidh.org/en/region/americas/mexico/mexico-murders-disappearances-and-torture-in-coahuila-de-zaragoza-are (accessed 8 June 2020).

Human Rights Clinic (2017), *Control over... the Entire State of Coahuila: An Analysis of Testimonies in Trials against Zeta Members in San Antonio, Austin, and Del Rio, Texas*, University of Texas, https://law.utexas.edu/wp-content/uploads/sites/11/2017/11/2017-HRC-coahuilareport-EN.pdf (accessed 8 June 2020).

Institute for Security and Democracy (INSYDE), Mexican Commission for the Defense and Protection of Human Rights (CMDPDH), and Citizens' Commission of Human Rights of the Northeast (CCDH) (2014), *Informe sobre el estado del marco normativo y la práctica de la tortura en México* (Mexico City, INSYDE), www.cmdpdh.org/publicaciones-pdf/cmdpdh-informe-sobre-tortura-relator-onu-abril-2014.pdf (accessed 23 September 2017).

International Criminal Court [ICC] (1998), Rome Statute of the International Criminal Court (17 July, entered into force 1 July 2002), www.icc-cpi.int/resource-library/Documents/RS-Eng.pdf (accessed 8 June 2020).

International Criminal Court [ICC] (2009), *Prosecutor* v. *Bemba Gombo*, case no. ICC-01/05-01/08, PTC decision on the confirmation of charges pursuant to article 61(7)(a) and (b) of the Rome Statute, para. 83, www.icc-cpi.int/pages/record.aspx?uri=699541 (accessed 8 June 2020).

International Criminal Court [ICC] (2010), Situation in the Republic of Kenya, case no. ICC-01/09, PTC decision pursuant to article 15 of the Rome Statute on the authorisation of an investigation, para. 95, www.refworld.org/cases,ICC,4bc2fe372.html (accessed 8 June 2020).

International Criminal Court [ICC] (2012), *Prosecutor* v. *Ruto et al.*, case no. ICC-01/-9-01/11, PTC decision on the confirmation of charges pursuant to article 61(7)(a) and (b) of the Rome Statute, paras 175–8, www.icc-cpi.int/CourtRecords/CR2012_01004.PDF (accessed 8 June 2020).

International Criminal Tribunal for Former Yugoslavia (2002), *Prosecutor* v. *Kunarac, Kovac and Vukovic*, Appeals Judgment IT-96-23-T and IT-96-23/1-A, paras 101–2, www.icty.org/x/cases/kunarac/acjug/en/kun-aj020612e.pdf (accessed 8 June 2020).

National Institute of Statistics and Geography [INEGI] (2016), 'Datos preliminares revelan que en 2015 se registraron 20 mil 525 homicidios', press release (25 July 2016), www.inegi.org.mx/app/saladeprensa/noticia.html?id=2779 (accessed 29 June 2020).

Ordorica, A. P. (2011), 'El Ejército y la ley', *Nexos*, www.nexos.com.mx/?p=14585%20 (accessed 23 September 2017).

Saenz, R. D. (2017), 'Confronting Mexico's Enforced Disappearance Monsters: How the ICC Can Contribute to the Process of Realizing Criminal Justice Reform in Mexico', *Vanderbilt Journal of International Law*, 50:1, 45–112.

Valdez, G. (2017), 'La senda del crimen', *Nexos* (1 January), www.nexos.com.mx/?p=30864 (accessed 23 September 2017).

Vázquez Valencia, L. D. (2019), *Captura del Estado, macrocriminalidad y derechos humanos* (Mexico City, FLACSO-Mexico, Fundación Böll-México y el Caribe, UNAM Instituto de Investigaciones Jurídicas).

# 17

# Forced Disappearances in the Inter-American Human Rights System

SANDRA SERRANO

THE HISTORY OF the Inter-American Human Rights System – (composed of the Inter-American Commission on Human Rights (IACHR) and the Inter-American Court of Human Rights (IACtHR)) mirrors the history of the Latin American region: the dictatorships, the internal conflicts, the recent processes of militarisation, and the rise of violent crime. Throughout the system's history, forced disappearances have been a severe and defining violation in the region, although the crime's specific characteristics vary depending on the context. The content and scope of forced disappearances have shaped the regional system's dynamics and evolution, from the structure of its authority to the specific mechanisms for protecting the rights of victims and their families. Put simply: to discuss the Inter-American System is to discuss forced disappearances.

This chapter describes the distinct mechanisms employed by Inter-American Human Rights System ('System') to address forced disappearances, understanding that the Inter-American jurisprudence is an instrument that is not only valuable for litigation in the regional system itself, but also serves as a fundamental tool for domestic litigation of public policies within member states, having been first adopted as law and then transformed into binding custom. The jurisprudential and institutional history of the Inter-American System has been shaped by victims and their families as well as by a human rights movement that was forged in the struggle against the gravest human rights violations of authoritarian regimes, often committed against political opponents.

Today, as illustrated in this book, victims, families, and civil society continue to mobilise against new forms of disappearances that have spread in post-transitional democracies in Latin America. The increase in disappearances has not solely been one of magnitude, but also differs in the variety of perpetrators and victims. The perpetrators include state actors but also criminal organisations whose actions are not sanctioned by the state. The victims, many of whom are depicted in this

*Proceedings of the British Academy*, **237**, 251–261, © The British Academy 2021.

book, tend to have little to no involvement in oppositional politics, and as such, it is difficult to characterise or identify them as a singular group. Further, many Latin American countries already have strong policies protecting human rights, and courts that are willing to uphold them. The Inter-American Human Rights System has taken some steps to respond to this new reality, but the challenges are still many. The System's greatest advantage is its enormous capacity for adaptability, which has always permeated its every action.

This chapter is divided into two sections; the first discusses distinct mechanisms of the System, particularly the IACHR, to prevent disappearances and raise awareness or draw governments' attention to them. The second section delineates the jurisprudence prohibiting forced disappearances, explaining relevant decisions of the IACtHR and their implications, along with the primary weaknesses of the jurisprudence in addressing the new dynamics of disappearances in the region. The chapter ends with brief final reflections.

## A System for Combating Forced Disappearances

The two bodies of the Inter-American Human Rights System, the Commission and the Court, respond to disappearances in light of their own contexts. As part of the Organisation of American States (OAS), they were established with the primary objective of protecting human rights, independent of the political interests of the member states. These two bodies have thus assumed the role of denouncing human rights violations since the 1960s, in spite of governmental interests, and even now, the System's evolution has been a constant struggle to imagine new ways to protect rights in an environment where the forms of the violations are constantly changing.

The IACHR was established long before the American Convention of Human Rights and, as such, its authority transcends that treaty and imbues the OAS directly with the defence of rights. Founded in 1959, barely 10 years after the Charter of the American States, the IACHR began to carry out its charge to promote respect of human rights without a rigid structure or standards. Since the beginning of its activities, the most difficult challenge faced by the Commission has been combating the grave human rights violations committed by military dictatorships in the Southern Cone – in particular, forced disappearances. While there were other serious violations such as torture and extrajudicial executions in the region, the international community already had structures to identify and sanction those practices. Forced disappearances, however, were seen as a relatively new strategy to defeat political opponents. The problem was defined as one where state agents would detain a political opponent and then deny arrest and knowledge of the person's whereabouts. The detained person remained in an extended situation of being 'disappeared', preventing anyone from finding information about them. The IACHR's challenge was to establish the relationship between the detentions and the disappearances.

Throughout its first years, the IACHR's role and responsibilities were not clearly defined. While the international community was increasingly concerned about disappearances, the Inter-American Commission had few tools to denounce the practice, and fewer still to find responsibility for it. In spite of this, in the decades that followed, one of the IACHR's greatest advantages was the election of individual experts to serve as its commissioners, who themselves often came from human rights movements. While the resolution that founded the IACHR established that the body should not meddle in internal matters of its member states, the Commission interpreted its mandate broadly and developed activities that were not strictly within its statute, such as issuing country reports and conducting on-site visits to address the situation of serious, massive, and systematic violations.

The IACHR established mechanisms to carry out independent evaluations of the general situation in countries in order to address systemic violations. The process permitted the Commission to investigate human rights violations, ask for information from the state with respect to its actions, and put forth recommendations regarding the general situation in the country. This gave the Commission the ability to assume an active role in soliciting information, investigating the facts by different means, and publicising their findings as a process for pressuring authoritarian governments, among other actions (Medina and Nash 2007: 49). Ultimately, these actions led to international visibility of the grave problem of forced disappearances. The OAS recognised the utility of conducting the investigations and releasing country reports.

Today, the IACHR practices the following human rights strategies:

- Country visits. When there is a special human rights situation, or one that is deemed to be particularly grave and needing closer review, the IACHR may carry out a visit to a member state to gather information necessary to evaluate the situation, with prior agreement of the government. After each visit, the IACHR drafts a report with the results of its assessment along with recommendations to the state. As mentioned, these state visits have been fundamental for elucidating the practice of forced disappearance in the different states in the region.
- Public hearings. A tool of a political nature, public hearings are used by the IACHR as a space for discussion among the government, civil society, and victims to evaluate issues of concern in a country or a group of countries. For example, Mexico has been called to appear at a public hearing to discuss what search activities it is using to find its more than 60,000 disappeared, as well as to locate and identify remains. These hearings serve the objectives of raising awareness about the problems, searching for concrete solutions from the states, and informing the IACHR about the situation in these countries.
- Annual and thematic reports. The IACHR issues reports on themes of particular importance to the region, either based on its own analysis of a situation prevalent in various states or from an analysis of inter-American

jurisprudence. In addition, in its annual reports, the IACHR evaluates the current situation in the states respecting the fulfilment of their international obligations. Both types of reports review disappearance cases of particular importance.

- Receipt of petitions. The IACHR serves as the first review stage in all contentious procedures before the IACtHR and, because of this, it receives individual petitions against States Parties and analyses them for the potential existence of a violation of the American Convention of Human Rights. As part of each petition process, the IACHR formulates a preliminary analysis of the facts of the case; offers the possibility of a friendly settlement; and, in case the parties cannot reach one, sends the matter on to the Court. In contrast with the previous mechanisms, which consider problems of a generalised nature, the petition process analyses individual violations.
- Precautionary measures. Faced with a situation of risk to a person or group of persons (for example, an indigenous community), or concern that the petition itself may be at risk because of the prevailing situation in a state, the IACHR may issue precautionary measures to safeguard the persons or the petition. These measures have been fundamental in cases of disappearance, particularly for demanding a search and the adoption of immediate measures to preserve elements of proof, but also for the protection of witnesses and family members who, on many occasions, find themselves at risk solely for denouncing the disappearance. When the situation is one of grave concern and there is already a formal petition before the IACHR, the Commission can transform the case into a request for provisional measures to the IACtHR to increase the compulsory nature of the decision.

These different types of mechanisms have left compliance regarding international obligations up to the states themselves, which resulted in some successes and many failures. Because of this, in the face of a new wave of disappearances in the region and, particularly, in the case of the disappearance of 43 students from the Isidro Burgos Normal School in Ayotzinapa, Guerrero in Mexico, the IACHR chose once again to carry out an institutional innovation. Within a framework of precautionary measures put in place in 2014 to search for the disappeared youths, at the instigation of their families and with the acceptance of the Mexican government, the IACHR created the Grupo Interdisciplinario de Expertos Independientes (Interdisciplinary Group of Independent Experts; GIEI) to assist with the investigations and the search for the students on Mexican territory. Never before had an international human rights body created such a technical assistance mechanism, which was authorised to provide direct, immediate, and on-site support in the case. The GIEI had the authority to review investigations, to propose new lines of investigation and search plans, and to accompany the families of the victims on the painful journey they faced. In addition, the GIEI succeeded in presenting an independent investigation that contrasted with the official truth about the disappearance of the students, emphasising the structural problems that served as obstacles to the investigation into the perpetrators of severe human rights violations and the dynamics of macro-criminality that plagued the country (Beristain *et al.* 2018).[1]

According to the 'Miguel Agustín Pro Juárez' Human Rights Centre (PRODH), the impacts of the GIEI can be summarised as follows: raising awareness about the centrality of the victims, their organisational capacity, and demands; reconstructing a complex criminal event; demonstrating the importance of using scientific methods to carry out a criminal investigation; prioritising scientific and objective evidence; identifying the context of macro-criminality underlying the events; and identifying a concrete and possible pathway for clarifying the whereabouts of the 43 students (Patrón *et al.* 2017). In sum, the members of the GIEI demonstrated that, within the framework of the Inter-American standards developed to address the prohibition of forced disappearances, it was feasible to carry out judicial investigations and searches for persons, as long as there was the capacity and the will to do so.[2]

However, this proactive attitude has not been constant in the IACHR in cases of disappearance. In 2017, upon the news of the disappearance of Santiago Maldonado in Argentina, as a result of an operation by the national gendarmerie in the face of protests by a Mapuche community, the IACHR issued precautionary measures to determine his whereabouts, as well as to protect his life and personal integrity (IACHR 2017). These were traditional measures that did not follow the logic of direct intervention in the Ayotzinapa case. In January 2018, once the body of Santiago Maldonado had been found, the IACHR lifted the measures and limited itself to reminding the Argentine state of its duty to diligently investigate the case (IACHR 2018a). The case advances the idea that the IACHR has a greater capacity for response if it is driven to a specific direction by the families and the organisations that accompany them.

Both the Commission and the Court constitute atypical bodies that have placed the interests of victims and their families at the centre of their systems of protection, sometimes with a structural view and sometimes with the individual in mind. The tools that these bodies use are complementary, in that they search for justice from above and from below. This perspective is not without critics (Neuman 2008), but in the end it has been the interpretive advances of these two bodies that have laid the theoretical basis upon which, both regionally and in a significant part of the world, countries have developed their mechanisms for search and investigation in disappearance cases (Dulitzky 2019).

[1] The official version about the disappearance of the 43 students was that they had been mistaken as members of organised crime, and that because of this they were killed and their bodies were incinerated by a criminal group in the zone. The GIEI succeeded in establishing that the youths had not been incinerated, as put forward by the Mexican government, and that their disappearance demonstrated the existence of structures of macro-criminality at large in the country, composed of state and non-state agents.

[2] Unfortunately, a little more than a year after its creation, the Mexican government decided to withdraw its support, so the IACHR had to devise a new follow-up mechanism that would seek to monitor compliance with the GIEI recommendations and the search for the missing students (IACHR 2018b).

## Inter-American Jurisprudence on Forced Disappearance

The creation of the IACtHR, which resulted from the adoption of the American Convention on Human Rights, opened up a judicial arena to reinforce the political control that the IACHR was already exerting against the authoritarian governments in the region. The new Court faced considerable challenges, from the IACHR itself, which had reason to distrust the creation of a new body that endangered its prior work, to the question of whether the new body had the capacity to confront the kinds of massive and systemic violations endemic in the region (Nash 2009). The first contentious issue resolved by the Court dealt with forced disappearance, in the case of *Velásquez Rodríguez* v. *Honduras* (IACtHR 1988). The Court's judgment on the merits in the case marked a milestone in the protection of human rights, not only for the region, but for the European and international systems of human rights protection as well.

From its beginning, the IACtHR has been marked by forced disappearance cases. The necessity of developing a normative framework to clarify state obligations permitted the Inter-American tribunals to establish guidelines to address both the content and the reach of the prohibition against disappearances, as well as the nature of the rights affected by disappearances, and the obligations regarding search, investigation, and reparation of the harm. By the end of 2019, the IACtHR had issued just over 50 judgments related to the disappearance of persons, largely with regard to enforced disappearance carried out by state agents or with their acquiescence or tolerance. The great majority of OAS member states that have accepted the contentious jurisdictions of the Court have received a judgment related to disappearance, including Guatemala (with 11 judgments) and Peru (with 10), the countries that have been most frequently sanctioned for this violation.[3]

The development of the jurisprudence on forced disappearance has been slow. Little by little and based on the characteristics of each case, the Inter-American Court has incorporated new elements and elaborated new rights, revealed to be violations of the underlying structures of human rights law. For instance, the Court took the simple idea of the detained disappearance and explained its complexity in response to the multifaceted harms that are part of this severe human rights violation, as well as the contexts in which it has occurred. Thus far, the IACtHR has applied its normative framework concerning forced disappearances in various contexts, including military dictatorships, the authoritarian processes of the 1970s and 1980s, internal armed conflict (such as in Colombia and Guatemala), the more recent processes of militarisation in the region (such as in the cases of Mexico and El Salvador), or the return or disappearance cases in post-transitional democracies (Argentina and

[3] Per country, the number of judgments in disappearance cases are: Argentina (2), Bolivia (3), Brazil (1), Colombia (8), Dominican Republic (1), Ecuador (2), El Salvador (3), Guatemala (11), Honduras (3), Mexico (3), Panama (1), Paraguay (2), Peru (10), Uruguay (1), and Venezuela (2). From information of the SUMMA/inter-American system online at Cejil, available at https://summa.cejil.org/, and the Inter-American Court of Human Rights, available at www.corteidh.or.cr/ (both accessed 11 February 2021).

Brazil). Some general features of this line of jurisprudence are presented here as tools that can be used in disappearance cases at the inter-American level, but also at the domestic level.

The IACtHR has found that a forced disappearance contains three elements: (1) a deprivation of liberty; (2) the direct intervention, acquiescence, or tolerance of state agents; and (3) the refusal to recognise the detention or to reveal the whereabouts of the disappeared person (IACtHR 2009c). These elements have been the consistent core of the Court's decision-making in disappearance cases, including in cases where state agents did not interfere directly or indirectly in the crime. In those matters, particularly in disappearances of women linked to gender-based violence, the Inter-American Court has distinguished between a 'disappearance' and a 'forced disappearance' (IACtHR 2017: para. 123). Thus far, the Tribunal has only accepted jurisdiction for cases of forced disappearance (or of particular agents with the acquiescence, authorisation, or help of a state agent), although it is understood that cases of disappearance by private actors might rise to the level of a responsibility of the state for an internationally wrongful act when the state has actual knowledge of an imminent risk confronting the victim and does nothing to impede the disappearance or to initiate a prompt search in the case (IACtHR 2006b; IACtHR 2009b). As such, the disappearance of persons in the Inter-American jurisprudence is necessarily related to the conduct of the authorities, and has not broadened to incorporate other possible perpetrators (with the exception of acquiescence, authorisation, or help), which is understandable given its nature as an international body.

Likewise, the Inter-American Court has identified characteristics respecting the juridical nature of a forced disappearance:

1 It is a complex violation of human rights because it implies a violation of multiple rights: among them the right to life, to recognition before the law, to physical integrity, and to personal liberty.
2 It is a continuing and permanent violation, insofar as the disappearance continues to be committed until the person is found or their fate is known (IACtHR 2010c).
3 It is an autonomous violation, because it is recognised as a violation in and of itself, independent of the rights of which it is composed (IACtHR 2009a).

Demonstrating violations of the multiple rights that make up a forced disappearance is not necessary, because generally the violation of these rights can be presumed circumstantially based on the facts provided to the Court. Therefore, advocates do not need to prove there has been a deprivation of personal liberty (which is illegal, arbitrary, or starts legally but becomes illegal). Instead, it is adequate if the facts support a finding that there has been a detention by a state official or with their acquiescence (IACtHR 2006a), or if the modus operandi is one known to be used in disappearances (IACtHR 2009c). The same circumstantial presumption is true for violations of the right to humane treatment. Such violations can be presumed in contexts of systematic or widespread violations where the torture and ill-treatment of detainees are well known (IACtHR 2004). A similar presumption supports a finding of harm caused by removing a person from access to legal protection as a result of a forced disappearance (IACtHR 2008). With regard to the right to life, the IACtHR understands that, based on the nature of forced disappearances, this right is itself at grave risk and that the majority of disappearances result in the execution of the detained person, in secret, followed by the hiding of the cadaver 'with the object of erasing all material traces of the crime and to seek impunity for those who commit it' (IACtHR 2012b: para. 169).

The violation of the right to recognition of the person before the law was incorporated as part of the multiple character of an enforced disappearance, with the case of *Anzualdo Castro v. Peru* in 2009 (IACtHR 2009a). Until that case, the IACtHR had been reluctant to incorporate this right, but it considered that the disappearance in that case demonstrated 'not only one of the most serious forms of abduction of a person from all areas of the legal system, but also [the denial of] their very existence and [leaving] in a kind of limbo or situation of legal indeterminacy before society, the state, and even the international community' (IACtHR 2009a). In addition, based on various cases analysed by the IACtHR, there are other rights that have been found to be violated, such as the right to freedom of association (IACtHR 2012a), political rights (IACtHR 2010a), and the rights of children and girls (IACtHR 2014).

Enforced disappearance violates the rights of the relatives of victims, including their rights to access to justice, personal integrity, and truth. Through its case law, the IACtHR came to recognise these rights, based on the facts and characteristics of enforced disappearances. Today it is presumed that the lack of access to justice and an effective remedy entails the suffering of the family, and that in any investigation their participation must be guaranteed in order to achieve the objectives of the right of access to justice (IACtHR 1998, 2009a).

Recent cases have been consistent in their recognition of the violation of the right to truth as an autonomous one. In general, the IACtHR has recognised that the right to truth is violated as a result of the lack of access to justice to the extent that, in the absence of investigation, the relatives of the victim have no possibility of knowing the person's fate or, where appropriate, the location of their remains. However, when specific actions or remedies have been carried out under the right to seek and receive information, the IACtHR has also come to recognise an autonomous violation of the right to freedom of expression established in article 13 of the American Convention on Human Rights (IACtHR 2010b).

Apart from establishing the content and scope of the multiple and complex violations implied by enforced disappearances, the IACtHR has also specified state obligations with regard to the crime. The most important of these, of course, is to refrain from committing the enforced disappearance of persons. The issue, however, that has consumed most of the Court's attention regarding enforced disappearances concerns the nature of the state's due-diligence duty to investigate cases. In this regard, the IACtHR has declared that the state's obligations extend to the investigation of potential perpetrators and the search for the remains of missing persons based on all facts presented. This means that the investigation of the facts should be carried out taking into account their complexity, the context in which they occurred, and the patterns that explain their commission (IACtHR 2009c). Therefore, when facing a case of enforced disappearance, the state must carry out a systematic and thorough analysis in order to reach a comprehensive perspective of the case that supports the ability of investigating authorities and the judiciary to reach a judgment based on the full complexity of the facts presented (IACtHR 2010c). That is why a constant principle in Inter-American jurisprudence on enforced disappearances is that the fundamental evidence must be considered within the context and circumstances of each case (IACtHR 2010c). By the very nature of a disappearance, in which not only the person but also the evidence about how the crime was carried out disappears, the IACtHR has emphasised the significance of the contexts in which the crimes took place. It thus gives importance to contextual factors, such as patterns of widespread or systematic violations, knowledge about the practice of potential perpetrators, the nature of the victims' activities, and the places and times in which the crimes occurred.

As for the search, the IACtHR gives priority to judicial search (although it does not dismiss search by non-judicial means) and to the immediacy of the steps taken, from the first notification of the disappearance, in order to increase the proof necessary to identify the whereabouts of the victim (IACtHR 2018). As part of this obligation, in the event of finding the victim's body, the authorities must identify the victim; recover and preserve the probative evidence; determine the cause, time, place, and manner of death; and return the deceased body of the victim to the family (IACtHR 2010b).

In investigations of disappearance cases, the Court sees it as an *ex officio* obligation of states to use all the logistical and scientific resources necessary to collect and process the evidence, as well as to ensure that investigators are authorised to follow up on evidence leading to the location of the victim and the perpetrators. In addition, the state must ensure access to all places of detention, to gather testimony and documentation. The objective of the investigation is to ensure that all material and intellectual perpetrators of the disappearance are identified and prosecuted. The analytical framework states use in these cases should reveal the structural context and systematic patterns that support disappearances in such a way as to ensure the fight against impunity (IACtHR 2009a).

Although the IACtHR has developed its jurisprudence through its process of monitoring the compliance of States Parties with the obligations of the American Convention on Human Rights, the standards concerning enforced disappearances have actually had to adapt to new contexts and new perpetrators. It is therefore up to each state to use these basic parameters in their own local contexts, which was shown to be feasible in the case of the GIEI's work in Mexico (Dulitzky 2019).

## Final Reflections

The development of standards and mechanisms of protection around enforced disappearance has focused on controlling the various forms of abuse of power that have been present in the region since the 1970s. That is why state power has remained at the heart of the discussion about disappearances, and the practice of hiding and inflicting suffering on certain kinds of victims, particularly those perceived as opponents of the state. Increasingly, however, these standards are used by the Inter-American System's own bodies in other situations of disappearance, such as women in cases of gender-based violence. The IACHR has also sought to test novel protection mechanisms such as GIEI to ensure immediate compliance with state obligations.

As noted at the beginning of this chapter, the Inter-American System has demonstrated its capacity to adapt to the new circumstances it faces. The disappearance of persons has once again struck the continent, with new dynamics, motives, and perpetrators, and in contexts that are quite different from those that gave rise to the original Latin American model of the violation. Today, governmental authorities act in collusion with criminal groups, but there are also disappearances being carried out by criminal groups with no state involvement. In the end, the suffering of victims and families is the same, whether the perpetrator is a state agent or not. The path advanced in cases of gender-based violence, based on the obligation to protect, has the potential to show the way to expand the content and scope of current standards in disappearance cases and to provide a more comprehensive response to the serious human rights violations that face the region today.

Undoubtedly, the GIEI is an example of a new type of international cooperation mechanism that ensures respect for human rights, but the region's fragile democracies are still steps removed from truly being able to interact with such mechanisms. Perhaps because of this, the IACHR has been reluctant to redeploy this mechanism extensively in other countries: the GIEI was the victim of its own success. It will not be the last time that the IACHR has to expand its actions in order to remove obstacles to the actual respect and guarantee of human rights.

## References

Beristain, C., M. Buitrago, A. Valencia, and F. Cox (2018), *Methodologies of Research, Search and Attention to Victims: From the Ayotzinapa Case to New Mechanisms in the Fight against Impunity* (Mexico City, FLACSO-Mexico, Themis, Jesuit University System, UNAM, Universidad de Deusto).

Dulitzky, A. (2019), 'The Latin-American Flavor of Enforced Disappearances', *Chicago Journal of International Law*, 19, 423–89.

Inter-American Commission on Human Rights [IACHR] (2017), *Precautionary Measure no. 564-17: Santiago Maldonado, Argentina* (Washington DC, Organization of American States).

Inter-American Commission on Human Rights [IACHR] (2018a), *Balance Sheet Report: Follow-Up to the Ayotzinapa Affair by the IACHR's Special Monitoring Mechanism* (Washington DC, Organization of American States).
Inter-American Commission on Human Rights [IACHR] (2018b), *Resolución de levantamiento de medidas cautelares 2/2018: Precautionary Measure no. 564-17. Santiago Maldonado, Argentina* (Washington DC, Organization of American States).
Inter-American Court of Human Rights [IACtHR] (1988), *Velásquez Rodríguez* v. *Honduras*.
Inter-American Court of Human Rights [IACtHR] (1998), *Blake* v. *Guatemala*.
Inter-American Court of Human Rights [IACtHR] (2004), *19 Merchants* v. *Colombia*.
Inter-American Court of Human Rights [IACtHR] (2006a), *La Cantuta* v. *Peru*.
Inter-American Court of Human Rights [IACtHR] (2006b), *Masacre de Pueblo Bello* v. *Colombia*.
Inter-American Court of Human Rights [IACtHR] (2008), *Ticona Estrada et al.* v. *Bolivia* (2008).
Inter-American Court of Human Rights [IACtHR] (2009a), *Anzualdo Castro* v. *Peru*.
Inter-American Court of Human Rights [IACtHR] (2009b), *González et al. ('Cotton Field')* v. *Mexico*.
Inter-American Court of Human Rights [IACtHR] (2009c), *Radilla Pacheco* v. *Mexico*.
Inter-American Court of Human Rights [IACtHR] (2010a), *Chitay Nech et al.* v. *Guatemala*.
Inter-American Court of Human Rights [IACtHR] (2010b), *Gomes Lund et al., 'Guerrilha do Araguaia'* v. *Brazil*.
Inter-American Court of Human Rights [IACtHR] (2010c), *Ibsen Cárdenas and Ibsen Peña* v. *Bolivia*.
Inter-American Court of Human Rights [IACtHR] (2012a), *García and relatives* v. *Guatemala*.
Inter-American Court of Human Rights [IACtHR] (2012b), *González Medina and Family* v. *Dominican Republic*.
Inter-American Court of Human Rights [IACtHR] (2014), *Rochac Hernández et al.* v. *El Salvador*.
Inter-American Court of Human Rights [IACtHR] (2017), *Gutiérrez Hernández et al.* v. *Guatemala*.
Inter-American Court of Human Rights [IACtHR] (2018), *Alvarado Espinoza et al.* v. *Mexico*.
Medina, C., and C. Nash (2007), *Inter-American System of Human Rights: Introduction to Its Protection Mechanisms* (Santiago de Chile, University of Chile).
Nash, C. (2009), *The Inter-American System of Human Rights in Action: Hits and Challenges* (Mexico City, Porrúa).
Neuman, G. (2008), 'Import, Export and Regional Consent in the Inter-American Court of Human Rights', *European Journal of International Law*, 19, 101–23.
Patrón, M., S. Aguirre, S. Brewer, S. Robina, and M. L. Aguilar (2017), 'A Novel Exercise in International Oversight', *SUR International Journal on Human Rights*, 14, 189–206.

# 18

# How to Create a Search Mechanism for Disappeared Persons: Lessons from Mexico

VOLGA DE PINA RAVEST

## Introduction

THIS CHAPTER SETS out the principal characteristics of the search mechanism for disappeared persons developed in Mexico. The mechanism is embodied in the General Law of Enforced Disappearance, Disappearance Committed by Private Parties, and the National System of the Search for Persons in Mexico (General Congress of the United Mexican States 2017), hereafter the 'Disappearance Law' or the 'Law'.

A tool to search for the disappeared is exceedingly important. However, creating and implementing a new tool within a previously developed and existing institutional architecture, as in the case of Mexico, presents challenges. The process for doing so in Mexico was historic. It involved the direct participation of collectives of the relatives of disappeared persons, civil society organisations, experts, and international organisms in defining the mechanism of and even writing the Law. Although not all their proposals were incorporated into the Law, the participatory process delivered a model that broadened the state's obligations regarding the search for the missing and incorporated many of the victims' relatives' demands.

Searching for the missing required mechanisms exceeding the capacity of the criminal investigation system that had traditionally controlled the process. Institutionalising an autonomous search mechanism confronted distinct challenges in a context such as Mexico's. It aimed to overcome the problem of persistent bad practices that characterised the pre-existing framework. That framework deepened the harm to victims by failing adequately to address or even recognise disappearances, as Payne and Ansolabehere show in Chapter 1.

Implicit in the new Law was a recognition of the magnitude of the existing problem and the deficiencies in the state's past responses to it. The new Law

*Proceedings of the British Academy*, **237**, 262–269, © The British Academy 2021.

established the duty to search as an independent obligation, and a search mechanism as an autonomous entity with responsibilities that fell under the control of the executive branch of government. As such, it broadened public policy approaches to addressing disappearances, replacing the previous and exclusive authority over disappearances by the law enforcement system.

The different phases of the process of mobilisation and the state response that led to the creation of the Disappearance Law are analysed in detail in Chapter 5. This chapter seeks to analyse the components of the Law that are fundamental to understanding the search mechanism tool in Mexico, particularly the conception of the search itself as an autonomous mechanism, the subjects or persons to be included in the search, and the principal requirements and tools created to conduct search actions.

The mechanism developed in Mexico does not provide a 'recipe' for replication in any context. In several ways, however, it offers insights into how to advance a search mechanism in the face of common state responses to disappearances in post-transitional contexts. Even considering potential problems of efficacy, the Mexican search mechanism warrants attention. It benefits from the experiences of hundreds of relatives of disappeared persons who for more than a decade have made progress in pushing for the development of search mechanisms within the Mexican state.

## Background

During the process of creating the Law, in which I participated as an expert, the need to design search mechanisms that would overcome the inefficiencies in the existing criminal investigation system became a priority. The overwhelming evidence presented by the families of the victims about distinct problems that had blocked their search for the missing was fundamental to the successful creation of new requirements and tools to carry out this work.

Previously, the *ministerio público* (prosecutor's office) controlled the search mechanism. The theory behind this was that the search for missing persons formed part of a criminal investigation, and, as such, the Constitution mandated that it was under the authority of the Public Ministry. The experience of victims' relatives from various entities throughout the country exposed the inefficiency of this model. In only a very few cases had it succeeded in locating the victims.

It also became clear that, in using the official designation system, a significant number of cases were never considered as disappearances. Because of different deficiencies associated with the complexity and 'hyperspecialisation' of national criminal legislation and procedure, many of the cases of people whose whereabouts have been unknown for years were registered not as disappeared, but as other types of crimes, such as kidnapping, trafficking, child abduction or other forms of deprivation of liberty, and more. As such, these types of cases did not require formal investigation, and search action was not deployed in a timely fashion.

Even in cases where there was a prompt investigation, little progress was achieved. The prosecutors were not able to locate the disappeared person because of a variety of deficiencies in the investigation system. These included poor investigative techniques, overly formal bureaucratic procedures, negligence, corruption, saturation of the criminal justice system, and the lack of resources and capacity to adapt to an exceedingly complex criminal context.

These problems justified the creation of a specialised mechanism autonomous from the prosecutor's office that employed a distinct methodology for carrying out the search for the missing. This process includes new definitions for disappeared and missing persons to avoid dismissing cases for investigation as a result of legal classification problems (as raised by Frey in Chapter 2). The goal of the new design is that searches will be carried out in a better way. The process also created a space for interested parties to have dialogue and interaction with the search commissions, because previous interactions with the prosecutors had not been productive.

The creation of these new search mechanisms does not mean that the Public Ministry has ended its role in the process. On the contrary, it must collaborate with the commissions and initiate its own actions to advance efforts to find disappeared persons. There are certain critical actions – such as search procedures, geolocation of electronic devices, communication tracking, and exhumations – that are integral to criminal investigations and, as such, prosecutors are obliged to carry them out under criminal procedures regulations (CNPP 2014: articles 251 and 252). This means that coordination between search commissions and prosecutors entails complex issues that have thus far not been successfully achieved.

Thus, while the Law has permitted the creation of new strategies and methods of conducting investigations, and it has opened up a space for dialogue, one of the principal lessons that has emerged from this process is the need to rethink concrete strategies for coordination. To create a more effective approach, the search commissions have developed a series of procedures. For instance, they propose to intervene at key moments in criminal investigations to generate the information necessary for a successful search.

## The Purpose of the Search

Article 79 of the Disappearance Law (General Congress of the United Mexican States 2017) sets forth the purpose of the search mechanism: to carry out all actions and processes necessary to determine the location, fate, or whereabouts of a person, including the identification of the remains if they are found. Establishing these objectives was not an easy part of the discussions that led to the Law. Some of the state actors who participated in the legislative process considered that execution of these activities was a natural part of a criminal investigation and that, as such, including them in the Law would be superfluous. They also felt that granting these functions to different actors encroached on the Public Ministries' powers.

As indicated, the experiences of relatives of disappeared persons who had carried out searches for their loved ones proved crucial, exposing the limitations of the criminal investigation model. The previous approach by law enforcement had focused narrowly on the analysis of evidence deemed directly material to the legal case and legal definitions. Yet families related successful experiences in obtaining relevant evidence that prosecutors were unable to acquire. Another fault of the previous system was that few witnesses were willing to participate in a process run by the prosecutor's office because of their lack of trust and the fear that they might themselves end up implicated in a criminal investigation.

The conceptual separation of the search process from the criminal investigation has been emerging for some time in the narratives and the actions of families, piloted by institutions created at a state level, such as the Specialised Group for Immediate Search in the state of Nuevo León. Comparative knowledge also contributed to refining this separation process, since search units or commissions have been created in different countries, using a similar logic.

The tendency to distinguish the specific tasks related to the search for disappeared persons has gained force. The Committee on Enforced Disappearance (CED) in the United Nations, for example, recently released its Guiding Principles for the Search for Disappeared Persons (CED 2019), in which it developed concrete tasks related specifically to the search process, showing the methodological features of each (discussed by Frey in Chapter 14 and Huhle in Chapter 15).

Although there is no definitive consensus on the definition of the search, it is possible to characterise it as an activity autonomous from a criminal investigation. Both the investigation and the search aim to clarify the facts related to the disappearance. The search mechanism, however, places emphasis – and the hope of a result – on determining the fate and the whereabouts of the victim. Criminal investigations are oriented toward the identification of responsible perpetrators. As such, criminal investigations can lead to the punishment of perpetrators, without necessarily finding the victim. In such a situation, in the eyes of the state, the case is perceived as successful and closed. If, in the process of an investigation, the victim is located, this is merely an accident or a fortuitous outcome, rather than its purpose. For this reason, the search is defined as a separate activity from the criminal investigation.

The process of creating the Law revealed an important discussion. For the families of disappeared persons, the search is the priority. Separating it from the criminal investigation has the practical purpose of trying to improve the specific methodologies for the location of missing people. This does not mean that the families renounce justice for wrongdoing. Indeed, they insist upon a parallel criminal investigation. If not, the attention will be oriented toward the search and the pressure on the prosecutor's office will diminish, and along with it the possibility of a successful investigation.

## The Search for Persons

As indicated in the background section, one of the recurring complaints of victims' relatives was that the state failed to categorise many cases as disappearances and, as a result, did not activate mandated search actions. It thus became imperative to broaden the definition of disappearance to expand the universe of disappeared persons who would be included in the commissions' searches.

The Disappearance Law includes definitions (General Congress of the United Mexican States: article 2) for two types of situations:

- disappeared person: a person whose whereabouts are unknown and where it is assumed, based on existing evidence, that the cause is related to a criminal act;
- missing person: a person whose location is unknown and whose absence, based on the information reported to the authorities, is not likely to be related to a criminal act.

These defining characteristics were at the centre of one of the most complex debates around the Law. The relatives were clear in their demand that search mechanisms should be carried out for all cases of missing and disappeared people, regardless of the judicial classification of the acts connected to their case. Because searches had been blocked in certain cases, such as kidnapping, the definition of a disappeared person in the Law now refers only to a 'crime' without specifying the type of crime. This open-ended definition provided a way to broaden the spectrum of persons included in the search mechanism, and covered other types of common cases and situations that also merited search action.

It is not uncommon for worried relatives to register with authorities that family members have failed to return home at an expected time or that they cannot be reached. These types of cases have frequently been dismissed by public officials who asked the relatives to wait 72 hours or more before filing a report because there was insufficient evidence to link these acts to a crime. As a result of the dismissal of these cases, searches were not initiated quickly enough, even though early searches are more likely to be effective. The dilemma was that, even if the majority of missing persons may have returned to their homes or established contact – informing their families that nothing had happened, that they lost track of time, that an accident occurred, or other explanations – in other cases, the persons reported missing were never seen or heard from again.

During the drafting of the Law, families emphasised their concern regarding the lack of attention given to missing person cases. Even though these may initially have looked like voluntary absences or other types of situations, family members' worries should have been a sufficient motive to activate the search. Sadly, many of the ones who remained disappeared were those who simply left their house one day and never returned. The search for them did not occur promptly, and thus the opportunity to find them was missed.

The inclusion of the term 'missing person' in Mexico's Law has proved controversial. Many authorities had previously used it, and other terms like it, such as 'lost person', wrongly. These terms were used to deny disappearances and to minimise their importance in criminal statistics. Despite these issues, the term was included with more precision in the Law to gain conceptual ground. It was considered useful to incorporate the term 'missing persons' in the Law to allow for distinctions between two types of situations: those where a crime was presumed and those where no crime was presumed. The inclusion of missing persons as a category also helped clarify claims that the authorities had 'located' thousands of disappeared persons when they were almost always referring to missing persons. The seriousness of all disappearances was minimised by those claims, which authorities presented as successes, even though they had actually played an insignificant role in locating the persons. Allocating resources to resolve these missing person cases is not wrong in a context such as Mexico's, where the simple fact of going out on the street implies certain risks. As such, creating a category that initiates search actions quickly has the potential to locate effectively those who might be victims of a crime. Moreover, such categorisation can lead to improved registries, statistics, and search and criminal-investigation methods.

## Search Commissions

The separation of the search mechanism from the criminal investigation system has been functionally and methodologically implemented through the creation of search commissions. The Law established the creation of a Comisión Nacional de Búsqueda (National Search Commission; CNB) and local search commissions in each of the 32 federal states in the country (General Congress of the United Mexican States 2017: article 2, IV). To avoid replicating the obstacles that previously delayed search actions, the Law stipulated that the commissions may instigate actions upon receiving reports themselves (article 80) rather than waiting for criminal investigations to be initiated.

Originally a single commission that covered the entire country was proposed to overcome the problems of the federal structure, particularly the challenge of coordination between different levels of government. This proposal was rejected by the executive and legislative branches on the grounds that it violated the autonomy of the states.

As a solution, the Law required the CNB and the local commissions to engage in search action that is jointly conducted and coordinated, and simultaneous (General Congress of the United Mexican States 2017: article 79). In practice, there are cases that require the instigation of actions in more than one federal state. In these cases, the CNB is expected to know about, be involved in, and coordinate search actions carried out by local commissions. This achieves the principal goal for the relatives, which is to prevent local authorities – who for many years have been able to protect perpetrators – from assuming jurisdiction in these cases. The Law mandates that the CNB form part of the Interior Ministry, which is, at least in theory, the most powerful ministry in the government. It tends to coordinate the actions taken by different presidential cabinet members. This placement was designed for the CNB to have a high-level role in the administrative structure of the government, and thus the ability to mobilise other governmental institutions. The Law, however, is not entirely clear on how this would occur. It was expected that the local commissions would have a similar administrative position within each state. In practice, this has occurred: 30 of the 32 local commissions created thus far have established this administrative structure.

The CNB possesses multiple and varied levels of power and obligations. The Law includes at least 54 distinct types of authority, many of which are replicated at the local level. It is important to note, however, that some of this authority is reserved for the CNB alone, as the national governing body. Specifically, the CNB has sole control over the creation and execution of the National Search Programme (General Congress of the United Mexican States 2017: article 53, I) and the issuance of guidelines that regulate the functioning and coordination of the National Registry of Missing and Disappeared People (General Congress of the United Mexican States 2017: article 53, II).

The Law stipulates that the search commissions must include, at the very least, the following entities: a specialised search unit, a context analysis unit, and a data management and processing unit (General Congress of the United Mexican States 2017: article 58). These units emerge from families' experience in promoting their cases before various authorities. The first unit attempts to ensure that the commissions have personnel to carry out fieldwork. The second develops teams that apply the methodologies that have proved more effective than the analysis of individual cases alone. The third provides for the capacity to process large volumes of information, given that the model largely hinges on access to these data.

The Law also includes a space for high-level coordination called the National Search System (General Congress of the United Mexican States 2017: article 44). The design and evaluation of public policy related to the search for the missing are under its control. It is tasked with establishing the principles and procedure for standardising the offices that are engaged in searches. An important exchange of information, good practices, and studies of progress on implementing the Law is at the core of the structure of the National Search System.

Finally, the Law defines a set of distinct tools proposed by the relatives. These tools aim to improve the quality of information necessary to achieve greater effectiveness in locating people as well as to establish the methodologies used in the search. The principal tools are the National Registry of Missing and Disappeared People, the National Forensic Database, the National Registry of Graves, and the

Standardised protocol for searching for disappeared persons (General Congress of the United Mexican States 2017: article 48). Although these tools have not yet been created, they are extremely necessary for the success of the commissions in yielding results.

## Lessons

The Law includes a remarkably complex set of innovative search mechanisms, including the expanded definitions of search subjects and new functions and tools. The implementation of the Law will not be simple or quick; it will require a large budget and significant planning and coordination work.

The experience of those who have faced every possible obstacle in searching for their relatives is embedded in this new mechanism, reflecting years of learning and stumbling blocks. Each one of the definitions, persons, public mechanisms, and tools included in the Law involved a profound process of consultation and discussion. This shows that, despite the families' exhaustion and frustration, accumulated over years of experience with one failed search mechanism after another, the motivation to construct a new system persists.

Much work remains to be done to ensure that the goals that families sought to achieve by promoting this legislation are met. Many authorities continue to pose obstacles to the process, refusing to provide information to the commissions, to collaborate in search actions, and to fulfil the obligations that the Law itself imposes. Because of this, it is important to maintain pressure on all institutions that can and should collaborate so that all the tools and requirements can function as envisaged. If the consolidation of this model is not achieved, then all of the effort put in by the families will be for nought.

## References

Código Nacional de Procedimientos Penales [CNPP] (2014), www.diputados.gob.mx/LeyesBiblio/pdf/CNPP_220120.pdf (accessed 20 April 2020).

General Congress of the United Mexican States (2017), 'Ley general en materia de desaparición forzada de personas, desaparición cometida por particulares y del sistema nacional de búsqueda de personas', www.dof.gob.mx/nota_detalle.php?codigo=5504956&fecha=17/11/2017 (accessed 20 April, 2020).

United Nations Committee on Enforced Disappearances [CED] (2019), 'Guiding Principles for the Search of Disappeared Persons', United Nations Document CED/C/7.

# Conclusions

SILVANA MANDOLESSI*

THIS BOOK FILLS an important gap in the study of current dynamics of violence by addressing the phenomenon of disappearances in post-transitional contexts in Latin America. It is striking that, while the dynamics of disappearances during past authoritarian regimes and armed-conflict situations in the region have been a sustained object of academic concern in the last decades, almost no research has been devoted to the disappearances that took – and are taking – place in democratic contexts.

It is striking, first, because far from being an exception, the phenomenon reaches, in some of the countries analysed in this book, crisis levels. The more than 60,000 victims in Mexico since the beginning of the 'War on Drugs', or the approximately 80,000 people who have disappeared every year in Brazil in the last decade, testify to the scale of this practice, which appears to have become part of a common feature of the dynamics of violence. Paradoxically, the numbers of disappearances in these countries are much higher in democracy than during past authoritarian rule. Second, the existence of disappearances in democratic contexts challenges the very status or, at least, calls into question the *quality* of democracy – how to reconcile the assumption that a democratic system guarantees the rights of its citizens with the widespread existence of disappearances, in which the rights to life, to be free from torture, to be free from arbitrary detention, to recognition before the law, and to fair trial are simultaneously and continuously violated?

The editors of this book set out to achieve two objectives. First, to *explain*, by describing and conceptualising the phenomenon of disappearances in democratic contexts. Because of the nature of the crime as marked by the absence of information, the data on who perpetrates the disappearance, the profiles of the victims, and the underlying motivations, are scarce. Human rights non-governmental organisations (NGOs), relatives, and 'colectivos de víctimas' carry out fundamental work in the field, producing and collecting information, often at risk to their own lives. Nevertheless, this information frequently appears scattered, and it is necessary to systematise it in order to grasp both the patterns and general logics, as well as local differences.

*This work has received funding from the European Research Council (ERC) under the European Union's Horizon 2020 research and innovation programme (grant agreement n° 677955).

This is the work that the Observatorio sobre Desaparición e Impunidad en México (Observatory on Disappearances and Impunity in Mexico) is conducting as a joint initiative between FLACSO-Mexico, UNAM, University of Minnesota, and the University of Oxford, which aims to fill the information void about disappearances in the country by collecting data from NGO case files; local media stories; and interviews with journalists, victims' groups, and relatives. Part of their findings are presented here by Karina Ansolabehere and Alvaro Martos in Chapter 4.

The second goal of the book goes beyond explanation, and focuses on the tools available to civil society and judicial actors engaged in efforts to stop disappearances and to obtain state responses to them. Both objectives are naturally related: we need to understand disappearances in order to address and stop them. At the same time, the emphasis on 'tools' demonstrates that disappearances are not only an object of academic enquiry, but are an urgent reality that we cannot fail to attend to. For this, a close collaboration between academia, practitioners, and civil society is crucial, and this book, which brings together voices of researchers, relatives, and practitioners, becomes a good example of that dialogue and the results that can be achieved.

To conceptualise the phenomenon, the book connects present-day disappearances with 'classic' disappearances committed during the region's past authoritarian regimes and armed conflicts. Since the 1980s, scholars from a vast range of disciplines have studied the way in which this repressive practice has been used in these circumstances. As a result, we know how these disappearances were perpetrated, by whom, against whom, and the long-lasting effect of the ambiguous loss (Chapter 1) that the uncertainty provokes, both on direct victims and on society as a whole. But the current scenario is different. It is not only the state that perpetrates disappearances with the objective of targeting political dissidents, but also non-state actors, or both acting in collusion. Victims are not mainly political opponents, as in the past, but marginalised populations – the young, black, poor populations in Brazil, as shown in the chapters by Débora da Silva (Chapter 6), Javier Amadeo and Raiane Severino Assumpção (Chapter 7), and Marlon Weichert (Chapter 8). The victims are the populations living in poor neighbourhoods controlled by gangs, as addressed by 'Wilson' (Chapter 11) and María José Méndez (Chapter 12) in the examination of El Salvador. Motives are varied, ranging from modern slavery and group fights for territorial control, to labour required by organised-crime groups. These dynamics occur in contexts of generalised violence, where disappearances coexist with summary executions, torture, and other types of violent acts, the boundaries between which can be blurred owing to the lack of investigation.

How can we use the knowledge developed on the enforced disappearances of the past to understand the current ones? And to what extent is the definition of 'enforced disappearance' provided in the 2006 International Convention for the Protection of All Persons from Enforced Disappearance suitable – and useful – when dealing with the current context?

In dealing with this question, recent studies have opted to outline the differences between both. This is, for example, the approach taken by Daniel Omar Mata Lugo, who contrasts the 'original idea of disappearance' with the 'vernacular idea of disappearance in Mexico', and provides a detailed explanation of the differences in terms of perpetrators, motives, victims, effects, juridical framework, diagnosis of the problem, and possible solutions (Mata Lugo 2017). In the same vein, the traditional understanding of enforced disappearance – considered too narrow to capture the diverse modes of the present – is replaced by others that seek to provide a more ample conceptualisation, such as the concept of 'a technique that consists of a remodeling of communication flows' (Yankelevich 2017), 'traceless deaths' (Albahari 2015), 'administrative disappearance' (Mata Lugo 2017), or 'social disappearance' (Schindel 2019).

The editors of this book opt instead to emphasise the continuities between both periods. This is reflected in all contributions, although it particularly stands out in the conceptualisation advanced in the initial two chapters. Leigh A. Payne and Karina Ansolabehere propose four overlapping logics, which include: (1) hiding wrongdoing from view through clandestine acts of disappearance; (2) disappearing populations deemed 'disposable' because of their social class, race and ethnicity, gender, geographic location, or political views; (3) disappearing those who potentially challenge the unfolding political economy of development; and (4) establishing social control through ambiguous loss (Payne and Ansolabehere, Chapter 1).

The fact that the violence is clandestine and less visible reduces the legal or reputational costs for states, and eventually also of non-state actors. In other words, the clandestine nature of the disappearance pursues above all the 'pragmatic' aim of avoiding responsibility for the crimes perpetrated. This is not substantially different from the instrumental aim pursued by authoritarian regimes, and it is even, in a paradoxical effect, reinforced, since open or explicit use of violence is less tolerated in democratic systems. With regard to the victims of disappearance, they are members of society who are marginalised or represented as a threat to the socio-economic order or the status quo. Again, the emphasis is placed on the similarities rather than the differences: if, during the previous period, disappearances targeted activists who fought against the social inequalities of the system, now the targets are those living under the logics of precarity, to use Judith Butler's term: 'the politically induced condition in which certain populations suffer from failing social and economic networks of support and become differentially exposed to injury, violence, and death' (Butler 2009: 25). However, the logic of building an 'enemy' that can – or even should – be eliminated in order to guarantee the social order or to protect the interests of the economic system is the same in both cases. Finally, disappearance serves the purpose of social control 'through ambiguous loss'. The psycho-social effects that characterise a disappearance – the uncertainty about the fate of the loved one, the lack of a body, and the consequent difficulty to mourn – do not change, regardless of who the perpetrator is, or the circumstances in which it is carried out. In this sense, the emphasis on continuities rather than differences shows, as Payne and Ansolabehere argue, that 'political contexts of disappearances transcend particular types of political regimes and conflicts. There is nothing about the post-transition that makes systems immune to the four logics of disappearance set out [in Chapter 1]'. And they add, 'The differences in the two periods may involve particular emphases – from a discourse of ideological threat to a discourse of criminal threat – rather than a shift in underlying logics of disappearance' (p. 32).

The logics described above strategically do not address the status of the perpetrator in the post-transitional context. The status concerns the core of the definition of 'enforced disappearance'. Furthermore, it represents one of the main problems that academics face in conceptualising the phenomenon, as well as those who litigate cases in which disappearances are perpetrated not by the state but by non-state actors – be it alone or in collusion with state actors. However, this topic is the object of the second chapter of the theoretical framework, which leads us to read both chapters together, as proposed by the design of the volume. Barbara A. Frey (Chapter 2) addresses the hurdle posed to the contemporary context by the definition of enforced disappearance in the 2006 International Convention on Enforced Disappearance in relation to the role of the state in disappearances committed by non-state actors.

Although the existence of other disappearances is acknowledged in article 3 of the Convention, which recognises disappearances committed by non-state actors, this separation of the 'same' crime into two different articles constitutes, according to Rainer Huhle, a 'logical incoherence', since '"acts defined in Article 2" are acts committed "by agents of the State or by persons or groups of persons acting with the authorization, support or acquiescence of the State" and can therefore by definition not be committed by non-state actors' (Huhle 2013: 22).

Frey argues that there is a need to rethink the state's responsibility for disappearances, especially in contexts of generalised violence. She proposes the overlapping concepts of acquiescence and due diligence to rethink the linkage of the state with the 'third category of disappearances in post-transitional states' (p. 44), encompassing those carried out by organised crime or other private actors without a verifiable connection to the state. Frey advocates for a new jurisprudence on acquiescence, which recognises a state's failure to search and investigate as constituting a direct connection to the disappearance itself, especially in a context of generalised violence and impunity, when the state knew or should have known the risks to the victim. In other words, the state's failure to search for the disappeared or to investigate the crime should be enough to prove acquiescence. Chapter 10, by Federman *et al.* on Argentina, and particularly the treatment of certain victims such as the Maldonado family (Chapter 9), further emphasise this point.

The responsibility of the state is addressed in other chapters, such as the analysis of the 'General Law' on Disappearances adopted in Mexico in 2017, with the specific aim of addressing the reality of disappearances in Mexico. In Chapter 5, Sandra Serrano and Volga de Pina Ravest outline the background of the law, based on the recommendations made by different international mechanisms such as the UN

Working Group on Enforced or Involuntary Disappearances, the Interdisciplinary Group of Independent Experts, and the Inter-American Commission, among others.

Four cases are analysed in detail: Mexico, Brazil, Argentina, and El Salvador. Choosing these cases, as the editors contend, does not mean that they are the only cases in Latin America, nor that the phenomenon of disappearance in democratic systems only takes place in Latin America – there are cases in other parts of the world. Latin America is, however, a key region because of the historic role it has played in relation to this crime, but also because of the social problems – extreme levels of inequality, violent crime, corruption – that characterise the contemporary period.

The four cases are paradigmatic of the logics described, and at the same time stand out for particular traits: Mexico for the magnitude of the phenomenon and widespread impunity; Brazil for the link to summary executions, which reveals disappearances as a tool in the framework of a security performance in which the state targets a specific class of people – poor, black males on the urban margins – as a way to demonstrate its commitment to fighting crime; and El Salvador for the way disappearances are also part of police abuse of power in relation to 'maras' and other criminal gangs. Argentina differs from Mexico, Brazil, and El Salvador, at least in the magnitude of the phenomenon. Only two cases – Santiago Maldonado and Luciano Arruga – are examined by Federman, Perelman, Cañas Comas, and Chillier in their contribution. They point out that these disappearances are 'paradoxical', since the social visibility they acquired was undoubtedly driven by the 'label' of enforced disappearance, although later, in both cases, the facts were insufficient to provide evidence of state responsibility.

Numbers, of course, are important. They tell us something about the scale of violence in a given society. They also settle positions, as evidenced by recent discussions in Argentine society regarding the 'exact' number of disappeared during the last military dictatorship. While some insisted that 'no fueron 30,000' ('there were not 30,000') as a way to minimise them, others emphasised the importance of the numbers to reveal precisely the characteristic logic of disappearance. Uncertainty about numbers is closely linked to the clandestine nature of the crime, and points to the role of the state to investigate in order to clarify the number and the fate of the bodies. On the other hand, the importance of numbers is debatable: not only because a single disappearance is enough to question the functioning of a democratic system, but also because, as Camilo Ovalle contends in relation to the Mexican 'Dirty War', the central point is not the number of victims, but how the state structures part of its institutional apparatus to eliminate dissidents. In Argentina, the two cases analysed help to illustrate continuities both with the past (the criminalisation of social protest in the case of Santiago Maldonado) and with the region (police harassment and 'disposable' victims in that of Luciano Arruga). Compared to Brazil and El Salvador, Argentina differs in the level of visibility and social support observed in the case of the disappearance of Santiago Maldonado, visible in his brother's letters (Chapter 9), in which he thanks civil society for the role it played in the fight for justice. This support is closely linked to the sensitivity of Argentine society to the subject, and can be considered as a 'positive' legacy of the memory work that was carried out in Argentina, something that did not occur in other countries in the region where both the applied transitional justice instruments and the collective memory elaborated around the disappearances were less impactful.

The third and final section of the book presents the 'tools' available to confront forced disappearance. The tools are diverse, ranging from the repertoire of activism to the legal instruments available. The chapters not only describe them as static objects but tell their story, their trajectories, their itineraries, how they were born and developed travelling across the region – and beyond. Besides telling their story, the chapters also examine them critically. Are they effective? Why, or why not? What could we do better?

Taken as a whole, the search for the disappeared is the central point of focus. Without relatives, there are no disappeared. Expanding on this idea, without a society that testifies to the existence of that person, the crime as such does not exist. It comes into existence only through the act of denouncing – and of searching. The act of search involves a complex set of diverse actions and actors, institutions and mechanisms. In analysing the use of photographs as an iconic tool in the search for the disappeared, Payne and Hunter Johnson (Chapter 13) show how the locus of vulnerability that the search implies turns into a 'tool of power'. Relatives have taken this long path, from finding themselves in the helpless position of having lost a loved one to becoming activists who unite with others to claim justice. The testimonies in this volume – Lulú Herrera (Chapter 3), Débora Maria da Silva (Chapter 6), the relatives of Santiago Maldonado (Chapter 9), 'Wilson' (Chapter 11) – teach us how to fight from the site of terrible pain and to continue fighting, despite a lack of response from the state and society's painful indifference. Visual images are central in providing a symbolic visibility of human beings that were obscured by the label of 'disposable person'.

Throughout the history of disappearances in the region, diverse legal mechanisms have been created in order to establish, and later to improve, the search process. The Latin American history of human rights violations, as is well known, has had an impact far beyond the region, influencing the creation and adoption of legal mechanisms at the international level. This interrelation is reflected in the chapters that deal not only with the regional bodies (Sandra Serrano's Chapter 17 on the history of the Inter-American System of Human Rights), but also with the adoption of international protocols (Barbara A. Frey's Chapter 14 on the Minnesota Protocol, which provides a standard of performance in investigating enforced disappearance) and international mechanisms (Rainer Huhle's Chapter 15 on the 'urgent action' procedures of the United Nations specialised bodies dealing with enforced disappearances). As Michael Chamberlin explains in Chapter 16, another international legal option has opened up in recent decades: the submission of a communication to the prosecutor of the International

Criminal Court that demonstrates a pattern of disappearances directed against a civilian population amounting to crimes against humanity. Even if these kinds of submissions do not result in prosecutions, Chamberlin suggests, they serve as vehicles to 'promote understanding within the general public, particularly about the victims, the crimes, and their perpetrators, to establish a context in which the struggle for truth and justice unfolds' (p. 249).

All chapters coincide in stressing the importance assigned to the search for victims. In view of the challenges that ongoing disappearances pose to holding states accountable, and the states' evasion of responsibility under the guise of not being the direct 'perpetrators', the emphasis on search and on investigation constitutes the main tool to force states to provide answers to the relatives – and to society as a whole. It is significant that the chapters address recent legal 'tools': the Minnesota Protocol, which provides 'best practices', dates from 1992 but was revised and updated in 2016; the 'Sistema de Búsqueda', which Volga de Pina Ravest analyses in Chapter 18, is part of the General Law on Disappearances adopted in Mexico in 2017; the 'urgent actions' procedure of the Committee on Enforced Disappearances dates from 2012; and we could also add the 'Guiding Principles for the Search for Disappeared Persons', which were approved by the Committee on Enforced Disappearances in April 2019. All these recent initiatives suggest that pressuring states to comply with their obligation to search and investigate is one of the central tools available to address the challenge of ongoing disappearances.

Although the picture that results from the chapters in this book is a testimony of a gruesome reality – a phenomenon that should be absent in post-transitional, democratic Latin American societies – the book itself testifies to the innumerable efforts by relatives in the first place, but also by academics, practitioners, and members of civil society to address this urgent problem and put an end to disappearances. If there is something to be learned from the terrible history of disappearances in Latin America, it is the lesson that when civil society mobilises and 'unites forces', it can put an end to authoritarian regimes and their practices. The tools that originated in Latin America later served to address the phenomenon of enforced disappearances beyond the region. In providing an insightful, multidimensional, and detailed picture of the phenomenon, this book not only contributes significantly to an enhanced understanding of the multiple ways in which disappearances continue to occur in democratic countries, but also offers a toolbox of best practices for civil society actors who carry on the fight against disappearances, not just in Latin America but also beyond.

## References

Albahari, M. (2015), *Crimes of Peace: Mediterranean Migrations at the World's Deadliest Border* (Philadelphia, University of Pennsylvania Press).

Butler, J. (2009), *Frames of War: When Is Life Grievable?* (London, Verso).

Huhle, R. (2013), 'Non-State Actors of Enforced Disappearance and the UN Convention for the Protection of All Persons from Enforced Disappearance', *Journal of International Law of Peace and Armed Conflict*, 26, 21–5.

Mata Lugo, D. O. (2017), 'Traducciones de la "idea de desaparición (forzada)" en México', in *Desde y frente al estado: pensar, atender y resistir la desaparición de personas en México*, ed. J. Yankelevich (Mexico City, Suprema Corte de Justicia de la Nación), pp. 27–73.

Schindel, E. (2019), 'Deaths and Disappearances in Migration to Europe: Exploring the Uses of a Transnationalized Category', *American Behavioral Scientist*, 64:4, 389–407.

Yankelevich, J. (2017), 'Introducción', in *Desde y frente al estado: pensar, atender y resistir la desaparición de personas en México*, ed. J. Yankelevich (Mexico City, Suprema Corte de Justicia de la Nación), pp. xi–xxi.

# Index

Page numbers in **bold** refer to tables and page numbers in *italic* refer to figures.